BY FORCE OF FANTASY

BY FORCE OF

fantasy

HOW WE MAKE OUR LIVES

Ethel S. Person, M.D.

BasicBooks

A Division of HarperCollins*Publishers*

Three lines and last two stanzas from "Daddy" from *Ariel* by Sylvia Plath. Copyright © 1963 by Ted Hughes. Copyright renewed. Reprinted by permission of HarperCollins Publishers, Inc. and Faber and Faber Ltd.

Copyright © 1995 by Ethel Spector Person, M.D.
Published by BasicBooks, A Division of HarperCollins Publishers, Inc.

Designed by Elliott Beard

Library of Congress Cataloging-in-Publication Data
Person, Ethel Spector.
     By force of fantasy : how we make our lives / Ethel S. Person.
        p.   cm.
     Includes bibliographical references and index.
     ISBN 0–465–02359–2
     1. Fantasy.   2. Psychoanalysis.   I. Title.
BF175.5.F36P47   1995
154.3—dc20   95-8649
                                                             CIP

95 96 97 98 ❖/HC 9 8 7 6 5 4 3 2 1

To my sons, Louis Michael Sherman and
Lloyd Andrew Sherman, with love and admiration
and in loving memory of their father,
my late husband, Barry Michael Sherman

CONTENTS

ACKNOWLEDGMENTS

FANTASIES ARE VERY PRECIOUS CREATIONS. I THANK MY PATIENTS PAST AND present for what they have taught me, and I am especially grateful to those who have generously agreed to let me recount their fantasies. For the sake of confidentiality, I have thoroughly disguised the life situation of every fantasizer. As to fantasies that are quite common, I have used composites, though with every effort to convey psychological authenticity. In addition to material from patients, I have drawn on interviews I conducted over the past four years with approximately forty nonpatients, a sample that comprised friends of friends and professional acquaintances. The interviews, geared toward fantasy life, ranged from one to three hours. Some interviews were structured, others open-ended. In addition, I have had access to fantasy material collected in a study on sexual fantasies (and corresponding sexual behaviors) of a nonpatient population, conducted at the Columbia University Center for Psychoanalytic Training and Research in collaboration with my colleagues Eugene Goldberg, Wayne Myers, and Nettie Terestman. We were assisted at various times by Carol Salvadori and Michael Borenstein. Though I have not used the interview data from that study in this work, our research findings have helped shape my thinking.

My efforts have been informed throughout by the generosity of friends and colleagues who have read and critiqued parts of the book, suggested references, shared stories, or discussed ideas. In particular I want to thank Shana Alexander, Brian Clarke, Dr. Arnold Cooper, Mindy Goldberg, Vicki Goldberg, Ann Stern Gollin, Dr. Marion Hart, Susan Metzger, Dr. Herman Roiphe, Judith Rossner, Prof. Joseph Sandler, Dr. Eleanor Schuker, Rhonda

Sherman, Robert Sherman, Lucy Simon, Gladys Topkis, and Prof. Claudia Zanardi. Ilene Lefcourt, Anne Roiphe, Daniel Stern (the novelist), and Caroline Stoessinger each have read long portions of the manuscript and their comments have been extremely cogent. Dr. Helen Kaplan generously allowed me to sit in on her sex therapy seminar and we have continued an ongoing conversation on the uses and meanings of sexual fantasy in and out of the treatment situation.

The Columbia University Psychoanalytic Center for Training and Research has long been an intellectual home—from the time I was a student there, through my first appointment to the faculty and my appointment as its director from 1981 to 1991. It is a home still and I continue to treasure its openness to new ideas and its spirit of inquiry. I thank my students there, my supervisees and analysands past and present, my former teachers, and my colleagues.

Though I have never specifically discussed fantasy as such with any of the members of a peer study group, CAPS Group Eleven, to which I belong, I have met with its members twice a year for more than a dozen years, and my psychoanalytic vision has been shaped by each of them. My thanks, then, to a group of psychoanalysts I consider among the most sophisticated clinicians in the country: Graziella Abelin-Sas, Maxine K. Anderson, Boyd L. Burris, David A. Carlson, Lawrence Chalfin, Carl L. Davis, Daniel A. Goldberg, Richard M. Greenberg, Joan Gross, Cornelis Heijn, Jacob G. Jacobson, Ruth K. Karush, George Moraitis, Barbara Rocah, and Sherwood Waldron, Jr.

My debts to the psychoanalytic literature, particularly to the work of Sigmund Freud and Hanns Sachs, are self-evident. Those to many important contributors to the psychoanalytic and the psychological literature are particularized in the bibliography. I am grateful to two mentors of my early professional life whose thinking has influenced this book: the late Lionel Ovesey, a distinguished psychoanalyst and my longtime collaborator, who taught me among other things about the theoretical importance of adaptation; and the late Hans Morgenthau, political theorist, intellectual companion, and sometime collaborator, who taught me about the role of power in human affairs.

My thanks go to my secretary, Linda Dagnell, who has typed and endlessly retyped my manuscript, and to Judy Kronenberg, librarian at the Columbia University Psychoanalytic Center, who has acted as research assistant and who checked the bibliography and the quotations.

I am grateful to my editor, Jo Ann Miller, who did the initial edit and who gently but firmly kept me to a deadline, and to Beth Rashbaum, who did an outstanding final edit—and who in her inimitable style "persuaded" me to rethink a number of issues, both substantive and stylistic. I am grateful, too, to my energetic and able agent, Joy Harris.

Most of all, my appreciation and love go to my family. My stepdaughters, Nancy Diamond Atwood and Jessica Diamond Schaer, each of them a creative force, have been open and sharing with their thoughts and extremely supportive of this book. Nancy and Jessica, along with my sons, Louis Sherman and Lloyd Sherman, have the warmth and generosity of spirit that have contributed to the creation of a strong and unified family. My husband, Stanley Diamond, is my best friend and most ardent supporter. Reading my manuscript, he always tempered his criticisms with kindness. It is his unique generosity that allows me to dedicate this book to my late husband without any sense of divided loyalties.

INTRODUCTION

FANTASIES—DAYDREAMS, CASTLES IN THE AIR, MENTAL SCRIPTS, AND scenarios—filter our experience of the inner and outer worlds to a surprisingly large extent.[1] Most of us believe these mental emanations are of little significance in our lives. They seem but puffs of smoke that diffuse into the atmosphere. And yet in truth, fantasy is as essential as air, forming the medium or the ether in which all the other activities of mind take place. Fantasy also impacts on the world outside the mind. Though early psychoanalytic formulations viewed fantasy as primarily providing substitute gratification, a retreat from the external world, fantasy in fact plays a major role in building that world, in guiding the choices and adaptations we make and the relationships we form. Fantasies are among the most powerful of the catalysts that infuse and organize our lives, dictating romantic, familial, and professional goals; fueling behavior; engendering plans for the future. In turn, our experiences, and the myths and stories of the culture in which we live, shape our fantasies. Moreover, fantasy, as embodied in the works of the great artists of our time, is one of the crucibles in which those myths and stories are forged, and is thus a key element in cultural evolution and change.

I've written this book to show that spinning fantasies is no idle pursuit, but rather that these products of the mind's alchemy are critical in shaping our behavior and personality, and ultimately the path we travel through life. My involvement in the topic was at first a by-product of my interest in romantic love.

1

Writing a book on love, I began to see several ways in which that emotion was fantasy-based.

The first element of fantasy relates to the choice of the lover, which always depends upon our having an image of the ideal other. In the course of growing up, each of us somehow creates within our mind that complex mix of qualities that seems to constitute the ideal lover. Borrowing a term from H. G. Wells, I have called this the fantasy of the lover-shadow.[2] The lover-shadow originates in our early life perceptions of our parents or relatives and our experiences with them and becomes more fully fleshed out as we venture forth into the world, interact with our peers, and gaze admiringly from afar at our elders. Our exposure to the larger community, including the books we read and films we see, also determines the shape of the lover-shadow.

Falling in love means bringing our perception of our actual lover into alignment with our internal image (fantasy) of the lover-shadow. This requires another imaginative act, through which we transform a living creature into the embodiment of this product of our minds. Along with our fantasies about the lover we have fantasies about romantic love itself. In Western culture we look to romantic love to satisfy a large range of underlying wishes: longings for attachment, dependency, sexuality, and companionship, and darker longings, too, such as the wish to devour another. All these subsidiary wishes, which are condensed as well as concealed in romantic love, can be symbolically (or actually) fulfilled in the act of falling in love. In non-Western cultures the same wishes push for gratification through other channels, for there is nothing universal about the fantasy of romantic love.

As I delved deeper into the subject of how our fantasies take shape and how they, in turn, come to shape our lives, I began to see how fantasy impacts all the relationships and all the great passionate voyages of our lives, our vocational and avocational choices, the way we spend our time and choose our causes. Its sources are both internal and external, rooted in the depths of the psyche and reflecting the culture around us.

My curiosity about fantasy is grounded in still another set of intellectual preoccupations—my long-standing interest in sex and gender and my commitment to feminism. Why, for example, in an age of women's liberation, do men and women still have rape fantasies? Are such problematic fantasies "hardwired," or, alternatively, are they the product of our individual histories or of our cultural scripts? Where do our individual fantasy scripts come from? And if they do affect our lives, can they be changed or enhanced?

Beyond these intellectual and professional concerns, my interest in fantasy arose from something personal, something I do not even now fully understand. When I applied for admission to an analytic institute many years ago, the admissions procedure included three in-depth personal interviews with each applicant. One of my interviewers asked me to tell him my fantasies. Eager though I was to be accepted, I said that I certainly did not know him well enough to share my fantasies and refused to answer his question. Discovering that I valued my privacy more than acceptance to analytic school was surprising even to me. I left that interview certain that I would be rejected, but somehow pleased that I had set limits. Much to my further astonishment, I was accepted for analytic training. I suspect that the interviewer was more interested in how I handled the question than in the answer: I was the one for whom the specific content of my fantasies seemed so meaningful. I had obviously intuited that fantasies were both intimate and revealing and that mine were precious to me. He was presumably more interested in my "ego strength."

So fantasy has had an important private meaning to me. Trying to understand why that private meaning is so powerful is part of the driving force behind this book.

Daydreams and reveries are virtually ubiquitous, floating in and out of consciousness. Sometimes they are no more than a flickering on the borders of awareness, sometimes prolonged, complexly plotted scenarios. Sometimes fantasies come to us spontaneously; other times we go with forethought to them, as when we flip through our private mental catalogue of imagined stories, looking for the one that will arouse us sexually or soothe our anxieties or lull us to sleep. Sometimes our fantasies are quite commonplace, sometimes completely idiosyncratic. Sometimes they borrow from our culture's warehouse of mythic stories; sometimes they relate only to us. Sometimes they appear realistic or close to future planning; other times they are wildly escapist or fantastical and bear no relationship to the immediate circumstances of our lives.

But they are never far from our innermost selves. Fantasies tell us something about who we are. This is one of the reasons why people are reluctant to share their fantasies with a stranger, and often with intimates as well. We may even be loath to look at our own fantasies too closely, fearing to know what they might tell us about ourselves, which might ruin the magical pleasure or comfort they offer us.

Although we may intuit how significant fantasy is to us personally, the subject of fantasy has not been a major theme in intellectual discourse (with the exception, of course, of the importance psychoanalysis accords to unconscious fantasy). While artistic creativity and other forms of imagination such as scientific ingenuity are honored in our culture, worshiped even, fantasy and fantasizing, another subspecies of the imagination, evoke a wide range of reactions, most of them negative. Fantasizing, sometimes dismissed as mere "daydreaming," is tolerated so long as it is only infrequently invoked to while away time that hangs heavy; more often, it is damned as idle wool gathering, a meaningless activity, or, worse, a dangerous one, evidence of a weak character insofar as an individual uses fantasy to avoid or substitute for reality.

Henry James's short story "The Beast in the Jungle" can be read as a cautionary tale against that kind of fantasy.[3] John Marcher, the protagonist of James's tragic story, believes that his life will be shaped by a remarkable experience, which he visualizes, metaphorically, as his being tracked by a beast in the jungle, a preoccupation he confides to a woman friend, May Bartram. Years later, when they again meet after a long separation, and May inquires whether the great thing has happened, John Marcher confesses that though it has not yet occurred, the expectation that it will remains the central belief of his life. Many years pass, during which May and John remain friends. Only after May's death does John realize that the real beast, the thing that has shaped his life, and emptied it of meaning, is his endless waiting for the partly feared, partly desired, transforming event. Unable to open himself to live until this event occurs, he has wasted his life.

Even the Near East, which Westerners often view as the dreamy East, has cautionary tales against being so immersed in reveries that one misses out on real life. "The Barber's Tale of His Fifth Brother" from *The Arabian Nights,*[4] is a classic example, in which the Barber tells the story of how his fifth brother, Al-Nashashar, came to be a beggar. When their father died, he left one hundred coppers to each son. The fifth brother, thinking to spend his inheritance on glassware and make a handsome profit, bought some glass and sat down on a bench at the foot of a wall to sell it. Leaning back, he soon fell into a reverie in which he fantasized selling his wares for two hundred coppers, buying more glass, making four hundred, and so on, until he had accumulated a great fortune. Then he began to fantasize buying and selling merchandise, tools, and perfume and eventually becoming so rich that he acquired a hundred thousand pieces of silver. In his mind, he sent out marriage brokers to look for the daughters of kings and statesmen, from among whom he might choose a wife. Finally he demanded a marriage with the eldest daughter of the prime minister, whom, if she refused to consent, he planned to take by force. In his fantasy, he attained his choice; but when his bride was brought to him, he refused to look at her so as to show his high status. His wife's mother came to beg that he pay attention to her daughter. She gave her daughter wine to take to the newly rich man. But he still refused to speak to his wife. Again she pressed him to drink, and just as she put the wine to his lips, he shook his fist in her face and kicked her. At that moment, acting out his fantasy, he kicked out with his foot and knocked over his entire tray of glassware, shattering it— and his hopes for the future—completely.

Paradoxically, fantasy also provokes fear, not because it takes us away from reality but because it may, in its portrayal of the future, bring us too close to it: our fantasy may come true. It is a belief (superstition) of our culture that we may have to pay a terrible price for those things we seek and find. This is the fear expressed in the well-known folk tale in which someone is given three wishes. In one version, "The Monkey's Paw," a couple first asks for great wealth, which they receive as a death benefit when their only child dies.[5] Their second wish is to restore him to them, whereupon he appears as a ghost. Terrified, they use their third wish to ask for a return to the very same conditions that obtained before they were given the wishes. Teresa of Avila sounds the same note when she observes: "More tears are shed over answered prayers than over unanswered ones."[6]

The bias against reverie, against fantasy, seems a straightforward argument for involvement in the workaday world as opposed to dreamy immersion in illusion. But no doubt the bias has deeper roots; it is fueled by all the mind's repressive elements arrayed against the threat of unconscious fantasies and preoccupations. Those feared and slimy creatures from the depths of the mind may enter into conscious life in the form of daydreaming, and, once there, may undermine our hard-won adherence to the duties of conscience and the customs of culture. We may live out our fantasies!

In contrast to both these cautionary approaches to daydreaming, however, is the belief that fantasy has great, sometimes magical, powers. For example, some believe that fantasy in the form of guided visualization can be invoked to overcome cancer, so they conjure up armies of white cells marching to annihilate the invasive malignant cells. Others celebrate fantasy as an inner resource that, if properly cultivated, will give even the ordinary person a wellspring of artistic creativity. This belief has resulted in the recent deluge of books on creative visualization and guided fantasy trips. For some people these approaches seem effective, for others not. One of my friends, working on visualizations with a therapist, found that he could only produce memories; he ended up feeling more deficient than enlarged when the therapist told him that all his *other* patients could create remarkable imaginary scenes.

But fantasy and the process of fantasizing are more central to our lives, indispensable really, than such narrow evaluations, negative or positive, would lead us to believe.

Psychoanalysts have long understood the underlying role of fantasy not only in neurotic disorders or the choice of specific sexual scenarios, but in character and behavior. Fantasy infuses all of our choices and behavioral patterns, not just the neurotic ones.

Fantasy should be understood as one of our major modes of adaptation. On the simplest level, it indeed provides substitute gratification for that which is otherwise lacking in life—just as the early psychoanalytic theories declared. Fantasies may be straightforward expressions of wishes, or, conversely, denials (or reaction formations) against conscious impulses. They may serve as consolations, compensations for what we lack in life. They may also heal or undo past defects, wounds, and old conflicts. Perhaps the most compelling function of fantasy is that it creates an ambiance of hope for the future, even in seemingly impossible situations, and gives us the strength to endure.

Beyond its role in emotional regulation, self-soothing, arousal, and formation of neurosis and even character, fantasy can act as a rehearsal for future action and can provide a template for life choices that may be either literal translations (enactments) or symbolic expressions of the fantasy's narrative content. Fantasy is a theater in which we preview the possible scenarios of our life to come.

At the heart of every fantasy are a germ of frustration and, consequently, a desire for change. The change we long for can be personal, or during extraordinary times of social flux, such as that just preceding the French Revolution, it can be culturewide. As often as not, fantasies are fantastic; that is, fulfilling them would be improbable if not impossible. But that does not mean they will not affect our lives. Fantasies, by definition, subvert the status quo and therefore always have a potential impact on the future, sometimes in the direction of radical change. Their role in personal and even cultural evolution is the subject of this book.

1

THREE TIMES HIDDEN:
THE SECRET WORLD OF
DAYDREAMS

THOUGH MANY OF US THINK OF THE MIND AS OUR ORGAN OF REASON, dedicated mainly to analysis, logic, planning, and other kinds of abstract thought, in fact, the mind carries on a large number of its activities by invoking stories: self-generated fantasies, memories, family tales, or the myths and folk tales of the culture that surrounds us. Fantasy, which constitutes a major portion of these stories, takes many forms—dreams for the future, daydreams, castles in the air, reveries, imagery, imagined scripts, scenarios, and scenes. A fantasy or a daydream—terms I use interchangeably—is an imaginative story or internal dialogue that generally serves a more or less transparent wish-fulfilling function, gratifying sexual, aggressive, or self-aggrandizing wishes and other wishes as well, or that transcribes our hopes.

Ever since the first psychoanalytic patient, Anna O., described her own daydreaming as a private theater, fantasy has often been called a theater of the mind, not a bad description considering that fantasies generally have a main character (most often the implied agent of action), a goal, an action, an object of the action, and a setting.[1] The fantasizer plays three roles, as the author of the fantasy script, as a player in the drama—often the star of it—and as the audience for whom the fantasy was devised.

The theatrical metaphor notwithstanding, fantasy is much more often private than public. The hiddenness of our fantasy lives is protean. Its most obvious form is secrecy. We consider our fantasies deeply personal, we choose whether or not to share them, and generally we guard them jealously. But the degree to which we keep them at a remove even from ourselves may surprise us. Relying upon fantasies as old friends and considering their meaning transparent, we may be unaware that we actually know little about them and do not appreciate their meaning, their importance in our lives, or their wellsprings. Even when we think that we understand how our lives revolve around a key fantasy, its underlying meaning is often much more opaque than it seems, its layering deeper and more complex than is at first apparent. Moreover, fantasies may not stay in our consciousness long enough to be attended to fully, like dreams that are quickly forgotten upon awakening, so that the fantasizer is barely aware of even having had a fantasy. Sometimes—as in unconscious fantasies—they are repressed completely.

Another important feature of our fantasies is also hidden from us. Thinking our daydreams singular, we do not realize how many of the story lines of our fantasies are drawn not just from the earliest life experiences that are common to us all, but from our family stories and myths, and from the fiction, art, and myths of the surrounding culture. Even our most apparently unique fantasy materials are probably shared by a great number of others. Since we talk with one another about our fantasies so rarely, however, we may go through life without ever discovering the commonalities.

The secrecy with which we guard our fantasies has long been recognized. Sigmund Freud understood that it was one of the hallmarks of fantasy life:

> The adult . . . is ashamed of his phantasies and hides them from other people. He cherishes his phantasies as his most intimate possessions, and as a rule he would rather confess his misdeeds than tell anyone his phantasies. It may come about that for that reason he believes he is the only person who invents such phantasies and has no idea that creations of this kind are widespread among other people.[2]

Conscious fantasies, then, are private property, personal secrets carefully concealed. Even in this age of psychological and sexual freedom, they are seldom explicitly shared.

Though casual friends have often startled me by their bold revelations of intimate details of their personal lives—affairs, life-threatening illnesses, abortions, and professional problems—seldom have even my closest friends told me about their fantasies. Lovers may share their fantasy lives, but even then they usually confine that sharing to sexual fantasies that they use as a mode of seduction or a tentative suggestion about what they find exciting. In fact, relatively few lovers tell each other much about their sexual fantasies.

However, many people readily relate their dreams. Freud himself was a prime example: he published fifty of his dreams, but recorded only a few daydreams.[3] Why are we willing, even eager, to share our dreams, but determined to hoard and hide our fantasies? One reason is that we feel more responsible for daydreams than for night dreams. Night dreams come unbidden, but conscious fantasy, because we conjure it up and are aware of manipulating it to suit ourselves, implicates us very directly. In some ways, fantasies seem more revealing of the self—its appetites or obscure, quirky desires—than dreams or even the most intimate narratives of the lived life. One feels shame in exposing certain fantasies to the outside glare, no matter how gratifying they are within the protected landscape of the mind. A particular fantasy, it is sensed, would reveal grandiose or obscene ambitions, infantile needs, otherwise well-disguised impulses to aggression, kinky sexual appetites, or, worst of all, some grotesque wish or need of which we ourselves are unaware. Moreover, since we assume that our fantasies are unique, that no one else would create such bizarre mental products, we are all the more reluctant to describe them.

Take, for example, the daydream with which one patient of mine regularly soothed herself to sleep, which she was able to reveal to me only late in her treatment. The fantasy depicted miniature creatures, human in form, that the patient liked to imagine inhabiting her gastrointestinal tract, for whom, rather like a dietician she planned imaginary meals that had to be made up of foods she had eaten within the past three days. Though partial to the fantasy's soothing quality, the patient, when she thought of it during the day, regarded it as primitive and was too ashamed to bring it into the treatment. And so for many months, the fantasy never bubbled to consciousness during her sessions. When she did finally reveal it, however, it proved immensely helpful to her self-understanding. In fact, I will return to an exploration of this multilayered fantasy later, as an example of the way in which conscious fantasy, explored and brought into fuller consciousness through analysis, may prove to be the Rosetta Stone that helps decipher a core conflict.

It is perhaps comforting to know that many fantasies that frighten the fantasizer or arouse shame are similar to other people's in one form or another, linking us to each other rather than setting us apart. Fantasies analogous to my patient's, in which the gastrointestinal tract constitutes a world unto itself, have been reported elsewhere in the psychoanalytic literature. For example, Belle, a patient of the psychoanalyst Robert Stoller, had fantasies of a peaceful underground world, to which people retreated in order to escape disasters on the surface. "The main thing about it was the marvelous, safe feeling, and yet it was sort of a sexual feeling."[4]

The underground setting of Belle's fantasy was eventually found to symbolize her gastrointestinal tract, with the fantasy evoking in her the urge to defecate. Together, Belle and Stoller exhaustively explored this fantasy, gaining insight into many events in Belle's childhood that fed into her fantasies.

Among the complicated antecedents was the fact that the woman Belle called the Caretaker (who looked after her when her mother left her) considered bowel movements of the highest importance, so that Belle's bowel habits became the major text of their communication. Over time Belle disclosed that the Caretaker checked her bowel movements and subjected her to rectal examinations and enemas, suppositories and thermometers, not to mention endless discussions of diet and threats of the horrors that would ensue should her bowel movements become irregular. Yet at the same time that she was extremely intrusive, the Caretaker provided Belle with security. Belle and Stoller came to understand the fantasies in a variety of ways. Stoller, having already interpreted the fantasies of large underground rooms and corridors, populated by silent people whom Belle did not know, as symbolic of her bowels and their contents, suggested further that "even if you experience all the people inside you as good and trustworthy, you don't trust any of us on the outside."[5] Belle's fantasies about the peaceful underground world counteracted her experience of being invaded, creating an imaginary world she could control. At the same time, imaginative reworkings of the anal indignities perpetrated on her also found their way into highly arousing sexual fantasies of sadistic assault, in essence imaginatively transforming the painful assaults of her childhood into evidence of being loved.

Certain parts of our life histories are of course unique. There is nothing universal or even common, for example, in Belle's experience of having a Caretaker focused so emphatically on bowel movements. And yet there will always be some similarity among our fantasies, because so many are engendered in earliest life by universal emotions (love or hate or fear) and are expressed in terms of the universal activities of infantile life (incorporating, expelling, destroying, and so on). Childhood emotions and early expressions of them will find their way into our behaviors and our relationships throughout our lives, with the result that the specific problems and conflicts we face will be shared by many others, as will our fantasies. These secret correspondences sometimes allow us to guess at someone else's fantasy.

Two women, standing at the edge of a turbulent ocean, almost simultaneously notice that the husband of one of them has swum out much too far and appears to be having difficulty getting back in. Turning to the swimmer's wife, the friend catches a fleeting enigmatic smile on her face, and says, "I know what you're thinking." Unhappily married people often entertain the same fantasy, although each generally guards it as a guilty secret: wishing for or fantasizing (sometimes almost continuously) the death or murder of the spouse. Despite its frequency, this fantasy is generally accompanied by so much guilt and shame that it is rarely freely expressed.

One man I know was suffering so much in his marriage, while feeling unable to leave it (or confront his wife with his unhappiness), that I did what the woman at the beach did (for me, a very odd thing, since I try to keep the professional and the personal spheres separate): I "guessed" at his fantasy of becoming a widower and shared my conjecture with him. I probably did it to relieve his guilt and help him focus on his problem. He was enormously relieved to discover that his was not a Satanic mind, and that he was entertaining a fantasy quite common when an unhappily married person feels helpless. My friend was human, not evil.

However, the meaning of the fantasy of the dead spouse, common and apparently self-evident though it is, is not in fact transparent, and it varies considerably from person to person. If a husband, completely convinced that his marriage cannot be improved, clearly wants to be rid of his wife, why does he not get a divorce (or fantasize one) instead of fantasizing about her death or about killing her? I cannot answer that question about my friend, since I know him socially, not analytically. However, I can address the meaning of a similar fantasy entertained by one patient whose treatment I was supervising (in fact, I could refer to several patients who have this common fantasy).

Mr. Rossmore enjoyed his fantasies of his wife's death because they gave him a way to imagine his freedom and an outlet for his hostility toward her. But he censored out any fantasies about divorce because he did not want to confront the social difficulties that divorce would entail, particularly since his wife is liked and admired by their friends. Moreover, because he (but not his wife) had previously been divorced, he felt sure that his friends would assign all the blame to him. If his wife were to die, however, he would be blameless and would garner the sympathy and support of his entire social world. He would not be alone, as he feared he might be if he got a second divorce. (As he sardonically put it, he would be able to "dine out on her death for a year.") Moreover, he would not have to give up half his money and his children would not rage against him.

As sensible as this explanation may appear, other fantasies were layered beneath this seemingly transparent daydream. Lurking in the shadows was the identification Mr. Rossmore made between his wife and his mother (or, more accurately, his image of the mother of his early childhood), which caused him to feel too dependent on his wife (more below the surface of consciousness than conscious) and revived murderous fantasies previously aimed at this mother, now directed at his wife.

Mr. Rossmore's dependency was often expressed in fearful fantasies about who would take care of him were he to leave his wife and then fall sick. And he expected to become ill, because he felt he would deserve some form of retribution for his evil thoughts. (He still felt guilty about his previous divorce, even though there were no children from that union and his ex-wife was remarried and thriving.) While Mr. Rossmore was in touch with his unhappiness and his desire to be free, he was less aware of the hostility he directed at his wife every day, through emotional withholding, mockery and contempt, and sly insults. His "crime" was in fact not wholly imaginary; metaphorically he *was* killing her.

Once, when his wife was away for some months, tending to her terminally ill father, Mr. Rossmore's sense of her goodness revived. He began to feel less frightened of her and less constrained by her, and his sense of claustrophobia decreased. These changes unexpectedly allowed him to feel a renewed attachment to her. This episode enhanced Mr. Rossmore's ability to understand his own role in his marital problem (how *his* dependency and *his* childhood experiences, and not any provocation by his wife, led to his hostility), and this insight ultimately relieved some of the tension between husband and wife.

People react to their fantasies in different ways. Sometimes they use them as clues to understand their current situation, but by and large, the man who wishes his wife dead will not discuss his fantasies. He is too guilty about having homicidal wishes and too ashamed of being unable to act by demanding that his wife change or by leaving her. (He may reveal his fantasies to a girl-friend to indicate how much he loves her.) Perhaps even more profoundly, he does not want to explore the fantasy's hidden subtext, fearing to see what it reveals about the hostile dependency he dimly perceives as weakness. He may also fear the implicit call to action—to confront his own problems, or his wife's, or the possibility of divorce.

But shame and guilt or fear of consequences in the real world are not the only impediments to revealing fantasy. Often, the fear of losing the power of fantasy—fear of the loss of its usefulness as a magic amulet that can soothe or assuage anxiety, stimulate sexual arousal, or produce pleasure—is the major obstacle to sharing a fantasy (or even looking at it too closely). Secrecy seems to add to the potency and piquancy of our fantasies. There is an extra little frisson of excitement in keeping one's inner life private. It sometimes feels like having an edge, keeping an advantage, to know something about oneself that is invisible even to our intimates. It reinforces our sense of ourselves as autonomous.

The inhibition about sharing conscious fantasies appears to be the general rule even in the psychoanalytical situation, where the patient is committed to an exploration of his or her inner life. Of course, a few exceptional patients disclose their fantasies early on, particularly those whose sexual arousal depends upon their summoning fantasies of one or another kind. Fantasies that are prerequisite to sexual arousal are sometimes too pervasive for the patient to ignore.[6] In general, however, patients hesitate a long time to introduce their fantasies in the analytic process.

Even when patients do reveal a fantasy, they may be either unable or unwilling to reveal the precise detail that will ultimately bring its meaning into focus. Generally, an analyst must hear a fantasy many times in many different contexts to identify the key elements, much as in looking at pornography one does not immediately grasp the specific detail that is exciting to the user. While a foot fetishist may be aroused by a photograph of a foot in a high-heeled shoe with a particularly high arch, shot at a precise angle, its impact rarely registers with anyone other than the fetishist, even a sex researcher. In general, one person's pornography is another's soporific.

One patient had a sexual fantasy that appeared in several different but related forms. In one version he could always get an erection by fantasizing having intercourse with his ex-wife; in another fantasizing having sex with a former lover aroused him. What emerged only slowly—and was not fully articulated even by him—was that the specific detail that led to his arousal in each fantasy script was the minutely imagined moment when his lover, on the edge of orgasm, cried out in total abandon, "Now" or "Take me now"—a moment he could illustrate with memories of actual events. From his point of view, his ex-wife and his lover had been out of control with excitement.

Though these memories were incorporated into and key to his basic fantasy, he never described them in his early accounts of it. Yet it was the precise memory of those cries that excited him and that linked these fantasies to his earliest remembered sexual feeling, which was the arousal he had experienced in an episode at a party his seventeen-year-old brother had hosted. One of the guests, his brother's girlfriend, got drunk and had to be put to bed, when the patient, then ten or eleven years old, glimpsed her nakedness and felt the first stirrings of desire. From then on, the image of a sexual partner being out of control—though in a different way—entered into his most intense erotic memories and into the construction of his predominant fantasy.

Why did this image "take"? That it was his brother's girlfriend helped (our rivalries may be played out as much with siblings as with parents—displaced perhaps). Moreover, his sense of his partner's loss of control overcame his fear of being harmed or castrated through sexual contact—a fear engendered by his relationship with his overbearing mother and his rivalry with his brother—and it was only under the cover of his partner's being "disarmed" by pleasure that he could allow himself the luxury of having an orgasm. This patient arranges his fantasy so as to arrive at the part where his sexual partner screams out "Take me now" just at the moment when he wants to ejaculate. (Many men require that a partner climax first, sometimes out of consideration, perhaps more often out of a need for psychological safety: They are afraid to be out of control while their partners are in command of their faculties.)

Many analysts focus almost exclusively on the reconstruction of unconscious fantasy, to the exclusion of any exploration of conscious fantasy. Trained to ask patients for their dreams and to explore those dreams for their latent meanings, they may not think of conscious fantasy as an equally rich source of meaningful material. But the rewards that can be reaped by this kind of exploration are many.[7]

•   •   •

Not only are conscious fantasies hidden from others, but, as already suggested, their deeper meanings remain hidden from the fantasizer as well. While a given fantasy may be an old friend we regularly call upon for soothing or sexual arousal, the inner working of the fantasy remains utterly mysterious to us, the reasons for its power unknown. Our internal censors prevent us from questioning its meaning, from "looking a gift horse in the mouth."

For example, a common male sexual fantasy is the so-called lesbian sex fantasy of having sex with two women. Some men are open to the fantasy but do not actually invoke it; that is, they are aroused by an image of two women having sex together if they encounter it by chance, perhaps while watching porn films. Others purposefully conjure it up as a sexual turn-on, and still others are driven to enact the fantasy, frequently with two prostitutes. But for very few of the men, either those who are passively susceptible to the fantasy or those who invoke it, does the question of *why* this particular fantasy has such a powerful effect arise; it is used without being scrutinized, without any thought of its possible meaning.

The manifest or surface content of a fantasy, like that of a dream, is always the result of a compromise between wishes and prohibitions against them. Like dreams, fantasies cannot be understood in terms of manifest content alone, but must be translated back into the language of desire. Even daydreams that seem relatively transparent—brief, unelaborated flash fantasies about fame, fortune, power, or love—may have a less obvious meaning than is apparent, an unconscious subtext that can be very hard to get at.

Because the wish is disguised, the fantasizer can enjoy it: he, in effect, hoodwinks himself. Therefore, understanding the fantasy entails certain dangers. By talking about it, for example, the fantasizer risks losing the pleasure in his fantasy: in the telling he may understand (or someone may suggest to him) more of the latent content than he wants to be aware of; he may then have to step back in horror or shame, and thus deny himself its pleasure. A Jewish woman I know daydreamed about bringing about world peace by having a sexual affair and winning over the heart of Yassar Arafat. Thinking about it by herself she could focus on the goodness embedded in her concern with peace. Speaking the fantasy out loud she became much too aware of the narcissism involved, not to mention what could be interpreted as a kind of betrayal of her own people (sleeping with the enemy—even if it is being done, Queen Esther–style, in the interests of those people).

Consider Mr. Jordan, an unmarried man in his thirties, who was quite articulate about the fact that his fantasy life revolved around rescuing a damsel in distress. When he is courting—in the first flush of the relationship—he likes to imagine himself playing Pygmalion to a Galatea less advantaged than he. It is not unusual for him to become involved with a woman of slender means and eventually set her up in her own business or encourage her to get professional training. (The childhood edition of his fantasy took the form of saving a little girl on whom he had a crush from being kidnaped.)[8] If things go badly in his relationships—as they have thus far—he toys with the idea of leaving his girl-friend, only to find himself almost paralyzed by a barely glimpsed fantasy that if he abandons her, she will be desolate and might even kill herself.

As a child, Mr. Jordan sided with his mother, who he felt was abused emo-tionally (though not physically) by his father. Experiencing himself as power-less (children always do in such situations) he developed a lifelong need to make restitution to a disadvantaged woman. His Pygmalion fantasy is based on an *underlying* fantasy of saving his mother from his abusive father and a companion fantasy that his mother was mistreated in part because she pre-ferred him to his father.

Mr. Jordan is aware of his desire to play the savior role, and he has noticed himself trying to enact such fantasies many times before. But the fantasy of a woman being so dependent on him that she may kill herself if he leaves is less available to him—one of those mental images that fade in and out of aware-ness, emerging only at certain moments. In Mr. Jordan's case, it emerges *only* when he begins to think about ending the relationship, and it expresses the unconscious contempt he feels for the weakness of his lovers, which is an echo of the contempt he earlier felt for his mother. (After all, part of him thinks, his mother was not blameless; she permitted herself to be abused. And he resents the guilt and sorrow her plight made him feel.) Yet his fears that his various lovers cannot survive without him stoke his guilt and serve to keep him in relationships longer than he wants to stay. Thus both fantasies are very pow-erful in shaping the trajectory of his life.

While Mr. Jordan was aware of the concern and sympathy underlying his rescue fantasies and their enactment, he was not aware of his contempt and anger toward the objects of his rescue projects. Thus at the beginning of his therapy, he was not at all disturbed by his fantasies; they seemed totally con-gruent with the male role as he understood it, and he saw no harm in them. Only when he could connect them to his subsequent disenchantment with his once adored lovers could he begin to understand their connection to his earlier experiences and to his underlying anger at women. Bringing more layers of his fantasies into consciousness has enabled him to free himself from the prison of these perpetually repeating patterns.

Although rescue fantasies often seem to have an obvious meaning, they are complex like all fantasies. They issue from many different levels of the mind and come together in a multilayered meshing of images that can be very diffi-cult to decipher. An adult's rescue fantasies may arise from various childhood and adolescent experiences and feelings.

A rescue fantasy may be a reaction formation against a man's unacknowl-edged anger toward his mother because he had at one time felt unloved by her. I know several men who during adolescence had conscious fantasies of rescu-ing their mothers from dreary lives, and who later transferred this fantasy onto other women. But the anger these men felt at having been neglected, dis-approved of, and criticized by their mothers, who had loved neither their hus-bands nor their sons, and the contempt they sometimes expressed for their mothers, who had never taken responsibility for their own unhappy fates, were also transferred onto other women, with the result that the rescue fan-tasy, like the original fantasy involving the mother, was accompanied by alter-nating wishes to save and to abandon the "beloved."

Other times, a man's need to rescue a woman may relate to unconscious guilt engendered by his fear that he damaged a sister or brother through his own achievements, which left his sibling at a competitive disadvantage. Or it may be that his guilt is stoked by knowledge that he was a replacement child, that he literally took the place of a brother or sister who died before he was ever conceived.

In still another scenario, a man whose father died early in his life and who grew up with a widowed mother may also feel a need to rescue a woman, but often that need may be paired with a wish to himself be rescued by a father fig-ure. The wish for rescue may get encoded in fantasy, for example, in day-dreams of being taken into his boss's business. Such daydreams may be real-ized if the fantasizer finds a mentor who is himself a rescuer.

Sometimes a rescue fantasy is a derivative of adolescent conflict and not pri-marily related to childhood problems. A young man, who, for whatever rea-son, feels unattractive in adolescence and who consequently feels uncomfort-able with women may feel safer (from rejection) in the powerful position of rescuer.

Of course women, too, entertain rescue fantasies. The wish to nurse a wounded or damaged man back to health is embodied in many works that appeal to the female imagination, *Jane Eyre* being one of the more famous examples. And many women feel a need to help "bad" boys straighten out, give up their alcoholism, or learn to hold a job. Consider, too, the fantasy of adopting children by the dozen, sometimes enacted à la Josephine Baker.

The fact that motives and emotions underlying our fantasies remain obscure to us does not necessarily doom us to a treadmill of repetition and frustration. Sometimes, even without deep understanding, one may achieve a fulfilling realization of a fantasy. One man spent fruitless years trying to res-cue women who could not be rescued because they were alcoholic or just neu-rotic. He finally worked out his problem, not by giving up his fantasy but by finding a perfectly competent woman who had inadvertently become roman-tically involved with an extremely clever psychopath. In essence, he "figured out" how to actualize his fantasy in the real world without the downside he had typically encountered.

Just as rescuers generally fail to connect their behaviors with their fantasies, many individuals with self-defeating patterns of behavior—for example, those who repeatedly put themselves in positions to be financially exploited—fail to connect their behaviors with their masochistic fantasies in another sphere, for example, with pleasurable fantasies of being cuckolded. And so on. It is easy to dismiss a fantasy as irrelevant or frivolous, and in so doing fail to understand its source and, even more important, where it is taking us: its impact on the way we live our lives.

It is no accident that fantasies are so difficult for even the fantasizer to penetrate. A fantasy is constructed to provide pleasure or safety or control, but it is very important to keep the scaffolding out of view; fantasy is a magic trick that the fantasizer performs without knowing how he does it. It acts to prevent one part of the self from knowing what another part wants. Through disguises one fools the repressive part of the personality into overlooking the hungry, desiring part.

There is yet another way of hiding fantasies, which goes beyond not sharing them with others or obscuring their meaning from oneself. Some individuals do not recognize fantasies as such, do not register their own fantasies, forget them almost immediately, or even totally repress them. While most people are attuned to both the outside world and the inner world of affective and imaginative life (modes referred to in the psychological literature as the external and internal channels of attention), the degree to which each individual attends to one or the other, and the quality of that participation, vary dramatically. People are not equally adept at accessing preconscious material, at looking inward, and this is true of their sensitivity not just to the realm of fantasy, but to the inner world in general.

Some individuals focus almost exclusively on the external channel, the hurly-burly of the world around them, sometimes as a defense against the conflicts and ambiguities that attention to the inner world might elicit. Rather than relying on the disguise afforded by the fantasized presentation of a wish, they try to preempt the very possibility of fantasy. They are so reluctant to risk any inward glimpse that they turn on the television whenever they are alone, go to sleep listening to the radio, or load their calendars with work obligations or social engagements, trying to crowd out any possibility of reveries that might surface in the absence of noise and commotion.

Consequently, sometimes fantasy is not only difficult to interpret or understand, but hard to access at all. Some people's daydreams may not linger long enough in consciousness for them to note them fully or remember them, just as nighttime dreams may fade so quickly upon awakening that they disappear from recollection. These people may be convinced that they do not dream— or fantasize—at all.

Although some people say they do not have fantasies, this is hardly ever so. One woman, who claimed that she never fantasized, revealed upon further conversation that she had once been an avid fantasist. Raised by a mother who treated her as a stranger of whom she was contemptuous, this woman grew up possessed by the fantasy of having many children, at least a dozen, and becoming such an incredible mother that everyone, including her own mother, would have to sit up and take notice. Hers was a fantasy that, while obviously compensatory in nature, also veered in the direction of a rehearsal for life: that is, it presented her with a life plan. Unfortunately, it was a dress rehearsal for what turned out to be an impossibility, for she was unable to become pregnant. She did go on to adopt two children, whom she loved very much, but in the process of suppressing her pregnancy and Supermom fantasies, she also buried the ability to fantasize consciously.

For many people like this woman, the value of a fantasy is that it *may* come true or will likely come true. Being forced, as she was, to confront the fact that a long-cherished wish (and accompanying fantasy) will never come to pass may cause them to withdraw from the hope that is implicit in fantasy, and thus from fantasy itself. In this way they protect themselves from future pain.

Hers is an extreme case of a common phenomenon: Many adults who in their early years spent a considerable amount of time in the realm of the imagination may, with the responsibilities of adulthood or the disappointments of failed dreams, cease to pay much attention to the inner channel. Out of self-protection, they eliminate fantasy. Someone who earlier longed for love and fantasized great love affairs may turn off the fantasy if it remains unfulfilled well into middle life. If such individuals fantasize, they have brief reveries in the period just after waking or just before going to sleep, or during intervals of solitude like driving alone. They might gorge on movies or popular fiction, enjoying the fantasies embedded in those narratives without having to claim them as their own.

Still other people who claim not to fantasize do not know that certain products of their minds qualify as bona fide fantasies. For whatever reason, they hide from themselves the fact that they fantasize—usually as an aid in further concealing the deeply disguised forbidden wish. Yet ask self-proclaimed non-fantasizers whether they sometimes have imagined conversations in which they come up with witticisms or put-downs that failed to occur to them in real life, and they will generally say yes, but they had not thought to label such scenarios fantasies. Imaginary dialogues, simultaneously wishful and reparative, are often regarded merely as passing thoughts or as rehearsals for coming confrontations. Other fantasies are so integral to the process of thinking that we do not always distinguish them from reality planning; for example, in arranging a party, fleeting fantasies of flirting or of showing up one's rival as an inferior hostess may be interspersed among thoughts about the menu and the seating.

People sometimes think of themselves in metaphoric images, which they regard as descriptive rather than fantasy-laden. Yet these self-descriptions also conceal fantasies that are very close to consciousness but too painful or threatening or "inconsequential" to acknowledge. One man grew up thinking of himself as the white enamel pole in the subway cars of his young manhood. This image was closely related to his belief that he was the pole to which his mother and siblings could cling (he was the son of an alcoholic mother and a dominant father with little or no interest in either his wife's problems or his children's). This man grew up to be a helper par excellence: member of the ski patrol and of the volunteer ambulance service, builder of bookcases for all of the neighbors, and so forth. But growing up as the pole left him with unspoken needs for nurturance, most of which he met by becoming an extravagantly devoted father and thus satisfying his wishes vicariously. (It may be his ambivalence about *being* the pole that prevented him from dwelling on the underlying meaning of that self-image.)

Similarly, a woman saw herself as a beautiful *objet*. She felt that her function was to provide pleasure for other people but that she did so simply by being; by virtue of her beauty and her undemanding manner, she was worthy of admiration. This image-fantasy concealed her feeling that were she to make demands, to transcend objecthood, she might be rejected. By seeing herself as a work of art she turned a negative expectation into an attribute—a kind of reversal in fantasy.

Some fantasies go by so quickly—flash fantasies, we might call them—that they do not register as imaginative material. People tend to equate fantasy with elaborate plot lines, not with the on-off flickerings of intense affect-laden imagery that are common to us all. As an example of a flash fantasy, consider the momentary fear-fantasy a lone woman might have on entering a deserted parking garage. Visions of knife-wielding assailants and gun-toting kidnapers move into and out of consciousness so quickly that she barely apprehends them. Such flash fantasies get lost in the cacophony of what William James aptly called the "stream of consciousness." In this ever changing stream, fantasy snippets readily find hiding places. They are like little fish that take on the coloration of the surrounding vegetation or hide behind rocks, plankton in the swirling currents of consciousness. Because consciousness is so complex—a shifting array of thoughts, feelings, images, and perceptions—fantasies that are not fully attended to can slip into and out of the forefront of attention, concealed just out of the range of awareness.

Not only may we fail to register fantasies; we may repress them because of their taboo content. Consequently, we may not just fail to understand our fantasies or attend to them, but totally fail to access them.

Much of fantasy remains buried in the unconscious. We know it is there because we see its traces in our daydreams, our night dreams, our symptoms, and our neuroses. But we are unable to invoke the underlying fantasy itself—the "ur" fantasy. At best we may be able to reconstruct it in analysis or to intuit its meaning. At worst we are enslaved by it. Certainly many people, with or without analysis, become sufficiently self-aware to achieve a measure of freedom from those parts of the underlying fantasy that are destructive.

In people poorly attuned to subjective life, attention to any available material from their imagination may be an important highway to the unconscious and may help illuminate the meaning of previously obscure patterns of behavior. While fantasy material is not always deeply revealing, awareness of it sensitizes the individual to the inner channel and therefore is always useful, particularly in therapy.

Such sensitization proved abundantly productive for my patient Mrs. Elgin, a highly accomplished, professionally successful middle-aged woman who had just returned from a college reunion, who reported that while visiting her old campus and looking at a plaque commemorating those of its students killed in World War I, she had suddenly burst into tears. She would never have thought to report the incident but for her husband's puzzlement and his insistence that she bring the incident into her analysis.

The emotion, which Mrs. Elgin attributed to nothing more than a generalized sadness over the lives lost in that remote war, was *too* severed from any narrative content or association, so we could not work with it at the time. Some months later, when Mrs. Elgin described a similar reaction she had while watching a movie, we had more to go on. The movie was *Chariots of Fire,* set just after World War I. During an early scene in which one of the film's protagonists is on his way up to Cambridge by train, Mrs. Elgin found herself crying uncontrollably at the sight of young baggage handlers who had obviously been maimed in the war. She was moved, too, by the ultimate Olympic triumph of the two main protagonists, young men who were initially conflicted because of internal struggles: Harold, the Cambridge man, felt himself an outsider by virtue of being Jewish even though he came from a wealthy cosmopolitan family; and Eric, born to a missionary family in China and committed to return there as a missionary, was troubled by the potential conflict between his commitment to running and his commitment to God. But her major emotional reaction, she said, was reserved for the crippled young men, minor characters who appeared only in the opening scene. (On another level, it was the ability of Harold and Eric to confront internal and external obstacles in realizing their dreams that accounted for her deep fascination with the film.)

By treating these two events (her responses to the plaque and the film) as dream fragments, Mrs. Elgin was able to associate to her reaction to the maimed railroad workers. She now revealed that she had kept a sort of mental index of all the images of amputees she had seen over the years (much as did one of the characters in the novel *The World According to Garp*). She did not know why these images had stayed with her so vividly, but she could recall the exact time frame, setting, details, and circumstances of the initial "encounter" with each amputee, and on a few occasions, she found herself weaving stories about the flash images, tales that always involved some "if only" element so that the maiming trauma might have been prevented. In essence, these musings were "undoing" fantasies.

The person for whom Mrs. Elgin truly grieved, as expressed in her tears for the dead and maimed of World War I, turned out to be (in her associations) not a young man at all, but her mother, a woman for whom, at least consciously, she had little regard. Nonetheless, her mother's effect on her was direct and ongoing, as her mother had actively stoked her highly developed and dearly cherished ambitions. Indeed, she often complained of feeling that she was living out her mother's dreams, which she had imbibed with her mother's milk. Though extremely close to her mother in earliest childhood, she had lost respect for her in later years, feeling that her mother had wasted her life. Thus, the conscious contempt she felt toward her mother, the necessity to escape her mother's domination (benign though it might seem), and the need to disidentify, to plot a life quite different from her mother's relatively impoverished one (incorporating a number of her mother's abandoned dreams) had eroded her original feelings of closeness and warmth. Such feelings could continue only at an unconscious level.

The patient's susceptibility to World War I tragedies arose, in part, then, from the fact that that time frame coincided with the early adulthood of her mother; it was her mother whom she saw as maimed, both in the pursuit of her own ambitions (growing up in a time that virtually prohibited professional achievement by women) and in her femininity (by virtue of her personal insecurities). Her mother was the important person who she felt had been so sorely deprived, and whose plight so moved her.[9]

As she came to realize that her response to the plaque and the film was an intense sorrow for people who, like her mother, seemed to have been robbed of their rightful opportunities, she began to reminisce about her mother's lost chances. She allowed herself to fantasize about what might have happened had her mother been widowed rather than divorced, for it was the divorce that consolidated her mother's sense of defeat and ushered in her deterioration. Only in the patient's fascination with amputees, and periodic fantasies about them, were to be found the remnants of that great affection and sorrow that she had once felt for her mother; only through these very fragmentary flash fantasies did she have access to the strong emotion that had once bound her to her mother.

Those fantasies that related to the guilt she felt over her loss of love for her mother were manifest indirectly in certain phobic preoccupations and avoidances. In essence, the patient avoided situations that she irrationally feared might maim her; as if she feared that she would be punished for rejecting her maimed mother, or that she herself, who identified so strongly with her mother, would be injured. Her new knowledge was freeing and relieving in several different ways; it fostered a reconciliation with her mother, it greatly diminished her phobic preoccupations, and it enabled her to pursue her professional ambitions with much less conflict and less drivenness.

Sometimes we can find unexpected avenues into the hidden fantasy life of an individual, even in someone who on the surface has only a very limited repertoire of fantasy. Another patient, Mr. Kenney, a successful executive who loathed the tensions of corporate life, was divorced and in his middle forties. He came into treatment because he was having an all too familiar problem with his new girlfriend: though he was very much in love with her he found himself losing sexual desire. This had been a problem in his marriage and in all his long-term affairs, but he had not thought about it in depth. Insofar as he had a fantasy life, it consisted of highly formulaic and repetitive sexual fantasies, all of them reveries of business trips where he would meet scintillating young women who would introduce him to an adventurous life that had thus far eluded him. In reality, despite frequent exotic business trips extending over some twenty years, only twice had he had the kind of magical encounter that was the basis of his fantasy life, and even then the episodes had been brief.

Though a very intelligent, creative, and insightful man, Mr. Kenney was not given to introspection. As it turned out, however, he was an avid reader, and through the books of one of his favorite authors we gained a better understanding of the dynamics that lay behind his sexual apathy and flight from commitment. Like many people who do not create many of their own, he metabolized and enjoyed other people's fantasies—fantasies that gave a narrative structure to his own longings—as they were encoded in the books he chose to read.

His fondness was for the Travis McGee series of mysteries written by John D. MacDonald. What appealed to him was the unfettered life of the tough detective McGee, who always gives as good as he gets. McGee is not bogged down in corporate life but lives alone on a houseboat, *The Busted Flush,* which he won in a poker game and is docked in Florida. McGee describes himself as a "salvage expert" who recovers lost property—usually for beautiful women—in return for half the recovered value. Each adventure is accompanied by some kind of romantic interest, which for one reason or another never proves enduring. In addition he has an avuncular older friend, Meyer, who lives on a neighboring boat, a man with whom he has no competitive rivalry but rather a mutually supportive friendship. Meyer, a semiretired economist, is well known in international circles for his expertise on currency exchange. Unlike McGee, he is safety oriented and not in very good physical shape; he is more reasoned, timid perhaps, and often exerts a calming effect on McGee, restraining his impetuousness.

Travis McGee stands as the prototype of a certain kind of footloose and fancy free American hero, who tolerates no put-downs and who always stumbles into adventures. He has good (male) friends—in McGee's case a benign, supportive, mild-mannered father figure—in the foreground and plenty of attractive, available women in the background. His unfettered condition saves him from any sense of being tamed, trammeled, or tied down. He doesn't have to take any nonsense.

My patient was able to work with these characteristics of the fictional McGee to reach an understanding of his own behavior, not just in his love affairs but in his business life. He saw that what caused his sexual alienation was a claustrophobia that he associated with any committed relationship, a fear of being controlled. He felt similar fear in his business life—avoiding confrontation and feeling somewhat frightened, manipulated, and overwhelmed by the predator entrepreneurs he dealt with daily. Our focus on the theme of claustrophobia led to a fruitful exploration of his early life, and revealed at least two important origins of his fear of being tied down or constricted: The first was related to a sense of being overcontrolled by an intrusive mother and unprotected by his always on-the-move salesman father. The second was a serious, three-month-long fight with a debilitating viral illness when he was ten. We also examined his conflict aversion, which seemed related to his fear of bullies and his reluctance to fight during his adolescence, a period when he was still recovering from the effects of his illness and had yet to grow into his limbs or his full strength.

His identification with McGee allowed him vicarious gratification of the wish to live free and unfettered and it undid—at least in fantasy—his aversion to confrontation. Nor is there any doubt that Mr. Kenney rehabilitated his father by identifying him with the benevolent figure of Meyer. As a bonus, he had discovered a series with no resident female, only lovers who drifted in and out, which helped him feel better about his own transient love affairs.

But closer exploration revealed that Mr. Kenney was divided in his identifications between Travis McGee and Meyer: McGee was his admired persona while Meyer was in many ways his real persona, prudent and successful, though not in his mind a desirably assertive macho man. There is reason to believe that John MacDonald, McGee's creator, embodied a similar divided identification. According to the psychoanalyst and literary critic Jay Martin, the dying MacDonald arranged that the last McGee novel be published posthumously. This choice suggested to Martin that MacDonald was in fact overtly identified with Travis McGee and that one might anticipate some overlap between their personalities.[10]

Martin's supposition was in fact borne out in psychological tests Dr. Raymond D. Fowler, a psychologist, had given MacDonald.[11] Fowler persuaded MacDonald, who had earlier suffered from acute anxiety, at which time he had become acquainted with the psychoanalytic literature, to agree to take the

Minnesota Multi-Phase Personality Inventory (MMPI)—indeed to take it three times. MacDonald filled out the questionnaire, once as himself, once as Travis McGee, and once as Meyer. And the results were more complicated than any one-on-one personality identification.

MacDonald's McGee questionnaire revealed him to be energetic, easily bored, impulsive, risk-taking, egocentric, demanding of others in a narcissistic manner, lacking in adequate conscience development, and therefore free of inhibiting guilt, anxiety, and remorse.[12] In contrast, MacDonald himself was closer in personality configuration to Meyer. According to Fowler,

> McGee is a creature of MacDonald's imagination who has almost no similarities to MacDonald in personality, behavior or life-style. Meyer, on the other hand, could well be called MacDonald's alter ego. Intelligent and thoughtful, with a great store of information and ability to stand back and consider before acting, Meyer plays a vital role for McGee and perhaps for MacDonald as well. Meyer provides MacDonald with an opportunity to enter McGee's life, to talk with him, advise him and react to him. Although McGee is the narrator, it is through the eyes of Meyer, and therefore MacDonald, that we see Travis McGee's world.[13]

Jay Martin uses William Butler Yeats's metaphor of the mask to conceptualize MacDonald's split persona. The mask is that which is "opposite to one's identity but identical with [one's] desire." Thus, Travis McGee functions as MacDonald's mask, "the fiction of his creator's desire."[14]

Looked at this way, my patient's involvement with the Travis McGee mysteries reveals the same kind of defensive function; his desire is encoded in the identification with McGee, but he experiences a paradoxical longing for a father figure like Meyer—ironically, a man much like him. From this perspective, the therapeutic task for Mr. Kenney is to integrate some of McGee's "in your face" bravado with Meyer's reasonableness.

Mr. Kenney's need to participate in the world of fantasy to a fuller extent than his own limited fantasy-making abilities allowed led him to a fascination with another fictional character—one who did in some ways bridge the gap between Travis McGee's reckless bravado and Meyer's intellectual calm. Horatio Hornblower, the hero of a series of novels written by C. S. Forester, attracted Mr. Kenney at a young age, and his fondness for this fictional character persisted into adulthood and found its way into our work together.

Horatio Hornblower was a swashbuckling British naval hero who distinguished himself during Britain's rule of the sea during the eighteenth century. Starting off as a midshipman on a British sailing frigate, he climbed naval ranks through a series of daring escapades; Forester's later novels depicted Hornblower as Captain, then Lord of the Realm, and finally Admiral. During all these stages of his life Hornblower was an intelligent and courageous leader, adored by his men and feared by his adversaries. However, Forester portrays him as an overly sensitive man, plagued by self-recrimination and doubt. Even as a French frigate flees in flames, Hornblower worries about his wounded men, obsesses about the appropriateness of his actions, and anticipates the response of the distant and disapproving naval authorities to whom he must soon answer in England.

Mr. Kenney would recount Hornblower's passions and fears with great emotion. Hornblower was conquering the world at the same time as he seemed to fear the shadows of his own insecurities. Here was a man about to be knighted by the Queen of England who trembled with embarrassment and worried whether he might trip over his ceremonial sword. As the decks vibrated under the rumble of the firing gun carriages, Hornblower fretted, not about the surrounding carnage, but about his suitability for the task given to him by a haughty British crown.

And there was hardly a woman in sight. Like the women in the Travis McGee books, Hornblower's women—including his two wives—veer in and out of sight. But unlike McGee, Hornblower feared the "mystery" of women almost as much as he felt his own inadequacy. Again, Mr. Kenney resonated with the feelings of his fictional hero, identifying with every crest in his career, every trough in his ego. These were stories about Mr. Kenney's feelings about his own life—particularly in the corporate world he had grown to loathe. He had designed and implemented some of the best known marketing campaigns in American life, yet he was "afraid someone would ask [him] a question at a board meeting." The similarity between him and his fictional hero was so great that one of his friends, a man to whom Mr. Kenney had lent one of the Hornblower novels, even remarked on it. "When I asked him later how he had enjoyed it," Mr. Kenney reported, "he responded 'I thought I was reading about you. You *are* Horatio Hornblower.'"

What I am suggesting is that people who do not create many fantasies of their own may nonetheless participate very actively in the world of fantasy, as consumers rather than producers. Moreover, knowing their favorite fiction (or movies, or plays, or whatever) can give clues as to their underlying personality themes and dreams that are just as meaningful as those that derive from the self-generated fantasy life of other people. Reading fiction is satisfying, in part, as Freud told us, because it puts "us in a position where we can enjoy our own daydreams without self-reproach or shame."[15] Whereas a spontaneously generated daydream may be experienced as shameful or guilt-provoking, a similar daydream expressed in the work of an author or filmmaker or other artist can be vicariously enjoyed without apparent self-implication. If we cannot generate fantasies ourselves, we may use those embedded in theater, book, movie, opera, television, and so on, as a substitute. The creator becomes our secret collaborator, giving voice to our longings. This is another way we can hide our fantasies from ourselves, and remain unaware even of *having* them.

However, we cannot be completely co-opted by someone else's longings. We only utilize those fantasies that speak at least in part to our own particular unconscious and preconscious inclinations, needs, and wishes. This is the reason that certain books appeal to some people and not to others. I suspect that both the Travis McGee and Horatio Hornblower series are more interesting to men than to women and appeal most strongly to a certain kind of man—one who is brave but uncertain, and who may feel edgy or anxious about the interdependency almost implicit in modern middle-class marriage.

The consumption of fantasy is not only the province of those who are limited as fantasists; in fact, fiction writers and other artists, who are generally superb fantasists, tend to be avid consumers of works of fantasy and narrative. They are responsive from early on to the game of "what if," to the imaginative envisioning of different possible selves, and they enjoy excursions into the make-believe world of others. For them as for all of us, fictional stories, in whatever form, make possible the construction of an alternate world, an imaginative space. The great fantasist writer Italo Calvino in "A Cinema Goer's Autobiography" writes about what film meant to him:

> I suppose: distance. It satisfied a need for distance, for an expansion of the boundaries of the real, for seeing immeasurable dimensions open up all around me, abstract as geometrical entities, yet concrete too, crammed full of faces and situations and settings, which established an (abstract) network of relationships with the world of direct experience.[16]

It is commonly observed that we misunderstand animals because we anthropomorphize them: that is, we project human characteristics onto them. What is less widely remarked upon is that our notion of human consciousness, other than our own, is beset by the same problem; we each tend to project our personal experience of consciousness onto others of our kind and assume that what is true for us represents the experience of all humankind. This kind of projection is yet another factor in the "hiddenness" of our fantasy lives. We won't, and, because of the many hard-to-communicate differences in the way our fantasies manifest themselves, we *can't* be effective in conveying our experience of our fantasy lives to other people. These differences pertain to every aspect of fantasy.

Access to fantasy varies from person to person, and for reasons generally having no relation to mental "health." Neurotics and nonneurotics may or may not be "good" fantasizers. The differences in the access people have to their fantasies is to some degree a matter of interest, attention, early life encouragement (or its lack), and only sometimes the result of inhibition or repression due to shame, guilt, or anxiety. Degree of access to the internal world and to fantasy depends on the way a particular mind is organized and its innate dispositions. Just as people differ in their talent for painting or writing or composing, so too are they variously endowed with the capacity for creating *conscious* fantasy or for reaching deep into the inner world. For some, the channel to the unconscious seems to open wider than it does to others. Some people are gifted fantasists, others occasional fantasists; some people use memory as a substitute for fantasy (reality plagiarists, as it were), while others borrow from the fantasies of the culture.

Not only do we differ in our access to fantasy, but in the modality in which our fantasies appear. Each of us has a unique mental pattern, a mental landscape with a characteristic profile, its various features related to specific patterns in the stream of consciousness, the predominance of one or another of the faculties of sense, and the relative prevalence of various modes of thought. The sum of these parts will help to determine the particular form in which our fantasies are cast.[17]

Consider the stream of consciousness, that mysterious, ambient medium in which all our fantasies emerge and float. For some the stream pushes up well-elaborated perceptions, images, emotions, memories, and fantasies; for others it seems to flow *toward* something and to culminate in a directed kind of thinking that includes planning, observation, and abstract thought; and for still others it is often given over to the act of "floating," which yields an apparently content-free meditative state. And of course, any given person's stream of consciousness can change course, from moment to moment, in response to either willed or involuntary dicta.

Those people whose minds appear to be blank a good part of the time, seem to need this floating or idling a few hours a day. But, interestingly, their most creative thoughts bubble to the surface during the floating time, good evidence for the creative thinking—including fantasizing—that goes on just below consciousness. If one of these types forces herself to think actively, she may have a kind of personality change, appearing much funnier, faster, or sharper, because of the greater number of conscious mental associations, but she is likely to feel exhausted.

Our reliance upon different primary sensory modalities is another source of the differences in our fantasy lives. There are few musicians, for example, who do not hear music in their heads a large part of the time. One young man always hears background music, as though it were continuously being played. The songwriter and singer Carly Simon said that she did not compose consciously, but rather that she selected and edited the best songs from among those tunes that were constantly piped into her mind. Artists, of course, have heads stuffed with visual images. But such predispositions are not limited to musicians and artists.

In the neurologist Oliver Sack's account of Temple Grandin, a brilliant biologist and engineer who was an autistic child, we have a good example of someone almost completely visual, and an excellent description of what that would feel like taken to an extreme. Grandin had a "near-hallucinary power of visual imagery."[18] Sacks remarks on

> the vividness of . . . memory . . . it seemed to play itself in her mind with extraordinary detail. . . . It was as if the original scene, its perceptions (with all its attendant feelings), was reproduced, replayed, with virtually no modification. This quality of memory seemed . . . both prodigious and pathological—prodigious in its detail and pathological in its affinity, more akin to a computer record than to anything else.[19]

But the capacity for such detailed visualization, however pathological in many respects, proved valuable in Grandin's work, allowing her to visualize the sequences in her animal husbandry designs, to create a kind of virtual reality. (Grandin thinks most autistics are visual thinkers.) In general, the differences in our ability to visualize scenes are remarkable, ranging from almost eidetic recall to a virtual blank.

People have been known to feel acute envy upon discovering that others have highly developed senses that they lack. Pity the would-be filmmaker who discovers the weakness of his capacity for visualization compared to that of idolized directors and cinematographers. Of course because our modes of thinking and fantasizing are cast so differently most of us do not know what we're missing. If one were to use a comic strip to portray consciousness, for some the main action would be portrayed in drawings with just a few words in the balloons; for others the dialogue-bearing balloons would overwhelm the images, entirely filling the comic strip. For many individuals, these patterns may be subject to change over the years; scientists, for example, often lose the capacity for visualization—and sometimes for fantasy, too—and come to think almost exclusively in abstractions.

Some of these differences in mental landscapes may be learned, some psychologically motivated, some undoubtedly inborn. Sometimes a mood can evoke a fantasy deploying a certain sensory modality. One woman hears music when she is feeling assertive or triumphant, and then it is always martial band music, while another woman hears strains of the "Merry Widow" whenever she is angry at her husband. "I saw red" is probably a literal truth for many people in a state of anger.

A motivational component may also shape the formal characteristics of fantasy life. For Ms. Jones, her fantasies assume the form of conversations because this is her way of overcoming her feelings of isolation and alienation. These ongoing conversations are edited versions of past conversations, wished-for talks that never happened and are not expected to or that may yet take place. Ms. Jones fantasizes conversations with her ailing mother, her therapist, her business partner, a production manager who works for her, her about-to-be ex-husband, and so on. What they all have in common is that Ms. Jones invokes them because she cannot bear to be alone. Uneasy with people, she is nonetheless terrified and lonely without them. On occasion, she even interjects fantasy scenarios, usually about being lonely or abandoned, into everyday conversation. One night at dinner she told several friends, "Twenty years from now you'll be sitting around this table. You'll be saying 'What ever happened to Janet [Jones]? She got a divorce. Nothing good happened after that. She was a lesbian for a while. She was out in the Hamptons for a while. But what do you think happened to her?'" Here her perpetual fear of being left out, of not being listened to or understood, leaked into an actual exchange with friends. Ms. Jones's description of this dinner table speech was, as it happened, the first indication her therapist had of her imaginary conversations. Further discussion of the scene led to an awareness of the degree to which Ms. Jones's inner life took the form of dialogue—a discovery that had many implications for the future course of her therapy.

Imaginary conversations are often not acknowledged as fantasy, but they are a very common form of fantasy, whether deliberately invoked or passively experienced. For some people, fantasy conversation is pleasurable; others may feel inundated by the continual buzz of conversation in their heads and may try to shake them off. Some people are so immersed in their inner world of fantasy that they walk the streets vocalizing their imaginary conversations. (Though we call them crazy, many of us can recall momentary lapses when we do the same, or stop just short of doing so. All mental experiences are on a continuum.)

Despite these major differences in the makeup of the stream of consciousness, we generally automatically assume that other minds are like our own. Projection accounts for part of this ignorance, but there is another reason. Because communication relies so heavily on language and most of us do not have the language skills to convey such complex and subtle phenomena, it is very difficult for us to get any sense of another person's inner life. Some writers, however, do have that skill. Thus much of what we know of the variety of interior monologues comes to us from gifted scientists/writers like Oliver Sacks, and also from modern authors. Early in the twentieth century writers took interior monologues as one of their main subjects of exploration, notably Virginia Woolf in *Mrs. Dalloway* and James Joyce in *Ulysses*. In rendering the streams of consciousness of Leopold Bloom, Stephen Daedalus, and Molly Bloom, Joyce gives us three distinct pictures of subjective life. David Lodge has elegantly described these differences:

> Whereas Stephen's and Bloom's streams of consciousness are stimulated and made to change course by their sense-impressions, Molly, lying in the darkness, with only the occasional noise of the street to distract her, is borne along by her own memories, one memory triggering another by some kind of association.

And whereas association in Stephen's consciousness tends to be metaphorical (one thing suggests another by resemblance, often of an arcane or fanciful kind) and in Bloom's metonymic (one thing suggesting another because they are connected by cause and effect, or by contiguity in space/time), association in Molly's consciousness is simply literal: one breakfast in bed reminds her of another, as one man in her life reminds her of another.[20]

Generally people who think primarily in terms of metaphor or metonymy are more likely to be prolific and inventive fantasists than those who think more concretely. And the tendency to think in metaphors may also be an early sign of creative ability, particularly in the area of writing. The portrait of Daedalus, of course, is that of the artist/novelist as a young man. Novelists are almost always gifted fantasists, and this was evident in the childhoods of many in their perpetual daydreaming or creation of imaginary companions. But creative people in a variety of other fields may be poor fantasizers.

Knowing the particular landscape of another person's mind can have consequences. No one should be more alert to the consequences than a psychotherapist, but this is a little discussed area of inquiry. I was surprised to discover, late in her analysis, that one of my patients always had an imaginary conversation running in her head, usually with her father or her grown son. (As a child this woman had had an imaginary companion.) The discovery of this fact led to an understanding of problems in separation, which had resulted in difficulties in being alone. A hunch: many therapists focus on the content of what the patient says, and not on the form in which it presents itself, because the primary mode of patient/therapist communication—language—washes out the formal characteristics. As a result therapists may overlook important characteristics of their patients' mental lives. Ms. Jones and her therapist (like me and my patient) had failed to note this habit of mind, though many of Ms. Jones's imaginary conversations took place with her therapist and encapsulated the major thrust of her transference feelings for her therapist.[21]

The hiddenness of our fantasy lives takes many forms, and the ways we keep other people ignorant of our fantasies go far beyond deliberately keeping them secret. Moreover, we often manage to remain unaware of them ourselves. Paradoxically, despite our determination to keep our fantasies private, we are wordlessly telegraphing them all the time. Indeed, the nonverbal (and sometimes verbal) communication of fantasy materials between and among people is the stuff of interpersonal communication. We enact aspects of our fantasies not only in our personal relationships but in the choices we make—the goals we aspire to, the paths we follow, the overall tone and content of the voyage we make from birth to death.

2

THE FANTASIES OF
EVERYDAY LIFE

WHILE FANTASIES ARE SOMETIMES HARD TO ACCESS, NONETHELESS, MOST OF us—about 96 percent according to a number of different researchers in the United States—report having had daydreams or reveries at one time or another.[1] The psychologist Silvan Tomkins's response to this finding makes an important point: "If daydreaming is a trivial activity, then most Americans are wasting some part of every day. If it is a pathological activity, then most Americans are sick. If it represents a sublimated drive gratification, then most Americans are either underfed, underwatered, or undersexed."[2]

If fantasy is not just an atavistic carryover from an earlier stage of our development—the mental equivalent of the superfluous appendix—what functions does daydreaming serve? Vital ones it appears, since many psychoanalysts have observed that an inability to fantasize is just as pathological as an excessive immersion in fantasy. Acquiring the capacity to fantasize (or to tap into the fantasy inherent in novels, movies, and other cultural materials) is a developmental achievement, without which one's life is bloodless, passionless, and sometimes lacking in hope and forward momentum as well. Ideally the lived moment is richly invested with fantasy and memory, even when we are unaware of the fantasy activity taking place just below the surface. If the investment is meager, however, then life begins to feel thin, mechanistic, detached.

Fantasy is situated within the context of imagination.[3] Imagination, which depends on ability to create and manipulate symbols, is the mental capacity to think of possibilities beyond the evidence of immediate sense perceptions. Imagination allows us to contemplate alternatives to the real world of people, places, and things; to the time-bound events of the past and the present.

The future itself is by definition an imaginative construct. Without imagination, consciousness would be locked into the sensory present or the remembered past,[4] denied the contemplation of infinite alternatives and possibilities, relegated forever to an animal-like existence. For this reason imagination is often referred to as the uniquely human gift, that which sets human beings apart from other species. The experiential life of a fourteenth century cow is essentially like the life of a twentieth century cow; not so for a person. Many species are programmed so that the individual is preadapted to its environment. In contrast, as pointed out by Anthony Storr, it is because humans are specifically *not* adapted to any one environment that they can, and must, adapt to many different environments. As Storr puts it, "Man's creative adaptability paradoxically derives from his primary lack of adaptation."[5]

Imagination is humankind's major adaptive tool. Without it, there could be no picturing of mental alternatives to current discomfort or deprivation, no planning of a future course of action, no creative rethinking of the past to make it pertinent to the present and future. Using the imagination to scan trial actions and conjure up a range of responses, and thus to predict the immediate and long-term future, is essential to both scientific thinking and fantasy thinking, and one of their common characteristics. Still, there are significant differences, even though some theorists have proposed that some form of fantasy attends all thinking. The psychologist Jerome Singer gives an example, which he calls fantasy, of a professor fumbling to open a door because he is preoccupied with thinking about which of two possible interpretations of an obscure text is more aesthetically pleasing. I would regard the professor as engaging in an intellectual pursuit involving imaginative alternatives, but not as fantasizing.

Fantasizing is a unique kind of imaginative thought that serves a psychological or emotional purpose rather than a primarily pragmatic one.[6] This description of the goal of fantasy enables us to distinguish fantasy from imaginative thinking as a whole. However, the dividing line can be blurry.

A common example from everyday life illustrates the way fantasy as a subspecies of imaginative thinking is sometimes hard to identify. A young woman whose relatively new boyfriend is away on a business trip finds herself visualizing him in her mind's eye as he goes about his morning rituals, eats breakfast, gets dressed, and takes a taxi, and she easily imagines the route he takes because she is familiar with the city where he is. She does not call this exercise fantasy. And yet, knowledge of her life history—her childhood fear of abandonment engendered during her single mother's illness and hospitalization, her vivid and painful childhood memory of being lost in a department store, her abrupt rejection by a former boyfriend who disappeared without warning—suggests that visualizing her boyfriend is a fantasy that allows her to feel emotionally anchored. Her imaginative thinking undoes the threat of separation; in her mind she is with him.

Margaret Atwood's novel *The Handmaid's Tale* provides another good example of the difficulty of distinguishing precisely between imaginative thinking in general and fantasizing in particular. Living under totalitarian rule in a kind of Orwellian regime, the protagonist thinks about what may have happened to her well-loved husband, Luke. Her three scenarios are all plausible, and she describes them as beliefs. In the first scenario, she says,

> I believe Luke is lying face down in a thicket, a tangle of bracken.... What is left of him: his hair, the bones, the plaid wool shirt, green and black, the leather belt, the work boots. I know exactly what he was wearing. I can see his clothes in my mind, bright as a lithograph or a full-color advertisement from an ancient magazine, though not his face, not so well.[7]

In the second scenario she visualizes Luke alive but imprisoned:

> I also believe that Luke is sitting up in a rectangle somewhere, gray cement or on a ledge or the edge of something, a bed or a chair.... He finds it painful to move his hands, painful to move, he doesn't know what he's accused of. A problem, there must be something, some accusation. Otherwise why are they keeping him, why isn't he already dead? He must know something they want to know. I can't imagine he hasn't already said whatever it is. I would.... Does he know that I am here, alive, that I am thinking about him? I have to believe so. In reduced circumstances you have to believe all kinds of things. I believe in thought transference, vibrations in the ether, that sort of junk. I never used to.[8]

And in the third scenario, she believes "that they didn't catch him or catch up with him after all, that he made it, reached the bank, swam the river, crossed the border, dragged himself up on the shore, an island, teeth chattering; found his way to a nearby farmhouse." If the third scenario really happened, she expects to hear from Luke.

The protagonist narrator goes on to muse,

> The things I believe can't all be true, though one of them must be. But I believe in all of them, all three versions of Luke, at one and the same time. This contradictory way of believing seems to me, right now, the only way I can believe anything. Whatever the truth is, I will be ready for it.[9]

Are these fantasies or are they examples of imaginative thinking in which a woman considers alternative possibilities? I think they are on the border, but veering toward fantasy because of the use to which they are being put. That is, they are fully visualized scenarios that are invoked for a specific psychological purpose—to protect the narrator against the horrible shock of surprise, of being unprepared and vulnerable. (Margaret Atwood may have introduced these alternative scenarios not primarily to represent the musings of a real person, but to inject suspense into her plot. Nonetheless, they constitute a very good description of the kinds of alternate scenarios that each of us conjures up to guard against being caught unaware.)

Imaginative thinking, then, is the more inclusive category and it comprises abstract thinking, problem solving, and fantasy thinking, overlapping but nonetheless distinct modes of mental activity. Imaginative thinking is often dispassionate, allowing the thinker to scan a number of alternatives in which he or she may have little personal investment, whereas the imaginative script in fantasy thinking is highly charged. Generally (though not always) fantasizing is associated with the pleasure of a wish or hope being fulfilled. Alternately, it may contain fear or mitigate some other uncomfortably strong emotion.[10]

Many gifted fantasizers intuitively understand that fantasy serves some psychological function. This is what Dominique Aury (pen name Pauline Réage), the author of Story of O, is telling us when she writes about the fantasy life to which she retreated in her mind, before she wrote it out for the man she loved (and ultimately the world): "I no doubt accepted my life with such patience . . . only because I was so certain of being able to find whenever I wanted that other, obscure life that is life's consolation, that other life unacknowledged and unshared."[11] She goes on to say about the fantasies she set down on paper: "All I know is that they were beneficent and protected me mysteriously"[12]—this about a series of sadomasochistic fantasies that were violent enough to horrify many people. Whatever a fantasy's form, its intended effect is "beneficent and protective."

Freud helped tease out the specific nature of fantasy by describing the mode of thinking it involves. Fantasizing is a mental process that the fantasizer knows to be an act of the imagination. However pleasing the fantasy may be, the fantasizer knows that it is imaginary, a self-generated fiction. In the process of generating fantasy and manipulating it, the fantasizer is almost always aware of creating and directing the script and able to distinguish fantasy from reality just as the child distinguishes make-believe play from reality. Imaginary material of waking life that is not recognized as such is not fantasy but merges into illusion, delusion, and hallucination.

Fantasies vary from fragmentary flash images to complexly plotted scenarios. Fantasy scripts are diverse; they may be sexual or angry, dreams of hope, or scenes of fearful encounter; sometimes they may be given over to the vicarious quests and victories not of the self but of an alter ego. Fantasy time may be in the present, in the near or distant future, or in the recent or remote past.

Some fantasies arise spontaneously during the waking state; others are invoked for a specific purpose such as sexual arousal or self-soothing. Unprompted reveries often occur when going to sleep or waking up (hypnogogic and hypnopompic fantasies, respectively), and fantasies specific to the therapeutic situation may arise in the course of treatment, especially fantasies directed toward the therapist. Whether a fantasy is purposely invoked or merely wafts into consciousness, it becomes part of waking life, though sometimes barely noticed.

Once a fantasy is invoked, the fantasizer savors, lingers on, or revises the most exciting, pleasing, or soothing part of his or her mental creation, whirling it around in the mind until arriving at the "version" that is most gratifying, often slowing the fantasy down at the most stimulating point, speeding it up at moments that have begun to seem boring, improving on the dialogue, adding new touches to glamorize the setting. A man may repeatedly play a sexual scenario involving a woman he has just met, picturing her in a number of different poses; a woman may conjure up a dozen different declarations of love from a man she is going out with that night; an office worker may come up with multiple witty, wounding responses to the boss's negative performance review; and so forth.

Not only did Freud describe the mode of thought involved in fantasizing, but he also analyzed the motive forces that cause a fantasy to surface. Fantasy is a compensation for what the fantasizer lacks in life. In "Creative Writers and Day-dreaming," still the touchstone for subsequent psychoanalytic definitions, he wrote, "We may lay it down that a happy person never phantasies, only an unsatisfied one. The motive forces of phantasies are unsatisfied wishes, and every single phantasy is the fulfillment of a wish, a correction of unsatisfying reality.[13] In this early formulation frustration with the external world triggers the process of fantasizing.

Gradually Freud and his followers discovered that fantasy can also be wish-fulfillment of a more complicated kind, originating not just as substitution for a deprivation or shortfall in the external world, but as an ingenious, often highly indirect, and disguised solution to conflict emanating from the internal world, from an individual's inability to gratify his or her wishes for aesthetic or moral reasons. In this formulation, frustration may result as readily from inner prohibitions as from external barriers. Fantasy then disguises our wishes to prevent conflict with these internal prohibitions, thus allowing imaginary gratification that does not arouse the fear of punishment. One may fantasize, for example, sleeping with one's brother's best friend, because the real wish—to sleep with the brother—is taboo. The wish—and its gratification in the mind—has to be disguised because otherwise the taboo would probably prevent us from employing our contemplation of the forbidden act.

In turning to unconscious conflict as the source of fantasy, analysts emphasized the primacy of forbidden sexual and aggressive drives that aroused anxiety and guilt and set conflict into motion. This formulation suggests that fantasy substitutes for a pleasure we long for: pleasure associated with the imaginary satisfaction of heavily disguised instinctual impulses, either erotic or aggressive, often laced with jealousy or the desire for revenge.

More recently the range of the underlying wishes fueling fantasy has been conceptualized more broadly to include more than the gratification of erotic and aggressive impulses. Some fantasies are motivated by the desire to feel good about oneself, that is, to maintain self-esteem at an optimal level (in the service of what is called narcissistic regulation), or to maintain a sense of safety. Others reflect the need to contain fears, to deny unpleasant realities, to regulate emotion, and to undo trauma. The uses to which fantasies are put are as diverse as the wishes that fuel them.

Fantasizing, despite its wishful imaginative core, plays a very real role in our lives, or rather, many roles. On the simplest level, fantasy indeed provides substitute gratification for that which is lacking in life and it may relieve tension or dispel frustration. Daydreaming frees us from the dullness of everyday life, from the strictures of time and place, from the trap of the stultifying present. Thus it may make minor corrections in our emotional lives, as when conjuring up the vivid image of a weekend party to counteract the boredom of weekday chores and provide a prospect of respite, change, or excitement.

Daydreaming may signal that something is amiss, revealing an emotional reality we may have denied: The "happily" married woman who begins to fantasize a sexual affair with a man she has only glimpsed on the bus may think to explore her unacknowledged marital disappointments and resentments, and that exploration may lead to confrontation and change of a helpful kind. Fantasy metaphorically expresses subliminal perceptions. For example, the illness of a friend may first make itself known to us through a fantasy that our friend has died. Thus fantasy is one way of apprehending not only an inner emotional reality but also an external reality.

Fantasy may address transitory emotional needs, functioning as a "safe house" in which to discharge feelings and impulses that would otherwise be unacceptable. For example, fantasies of mortal combat can express the urge to vanquish, kill, or maim the object of a current rage. (This *cathartic* function was long considered one of its main purposes.) Or fantasy may be invoked to divert us from flickers of psychic pain. It may redress feelings of personal inadequacy, reversing passive into active—the kind of wish fulfillment encoded in the transformation of Clark Kent into Superman. Such fantasies aim to overcome helplessness or patch over a narcissistic injury (a blow to one's self-esteem).

Fantasy may serve a deeper healing function, undoing past defects, wounds, and internal psychological conflicts. As the psychoanalyst Robert Stoller expressed it, "The function of daydreams is to state a problem that has been disguised and then to solve it, the problem and the solution being the poles between which excitement flows."[14]

Although Stoller's theory deals mainly with sexual fantasies, the same dynamics are at work in many other fantasies. Fantasy tries to assuage today's needs, whether for mastery, separation, autonomy, or self-expression, simultaneously ameliorating the scars of the past. So, for example, the fantasy of perfect (romantic) love undoes the narcissistic wound of not having been the "chosen" of one's mother or father, at the same time that it posits a new life with the lover.

Fantasy may be invoked to master trauma. Stoller discusses a patient who, through a repeating masochistic fantasy in which she is forced to make love with a stallion while a "Director" looks on, is using it (somewhat paradoxically) to undo her father's absence early in her life. The Director is devoting all his time and attention to her. (This is the same patient, Belle, whose fantasies of a peaceful underground world were mentioned earlier.) Of course the genesis of this particular fantasy is infinitely more complicated than can be conveyed here, the wounds it undoes too varied to be understood without much more detail.

Perhaps most important of all, daydreaming lends solace in sorrow and pain. Fantasizing a happier future may permit us to bear an untenable present rather than be overwhelmed by depression and feelings of hopelessness. Therefore fantasy's chief benefit may be that it allows the fantasizer to hope, to trust in the future, even in a seemingly hopeless situation. To the degree that daydreaming offers a blueprint for a better future, it acts as a lifeline. Several of the American hostages released from captivity in Iran attested that internal fantasy stories (vacation trips for one of them) were their major tool in maintaining sanity during long periods of isolation. Victor Frankel, imprisoned at Auschwitz, described in *Man's Search for Meaning* how when he was cold and night had fallen, he would imagine himself in a warm, comfortable, and well-lit room addressing an audience seated on comfortable chairs. His imaginary talk was on the topic "the psychology of the concentration camp."[15] Similarly, the unhappy or abused child who can imagine better parents, happier times, a different world, may grow up relatively unscathed, the good life still within the realm of imaginative and thus actual possibility.

Fantasy, then, is not only a compensation or a palliative for a current unhappiness or fear or a disguised expression of forbidden wishes or narcissistic restitution; it is a major mode of adaptation in which hope and investment in the future remain alive. Fantasy postulates a better tomorrow.

Moreover, fantasy may help make that tomorrow possible, insofar as our expectations and hopes for what is yet to come, much of which is encoded in fantasy, fuel our behavior and thinking in the present. Thus, in addition to creating a general ambiance of hope, fantasy may lay a practical foundation for it. In scripting the future, our focus is different at various stages of development. In early adolescence, our hopes for what we may become (what psychoanalysts often call the ego ideal) take the form of grandiose fantasies of mastery and mighty deeds. But at every stage of life fantasy can act as a rehearsal for future action, a story line that can be incorporated into a life plan, a template for behaviors that are either literal translations (enactments) or symbolic expressions of the fantasy's narrative content.

Taking into account both Freud's original formulation and subsequent psychoanalytic modifications, let me propose a working definition of a conscious fantasy: It is a daydream that surfaces in the stream of consciousness, a narrative compounded of emotion, thought, internal dialogue, and (predominantly visual) sensory impressions. Sometimes highly schematic and abbreviated, sometimes minutely articulated and detailed, it is shaped by the imagination to coalesce ultimately around wish-fulfillment, emotional regulation, assurance of safety, containment of unpleasant emotions, working through of trauma, crystallization of perception, or aspirations for the future. The goal of fantasy is to achieve an overall change in state—a change in how one feels.[16] To invoke Pauline Réage again: Whatever the fantasy's form, the effect is beneficent and protective.

Whatever the motivation that initiates them, fantasies draw on both the memories and the events of our own lives and the stories of our fictional heroes, altering that material according to our underlying longings so that they transcend their origins. Indeed, as it is reworked by the imagination, the raw material may be altered beyond recognition.

The wish component that fuels our fantasies may be ingeniously disguised. Occasionally, especially with young children, they may be relatively transparent, as when the wish to eat strawberries leads to the fantasy of eating strawberries (sometimes a cigar is just a cigar). But more often, and certainly after childhood, fantasies take shape as elaborated, metaphoric, and symbolic expressions of wishes, so that their surface or manifest content disguises their underlying meanings. The deepest wishes underlying fantasy are often contradictory, conflictual, and possibly taboo.

The fantasy's superficial story line acts as a screen, concealing other stories, cloaking the underlying, perhaps forbidden wishes in an acceptable narrative. Hence a fantasy is almost always multilayered, reflecting the mind itself, which is divided into conscious and unconscious elements; into wishes, prohibitions, and defenses.

Fantasies are like sea glass, perfectly beautiful jewels washed up on the shore, a pleasure to contemplate, but on close scrutiny bearing traces of the original shards of broken glass thrown into the sea years before. The mind, like the ocean, works its magic and transforms these sharp edged and dangerous shards into treasured fantasies that wash up into consciousness.

Not only unconscious wishes and feelings, but the fantasizer's current life situation, longings, conflicts, and hopes shape and infuse daydreams. The following daydreams, reported by the same woman from different stages of her life, suggest how one's immediate discontents and emerging needs trigger day-dreams, and how the resulting wish-fulfilling fantasies are balm to those specific disequilibriums, sometimes pointing the way to new adaptations. The construction in these daydreams ranges from the relatively transparent to a very simple kind of symbolic transformation to a fairly complex symbolic structure, the range in part related to the age at which the woman had the fantasy.

FANTASY NUMBER ONE
Circumstances Surrounding the Fantasy

My brother was born when I was three and one half. After that I did not play with dolls, only stuffed animals.

I had sometime long before entering first grade wanted a dog—a dog to walk in the woods, a dog to curl up with me beside the fireplace, a dog for me to feed and brush. My mother was afraid of dogs, my baby brother allergic to all life-forms, and the nanny had had enough on the farm where she was born. Only I longed, and wished on each star and every birthday candle, for a dog. . . . I would not play with dolls. I only played with stuffed animals. My play, of course, was maternal. I wanted to be a mother dog.

The Fantasy

By the time I was seven I despaired of receiving my dog. One day I was in music class. I was asked to refrain from singing and simply move my lips. I am tone-deaf and must have been singing out of tune with the others. I was bored. Music always bored me. I imagined a black and white dog: a dog with one ear down and one ear up who appeared in the middle of the circle we were sitting in and ran to me. I scooped him up into my lap and imagined holding, petting, kissing him. He became mine. At first I only played with him in music class, then other times. I knew it was a game. But it was a game I loved. I can't remember the name I gave him or exactly what we did together, but the dog was mine.

FANTASY NUMBER TWO
Circumstances Surrounding the Fantasy

I had always planned to be a writer. From age five on I knew it was what I would do. I read in order to write. I looked at everything in order to write about it.

I was born on Easter Sunday and had a religious, Southern Baptist nanny until I was fourteen.

When I was around thirteen, my mother took me to see the film of
Laura Hobson's *Gentlemen's Agreement*. The Holocaust pictures had
already been in *Life* magazine. As I was leaving the film, which is about
the cruelties of anti-Semitism, I decided I would someday end prejudice
and poverty and inequity in the world.

The Fantasy

From the time I saw the movie until the time I went to college, I would
daydream about how I could save the world from nuclear disaster, hunger,
disease, injustice through writing a major book—a kind of modern *Uncle
Tom's Cabin*. This "I will save the world fantasy" was shockingly out of
keeping with my general sense of reality and ordinary life. But I didn't
even notice how grandiose and peculiar it was.

FANTASY NUMBER THREE
Circumstances Surrounding the Fantasy

My father was an athlete and in particular a swimmer. He had supported himself through college by working as a lifeguard at a Catskill
hotel.

When I was about four, he insisted that I dive into the water. Although
I was frightened, he insisted. I dove, but then vomited out of fear. I was
then embarrassed. I never quite got over my fear of diving, but I became a
champion long distance swimmer—perfect form and so forth. I was
always ahead of my age group at camp.

Also by high school age, I knew about the Greek gods, and the story of
Persephone was particularly interesting to me.

The Fantasy

My high school was on the East River. I could walk to and from school
on the esplanade past Gracie Mansion. I would lean over the edge of the
rail and watch the water. I imagined that a dark and terrible god who
lived in the water would pull me in and drown me, take me to his kingdom under the water, and make me his slave. There were many small
variations of this story: he would love me; he would hate me. He would
simply drown me and I would die. The fantasy was frightening and interesting. I also thought about jumping into the water. He would pull me
down under, and so on.

When I was upset, I would go to the river and stare at the water, contemplating, waiting for the god to appear. I knew it was a fantasy but it
somehow drained my emotion away.

In these daydreams, and in fact in all daydreams, it is not only the narrative that gives us a glimpse into the daydream's coded meaning, but the fantasy's context, its effect on the daydreamer ("it somehow drained my emotion away"), and its meaning to the daydreamer. The dog fantasy serves to establish a make-believe bond between girl and imaginary dog that in some way substitutes for the bond she lost when the birth of her brother displaced her in her mother's affections. The fantasizer also takes the maternal role, but in relation to a dog, not to a baby, thus repudiating the mother-child bond on one level, duplicating it on another (with reversal of roles). She invokes the fantasy at a particular moment, in a singing class in which she feels inadequate and rejected (she's been told not to sing) and is therefore in need of affection, of feeling connected. The save-the-world fantasy is a typical daydream of ego enhancement, embracing two poles—the wish to feel important and the wish to feel virtuous. The background material (the reference to being born on Easter Sunday) suggests that there may be an unconscious identification with a religious savior. (A conscious or unconscious identification with famous people on whose birthday or other significant anniversary we happen to be born is not at all uncommon.) Feeling important is also a balm to being ignored or abandoned.

In the River God fantasy, it is readily apparent that the fantasizer's somewhat problematic relationship with her father has become linked to unconscious Oedipal longings and is sexualized in her daydreams, though symbolically—the sexual version ("he would love me") alternating with a self-punitive variation ("he would simply drown me and I would die"). As this fantasy reveals, the nature of the pleasure attached to fantasy is sometimes ambiguous.

All fantasies, simple though they appear, generally conceal a wish, defenses against the wish, a latent self-identification (in the example cited with the Christ figure), an experimentation with wished for new relationships, or a modification or reversal of old ones. Each uses past experiences or stories that the fantasizer has been exposed to as part of the narrative structure.

Insofar as fantasies always push toward direct or indirect actualization, each also has implications for the future life of the fantasizer. The woman just described got her dog, achieved a very successful career in addition to being involved in socially conscious activities, and although she first married a man who metaphorically tried to drown her, the second time around married someone who loves her devotedly. By their very nature, fantasies (except those that are fixated, neurotic as it were, or fantastic in their construction) are capable of evolving, of moving in a direction that allows for—indeed paves the way for—some measure of gratification in the real world.

Conscious fantasy can be classified according to three different aspects or parameters, which are overlapping, rather than mutually exclusive.[17] These categorizations help us understand the many roles of fantasy in our lives.

First, we can categorize fantasies according to our emotional experience of them. While many fantasies are intensely pleasurable, others are not. Because our fantasy life is not dictated by simple wish-fulfillment, many fantasies are experienced in some emotionally negative way and might well be designated as *negative* or *dysphoric* fantasies in contrast to *pleasurable* ones.

Second, we can distinguish between fleeting and repeating fantasies. What we often refer to as daydreams are *fleeting fantasies*—brief, evanescent, generally nonrepeating, entering our minds unbidden and clearly triggered by an event or stress of the moment. In contrast, *repeating fantasies,* those we invoke regularly in our daily lives, are more central to our personality. Whether masturbatory, self-soothing, or tied to self-identity, they have a long history, often beginning in latency or adolescence and continuing in some form far into adulthood. This latter group sometimes have a more archaic quality, closer to unconscious fantasy, than the simple daydreams of everyday life.

In addition, there is an important intermediate group of fantasies, which I call *generative fantasies*. They have durability in that they are repeating fantasies, but they are not lifelong. Looser and more variable in form than repeating fantasies, they often have content related to securing self-esteem and narcissistic gratification. They speak, by and large, to our hopes and dreams, often with regard to career, family, or romantic goals. Given their future-orientation and their focus on issues of self-esteem, generative fantasies often serve as guides, pushing us down certain paths, helping us make necessary adaptations.

Third, fantasies may be either *substitutive* or *preparatory:* that is, sometimes they provide a retreat from reality (while affecting it indirectly), and at others they press for some form of actualization or enactment.

Looking at conscious fantasy from these perspectives gives insight into their role in modulating momentary distress, in shaping current emotional and behavioral patterns (particularly those that affect our personal relationships), in promoting sexual arousal and self-soothing, and, finally, in encapsulating future-oriented desire, ambition, and hence, strategies for the life to come.

Self-evidently wish fulfilling, pleasurable fantasies are the most readily recognized daydreams. Many fantasies *are* experienced as pleasurable or soothing. We have the sense that we can control them, summon them up, or turn them off. The reason for the pleasure is generally self-evident. Many are sexual; others involve bonding or emotional contact. Still others serve to plump up the ego; take, for example, all the Walter Mitty fantasies of future glory. Pleasure may also be achieved indirectly. Some fantasies establish safety; these include fantasies of being rescued, being protected, finding a benign and loving mentor, or gaining financial security by winning the lottery. Or they may involve wishes to retreat from interpersonal demands, for example, wilderness reveries and on-the-road fantasies or daydreams of dropping out of one's current life and assuming a new identity elsewhere.

Pleasurable fantasies may also express hostility. Some appear so brutal, so filled with revenge, anger, hostility, and violence, that they may be abhorrent to the listener though they bring pleasure and relief to the fantasizer. Individuals have a wide range of ability to conjure up hostile fantasies, depending on the nature of the defenses erected against rage, the fear of retaliation, the strength of conscience, and, of course, the amount of anger that can fuel such fantasies. For some people, to wish other people dead or to imagine killing them is quite commonplace, whereas others are unable to tolerate any conscious experience of such a hostile intent. One woman fantasizes a ray gun that she can point at someone who angers her to make that person disappear. (This fantasy illustrates one of the defenses built into fantastic fantasies: they reassure us of their wholly imaginary nature—the safeguard in this case that no such gun exists or ever could). Another man is so loath to experience hostile feelings that the furthest he can go in the direction of wishing someone "disappeared" is to float a Flying Dutchman fantasy: He wishes his "victim" restricted to a boat from which he may never reach shore, but his conscience is so rigorous that the boat be filled with all possible amenities, including movie houses, restaurants, and shuffleboard.

Sometimes hearing someone else's hostile fantasy may permit the overly conscience-driven listener to construct (or access) a similar daydream. Ms. Taylor was very inhibited in her freedom to express competition, assertion, or anger, avoiding the expression of any hostile feelings whatsoever. But one day her mother told her one of her own fantasies—of putting poison into the heroin supply, thereby killing all the drug addicts and ending the drug problem. (Ms. Taylor's mother was a social activist and in the fantasy she was saving society.) Hearing her mother's fantasy allowed a similar daydream to surface in the daughter: Conjuring up a much publicized crime in New York City in which a young jogger had been brutally raped and left for dead in Central Park, she fantasized castrating the rapist—a fantasy that she quite consciously enjoyed. Like her mother's, it was manifestly concerned not with personal rage at men, but with punishment meted out to perpetrators of a crime. The daughter had been granted permission by her mother to become aware of suppressed fantasies. But social retribution remained easier to imagine than personal revenge.

Other fantasies give us pleasure by providing reassurance (however illusory or misguided); consider the case of a woman who holds on to the belief that the rock hard lump in her breast is assuredly a benign cyst, requiring no evaluation. Fantasy: If I pay it no mind, it will go away. Mind over matter. This is a *denial in fantasy*.

A fantasy may be invoked to turn something that was painful in the past into something positive, for example, to undo the impact of an event experienced as traumatic. People who were abused in childhood frequently construct sexual fantasies with sadomasochistic elements that duplicate their childhood traumas, but with the proviso that the action, once administered to cause pain, is now administered in the service of pleasure. Even in childhood, concurrent with the abuse a young child may rationalize, "My father is beating me because he loves me," and conjure up the fantasy of being beaten as a pleasure in and of itself. One now middle-aged man takes great solace in recasting memories of his mother. He has persuaded himself that his manic-depressive mother's manifest lack of interest in him was illusory. As he now sees it, she remained aloof to protect him from the potentially negative impact of her own problems. He has rewritten his personal history by fantasizing his mother's love and concern for him.

Many of us entertain recurring fantasies that are experienced as pleasurable even though their content would lead us to expect they would be painful—for example, daydreams of being raped or of the death of a beloved. In fact, the reasons why a fantasy is pleasurable may be inexplicable or paradoxical without recourse to intense psychological scrutiny. But knowing that daydreams offer *symbolic* gratification helps us to understand in a general way how such fantasies might be pleasurable (even when we are unable to penetrate the symbolism of a particular daydream). A rape fantasy may be invoked as a pleasurable masturbatory fantasy, pleasurable either because narcissistic attention is provided by the rapist or because the fantasy displaces desire from the fantasizer—"*I* do not want sex; *he* wants it"—thus freeing the "victim" to enjoy it.

Some fantasies, however, yield no conscious pleasure: they are experienced as painful rather than pleasurable. Just as there are punishment dreams and anxiety night dreams, so, too, there are comparable daydreams that appear more painful or anxiety-provoking than soothing or pleasurable. Consequently, the (conscious) pleasure quotient or the sense of relief that so often accompanies fantasy is not necessarily part of its essential nature.

Those fantasies from which we do not derive any manifest pleasure veer toward fearful, self-punitive, or otherwise dysphoric themes. For example, many people report fearful flash fantasies that surface in particular circumstances: upon entering an elevator they see themselves being attacked by a hidden assailant or picture the elevator stalling between floors and trapping them for hours; at take-off in an airplane they are flooded with images of their flight going down in flames.

Exploring negative fantasies, one uncovers a whole skein of imaginative life that constitutes "fantasy" in that the stories and images are imaginary though they are not altogether under voluntary control and are not consciously pleasurable. *Negative fantasies,* as I propose to call those fantasies that yield no subjective sense of pleasure but are accompanied by fear, humiliation, or some other negative feeling, seem to negate the assumption that fantasies are always wish fulfilling.

At least some of these negative fantasies, however, can be seen as indirectly pleasurable if understood within the context of the conflict theory of the mind—the idea that in fantasy wishes unacceptable to the conscious mind are disguised or otherwise defended against. To get past the internal censor, the underlying wish is symbolically disguised. Thus the fantasy becomes a complex symbolic construction incorporating both the wish and the defenses against it. For example, a fantasy of being beaten may or may not be consciously pleasurable. If unpleasurable, the fantasy may still carry unconscious narcissistic gratification (as noted, about the pleasure of having been singled out for attention), or alternatively the pleasure may consist of the preconscious (not consciously experienced) moral pleasure of suffering a sexual punishment for a sexual crime.

Consider the vivid fantasy that one woman remembers from her childhood, one that emerged sometime between the ages of six and ten. "I remember lying in bed at night in a state of terror, fearful that my mother was not really my mother at all, but an Indian disguised as my mother, someone who was going to come in and scalp me. I knew that it was my imagination, but it scared me anyway."

Even those of us who question the universality of some Freudian theories about female development cannot help but be impressed that the scalping suggests castration, and that this fantasy likely portrays a sexual punishment for a sexual crime, probably an underlying fantasized Oedipal transgression. It also posits the "disappearance" of her real mother, so it incorporates elements of matricide. (It is also a form of a family romance fantasy; her "real" mother who is good and loving is understood to be elsewhere.) Her fantasy, though negative, is a good example of disguised wish-fulfillment, leaning on the moral pleasures of suffering for one's crimes and perhaps even more so on the preconscious pleasures of the imagined crimes themselves—incest and matricide.

Shortly after puberty, this same woman experienced an outbreak of phobic anxiety that took the form of a fantasy so intense that it bordered on delusional. Walking home from school, she always made a detour around an apartment building because she vividly imagined that it was about to erupt into flames. This phobic fantasy, like the retribution she had earlier feared from her mother, appears to represent a sexual punishment for a perceived sexual crime—the burning building symbolically linked to the burning or flamelike sexual desire awakened at puberty. In adulthood, she had many minor phobias, including social anxiety. Hers is a classic fearful fantasy in that the wish is well disguised, its pleasure aspect out of consciousness, its fearful elements readily accessed. Very different from pleasurable daydreams, negative fantasies may be experienced as terrifying and sometimes evolve into obsessive or phobic thinking.

Consider another example. One patient, who had recently indulged in fleeting fantasies about his wife's death, started to take his pulse quite conspicuously during a session. This was not a man given to hypochondria, but when asked what occurred to him in reference to the palpation, he replied:

> It's something I didn't want to tell you about. I keep taking my pulse. I think I
> have heart disease, like the kind my friend David died of. This thought about
> whether or not I have heart trouble also enters into my decision about whether
> or not to break up with my wife. I think I will need someone with me if I'm sick,
> so it's no time to break up. Then I think there's no need to break up because I'll
> be dead anyway, and if I die, I will not have aggressed against my wife. Then I
> think maybe I deserve to die because I've been so aggressive toward her. I identify with David. He was no good to women either. But perhaps there's something deeper behind it; if I don't go to the doctor, there is no heart disease
> because after all there is no reality outside my head.

He stopped talking for the moment, struck by the realization of the extent to which he had been indulging in "magical thinking"—those flights of fancy we use to deny the power of reality. At that very moment, he reported an intrusive thought. He was visualizing himself skewered and roasted over an open pit—a fantasy I would interpret as a punishment for the "crime" of betraying his wife through his longing to desert her or see her dead. This interweaving of wishful fantasies and fearful fantasies demonstrates the inadequacy of any theory that posits fantasy as simple wish-fulfillment; such a theory would not account for manifestly self-punitive and fearful fantasies.

The fact is that many motives other than the search for pleasure may spur fantasies, and some "negative" fantasies are not pleasurable even in the disguised way I have been discussing, where the pleasure is out of consciousness but nonetheless is quite real. Some negative fantasies, for example, appear to provide mastery rather than pleasure. That is, they may be invoked to minimize the possibility of unforeseen circumstances taking the fantasizer by surprise, even when the process requires the fantasizer to entertain the most dire scenario. For a person like Atwood's narrator, protecting herself against surprise takes priority, even over denial.

Very importantly, fantasies may regulate strong emotions (affects), helping to contain anxiety or other dysphoric sensations. We may say of these fantasies that their content appears to be affect-driven rather than wish-driven. Affect-driven fantasies include the murderous fantasies so often evoked by rejection and the fantasies of impoverishment fueled by depression.

One woman suddenly felt overwhelmed with anxiety in her dance class. She did not know why, but in fact there were several real situations in her life that might have served to make her anxious. However, she handled her anxiety in a very interesting way, through fantasy. She produced a fantasy in which another, unnamed woman in the class was reluctant to perform a certain step for fear of injury, but, ignoring her premonition, proceeded to execute the step, in the process twisting her spine in such a way that she became paraplegic. In the fantasy, the injured woman goes to bed every night and has a repetitive dream, in which she relives the moment of her injury and does not make the fateful step. But then she wakes and finds herself still paralyzed. The fantasizer has fantasized a trauma, complete with the repetitive dreams that are characteristic of trauma. By so doing she has somehow quieted her own anxiety, mainly by displacing it onto a fictional woman.

Though one could connect this fantasy to many different behavioral parallels in the woman's life—for example, the way she ignores her intuition that an ultimatum she is about to deliver to her adolescent son is so worded as to provoke a major confrontation—here it illustrates how negative affect can be contained in fantasy, and in this case displaced onto a fictional persona of the fantasizer's own creation, thus relieving the fantasizer's anxiety. (The ability to displace emotion onto an imaginary character that one has created begins in children's doll play. Child therapists take advantage of this ability by having children engage in such play during therapy sessions. The ability to invoke a kind of displaced fantasy is particularly well honed in fiction writers.)

An analyst friend tells me he has more negative fantasies if he is awakened in the middle of the night than when he "floats" during the day. If he wakes, for example, and worries that his elderly mother is about to die, his explanation is not that he wishes her dead, the hackneyed interpretation, but, rather, that his fear that his mother is dead is the present-day counterpart of an ancient infant fear, that of being abandoned, which is released only when certain parts of the brain are asleep or just waking. Awakening alone, he is cast back in time to the plight of the helpless infant, though the secondary revision (the image of the mother as old and frail) imposes a modern narrative on his earlier fears.

In sum, then, though many fantasies are indeed pleasure-driven, evoked in the service of wish-fulfillment and substitute gratification, others are directed more to achieving emotional mastery—creating a feeling of safety, containing fears and anxieties.

Negative fantasies have real life sequelae. Just as pleasurable fantasies lead us into new situations, fearful fantasies often curtail our activities. In fact, phobic symptoms crystallize around fearful fantasies—for example, the fantasy of being stuck or locked up and unable to get to a bathroom (hence, incontinent, out of control) that infuses so many elevator phobias. Some fearful fantasies, such as the fantasy of crashing in an airplane, are layered over with counterphobic fantasies. The counterphobic begins to fantasize taking flying lessons and may actually learn to fly—sometimes only to be awakened from sleep in the middle of the night with a vivid nightmare about a plane crash.

•   •   •

The second means of classifying fantasies is related to their durability and the nature of the occasion (or trigger) that prompts them. Fantasies may make one-time appearances or they may be repeating. And they may repeat throughout a lifetime, or only for a limited period of time. The latter kind are what I have called *generative fantasies.*

Transient daydreams, by definition fleeting, are contingent: they surface in response to a particular external stress, problem, or situation. Envious when someone else receives a coveted prize, different fantasizers may conjure up winning the lottery, being offered a prestigious job, or going to bed with the rival's spouse. Like dreams, such evanescent mental products may be very hard to remember. But they still serve the immediate purpose of restoring a lost equilibrium (whether due to stress, anxiety, or the loss of pride) by providing a remedy.

In contrast are those durable, repetitive fantasies that recur unchanged from childhood through adult life or, keep appearing in reeditions or remakes, sometimes even after long periods of banishment. A daydream that is repeated unchanged or with only slight modifications from adolescence or even latency into adulthood becomes a familiar friend, one whose benefits such as self-soothing or sexual arousal are cherished.

Ever-recurring hungers, rather than contingent events, stimulate fantasies of this type. Masturbatory fantasies, for example, are often lifelong aids to sexual arousal and performance, invoked at frequent and predictable intervals. Many of these enduring fantasies are *organizing fantasies*—that is, they play an essential role on a day-to-day basis in solving those central unconscious conflicts and problems of early life that continue to exert an influence in the present.

Sometimes it is easy to see that a whole life revolves around one of these organizing fantasies, for example, for the man whose intimate life revolves around the wish (need) to beat out a competitor, which is based on an underlying fantasy of vanquishing a rival brother or father. Such a fantasy preoccupation may be very evident in a person's choice of conversational anecdotes. One unusually intelligent man constantly regales his companions with tales of how he has successfully confronted a variety of bureaucratic hacks who have in some way inadvertently challenged his autonomy or tangled him up in red tape. His immersion in telling this kind of story, rather than describing other kinds of encounters, is a clue that some early competitive struggles still encroach on his imaginative life, despite the fact that professionally he has left his competitors far behind.

The distinction between fleeting and repeating fantasies is theoretically useful, but sometimes difficult to apply clinically, because of their overlap. Moreover, this distinction suggests that fleeting daydreams are too evanescent to have much meaning. But fleeting fantasies may be revealing of underlying psychic conflicts and motivations and can be extremely useful in deciphering what we are currently feeling in our relationships. One young woman whose babysitter was sick, in a pinch, asked her mother to substitute; she was immediately overtaken with a flash fantasy that the job would be so taxing that her mother would drop dead. Loath to ask anything of others, her fantasy could be traced to a generalized fear that her underlying needs were so all consuming that she could not express them without causing dire harm. Fleeting fantasies are particularly revealing in the therapy setting, because they often carry important transference information. When carefully attended to by therapists, they may indicate a great deal about the patient's current attitudes toward the therapist.

The other problem with trying to draw a rigid line between fleeting and repeating fantasies (what some analysts refer to as daydreams and conscious fantasies, respectively)[18] is that doing so leads us to overlook reverie, or what I call generative fantasy.

This third group is intermediate between the other two in terms of frequency and consistency, being relatively stable over varying periods but not so stable or structured as repeating fantasy. *Generative fantasies* are generally future-oriented, responses to future desire and intentionality. Thinking about one's future (like all future thinking, an imaginative pursuit) is inevitably chock-a-block with fantasy, some well formed and highly articulated, some mere snippets of imagery. For example, a young woman repeatedly fantasizes getting married, visualizing the ceremony, the dress, and the veil, with changing representations of the groom depending on the person who interests her at the moment. Such fantasies appear at varying intervals from adolescence until she actually marries. While stable over time, this fantasy does not have the tenacity of a lifelong repeating fantasy. (But it may reappear in altered form, the narcissistic component of the fantasy resurfacing in the form of "mother-of-the-bride" fantasies when her daughter becomes engaged. She may well spend twice as much thought and money on her own outfit as on her daughter's wedding dress.)

Generative fantasy is a very important area to explore because it provides the major locus (along with preconscious thinking) for imaginative dress rehearsals and trial-actions, thus a route to understanding the fantasizer's hopes, dreams, and plans. Sometimes ambition-linked fantasy is cast backward in time, prompted by the thought that the future is totally limited by the past. A young man, feeling insecure in his new job on Wall Street, fantasizes a desired past at variance with his real childhood. This is a fairly typical example of a "what if" or an "if only" fantasy.

While there are major differences between lifelong repeating fantasies and future-linked reveries, they also overlap, bleeding into one another. At the extremes of the continuum, repeating fantasies have a more primitive, dreamlike quality, while future-oriented fantasies are often more practical and realistic, indicating plausible scenarios, generally desirable ones. The two kinds of fantasy rest on different primary roots. Repeating fantasy appears closer to primal unconscious fantasy, with relatively little current input from the outside world, while reverie or generative fantasy appears closer to the more logically articulated thinking processes of waking life. Repeating fantasy, formed early in life, is more drive-instigated and more often uses body metaphors to express itself. Reverie, or generative fantasy, while ultimately shaped by unconscious fantasy as all fantasy is, is further from it, more responsive to current issues of mastery and narcissistic regulation, to the contours of ambition and future possibility.

Because generative fantasy is cast more realistically, it is more susceptible to external influence: that is, it is more changeable in response to cues from the surrounding culture, and to changes in that culture. But both generative and repeating fantasies may be enacted, and both play significant roles in the course our lives take, characteristics that provide another criterion for classifying fantasy—the capacity for or likelihood of its conversion into real-life scripts and behavior.

Daydreams have scripts that range from the impossible—such as fantasies of being invisible or being a vampire—to the more or less possible or even probable variety (such as romantic fantasies or achievement fantasies). In the first instance, the fantasies are known to be fantastic; they are scripts that provide substitute gratification with no possibility for being literally enacted. Even so, they may relate directly to everyday feelings and attitudes. For example, one woman who pleasurably fantasized about being invisible and using her invisibility to inflict harm on others without incurring any risk, nonetheless, in a totally different context, complained that she was sad because she felt that no one ever noticed her. One might interpret her fantasy as rationalizing or making palatable her sense of being overlooked, or, alternatively, view her perception of being unacknowledged as a *misperception* based on a need to be punished for her underlying hostility (as expressed in her fantasy).

Quite different are the fantasies cast in probable scripts capable of being enacted. Nonetheless, a potentially realizable fantasy may remain restricted to the realm of the mind as an imaginative scenario. While some potentially realizable fantasies may provide dress rehearsals for real life, others serve primarily as wish-fulfilling substitutes. To engage in a new venture or to enact a script, one generally needs to imagine it first. But not every imaginative script is enacted.

Take the case of a repeating masturbatory fantasy. Sometimes it serves as the main event, used as an aid to arousal, and sometimes as a dress rehearsal, that is, as something to be enacted. Perhaps the most common example is the invocation of some kind of sadomasochistic sexual activity: the fantasy in itself may be exciting, it may even be a prerequisite to excitement; however it may or may not be acted out, and the likelihood may depend on the fantasizer's partner as much as on the fantasizer himself. For example, enactment of a fantasy may be initiated by a partner who requests to be spanked, to be tied up, and so on.

The so-called perverse fantasies, in particular, are very often a prelude to action; they present a powerful script pressing for enactment. Yet it remains a puzzle why a sexual fantasy is sometimes gratifying in itself, but at other times moves the fantasizer to try to translate it into real experience. Conversely, often acting out of a fantasy, particularly a sexual one, proves less gratifying than the fantasy that inspired the enactment. In part, this is because one knows that the acted out scenario has been planned and therefore lacks spontaneity, which for some is the hallmark of authenticity. (Paradoxically in taking shape in reality, the fantasy loses its genuineness, becomes artificial.)

Future-oriented reveries in the form of rehearsal fantasies often are lived out in one form or another. Many children create explicit fantasies of their successful lives as adults, often as a way to assert hope for the future, sometimes to imagine how to please a parent; many such fantasies become grooved into literal life plans. Many of the choices made in adulthood are rooted in early life fantasy, as in the case of a career choice made by a woman whose mysterious father had been attached to military intelligence during World War II. During an unhappy childhood, she "absented" herself from an emotionally abusive mother by means of an active fantasy life. An avid consumer of Nancy Drew mysteries, she apparently identified both with Nancy Drew and with her own elusive father, whom she thought of as a spy. This dual identification helped her to "disidentify" from her mother and patched over her loneliness by allowing her to feel close to her father. She did not grow up to become either a spy or a detective but was very successful in the field of information retrieval and data fact-finding for business clients—an activity she regards as similar to spying because it involves gathering difficult-to-find information that serves as a basis for future action. In essence, her well-developed childhood fantasy of being a spy was later incorporated into a future-oriented reverie (a rehearsal fantasy) and ultimately into her choice of profession.

Anna O. (the first "psychoanalytic" patient, mentioned earlier) indulged in systematic daydreaming, described by her not just as her "private theater," but as "chimney sweeping." Her fantasies, as Freud noted, were of a largely substitutive, wish-fulfilling nature, and intimately connected to her psychological symptoms. Because Freud first focused on daydreams in this context—that of illness—his emphasis from then on concerned their role in symptom formation. And the emphasis on neurosis has set the tone for most of the subsequent considerations of fantasy in the psychoanalytic literature.

There is no denying that daydreaming plays a negative role in some people's lives. The more archaic the content of repeating fantasies, the more likely they are to act as the immediate precursors to a variety of neurotic symptoms or to serve as the habitual mode of conflict resolution. The dysphoric fantasy, particularly the fearful fantasy, may crystallize a number of different phobias around it, thus inhibiting the fantasizer's behavior in certain directions. Moreover fantasy can be used to deny reality. A woman in a hopeless marriage, rather than fantasizing alternatives and then acting on them, may relive the past happiness of the courtship, fantasize a metamorphosis in her husband's personality in accordance with her memories and wishes, and, mistaking her hopes for reality, harbor unrealistic expectations for the future, which lead her further into passivity rather than activism. (At the extreme are those who retreat into daydreaming as an alternative to a "real" life or trade in their own identities for imaginary ones.)

Although psychoanalysts have come to appreciate the role of unconscious fantasy in character and behavior, in clothing and self-decoration, indeed in everything that constitutes what we think of as our very essence, many analysts, following Freud's lead, still focus primarily on the negative role of fantasy. In fact, the search for the unconscious fantasy material that fuels neurotic symptoms is at the heart of psychoanalytic therapy.

The pathological perspective is much too narrow; because of it, the many varieties of conscious fantasy, and the many positive, adaptive purposes they serve, have received too little attention, even though we now acknowledge conscious fantasies as part of normal psychology. Freud himself gave us some key insights into the adaptive aspects of fantasy. For example, he was aware early on that the author uses daydreams in writing fiction, and that fantasy themes disseminated through stories are key to the construction of a culture's myths. Even so, he never focused on the essential role of daydreams in individual adaptation. Following his stance, most analysts have failed to theorize the multiple functions of conscious fantasy and to understand its pervasive influence on how we make our lives. Yet daydreams have major importance in their own right, quite apart from the impact of unconscious fantasy. In fact, fantasy is prerequisite to a fulfilled life.

The purposes of fantasy are many, but fantasy is more than an emotional corrective, a pathway to hope, the key to unlocking sealed off mental compartments, or even a template for future adaptations. No matter how bizarre or how commonplace the fantasy, each is ultimately a uniquely individual expression of the fantasizer. It indicates the person's current wishes and hopes, underlying needs and past history, scripted in her or his special imagery or style. Fantasy, no matter how remote it may be from our actual life or who we appear to be on the surface, means something, tells us something about who we are—if only we can find the courage to contemplate it and the psychological insight to decipher it. Through our fantasies we may glimpse our desires and sometimes our most authentic self-portraits.

3

DAYDREAMS, NIGHTDREAMS, AND PLAY

BOTH RESEARCH PSYCHOLOGISTS AND PSYCHOANALYSTS HAVE BEEN AVID students of fantasy in recent years. To the research psychologists we owe a rich array of descriptive data about daydreams—their frequency, their variations over the life cycle, their triggers, and a host of their other characteristics.[1] To the work of psychoanalysts we owe our knowledge of fantasy in the context of a depth psychology. Both bodies of work help us better understand the sources of fantasies and their function as rehearsals for life and not just substitute gratifications or precursors to neurosis.

The discovery of the importance of fantasy in our lives was Sigmund Freud's. He first recognized the power of fantasy, its influence on our lives, when he was studying hysterical patients, all of whom were women. They suffered mainly from conversion symptoms (including paralysis or tics, unusual feelings in their arms and legs, blindness or deafness), amnesia and fugue states, or "hysterical fits" without any discernible organic basis. It was Freud's great insight that the cause of their hysterical symptoms was psychological rather than physical. Initially Freud concluded that the source of hysteria was real events, not fantasy. Early life sexual trauma was the culprit in his patients' neurosis, he believed, and their hysterical symptoms were symbolic representations of their sealed-off traumatic memories. Writing in 1896, in *The Aetiology of Hysteria,* Freud proposed that

at the bottom of every case of hysteria there are *one or more occurrences of premature sexual experience,* occurrences which belong to the earliest years of childhood, but which can be reproduced through the work of psycho-analysis in spite of the intervening decades. I believe that this is an important finding, the discovery of a *caput Nili* in neuropathology.[2]

However, Freud soon abandoned the seduction theory to argue instead that his patients' apparent "memories" of being seduced were, in fact, fantasies— derivatives of unconscious childhood wishes rather than distorted memories of real experiences. As early as 1897, in a letter to Wilhelm Fliess, Freud indicated that discovering the role of fantasy in hysterical illness made him realize that it occupied as large a role in mental life as any external reality.[3]

Thus, Freud arrived at a totally new theory: he proposed that the girl invoked seduction fantasies to disguise her own sexual impulses and thereby avoid guilt. Scenes of seduction were in fact products of the child's wish-fulfillment fantasies, disguising her autoerotic activity. (The girl is essentially saying: "I do not lust for my father; it is he who lusts for me.")

Freud's 180-degree theoretical turn in his understanding of the cause of hysteria marked the beginning of his conceptualization of *internal, psychical reality* as distinct from *external, material reality*. Freud now refuted his former interpretation of real events, particularly traumatic ones, as the causative factor in the formation of hysterical illness. No longer did he believe that hysterics suffered from terrible buried memories; rather, they experienced terrible conflicts associated with childhood fantasies that emerged from their own infantile sexual desires. By 1908, Freud had concluded that fantasies of seduction rather than actual seduction fueled hysterical symptoms: "Every hysterical attack which I have been able to investigate up to the present has proved to be an involuntary irruption of daydreams."[4]

In Freud's revised view, the patient's creation of seduction fantasies was

> of scarcely less importance for [her] neurosis than if [she] had really experienced what the phantasies contained. The phantasies possess *psychical* as contrasted with *material* reality, and we gradually learn to understand that *in the world of the neurosis it is psychical reality which is the decisive kind*.[5]

Freud no longer regarded fantasy as purely imaginary; it impacted on reality, creating what he called psychical reality. Fantasy could no longer be viewed as wool gathering, or spinning one's wheels; it was real and it had real-world consequences.

Freud's motives for rejecting his previous interpretation have been attacked from two different sides. Some have criticized him for basing his original seduction theory on inadequate data; they question whether Freud's patients actually reported scenes of seduction or whether Freud reconstructed these scenes in the course of analysis.[6] The opposite camp argues that Freud retracted his ideas not because of new observations or fresh insights, but because he feared the disapproval of his community.[7] Whether Freud's seduction data were reported directly by his patients or reconstructed by him, it seems clear that he genuinely came to doubt that sexual trauma was the primary cause of hysteria. Several considerations caused him to change his mind, among them the fact that hysteria was so common at the time that if its causes were inevitably related to early-life seduction, then many fathers (or other relatives) of seemingly impeccable respectability and decency were the seducers. Considering this implausible, Freud sought a different explanation for what he now took to be seduction fantasies, one that would explain what initiated the fantasies and why they were so prevalent.

Freud's conclusion that repressed fantasy was the ultimate source of hysteria illuminated the underlying causes of many other disruptive mental phenomena as well. All of them, he believed, shared a source in the forbidden wishes of early childhood, and all provided a defense against the forbidden, the unbearable. Being unbearable, these wishes had been buried—a process Freud later termed *repression*. But once buried, they still craved expression, which took the form of symbolic representation in hysteria and hysterical paralysis, and in phobias, obsessions, delusions, hallucinations, and so forth.

Freud's reformulation of hysteria was essential to the birth of psychoanalytic thinking, grounding it in an appreciation of innate desires and the fantasies they generate, and particularly emphasizing *unconscious* fantasy.[8] One result was to almost negate the impact attributed to memories and external events on the formation of fantasy. As incorrect in certain respects as his new formulation turned out to be—particularly from the perspective of today, when the focus is again on real life trauma—it did prepare the way for Freud's profound insights into dreams and into the key role of conscious and unconscious fantasies in our lives.

Dreams proved to be Freud's royal road to conceptualizing the way the mind worked. He wrote to Fliess in 1897 that no matter where he started, "I always find myself back again with the neurosis and psychical apparatus. . . . Inside me there is a seething ferment, and I am only waiting for the next surge forward. . . . I have felt impelled to start writing about dreams, with which I feel on firm ground."[9] In part, this was because his hysteria patients had already drawn dreams to his attention when he asked them to associate freely and he was able to observe how the dreams themselves stimulated still more associations. But perhaps more important, it was through his own dreams that Freud was able to conduct his own self-analysis—in which he was both patient and therapist. And that self-analysis revealed to him the multilayered nature of the human mind. Thus, through Freud's investigation into dreams, psychoanalysis evolved from a treatment method into an overarching theory of mind, a depth psychology that conceived of the mind as existing on a continuum from unconsciousness to preconsciousness to consciousness, this division of the psyche corresponding to what is available—and acceptable—to personal consciousness.

DAYDREAMS AND DREAMS

In studying dreams Freud first worked out the relationships among daydreams, night dreams, and unconscious fantasy, and between wish-fulfillment and fantasy. For Freud the wisdom of language had established the fundamental connection that existed between *daydreams* and nighttime *dreams*. Daydreams, he believed, are like nocturnal dreams because both originate in the wishes buried in unconscious fantasy and both are vehicles for wish-fulfillment.[10] (Recent findings of research psychologists, who are generally uninterested in unconscious fantasy in the Freudian sense, support the idea that daydreaming and night dreaming form part of a single and continuous flow.[11] Several observations illustrate this relationship: In any individual, daydreaming and night dreaming have the same style and are triggered by the same kinds of external—sometimes internal—stimuli; they share some of the same imagery; and they both appear to peak in ninety-minute cycles.[12] According to the research psychologist Eric Klinger, daydreaming and night dreaming "make up a single continuum of human consciousness in which one continually shades into the other—much as each day the varied world of daytime shades into the equally variable world of night.")[13]

In the opening paragraph of *The Interpretation of Dreams,* the great work he published in 1900, Freud set out his far-reaching intentions:

> In the pages that follow I shall bring forward proof that there is a psychological technique which makes it possible to interpret dreams, and that, if that procedure is employed, every dream reveals itself as a psychical structure which has a meaning and which can be inserted at an assignable point in the mental activities of waking life. I shall further endeavour to elucidate the processes to which the strangeness and obscurity of dreams are due and to deduce from those processes the nature of psychical forces by whose concurrent or mutually opposing action dreams are generated.[14]

And this he proceeded to do.

Some have claimed that Freud's seminal work might just as well have been "The Interpretation of Daydreams" or "The Interpretation of Jokes"; I disagree. It was probably inevitable that dreams rather than jokes or daydreams would prove the key to understanding the workings of the mind and the importance of unconscious material because jokes are considered trivial (and not everyone makes jokes) and daydreams have been so seldom communicated that we have a limited number from which to theorize.

Moreover, because we think of daydreams as conscious creations, transparently embodying the daydreamer's most personal wishes, we tend to attach moral judgments to them. As a result they are more often objects for suppression than for exploration.[15] In contrast, because dreams are considered involuntary productions of the mind, for which the dreamer cannot be held accountable, and because the wishes underlying them are much more disguised, people have been more willing to relate them and to open them up for analysis. Paradoxically, because dreams are even *more* disguised than daydreams they ultimately have been the route to revelations about the mechanisms of the mind.

People have always talked about their dreams, and we have a very long tradition of dream interpretations, which have afforded some seminal insights into their meaning. Dreams were long believed to deliver important warnings, predictions, and portents—a whole array of prophetic messages. Though in some periods dreams were dismissed as nothing more than inexplicable effluvia, the predominant view in antiquity emphasized their importance as relaying insights from the great beyond, from supernatural or divine sources.[16]

Freud's magisterial *The Interpretation of Dreams* was not the first important book by that name. Artemidorus, a second-century Roman soothsayer, author of *Oneirocriticon,* had profound insights into the nature of dreams, exploring "the question of recurrent dreams, . . . the intensity of emotion that different dreams evoke, . . . the manner in which prodromic dreams seem to anticipate illness and . . . the way in which dreams were related to such similar phenomena as visions, oracles, fantasies, and apparitions."[17] But the prophetic nature of dreams—their perceived similarity to pronouncements from the Delphic Oracle, to auguries, to the reading of entrails, and to other ways of receiving messages from the gods—was for hundreds of years the prime motive for studying them.

In the eighteenth and nineteenth centuries, an age dominated by the positivists, who sought to reduce all human experience to the logical, the measurable, and the material, the interest in dreams declined. Dreams were taken away from the gods and other supernatural sources and assigned to human beings, their origins consigned to physiological processes. A dream of being crushed to death might result from heavy bedclothes; a dream of being chased by a beast whose pounding hooves are getting ever closer might arise from indigestion and the pounding heart that often accompanies it; and so forth. Boiled down to such basics, dreams were seen as essentially marginal.

But there were some exceptions to this reductivist approach and when Freud began his work he was able to utilize some of his predecessors' insights. For example, Freud refers to Karl Albrecht Scherner's *The Life of Dreams* as "the most original and far-reaching attempt to explain dreaming as a special activity of the mind, capable of free expansion only in the state of sleep."[18] Among Scherner's profound insights, he described how the dream fantasy lacks a conceptual language—what it wants to say it must paint pictorially. . . . The clarity of its language is impaired by the fact that it has a dislike of representing an object by its proper image, and prefers some extraneous image which will express only that one attribute of the object which it is seeking to describe. Here we have the symbolizing activity of fantasy.[19]

Coming out of a positivist tradition, Freud, too, saw dreams as emanating from within (not from the gods), but his profound insight was to see beyond the boundary of physiological processes into the psychological properties of dreams. Although at various times Freud acknowledged the role of the body in triggering dreams, he recognized that the dream's meaning transcends what gave rise to it. Dreams are significant because they reveal the deepest wishes of the dreamer. Thus Freud gravitated to a study of dreams as passionate as that of the ancients—in part to facilitate his own analysis.

Freud's central idea was that the dream is layered: the manifest content (what we remember) expresses the fulfillment of a hidden wish, the disguised gratification during sleep of a buried desire; the latent content is the underlying wish. Freud emphasized that whatever triggers a dream—and this might be a sensory stimulus or a physiological condition—its importance lies in its meaning. Noting the relationship of dreams both to some incidental trigger (the "day residue") and to early life, Freud described the fundamental nature of dreams as wish-fulfillment. But when the forbidden wish or desire attempts to surface, some other part of the mind attempts to distort and disguise it. This "Dream Censor" dictates the disguise in which the unacceptable unconscious material will appear.

Thus far, I have described the process of forming a dream. But what is the nature of the wish that infuses the dream? The motive for the dream? Though he primarily focused on sexual motives—on the developmental stages of sexuality and the wishes and fantasies that derive from them—Freud was quick to point out that "there are numerous dreams which satisfy needs other than those which are erotic in the widest sense of the word: dreams of hunger and thirst, dreams of convenience, etc."[20]

To identify the wishes that shape dreams we must examine their links to current concerns and to the underlying wishes and conflicts of childhood. Only then can the meaning of the dream be revealed. Consider, for example, a man insulted by his boss during the day who dreams that night that the office of the governor of his *home state* (where he was born) is blown up by a terrorist bomb. The exchange with his boss constitutes the day residue; it triggers the dream. The events, characters, and common images of the dream, along with the internal commentaries that accompany it and the affect associated with it, are its *manifest content*—everything the dreamer can tell us about it. However, the dream is not transparent. Its manifest content is but a disguised version of the various repressed impulses and feelings—the *latent content*—that stoked it. Perhaps the dreamer is so quick to intense anger because he still harbors a deep grievance against his authoritarian father. If so, his unconscious wish is twice disguised: manifestly the dream is about killing the governor, not his boss or his father (though his current anger at his boss, who in some ways resembles his father, provokes the dream and the assassination of a man whom he explicitly identifies as governor of his home state suggests a connection with his early life); it is further disguised by the fact that in the dream the agent of death is a terrorist, not the dreamer himself.

Dream-work is the censorship process that disguises the underlying unconscious wish. The Dream Censor translates forbidden wishes into dream language—a language that bears many resemblances to poetry, for its signature modes of expression are condensation, displacement, indirect representation, and symbolism.

In *condensation,* an event or person or even a single word can contain levels and kinds of meaning accruing from a number of different sources. For example, in one of Freud's own dreams, the "Irma" dream, the figure of Dr. M., one of his senior colleagues, spoke and acted as he did in real life, but his physical appearance and his infirmity were those of Freud's older brother. Recognizing the connection allowed Freud to use associations to both men to deepen his understanding of his dream.

Displacement transfers feelings from the original object to which they were directed to a substitute. For example, the dream about the bombing of the governor's office transfers feelings stoked by the boss onto the governor.

Through *indirect representation,* images that go to make up an action appear out of sequence, because dream language lacks an equivalent to conjunctives such as *and* or *therefore*.[21] Dream representation has been compared to those medieval paintings that depict events that occur at different times together, as if they are occurring simultaneously, or to a triptych in which each panel represents one part of the story being represented.

A *symbol* is another form of indirect representation. Freud tended to see many symbols as having fairly fixed meanings, which have become familiar from his writings: those elongated objects, such as cigars, sticks, tree trunks, and umbrellas, that he equates with the phallus; containers, such as boxes, cases, chests, and ovens, that he interpreted as representations of the womb; and so on.[22] But many symbols are so idiosyncratic that they are not amenable to such generalization. Hanna Segal gives an example of a very ingenious symbolic mode of representation: "As part of a long dream a patient dreamed *of a column of soldiers marching eight abreast.* Rather perplexed by that part of the dream, [Segal] asked her what she thought. She answered immediately: 'ATE a breast, of course. What else could it mean?'"[23]

The Censor's use of dream language to disguise underlying wishes is further enhanced by what Freud called *secondary elaboration*—the rationalizing mechanism through which, in recollecting a dream, we attempt to make it more logical. Memory is a master of concealment.

Freud's great thesis, then, was that the unresolved conflicts and ungratified impulses of infancy, which take shape as unconscious fantasies, press continually for some form of gratification—often in dreams, though in dreams that are heavily disguised versions of those wishes and needs. From this point of view, all the derivatives of unconscious fantasy—fantasy, dreams, symptoms—look backward: they all express unfinished business.

Nonetheless, Freud recognized that the dream does contain some future orientation as well. The ancients' view of dreams as prophecies had some validity. In one of the more famous prophetic examples reported by Artemidorus, and noted by Freud, Aristander interpreted a famous dream of Alexander the Great in which he saw a satyr. Aristander interpreted the satyr as *sa tyros,* which in Greek means "Tyre is thine."[24] The storming of Tyre in 332 B.C. is considered to be Alexander's greatest military achievement: for him, a wish come true. Thus we have a perfect example of the dream as both prophecy (as the ancients understood it) and wish-fulfillment (as Freud intuited).

Freud understood how the future orientation of a dream could have self-fulfilling consequences: "Dreams are derived from the past in every sense. Nevertheless, the ancient belief that dreams foretell the future is not wholly devoid of truth. By picturing our wishes as fulfilled, dreams are after all leading us into the future."[25] And dreams have proved to be future-oriented in broader ways than as guides to future gratification. They are attempts to solve problems, to master traumatic experiences, to process information, all of which affect the future. Of course, these are also characteristics of fantasy: Both dream and fantasy have roots in the past and momentum into the future; both look in two directions, backward and forward. Both use the past to plot the future.

By way of dreams Freud glimpsed the shores of unconscious fantasy. But even though he postulated that dreams could only be understood as the symbolically disguised manifestation of an unconscious fantasy—and this was the very centerpiece of his whole psychological theory—he never worked out a full-fleshed theory of fantasy comparable to his theory of dreams.[26]

THE SOURCES AND CONTENT OF UNCONSCIOUS FANTASY

Unconscious fantasy can only be an inferred construct: what is unconscious cannot be directly observed. Nonetheless the concept is indispensable to understanding the mind. Just as we assume a grizzly has passed by when we see its tracks in the ground, though the grizzly itself is nowhere to be seen, so we infer the existence of unconscious fantasy through the tracks it leaves in mental life—for example, in conscious fantasies and dreams and in neurotic symptoms.

Freud was not the first to propose the existence of the unconscious; most of his contemporaries and predecessors believed that there was some unconscious aspect to mind.[27] But whereas Freud's predecessors viewed the unconscious as ancillary to consciousness, Freud suggested the exact opposite interpretation— that the most important mental processes take place in the unconscious. The unconscious is the storehouse of motivation, which feeds into dreams and daydreams, jokes and slips of the tongue, neurotic symptoms and artistic productions.

But what is the source of unconscious fantasy and what is its nature? For Freud, daydreams are not just an outgrowth of the unconscious fantasy but one of its major sources. Daydreams, like dreams, have their sources in wishes. In both, fantasy originates in that period between the arousal of an appetite or need and its gratification; any delay in the longed-for gratification generates an acutely painful state of longing, of desire. Originally, early in life, desire creates a hallucinatory form of gratification, but later in development this gives way to fantasy, which has the function of providing imaginary (rather than hallucinatory) wish-fulfillment. Freud postulated that fantasies (daydreams) are conjured up as the imagined fulfillment of wishes, their purpose to relieve the anxiety and pain of undischarged instinctual tensions and unfulfilled needs. And if a conscious fantasy is unacceptable to the fantasizer, it is buried (repressed) and transformed into an unconscious fantasy.

Freud suggests, "Just as there are phantasies . . . which are conscious, so, too, there are unconscious ones in great numbers, which have to remain unconscious on account of their content and of their origin from repressed material."[28] When a wish-fulfilling fantasy unacceptable to consciousness is repressed, it becomes part of the unconscious, whose mental processes are very different from conscious processes.

One of the ways these processes differ is related to the awareness of what is real and what is imagined. In its early hallucinatory mode of mental activity, the infant does not distinguish between its wishes and reality: it engages in magical thinking in which its wishes reign supreme and are accepted as their own form of reality. But ultimately the hallucination or the fantasy fails to be gratifying, and the infant painfully comes to learn that imaginary substitutes do not bring real gratification. A hallucinated breast and imaginary milk fail to satisfy real hunger pangs. In the face of deprivation, the young child learns to accept reality, to identify a causal sequence leading to gratification or deprivation, and to distinguish between what is and what is not possible. In the process the child gives up the belief in the omnipotence of its own wishes. Thus, to some degree, the child traumatically gains some perception of reality and the reality principle, which leads it to conform to the demands and limitations imposed by the external world.[29] Of course, as we now understand, we also gain our knowledge of reality by virtue of innately developing cognitive capacities.

Only gradually and incompletely do infants and children give up wishful, magical thinking. But Freud knew that we never fully renounce anything, and that fantasies from this early stage persist, sequestered in what he called the "nature preserve" of the unconscious. In that realm where unconscious fantasy lives, "everything, including what is useless and even when it is noxious, can grow and proliferate . . . as it pleases."[30] (And here is the insight that fantasy can be dangerous—radical in its implications.)

The eventual result is that in each of us, two different and simultaneously existing forms of thinking evolve: what Freud called *primary-process thinking*, or magical thinking, which employs an archaic, prelogical mode and is characteristic of both infantile thought and of the unconscious; and the more objectively oriented *secondary-process thinking* characteristic of consciousness (and to some extent of the preconscious system), which encompasses the ability to make realistic judgments.

Daydreams partake of both kinds of thinking. Though wish-fulfillment fuels them, because they are products of the conscious mind, and because we know they are imaginary, they are bound by a more rational kind of thinking than is believed to take place in the unconscious. Thus daydream scenarios are generally characterized by at least a superficial semblance of logic, and an awareness that they are products of the imagination.

In contrast, when fantasies are repressed and become unconscious, no knowledge remains that the fantasy is imaginary. If it is retained at all, it exists in an encoded form, as a memory, as reality. Here is the fundamental problem in the ongoing debate about how to distinguish seduction that took place in reality and seduction that took place in the imagination. According to Freud's theory, there is no way to distinguish unconscious fantasies from repressed memories.[31]

Freud concluded that unconscious fantasy originates in childhood wishes unacceptable to consciousness that are repressed and relegated to the unconscious, where they function according to primary-process thinking. But his early model actually embraces two origins for unconscious fantasy: "Unconscious fantasies have either been unconscious all along and have been formed in the unconscious or—as is more often the case—they were once conscious fantasies."[32] Freud is suggesting two alternative explanations of the source of unconscious fantasy. While some fantasies are specific to an individual, others are inborn and well-nigh universal. Here he raises the possibility that certain fantasies—for example, primal scene fantasies (scenarios of parental intercourse, often perceived as sadomasochistic) and Oedipal fantasies (relating to the

Oedipal complex and denoting desire for one parent and fear of the other)—might be independent of experience. Some unconscious fantasy could be innate (endogenous)—a mental representation of instinct, not always the product of fantasy repression.[33] Freud proposed still another explanation for the ubiquity of certain fantasies—that unconscious fantasy in the form of myth is essentially the memory not of the individual but of the species. Thus, Freud came to entertain the possibility of fantasies that were either primal or original.[34]

Over the long haul the idea of the inheritance of specieswide memories in the form of myths became less important to Freud's thinking (though he never entirely rejected it). Ultimately he would return to the theory that the child's core wishes (primarily sexual) and the fantasies that issue from them are the true organizers of unconscious fantasy life. Believing libido—the energy of the sexual drive—to be the major motor force in life, Freud posited that the individual develops in accordance with the expression of sexual impulses (and wishes), which are innate and unfold in a regular developmental sequence. As the child is socialized and increasingly restricted by the conventions of the world (internalized as superego) these sexual wishes cannot be directly expressed and are therefore repressed, subsequently appearing only indirectly as disguised manifestations of an underlying, now buried wish. Later Freud came to consider aggression as another major energy source of fantasy.

For many years, psychoanalysts equated the *unconscious fantasy* with the *unconscious instinctual wish,* and a consensus existed that the wishes expressed in unconscious fantasy were primarily sexual or aggressive. However, with the shift to the *structural theory* (the theory that the mind is composed of ego, id, and superego), the understanding of what constitutes unconscious fantasy has changed. The newer view suggests a broader range of wishes and a different structure of unconscious fantasy. As already suggested, it has been recognized that many underlying wishes and motives operate in fantasy, including the need for the regulation of self-esteem, the need for a feeling of safety, the need for regulating affect, and the need to master trauma.

Moreover, in this more recent view embraced by ego psychologists (but not by all contemporary analysts), fantasy encompasses not only the original wish but the defenses erected against it. All fantasies show the mark of the ego's synthesizing function and, therefore, are more or less composites of wishes, defenses against them, superego directives, and reality considerations.[35] In this view, an unconscious fantasy is not just a wish but a compromise formation, the result of a struggle between mutually exclusive wishes (contradictory drives and impulses simultaneously striving for expression) or between wishes and the opposition mounted by either internal (psychic) reality or external reality.

Whatever the source of unconscious fantasy—in repressed fantasy or experience, in instinct, in primal or species memory—there is some consensus today about the universality of much of its content and the possible range of that content. As the psychoanalyst Harry Trosman says,

> We need not get into the ancient argument about whether the universality of these fantasies is to be accounted for on the basis of a phylogenetically transmitted inheritance. It is enough . . . to indicate that psychoanalysts have developed a kind of shorthand, or gloss, to account for a broad range of fantasy structures. They are about intrauterine existence, primal scenes, castration, seduction, and other vital matters which are common, emotionally laden, basically wishful.[36]

Differences in emphasis notwithstanding, the literature on fantasies reflects some consensus on the content of universal fantasies. The psychoanalysts Jean Laplanche and Jean-Bertrand Pontalis describe fantasies of origins that they liken to myths in their ability to solve mysteries and address children's pressing life concerns. They posit three fantasies of origins: the primal scene fantasy depicting the origin of the individual, seduction fantasies depicting the origin and upsurge of sexuality, and fantasies of castration accounting for the origin of the differences between the sexes.[37] Although the psychoanalyst Scott Dowling sees fantasies as constructed rather than as innate, the basic fantasies he describes overlap with those described by Laplanche and Pontalis. Dowling proposes "two closely interrelated groups" of psychological issues that stimulate the formation of fantasy.[38] The first group arises from the drives and encompasses "issues of physical and emotional stimulation and intimacy and oral, anal, phallic, and genital levels, together with related feelings of curiosity concerning conception, birth, competition, retribution, and death," and results in fantasies such as oral or anal conception and birth.[39] (It is this group that overlaps with Laplanche and Pontalis's fantasies of origins.) The second group Dowling describes is stimulated not by drives but by life experiences that engender feelings of abandonment, loss, separation, anxiety, and helplessness, which act to stimulate fantasies of omnipotence and control to counter the painful feelings.[40] Taken together, the two groups of fantasy—both products of the human condition—depict universal themes that include Oedipal fantasies, omnipotent fantasies, oral-dependent fantasies, and masochistic fantasies.[41]

While each individual's "universal" fantasy has its own unique coloration, generalized fantasy themes that are incorporated into art speak to many. The child analyst Lili Peller shows how the fantasy solutions to the problems of early life often appear in children's favorite books. The books depict, among others, such reparative fantasies as the fantasy of maternal loss and return (*The Tale of Peter Rabbit, Curious George*); the fantasy of a group of loyal friends looked after by a protector (*The Wind in the Willows*); and fantasies of twinship, in which the twin provides escape from loneliness or from sibling rivalry (*Max and Moritz*). Comic books serve the same functions, providing fantasy solutions to counter age-specific problems and conflicts. As the psychoanalyst

Martin E. Widzer points out, comic book heroes provide models with which children identify as those heroes "perform acts of retribution, retaliation, and repair." For Widzer the variety of comic book themes address unconscious fantasies typical of every level of psychic development.[42] And so on, throughout life.

Unconscious fantasy is critically important because it involves psychic material so powerful, basic, and primal that it exerts an ongoing influence on perceptions, subjective experience, and behavior throughout a lifetime.[43] Fantasy becomes intertwined almost imperceptibly with our views of reality. We know, for example, that any given memory is a composite of "real events" sifted through the sieve of imagination, that memory is not a videotape of what literally happened, and, moreover, that any given memory is modified— or at least shaded—by the circumstances in which it either spontaneously surfaces or is invoked consciously.

Similarly, even the most apparently simple perception is colored by subjectivity, wish and feeling. Perception of the external world is never strictly "objective"; it is in effect constructed. A much-cited example of this involved one of Jacob Arlow's patients, who, feeling angry, misread the word *Maeder* (the name of the store's owner) on a familiar shop's sign as *murder*.[44] The degree to which strong emotion affects perception is highly variable. But emotion is a sufficiently powerful and pervasive factor that it makes the doctrine of "immaculate perception" untenable.[45]

Just as emotion-mediated fantasy colors memory and perception, so fantasy exerts its impact on almost all other aspects of the mental life. Fantasy and reality are not opposites; rather, the former is a significant factor in our mental construction of the latter. The centrality of unconscious fantasy to mental life—its influence on thoughts, intentions, and feelings—is generally acknowledged by all contemporary schools of psychoanalytic thinking. A guiding force in motivating us, unconscious fantasy is also the headwater from which flow the rivers of neuroses and other symbolic mental products, including dreams, daydreams, and artistic productions.

Fantasy may or may not become (or remain) conscious, depending on whether it is jacketed in scripts acceptable to the individual's internal censor, that is, whether it is acceptable to his or her conscience and taste. When it does become conscious, it plays a vital role in the direction our lives take but one that is much less emphasized than the role of unconscious fantasy.

DAYDREAMS AND PLAY

Freud presented two different models for understanding the function of conscious fantasy: a model relating daydreams to dreams (in *The Interpretation of Dreams*) and a model relating fantasy to children's play (in "Creative Writers and Day-dreaming"). Both models illuminate the function of conscious fantasy, but their focus and implications diverge.

Freud's dream model focuses more on the origins of fantasy in early childhood and its role in substitute wish-fulfillment and in symptom formation; it comes closer than the play model to illuminating the origins of repeating fantasies, and it relates primarily to the daydream's function of undoing the conflicts and wounds of the past.

Freud's play model looks more to the future. Even though one of the important functions of play is to repeat the past (for example, in mastering trauma), its major function is assuaging current emotional needs and devising current and future adaptations. Freud's play model is more useful in explicating generative fantasies and the purposes they serve in future planning.[46] There is, of course, considerable overlap between the two models.

Freud's play model of fantasy appeared first in 1908 and again in 1911.[47] Drawing a parallel between play and fantasy, he proposed that both issue from the same motives, insofar as both offer a vehicle for imaginary wish-fulfillment; moreover, the results are often parallel, insofar as both are highly pleasurable. Play and fantasy are similar in yet another way. Neither the child at play nor the fantasizing adult has obscured his basic reality. Both are simultaneously aware of external reality and able to enjoy the make-believe or fantasy. But to reap the pleasures of make-believe, both momentarily suspend their immersion in reality. (To the degree that the sense of reality is eroded, and a fantasy experienced as reality, one enters the domain of delusion.)

Freud saw yet another function—other than simple wish-fulfillment—in play and in fantasy too. Whereas theorists prior to Freud had considered play as practice for useful skills, Freud perceived that one of its primary purposes was to work through anxiety and other current emotional stresses. He saw that both play and fantasy were invoked as solutions to current problems in the child's emotional world. Having observed a year-and-a-half old boy engaged in a game of a disappearing spool (the Fort Da game), Freud wrote a charming account of play invoked for purposes of mastering separation anxiety.

> This good little boy . . . had an occasional disturbing habit of taking any small objects he could get hold of and throwing them away from him into a corner, under a bed, and so on, so that hunting for his toys and picking them up was often quite a business. As he did this he gave vent to a loud, long-drawn-out "o-o-o-o", accompanied by an expression of interest and satisfaction. His mother and the writer of the present account were agreed in thinking that this was not a mere interjection but represented the German "fort" ["gone"]. I eventually realized that it was a game and that the only use he made of any of his toys was to play "gone" with them. One day I made an observation which confirmed my view. The child had a wooden reel with a piece of string tied round it. It never occurred to him to pull it along the floor behind him, for instance, and play at its

being a carriage. What he did was to hold the reel by the string and very skill-fully throw it over the edge of his curtained cot, so that it disappeared into it, at the same time uttering his expressive "o-o-o-o". He then pulled the reel out of the cot again by the string and hailed its reappearance with a joyful "da" ["there"]. This, then, was the complete game—disappearance and return. As a rule one only witnessed its first act, which was repeated untiringly as a game in itself, though there is no doubt that the greater pleasure was attached to the sec-ond act.[48]

Freud understood the thrusting away as the boy's attempt to transform an event in which he experienced himself as passive (his mother's occasional and to him inexplicable disappearances) into one in which he was active (*he* was the one who did the abandoning or casting out). Most analysts agree that one or another form of this game—throwing and sometimes retrieving an object—is widespread, if not universal, in young children's play repertoire. The game is pleasurable because it symbolizes control over the mother's whereabouts, reas-suring the child that he or she can will the reappearance of the disappeared person or object.

Other examples of anxiety-assuaging fantasy play, some of which occur even in the preverbal period, are peek-a-boo games, the child's repetitive throwing down of items in order for the mother to retrieve them, and role-reversal play enactments in which the child plays the role of the mother, for example, feeding, scolding, or comforting.

These various games are pleasurable because they help the child deal with uncomfortable feelings such as separation anxiety, dependency, and power-lessness. They permit the young child to feel more in control, to replace pas-sivity with activity, helplessness with mastery. Gradually such games evolve into the fantasy playlets or make-believe games of later childhood in which the child instructs the parent to play a certain role or introduces an imaginary companion, human or animal, into the family with the assumption that the family will respond to it.

These more advanced pretend or make-believe games have important developmental functions: They provide a mode of mastery in response to anx-iety or a solution to emotional conflicts current in the child's life; they counter unpleasant feelings and the sense of helplessness. They may also serve as life rehearsals insofar as they project the child's goals and an image of what the child wants to be. Freud believed that one of the primary motives in make-believe was the wish to be "big"—and one certainly observes children spend-ing considerable time trying on adult roles, playing at being Mommy or Daddy, firefighter or nurse.

Not everyone considers play, at either the preverbal or the verbal stage, equivalent to fantasies as strictly defined. Even so, play must surely be on a continuum with fantasy, for they both address similar wishes and problems, posit solutions to these problems, and draw on unconscious fantasy. As Eric Klinger sees it, both "play and fantasy reflect current focal concerns of the individual—unresolved current problems, unfinished tasks, role conflicts, and prominent affective responses, as well as the challenges of identity and commitment posed by the individual's social relationships."[49]

There comes a time when fantasizing begins to displace play. Beginning at about age eight, the child gradually becomes ashamed of his or her make-believe play and internalizes it in the form of fantasy. (I remember even now how I reluctantly gave up playing with paper dolls at a time when I still enjoyed them, but had come to see the play as infantile, at least as regarded by others. For a while I played with them on the sly, but gradually I abandoned them. Sometimes these early pleasures can be retrieved. For many parents, one of the surprise bonuses in raising children is the permission it gives to return to the make-believe pleasures and play of one's early life. Think of all the fathers trying to encourage their sons to take as much interest in electric trains as they did in their own childhood, or mothers passing on to their daughters the treasured dolls of their youth.) Shame is not the only factor in this change-over; the child's increasing capacity for narrative makes fantasy an ever more viable substitute.

Sometimes dramatized play lasts well into the teens. The recent movie *Heavenly Creatures* brilliantly depicts two lonely teenaged girls who overcome their feelings of isolation by jointly participating in an elaborate game of make-believe involving sex, romance, and murder. (In this case, murderous fantasies are enacted!)[50] But for most of us, fantasies (internal, mental) largely replace play (dramatized, enacted) earlier.

At puberty, as play becomes even less important, fantasy activities become comparably more important.[51] Fantasy continues to address current problems and emotional discomforts and to sculpt the individual's future dreams and plans.

THE TWO-WAY LOOP BETWEEN THE INNER AND OUTER WORLDS

Fantasy influences our relationship to the external world in many ways: It impacts on our perceptions, on our behaviors and relationships, on character, on neurosis, and on our adaptations. It even affects what we wear, where we live, and what we do with our leisure time. Referred to as a centrifugal approach to the study of mind[52]—one that moves from the central core to the surface—the psychoanalytic perspective traces the many ways in which unconscious and conscious fantasies are expressed in everyday life.

But equally important is what one might call the centripetal point of view, which focuses on the way in which the external world influences the forma-tion of fantasy—the way events impact the psychological core—thus creating an endless loop of feedback.[53] Freud was well aware of daydreaming as a potentially adaptable as well as adaptive force in our lives. In 1908, he remarked how fantasies were responsive to one's current situation and how they could also sometimes be malleable, evolving over time in response to changing circumstances in the external world.

> We must not suppose that the products of this imaginative activity—the various phantasies, castles in the air, and daydreams—are stereotyped or unalterable. On the contrary, they fit themselves into the subject's shifting impressions of life, change with every change in his situation, and receive from every fresh, active impression what might be called a "date-mark". . . . Mental work is linked to some current impression, some provoking occasion in the present which has been able to arouse one of the subject's major wishes. From there it harks back to the memory of an earlier experience . . . in which this wish was fulfilled; and it now creates a situation relating to the future which represents a fulfillment of the wish. . . . Thus past, present, and future are strung together, as it were, on the thread of the wish that runs through them.[54]

Here Freud clearly indicates that many fantasies change—evolve or adapt—over time. This observation gives us a model whereby a fantasy does not necessarily repeat itself unchanged but alters in accord with changes in both intrapsychic and cultural conditions. This capacity for change is the very essence of what I call *generative fantasies*.

Although Freud acknowledged the impact of external circumstances on fantasy, only recently has there been a major paradigm shift in both psychology and psychoanalysis to a specific focus on the important role of communal life in the way our minds are formed. As the psychologist Jerome Bruner puts it,

> When we enter human life, it is as if we walk on stage into a play whose enactment is already in progress—a play whose somewhat open plot determines what part we may play and toward what denouements we may be heading. Others on stage already have a sense of what the play is about, enough of the sense to make negotiation with a newcomer possible.[55]

Part of that negotiation concerns the newcomer's ability to create fantasies that are compatible with those of others in his or her world. The boundaries between our inner and outer worlds are porous, and they remain so long past childhood, indeed throughout life.

This observation, of course, does not mean that what happens or what we absorb from the external world passes unmodified into consciousness or unconsciousness. The psychoanalyst Arnold Cooper gives a very good example of the difficulty in distinguishing material reality (what really happened) from psychic reality on the basis of retrospective data:

A toddler ... spoken to sharply by his mother, runs to his father and says, "Mommy pushed me down and bit me." The discrepancy of fact and report is clear but the child may internalize his fantasy version rather than the realistic one, since at the moment a feeling of overwhelming injustice done to him is more satisfying to his injured narcissism than an admission of being a bad boy who is too small and helpless to ward off punishment. It is that genetic past— the past as experienced, including the distorting defenses that make experience tolerable even at the expense of some observable truth—that his future analyst will attempt to unravel.[56]

This is why analysts have emphasized psychic reality as opposed to material reality. Nonetheless, the historical lived reality does feed back into the unconscious, from which it later ramifies outward again. We know, for example, that our early life relationships reconstitute themselves not just in our inner world, but in the external world as well, in the way we live our lives.[57] The very theory of transference is based on observations that patients experience feelings toward their analysts which recapitulate those they had experienced toward the significant personae of their early lives. That one recapitulates in one's intimate relationships aspects of early relationships is commonly observed when an individual marries someone very like his or her mother, father, or sibling.

Lived experiences affect fantasy throughout life. One of the arguments I make throughout this book is that whatever the fate of unconscious fantasy— and this we can never know with certainty because what is unconscious can only be inferred—fantasy narratives are continually modified by new input from the external world.

That input includes cultural material. There is always potential for reconfiguring one's fantasy life and one's psyche, not just through new experience or therapy but through exposure to art. Many literary critics, including Jean Wyatt, have pointed out ways books can change their readers.[58] In part we can use what we read as a change agent, because "different parts of the self respond to different registers of language—and to the different narratives they encode."[59] And perhaps the different parts of the self that respond to art are also responding to the different parts of the artist's self.

In a passage about the novelist George Eliot, Jean Wyatt addresses the issue of changing one's mind:

How can one give up one's habitual orientation to reality, one's reliance on distinct categories of thought, to slide back into a less differentiated way of thinking? An adult used to defending the line between inner and outer worlds, between self and other, may need some special solvent to diffuse the habitual containments of mental and emotional life.[60]

One such solvent, she suggests, may be emotional and sexual intimacy. By recreating that magical, timeless zone of playfulness and freedom shared by a mother and her small child, such intimacy may facilitate other kinds of freedom as well. As an example she quotes George Eliot's essay "How I Came to Write Fiction," in which she spoke of the bed she shared with George Henry Lewes as a creative space. Under the aegis of his permissive presence she was able "to relax into a fantasy of writing a novel, to acknowledge that daydream, and, with his enthusiastic affirmation, to make it part of her ongoing self-definition."[61] I have elsewhere written of the creative psychic flux that occurs when passionate love allows two people to recreate in new, improved form the intimate relationships of their past, and so to revision the world.[62]

The reworking or the revisioning of cognitive material goes on all the time in the preconscious, as we know from reports of the various ways people arrive at creative solutions to intellectual problems. Though we tend to credit the conscious working mind with getting us where we need to go, a number of artists and scientists have described problems they worked out and fully elaborated in the preconscious, by utilizing a secondary-process mode of thinking. Walter B. Cannon, for example, in preparing for a public address, would make a rough outline highlighting certain central points. Then over the next several nights he would experience spells of wakefulness during which fresh, fully articulated ideas that fit brilliantly into his paper would come to him.[63] His ability to delegate a task to his preconscious, and have it performed successfully in almost every instance, led him to believe that his was a universal mode of mental work. Many scientists acknowledge that their major contributions rest on intuitive hunches (which they must then of course test and prove).

Not all of us are so well endowed in working out creative solutions to scientific and artistic puzzles; but each of us does relegate—even if we do not actively delegate—certain kinds of mental work to the preconscious. There the job of modifying current cultural scripts to suit our own purposes, our underlying wishes and needs, takes place; in the laboratory of the preconscious we fashion our rehearsal (or preparatory) fantasies, fantasies that may be actualized. All of us are creative to some extent in spinning fantasies as guides that hold out the possibility of future gratification.

Because Freud implicated fantasy as the cause of hysteria, there has been a tendency in psychoanalysis, which has been adopted by the culture at large, to focus on the role of fantasy in neurosis (symptom formation). Moreover, because Freud worked out the psychology of fantasy in the context of his study of dreams, psychoanalysis has emphasized the wish-fulfilling nature of fantasies, an emphasis also absorbed into the culture. As a result, the repeating fantasies, part and parcel of the dream-related model of fantasy, have had the lion's share of the attention. Issuing from and oriented toward the past, they recur throughout a lifetime, and their relative stability (along with that of our unconscious fantasies) is reflected in the relative stability of our personalities.

Meanwhile, generative fantasies, which are best understood through the play model of fantasy, have been slighted. Changing according to the needs and dictates of our lives and times, generative fantasies are much more mobile than repeating fantasies. Freud's work on the play model noted this mobility and gave us another way to look at the impact of fantasy on the way we live, emphasizing dress-rehearsal and future-oriented plans.

Both kinds of fantasy are crucial to our lives, for we need both stability and continuity, on the one hand, and the capacity for adaptive responses, on the other. Fantasy acts to connect the inner world of the psyche to the outer world of reality; it also constructs a bridge from our past histories to our current situations and future hopes.

Understanding the impact of fantasy—both generative and repeating conscious fantasy, as well as unconscious fantasy—is the very lifeblood of psychoanalysis. How fantasy manifests itself in our lives is a wondrous and complicated subject. But perhaps even more critical to our self-understanding is an awareness that the influence works two ways. Our unconscious is always leaking into our everyday lives, and the external world is in turn finding its way back into the many levels of the psyche. It is a circular, ongoing, lifelong process.

4

EROTIC, SELF-SOOTHING, AND OTHER REPEATING FANTASIES

ALL THROUGH LIFE WE REPLAY AND REVISE A CORE GROUP OF FANTASIES, each organized around one of a relatively small number of infantile and childhood wishes.[1] In each series, a given fantasy portrays slightly different renderings or reeditions of one basic theme. The age and the circumstances of the fantasizer dictate specific details, but the revisions are generally minor. Of course, the various sequential editions of the fantasy may overlap, merge, or coexist, with one version in the ascendancy for a while, only to be supplanted by another. One man describes his collection of fantasies as a kind of lending library where there is a run on one fantasy for a time, while another sits on the shelf. (He, of course, is the only borrower from this particular library.)

These repeating fantasies are of three basic kinds—erotic, self-soothing, and global—the first group virtually universal, the other two less common. The masturbatory fantasy (I will use the terms *erotic, masturbatory,* and *sexual* interchangeably) is the source of both sexual and nonsexual gratification, and though often repressed in latency, it reappears in later life as our central erotic fantasy. Self-soothing fantasies comprise the second type that may continue throughout a lifetime, their durability reinforced by their capacity to quiet and console us, to assuage anxiety. Closely related to them are fantasies so central to our sense of who we are that they permeate every aspect of our lives; these are *self fantasies,* described in different psychoanalytic frames of reference as either *global fantasies* or *personal myths.*[2]

73

Other repeating fantasies may be narcissistic fantasies of glory or power or aggressive or sadistic fantasies encompassing the subsidiary themes of vengeance or preemptive strike, domination or total subjugation. Alternatively, they may be masochistic or submissive. Or they may be depressive in content, accompanied by suicide fantasies.

Many of these fantasies persist throughout a lifetime for reasons that go beyond their immediate use in achieving pleasure or emotional relief. They are *organizing fantasies,* which play an essential role in solving the central unconscious conflicts and problems that each of us carries with us from infantile life, and as such they become integral to our sense of identity. They are often adaptive, but they may be maladaptive as well—associated with neurotic symptoms or character disturbances.

Given their connection to the central issues of our psychic lives, repeating fantasies have special interest for psychoanalysts, who primarily view them as signposts to the mysterious world of the unconscious, as superego- and ego-edited derivatives of unconscious fantasies. Always the ultimate goal of analyzing them is to decipher the underlying unconscious fantasy, the key to understanding character traits and neurotic symptoms, to resolving unconscious conflict, and, ultimately, to achieving change.

But the repeating fantasies are more than pointers to something else: They have weight and meaning of their own. The psychoanalyst Harold Blum describes them as "linked to elusive but important aspects of self, identity, and character."[3] Because they are integral to our conscious sense of pleasure and agency, we cannot abandon our repeating fantasies at will. Considerable evidence indicates that many people spend much of their lives consciously attempting to enact their repeating fantasies or to live them out in slightly disguised forms—or, alternately, to protect themselves from the negative implications of realizing those fantasies. Moreover, such fantasies are often enacted in ways that the fantasizer does not perceive, because the enactment is such a heavily disguised version of the daydream's script.

Contemporary analysis is directing increasing attention to repeating fantasies not only for what they reveal about unconscious fantasy, but for what they indicate about how we see ourselves and others (in terms of persisting self- and object representations) and the relationships we are prone to form. Tracing the ways in which they are or are not enacted helps us understand ourselves and our life choices much more fully. We come to see how many of our everyday choices, quirks, and characteristics are fantasy-driven.

EROTIC FANTASIES

Erotic fantasies have received more attention than other conscious fantasies, in part because of their sheer abundance. The preeminence of sexual fantasy—in the sense that more sexual fantasies are generated than other kinds and more are repeating fantasies—is at least partly due to the enormous pleasure of the orgasm accompanying the fantasy, which serves as a powerful reinforcing agent. Sexual fantasies are particularly durable in those people for whom they are a prerequisite to sexual arousal. Within the category of sexual fantasy, "perverse" fantasies may be the most persistent, because they, more than others, are often obligatory in achieving sexual arousal and orgasm.

But sexual fantasies are also important, profuse, and persistent because they are organizing fantasies that condense and incorporate in their scripts our early identifications, childhood sexual theories and fantasies, experiences, and solutions to important childhood conflicts. The way erotic fantasies act as helpful (sometimes necessary) adjuncts to sexual pleasure is a mystery, but they constitute part and parcel of the uniqueness of each individual.

As adults we each have a specific erotic pattern—what I have elsewhere called a *sex print*[4]—that includes the specific sexual fantasies we invoke as a means to arousal in masturbation and often as an ancillary or obligatory aid to intercourse and other kinds of interpersonal sex. Our central erotic fantasy condenses in symbolic form certain key information about us.

The range of erotic fantasies is very wide. Fantasy variables comprise such factors as partner specifications (loved one or stranger, older or younger or sometimes a child, one or more partners or an orgy, intact or amputated, comely or disfigured, living or, very rarely, dead, and so forth) and place preferences (in public or in private, on the floor or in the spousal bedroom with or without the spouse). Fantasy scenarios may be homosexual, heterosexual, or bisexual. They may also depict acts that are generally described as perverse—defecating or urinating on one's partner or being the object of these activities, masturbating into a handkerchief or shoe belonging to a fantasy partner, spying on someone, or exposing oneself in public. Fantasies may feature sex in a costume or masturbation in front of a mirror. Important themes include exhibitionism (a woman fantasizing herself as a belly-dancer surrounded by a crowd of aroused men tucking dollar bills into her bra), humiliation, and degradation. In some fantasies, the self may be depicted as a torturer, humiliator, rapist, dominatrix, or benevolent master to a sexual slave.

Preferred sexual fantasies may not even appear to be sexual, entailing no more than a walk on the beach holding hands or nursing someone back to health. And on and on. While most people have conscious erotic fantasies, the nature of the preconscious sexual fantasies of others must be inferred from their choice of a sexual partner and activity or a close look at the nature of their favorite pornography.

People's attitudes about their own fantasies also vary widely. For some, sexual fantasies seem to be natural extensions of the people they experience themselves as being and feel quite comfortable. Their sexual fantasies and everyday personalities are more or less of a piece.[5]

Sometimes, however, sexual fantasies entail scenarios that appear to be completely at odds with who people are in their everyday lives. As a typical example consider the masochistic scenario of being tied hand and foot that may be the preferred or even obligatory sexual fantasy of a successful and assertive businessman. The apparent anomaly of the fantasy does not necessarily dictate that the fantasizer will be uncomfortable with it, however. Such a man may be completely at peace with his masochistic fantasies, viewing them as a welcome respite from his daily experience of always having to be in charge.

For other people, however, the discrepancies between who they are or wish to be and how they appear in their own erotic fantasies may be deeply troubling. Because of her political beliefs a feminist may disapprove of her own almost involuntary masochistic fantasies but be unable to concoct a pleasurable substitute. What from the political point of view are considered to be some of the most problematic fantasies may form her pleasure base. The problem is that even when masochism is deplored as a socially constructed box into which some women feel they have been herded, they may still feel its lure.

Because sexual fantasy often uses as its material motifs of pleasure and power that relate to early life conflicts, masochistic pleasures are the stuff of fantasy for many women and men, in about equal numbers. In a questionnaire study that some colleagues and I conducted with a college population, we found that both sexes reported the same level of masochistic fantasies ("Being sexually tortured by a partner," 10 percent of women, 11 percent of men); "Being whipped" (15 percent of women, 14 percent of men); "Being brought into a room against one's will" (20 percent of women, 16 percent of men); "Being tied up or bound during sex activities" (30 percent of women, 31 percent of men); "Being forced to submit" (31 percent of women, 27 percent of men).[6]

To understand and forgive ourselves for erotic fantasies of which we disapprove, we must remember that the self is not always—or in fact ideally—unitary, though in the more conscious regions of personality it often appears to be. A repeating sexual fantasy sometimes carries a part of the personality that has been disavowed in all other arenas. Occasionally enacting it may be pivotal in reclaiming, and subsequently rechanneling, a disavowed part of the self. The following vignette portrays a man already in analysis who began to enact his fantasies only when he encountered a sexual partner who led him down a path that he had previously traveled only in his mind.

Mr. Franklin was a happily married man who had entered treatment for work-related problems. While socially extremely adept, he had earlier in life suffered from demoralizing work inhibitions, including an inability to concentrate, and a sense of professional malaise. These symptoms had ameliorated to some degree after his marriage, which seemed in some way to steady him. But nonetheless his remaining inhibitions continued to interfere with his achieving his potential and caused him to seek analysis.

Mr. Franklin had grown up extremely sympathetic to a mother he felt had been ill used by his aggressive, argumentative, verbally threatening and abusive father, a man he disliked. Clearly his primary bond was with his mother, her values and interests, and he desperately avoided any behavior that would connect him in his own mind to his father.

He had no history of sexual problems with his wife or with those sexual partners who had preceded her, and during his sexual encounters with them he never had any conscious sexual fantasies whatsoever. However, he always maintained a secret masturbatory life, accompanied by fantasies that, though varied, centered around scenarios in which he was dominant and sadistic. These fantasies dated back to adolescence and first appeared in response to his chance exposure to sadomasochistic (S-M) pornography.

The complete separation between interpersonal sex without fantasy, on the one hand, and masturbation accompanied by S-M fantasies, on the other, continued until one of his firm's clients made known to him the fact that she prided herself on living on the sexual edge. Soon, at her instigation, they began an affair and fantasized together what they might do in subsequent encounters. When he tentatively broached the subject of bondage, she eagerly agreed and encouraged him to explore all the various facets of his dominant and sadistic fantasies systematically. She fell in love with him and entered into his fantasy world with abandon. She imagined being tied up and bought herself a nipple ring in order to become more fully his slave so as to increase his pleasure. For his part, he never loved her, but the affair led to a change in his nonsexual life, one that seemed to be associated with the acting out of qualities he had previously relegated exclusively to the realm of fantasy life.

His sadistic fantasies carried his assertiveness, which he unconsciously connected to an unacceptable identification with his despised father and erroneously equated with sadism. His ability to preserve the disavowed part of his personality within his fantasies, while frightening, did serve to stabilize his self-esteem insofar as it partially compensated for his feeling nonassertive. But it also meant that he closed the door on any kind of assertive behavior, and that course cost him dearly in his professional life.

Through analysis he came to understand the meaning of his secret masturbatory life and learned to rechannel some of the energies released in his affair into his work life. In the process he was able, in part, to rehabilitate his extremely skewed view of his father and, thereby, to integrate a split-off part of himself.

Though Mr. Franklin enacted his fantasies with his partner's sanction—indeed he seemed to need that sanction—some men with sadistic and violent fantasies are justifiably frightened that they might act out such fantasies without partner consent. (Although masochistic fantasies occur to the same extent in both sexes, sadistic and violent fantasies are more the province of men.) One man entertained violent sadistic fantasies that were obligatory—that is, he was unable to get an erection unless he invoked them. But he was too frightened to put his wife's image into his sexual fantasies for fear of losing control and hurting her, for he sensed the rage that lay behind them. The result was that just a few years into the marriage he became totally impotent with her, and the situation caused him to feel self-loathing (shame) and even self-hatred (guilt). Thus, even while he was trying to stifle the aggression he felt toward his wife (and women in general, beginning with a hatred for his mother), he was expressing it—not through violence but through sexual withholding. Though a therapist might ordinarily encourage a patient to invoke whatever fantasy he enjoys, such a situation can present a real dilemma, because sometimes an individual is correct in fearing a loss of control.[7] The problem is not generally in the nature of the fantasies themselves, but in the strength of the fantasizer's ego: Is it strong enough to confine the fantasies to the realm of imagination rather than enactment?

Where do erotic fantasies come from? Generally the erotic fantasy of our adult lives, which crystallizes into its more or less final form in late latency or adolescence,[8] is a reedition of a childhood masturbation fantasy. It expresses a condensation of our erotic dispositions as they are shaped, according to Freud, "through the combined operation of [the individual's] innate disposition and the influences brought to bear on him in his early years."[9]

What this means is that we all have one or more signature erotic fantasies, each with a particular developmental history. Each fantasy draws on specific childhood experiences, thoughts, and theories, but it is the resolution of the Oedipus complex that shapes the final form of an erotic fantasy. While there are as many different Oedipus complexes as there are people, psychoanalysts have charted "normative" pathways for boys and girls destined to become heterosexual and "normative" pathways for those destined to become homosexual. (For purposes of brevity I will outline here only the heterosexual variety.)

During the course of the Oedipal phase, the boy intensifies his feelings of mother-love and father-competition. But this situation presents him with conflicts. Although competitive with his father, he also loves him. Moreover, feeling guilty about his sometimes murderous wishes toward his father, the boy fears paternal retaliation and castration. The resolution of this conflict comes about when the boy renounces his incestual wishes, strengthens his identification with his father, and forms a plan to follow in his father's footsteps and eventually win a woman of his own. The erotic fantasy he constructs expresses not only his lingering mother-love but his future-oriented longings, and it safeguards against his fears.

In contrast, the girl longs for her father and fears her mother, dreading castration or body mutilation less perhaps than the loss of maternal nurturance. The resolution of her Oedipal complex is brought about by a father renunciation and an intensified identification with her mother. She too will construct a fantasy that expresses her longings and assuages her fears.

The degree to which the Oedipal complex is fully resolved and the nature of its resolution varies. Each erotic fantasy condenses, symbolizes, and resolves (or fails to resolve) the conflicts among the child's sexual, competitive, and aggressive wishes and impulses directed toward both parents through the different developmental stages of childhood. (These are encoded in both positive and negative Oedipal configurations.) It does so in such a way—through defenses, reversals, denials, and reaction formations—that the wishes fueling any fantasy may be disguised beyond all recognition. Because its construction is so dense, sexual fantasy is often hard to interpret and difficult to change even if we want to.

While it is possible to analyze the root causes of a fantasy, such analysis may only denude it of its pleasure rather than eliminate or replace it. But during the process of analysis, tracing the relationships among a masturbatory fantasy, early life experiences, and the structure of the Oedipal complex can be enormously helpful, as it was for Ms. Eastlake, a twenty-six-year-old lawyer. A recent transplant to New York from San Francisco, she had entered treatment for reasons having no relation to her sex life. Eventually she confided that she could only have an orgasm during intercourse if she fantasized walking through the door of a pale yellow Victorian house, a fantasy that first appeared in her early adolescence as a masturbatory fantasy.

The image of the yellow house turned out to carry a heavy freight of symbolic meaning that unfolded only gradually during the course of the analysis. The color yellow referred symbolically to her preference for Asian men as sexual partners: in essence, she was less readily aroused by men who were not Asian. Over time we traced this strong preference to the historical circumstance that from the time she was three until she was six her father had been stationed in Vietnam; on an unconscious level, she associated Asian men with her father. In treatment she discovered that her preference concealed an underlying father fixation. (On the surface, a Caucasian girl's almost exclusive preference for Asian men might look like father rejection.)

However, her preference was more complicated and drew on pre-Oedipal considerations. When Ms. Eastlake was finally able to talk about her fantasy and begin to analyze it, it was key to her tackling a much deeper and more painful problem than father fixation. She revealed that she was disturbed by the fact that while she was sexually drawn to Asian men, she was at the same time deeply ashamed of being with them, viewing her partners' smooth, relatively hairless bodies as a sign of effeminacy. Nonetheless, seeing her partner as feminine (castrated) was essential to her ability to reach a climax. It allowed her to maintain an underlying fantasy that she was the partner with the penis, her lover feminine. Hence her orgasm was tied to the moment that she, as a kind of body phallus, traversed the doorway of the yellow house, symbolically establishing her phallic prowess.

The underlying wish in the Victorian house fantasy is to posit herself as the active, penetrating participant during sex, and to deny any sense of being passive and penetrated; it is she who crosses the threshold, not a man who enters her. The fantasy image disguises her underlying repudiation of what she deems the passive feminine role while still allowing her to enjoy sex, so long as it is with Asian men. The fantasy, then, encompasses a kind of cross-gender identification—though a minimal one (that is, she never consciously wanted to be male, never consciously hated being female, as would a woman with a more pronounced cross-gender identification). The masturbatory fantasy expressed an underlying wish attached to her sense that her mother had wanted her to be a substitute husband during her father's absence, and also to a need to differentiate herself from an older and very feminine sister with whom she felt inadequate to compete. As it turned out, her shame concerning the "effeminacy" of her Asian partners arose because she projected her own sense of impaired gender adequacy onto them. She had not been either "man" or "woman" enough to please her mother. Adding to the complexities of the Victorian house symbol was the fact that her mother had grown up in such a house, which thus also symbolized her mother.

Analysis of the conscious fantasy was pivotal in her treatment, leading her to recognize her repudiation of femininity in many areas of her life, not just the sexual one, and to deal with its causes in her early life. The process ultimately freed her to interact with men from different backgrounds (not excluding her own), to accept her own sexual identity as female more completely, to connect with a man both as a sexual partner and as an equal, and to regard Asian men as *men*. However, the fantasy itself was never entirely eliminated, nor was that ever the goal. The point of analyzing a fantasy is rarely to eradicate it (except in those few instances when enactment would be devastating, for example, when pedophile fantasies are on the verge of being enacted). Rather, the goal is to use it to delineate and resolve core conflicts that continue to impede the patient's life. Sometimes the fantasy fades under the spotlight of analysis, sometimes not.

Just as in the case of Ms. Eastlake, the erotic fantasy always draws on more than Oedipal configurations. For example, in those people who were sexually or nonsexually abused, the masturbatory fantasy often incorporates elements of the traumatic events. One woman whose mother had hurled insults and objects at her throughout her childhood referred to her as crazy, but for a long time in her treatment remained unaware of the connection between her mother's abuse and her adult propensity to fantasize sadomasochistic love relations that duplicated those early abusive encounters. During analysis another woman, whose masturbatory fantasy was to be naked and tied spread-eagle to a bed in the middle of a circle of men with erections, related it to a long-suppressed memory that when she was a young adolescent her father held her down until she agreed to perform fellatio on him.[10] Sometimes the fantasy process allows the mind to deny or forget the traumatic event and rearrange the memory traces in such a way that what was painful becomes pleasant, and what was humiliating becomes a narcissistic triumph.

Sexual fantasies are umbrellas for many subsidiary fantasies. They are a magnet to pre-Oedipal sexual fantasies and to nonsexual fantasies as well; they are the primary medium in which fantasies of different origins can nestle and find nourishment (sometimes in direct expression, sometimes not). The reasons why are to be found in the nature of developmental life.

Erotic history precedes genital activity. Sexual fantasies incorporate elements of our entire erotic life, beginning with the history of our sensual pleasures (and pains) of the skin, the oral and anal mucosa, the internal organs, and the sensations of the genitals themselves; they draw on the feelings we experience in our body parts—not just the genitals, but the mouth, the anus, the arms and the legs, and on the comparisons we make of our body parts with those of others.

Because sexuality encompasses body surfaces that have nonsexual as well as sexual functions, sexual experience is symbolically interlocked with other sensual activities or aims. Consequently, these activities may become sexualized and sometimes inhibited. For example, a person may sexualize and then defend against eating, as do some anorexia nervosa patients.

The psychoanalyst Heinz Lichtenstein questions why from an evolutionary point of view pregenital sexuality (that is, nonprocreative sexuality) and the pleasure it yields should exist at all; he suggests its specific purpose may be to promote bonding between the infant and its caregivers.[11] And this bonding takes place in the context of pleasurable skin contact.[12] Inevitably, then, the physicality of our erotic history carries the emotional connotations of our early interpersonal relationships (represented in our minds as "internalized object relations"). The infant sucks its thumb not only for the inherent pleasure and comfort it offers, but as a substitute for what it is missing—generally the breast and ultimately the absent person, the mother.[13] Autoerotic activities are "comforters and means for drawing a kind of mothering from one's own body."[14] Such activities (and the fantasies that invariably accompany them) are erotic acts later incorporated into the masturbatory fantasy.[15]

In general, sex and sexual fantasy constitute a primary "arena in which relational struggles and issues are played out."[16] For example, a boy may have an unconscious fear of being castrated by his mother; this fear may symbolically represent his sense in early life of his mother's rejection of his maleness or of her hostility and intrusiveness, or sometimes it may signify a fear of retaliation for his own aggressive impulses toward her.[17] A consequence of this fear may be vagina dentata fantasies—that his partner's vagina has teeth and may bite off his penis during intercourse. A conscious fantasy, a dream image, or impotence may be the manifestation of this unconscious fantasy.

Several other factors predispose sex to be the setting, the hospitable stage, on which so many fantasies and feelings are acted out.[18]

First, sex, with its intense physical sensations, is ideally suited to symbolize some of our later interpersonal experiences.[19] Because sexuality involves contact between and mutual penetration of bodies, it presents a premier stage for the symbolic enactment of fantasies related to intense interpersonal impulses and longings—submission, soothing, merging, and a host of others. Moreover, the sense of drivenness in sexuality provides the body language to express high-voltage interpersonal dynamics—conflict, passion, rage.[20] Consider, for example, the rage a man expresses in the "sexual" fantasy of pinning a woman down with his penis, or in the rape fantasy he invokes as an antidote to feeling unmanned at work.

Second, sexuality is so often shaped by the primal scene fantasy, in which parental sex takes place behind a closed door and the child feels excluded, that sexual fantasy—in which the fantasizer takes the place of the excluding parent—can be mobilized to compensate for feelings of humiliation, inadequacy, or rejections.[21] (The legacy of the primal scene fantasy helps to explain the apparent paradox that a fantasy of an unavailable or unattainable partner sometimes has more aphrodisiacal power than an attractive sexual partner we have chosen who is lying in our own bed. In such cases, a derivation of the primal scene fantasy has become a prerequisite to excitement.)

Third, because life is divided into the private sphere, in which sexual experiences by and large take place, and the public sphere, in which overt sexual acts are generally taboo, sexual fantasy is ideally suited to express the wish to transgress social norms.

There is yet another reason sex so readily absorbs nonsexual fantasies. Because fantasy is rarely sufficient gratification itself but always presses for direct or indirect actualization of some kind, sexual fantasy, which generally leads to sexual activity, can be particularly rewarding. Orgasm validates sexual fantasy, converting it into a kind of virtual reality, even when the fantasy takes place during masturbation. (In fact, masturbation is extremely important developmentally, not only for its physical gratification but for the gratification of the many wishes expressed in the accompanying fantasy. Masturbation is also powerful because it provides an independent and autonomous source of satisfaction; we are no longer entirely dependent on another person to fulfill our needs and desires.)

Ease of enactment ensures that sex is an ideal means by which to express a variety of fantasies. Sexual activity is always possible because one can always close the door and masturbate. And if there is no partner available, one can rent a partner. The pressure to enact sexual fantasies ensures that there will always be a demand for prostitution.

Sexuality as the vehicle for expressing diverse fantasies has the further advantage of seeming adult—apparently unrelated to childish impulses. One can actualize a good many regressive fantasies by embedding them in sexual scripts, thereby passing them off, both to the self and to others, as expressions of mature interests. Sexual fantasies may be invoked to stabilize one's sense of self, assuage anxiety, or restore self-esteem. Those individuals driven by sexual desire who engage in some form of compulsive sexuality clearly demonstrate the nonsexual aims to which sexual fantasy lends itself, among them the stabilization of one's sense of gender adequacy. For example, a blow in the work arena may trigger castration anxiety; this may then be warded off through recourse to a bout of fetishism. Thus a man turns to sexual arousal to counter anxiety and reaffirm his masculinity and his body intactness, which were threatened in a nonsexual context. Consider, too, the Don Juan: he is never in search of sex alone. Narcissistic restitution almost always plays a role in his adventures, as does the symbolic defeat of all those other men with claims to his conquests.

Sexual fantasies also influence ongoing, nonsexual aspects of personality. The following vignette illustrates how the manifest content of an organizing sexual fantasy can color both the erotic life and the professional life of the fantasizer. I supervised the treatment of Mr. Daniels, a never-married man in his middle thirties who sought therapy to overcome his inability to commit himself to the woman with whom he was living. He had had a series of long-term relationships that inevitably ended in disappointment with his partner. Whenever he became distant from or angry at a girlfriend, he experienced sexual revulsion. (Or, more accurately, the sexual revulsion was usually the clue to his unacknowledged anger.) From the very beginning he had felt ambivalent toward his current girlfriend because he considered her less worldly than he, and what he considered her narrowness irritated him. Nonetheless, he found himself extremely drawn to her and dependent upon her. His complaints against her appeared somewhat exaggerated even to him, and he feared he was using them as a self-protective, distancing mechanism—as he was. His reasons for doing so remained obscure, for he was unable to get to much of his inner life in the beginning. Although he had formed a somewhat conventional good-patient relationship with his therapist and was superficially cooperative, he was unable, for example, to remember any dreams.

Nor was he readily in touch with his fantasy life. When the analyst inquired closely about his conscious fantasies, he at first denied that he had any, as he believed to be true. Only gradually could he remember, and acknowledge to himself, the following sexual fantasy, which had recurred periodically since late adolescence. Whenever he was feeling repulsed and impotent—with his current girlfriend or previous ones—he would envision his partner having intercourse with someone he admired, while he watched. Invoking the fantasy generally enabled him to perform satisfactorily (though without much passion). This fantasy, very common among men, is particularly interesting because it is manifestly paradoxical: a man is relieved, even empowered, by the fantasy of an event that he would experience as a humiliating defeat in real life.

The exploration of this fantasy led in several important directions. First, the

patient came to recognize its connection to certain otherwise inexplicable anxieties and behaviors. The fantasy that ensured potency had become a source of
insecurity concerning his lovers: he doubted that they really loved him. The
resulting suspiciousness led to distrust and distancing and—in one of the typically vicious cycles that can enmesh us—sexual withholding. This is but one
example of the way fantasies take on a life of their own and affect our feelings
about ourselves and other people.

As it happened, before entering therapy, Mr. Daniels had engineered a situation in which his fantasy was quite literally enacted. Without being aware
of doing so, of course, he set up a sexually charged, drunken evening during
which he himself passed out (though generally he drank very little), leaving
his girlfriend alone with the friend with whom he shared a beach house. In
part, he was trying to end the relationship, in part literally to act out his fantasy, in part to prove his absolute control over his lover through manipulating
her to do his will, in part to prove her unworthy and untrustworthy—a typically complex and self-contradictory assortment of motives, wishes, and needs.

For other men, the same fantasy can have other antecedents and meanings.
It can be a kind of primal scene fantasy, or a derivative of an Oedipal triangle.
For men bent on Oedipal revenge their most gratifying sexual relationships
may be those with women who have previously slept with or are currently
married to close friends. (Such men are numerous enough to have inspired the
term of derision "buddy fuckers.") The act itself is symbolically a kind of
Oedipal triumph over a competitive male figure—generally a father, step-
father, or brother.

For Mr. Daniels, however, the fantasy was an antidote to the feeling of sexual inadequacy that his father's browbeating and his mother's idealization of
his father and neglect of him had provoked. The fantasy let him simultaneously hide behind the prowess of another male and know that in reality *he* had
won the woman. The fantasy provided an Oedipal triumph, but with a twist:
Such a fantasy, or its enactment, is often a variation on the Oedipal scene; it is
related to what Lionel Ovesey has called a *pseudohomosexual fantasy,* in which
a man secures his masculinity from another male, sometimes through anal or
oral submission to him (for example, performing fellatio on another man to
steal his strength).[22] It is considered pseudohomosexual rather than homosexual because although the imagery may appear homosexual, the purpose of the
fantasy is not primarily homosexual: rather it incorporates the other man's
phallic strength for use in a heterosexual relationship. In his fantasy, too, Mr.
Daniels is borrowing the other man's manliness, though not through sexual
congress; instead the other man is performing his sexual "work" for him.

Unfortunately Mr. Daniels's fantasy device, though initially facilitating,
ultimately undermined him in his own eyes, making him question the authenticity of his girlfriends' feelings toward him and leading him to doubt his own
sexual competence. What began by being adaptive—at least in the short run

insofar as it increased his potency—turned out to have a negative after-jolt, as his jealousy and sense of rejection reemerged and the fear of impotence resurfaced, particularly after he literally set up his lover with his friend, essentially terminating his affair.

Mr. Daniels's sense that he relied on another man's strength was an important dynamic in nonsexual areas of his life. Working in the administration of a large business, he was unable to do anything out of the routine, even write an ordinary business letter, without first running it by a man whom he both greatly admired and resented. His lack of self-reliance interfered with his advancement, despite his above-average ability. Here, too, his symbolic use of another man's strength simultaneously empowered and undermined him.

Mr. Daniels's story illustrates the way fantasies sometimes not only *reflect* life issues but *create* them. Having fantasized that his girlfriend had sex with another man, Mr. Daniels began to have doubts about her and then made sure those doubts were realized. Exploring the incident in therapy illuminated the underlying fantasy and tracked its behavioral derivatives in his professional and sexual life.

In some people, erotic fantasies are sublimated (unconsciously modified) so as to reappear in manifestly nonsexual forms. Once sublimated, the revised fantasy material continues to have an impact on a life trajectory, as revealed in the fantasizer's aspirations and vocation or character.

A major contribution to our understanding of the phenomenon of the sublimation of a masturbatory fantasy—and to our view of it as potentially benign and transformative in its effects—comes down to us through Anna Freud.[23] Interestingly enough, it appears that the case material she used was based on her own analysis. At least this is the conclusion of her biographer, Elisabeth Young-Bruehl, who points out that the paper in which Anna Freud describes how a sexual fantasy came to be sublimated was written as a prerequisite to her acceptance to the Berlin Psychoanalytic Society.[24] But her paper was completed six months before she first saw a patient! Young-Bruehl notes that in the written version of her lecture, Anna Freud indicated that the patient had had a rather thorough analysis, but she did not say with whom.[25] (The analyst, of course, was none other than her father, Sigmund Freud.)

Anna Freud's essay had three parts that showed sequential developments in the history of a beating fantasy. The girl's conscious fantasy of a man beating a boy was accompanied by masturbation, and the climax of the beating coincided with orgasm. The process of analysis indicated that the fantasy symbolically represented a love fantasy of a girl for her father that was twice disguised, with substitution of the girl-fantasizer as boy and "by repression and regression to the anal-sadistic phase."[26] Beginning between the ages of five and six, these masturbatory beating fantasies continued until they were replaced by what Anna Freud called "nice stories," which appeared between the ages of eight and ten.

During her analysis, the patient (Anna Freud) recognized that the nice stories and the beating fantasies in fact shared similar plot lines. In the nice stories a young man breaks some rule and a stronger, older man confronts him about his transgression. First threatened, he is finally forgiven and reconciled with the older man. According to Anna Freud,

> In the beating fantasy, too, the protagonists are strong and weak persons who in the clearest delineation oppose each other as adults and children. There, too, it is regularly a matter of a misdeed, even though the latter is left as indefinite as the acting figures. There, too, we find a period of mounting fear and tension. The decisive difference between the two rests in their solution, which in the fantasy is brought about by beating, and in the daydream by forgiveness and reconciliation.[27]

When the beating fantasy metamorphosized into "nice stories" their association with sexual excitement and masturbation ended. The underlying masochism lost its connection to sexual gratification and was transformed into an affectionate bond.

The beating fantasy gratifies the sexual drives, whereas the nice stories gratify what Anna Freud called the aim-inhibited drives—a very effective sublimation, under the aegis of what we would now call ego and superego modifications. Thus the sexual impulse is transformed into an affectionate, somewhat masochistic tie. But that was not the end of the evolution of the fantasy.

In the final stage of the fantasy's metamorphosis, the "patient" left behind even her nice-story fantasies and began to write short stories instead, still utilizing the same kind of plot. She could now share the previously forbidden fantasy in its disguised form (the short story) with an audience, giving herself a totally new kind of pleasure.

This sequential transformation of the beating fantasy allowed internal approval instead of guilt; additionally it provided social and professional recognition. Thus, narcissistic gratification replaced sexual gratification. Young-Bruehl points out, "Anna Freud's paper is both a study of sublimation and an act of sublimation," since in fact the paper was the "disguised form," now being employed by the patient/writer/analyst.[28]

Ultimately Anna Freud used her self-understanding to develop the very important concept of altruistic surrender as a possible end point of unconscious sadomasochistic longings such as her own. She herself practiced altruistic surrender throughout her life, never marrying, devoting herself to her father, to the psychoanalytic movement, and to a profound interest in the psychology and welfare of children.[29]

Knowing from her own experience how fantasies were invoked to solve psychological problems, Anna Freud went on to apply her insight to other patients. It is surely not accidental that she contrasted two of her child patients with Little Hans, one of Freud's famous cases. Freud had interpreted the source of five-year-old Hans's horse phobia as a displacement of his fear of his (rivalrous) father onto a horse. But Anna Freud found other, happier fantasy resolutions of the Oedipal struggle in two of her little patients.[30] One of her patients, a seven-year-old, had also perceived his father as a rival and consequently hated and feared him. But instead of an animal phobia he produced an animal fantasy that seemed to solve the problem for him; he invented a tame lion—a stand-in for his father—who loved only him and who frightened everyone else (a reversal in fantasy, a denial of reality).

Still another boy, ten years old, in his fantasy was master of a circus of animals trained to be good and not to attack people. These animals symbolized his father. By taming them, he had incorporated their strength into himself, so that they were rendered harmless to him and in fact protected him.

Anna Freud postulated that both boys' fantasies were successful in denying the reality of their weakness vis-à-vis their fathers, allowing them to avoid undue fear and castration anxiety, and thus to finesse the production of any neurosis. She noted, too, the widespread theme of protective or helpful "wild" animals in fairy tales and myths, which was echoed in novels for young adults in which a small child tames a threatening or crotchety, powerful, and rich old man (for example, in *Little Lord Fauntleroy* and *The Little Colonel*). Perhaps because she could see in herself the beneficial effects of fantasy, Freud was able to use her insights to theorize fantasy as part of normal, not just pathological, development, and to understand its positive uses in psychic life.

SELF-SOOTHING FANTASIES

The developmental capacity to soothe oneself in the absence of a caregiver is a major achievement of infantile life, and it occurs through the invocation of an image. In essence the young child becomes capable of invoking a mental representation of its mother. One of the most dramatic such occurrences caught the public eye when it was written up as a human interest story in a variety of newspapers in 1987.[31] Jessica McClure, an eighteen-month-old girl, fell into a well, where she was trapped for fifty-eight hours. First crying and sobbing for her mother, she then began to sing to herself songs that her mother had sung to her, in essence doing for herself what her mother was not present to do in this extremely traumatic situation. People often develop fantasies that perform this kind of immediate, self-consoling function. Many self-soothing fantasies, however, serve much more complicated needs and longings, as the following case illustrates.

Mrs. Farber entertained what she considered to be a somewhat primitive daydream with which she regularly soothed herself to sleep but which she was able to reveal to me only late in her treatment.[32] As described briefly in chapter 1, this fantasy depicted miniature humanlike creatures, which the patient imagined lived in her gastrointestinal tract and whom she fed imaginary meals made up of the foods she had eaten in the previous three days. Though she invoked it almost every night, when she thought of her fantasy during the day, she regarded it as primitive and gross, and was for a long time too ashamed to bring it into treatment.

The patient, an academic, married and in her early thirties, modestly successful but somewhat inhibited in her professional activities, had entered treatment primarily for interpersonal problems. Her angry encounters with friends and colleagues were threatening the stability of her social and professional life. In the course of treatment, she revealed a long-standing fear of plagiarism, her obsessive preoccupation triggered by her discovery that she had inadvertently plagiarized a phrase from a paper on a subject similar to the one she was working on. Subsequently, each time one of her articles appeared, she obsessed over the fear that she might again have unknowingly stolen an idea or phrase from someone else. She was also very proprietary about her own work, frequently suspicious that she was herself being plagiarized by others. The fear of unconscious plagiarism, which she at first reported only as an incidental and minor preoccupation, turned out to be linked to a whole series of conscious fantasy fragments, and ultimately to a central unconscious fantasy.

Far into the treatment, but before she revealed the intestinal fantasy, she told me that she sometimes soothed herself to sleep with another fantasy, in which she planned imaginary wardrobes for herself, composed of items belonging to women she knew and admired; she allowed herself to "confiscate" ten items of clothing or jewelry from each woman. (Why only ten items? Setting some finite limit, even in a "fantastic" fantasy, seems to bring the requisite amount of reality that leads to a momentary suspension of disbelief and permits the consoling function of the fantasy to take place. Similarly, all the superheroes of the comics have some limitation; they are never all-powerful.) Later in the treatment she hesitantly revealed the fantasy of the miniature people.

What was particularly interesting about the intestinal creatures was her caretaking attitude toward them, the feeling that she must look after them; for example, she obsessed about her food intake to make sure she was providing enough variety in their diet. This attitude totally disguised her hostility, which at first could only be inferred because in the fantasy she reigned over those little people and had implicitly swallowed them whole. Though on the surface she had been invaded, she was ultimately the one in control, via her total command over her invaders' sustenance. She rationalized and denied her hostility through a pseudocaretaking fantasy. Her emphasis on feeding the little creatures, not cannibalizing them, was a reversal in fantasy, proof that she was good and not a killer.

Though the imaginary intestinal creatures were in part unintegrated little "selves," in part derivatives of pregnancy fantasies (with unconscious fears of being devoured by a fetus, a projection of herself as the greedy starving embryo), essentially the fantasy magically attempted to resolve her core conflict—the longing to perpetuate a symbiotic relationship with her powerful mother versus the wish to destroy (or incorporate) her mother's power. Her ambivalence was related to her simultaneous need for and fear of the envied and intrusive mother of her earliest childhood. By way of resolution she created a fantasy of a symbiotic relationship with herself in charge.

Mrs. Farber's earliest life had been lived in tandem with a mother who regarded her as special, but who was intrusive and insensitive to her child's needs. Her mother's entire focus was on grooming Mrs. Farber to grow up to be the successful woman she believed she herself, given the opportunity, would have become. In part, Mrs. Farber's impulse to plagiarism (whether the theft of ideas or of clothes) represented an identification with her mother, who had superego lacunae of her own, including a tendency to tell white lies and commit other small acts of dishonesty. But more central to the genesis of her core pathology was her sense of having been robbed of her autonomy by fealty to her mother's dreams for her. Gratified only through her submission to her mother and her tacit agreement to live her life to gratify her mother vicariously, she took her revenge through reversal in the fantasy—one fantasy that entitled her to the property of others and another fantasy in which she controlled an army of miniature people. But her unconscious incorporative and cannibalistic impulses perpetuated her sense of needy dependency, locked her into an envious stance, and prevented her from enjoying the authentically creative impulses in her life and work.

In the course of treatment, Mrs. Farber began to recognize her fantasies of theft (of clothes or ideas) as emblems of her envy and oral aggression and the source of her suspiciousness of others (the fear that others would do to her what she wished to do to them). Through our analysis of her two fantasies her cannibalistic impulses and fear of being devoured in retaliation emerged into consciousness, finding expression in dreams and transferential fears (fears that I would harm her in retaliation for her cannibalistic impulses aimed at me). Probably her most difficult moment was retelling a dream/nightmare which had awakened her with imagery so intense that she felt she almost hallucinated the following image: She was shipwrecked on a deserted island, where she was able to survive only by eating the arm of a drowned companion. This cannibalistic image was in her mind's eye when she awoke in a cold sweat. And she was able to relate the dream to the fantasy of the little people.

Traces of her envy and oral greed and the fear of retaliation they engendered were obvious in her social relationships. Although she admired other women, her admiration was often mixed with envy, hostility, and fear of rejection or condemnation. The patient was extremely competitive with her peers, particularly females, to the detriment of her relationships with them. She also coveted married men and suspected other women of having designs on her own husband. Though she was in touch with her conscious fears of rejection, she remained out of touch, until late in the treatment, with those hostile, destructive fantasies that colored all her relationships.

Through the analysis of her conscious fantasies and the reconstruction of her unconscious fantasies, Mrs. Farber was able to modify her envious and destructive impulses. She stabilized her relationship with her husband, with whom she had had a troubled relationship. Supportive in many ways, although somewhat closed off, he had tried to give her the sense of security she seemed to need, but her fears of being swallowed up in close relationships had made her react with anger. Once she could accept more from him without feeling so impinged upon, much of that anger disappeared. The diminution in her preoccupation with what belonged to whom led to more creativity in her work. And although the fact of her being slightly overweight had never been discussed, the tempering of her oral rage and greed resulted in her losing fifteen pounds with no apparent effort—much to her pleasure.

A self-soothing fantasy often reverses a deeply troubling one. At a recent panel on fantasies, Peter Neubauer presented the case of a middle-aged man who had had a very unhappy childhood, characterized by economic and social deprivation, a family history of neuroses, and an undiagnosed learning disorder.[33] Now highly successful, married, and the father of five children, he had entered treatment mainly for two reasons: his concern about his excessive involvement in extramarital affairs and his fear of professional failure.

From latency on, the patient had enjoyed the fantasy of being a leader on a white horse surrounded by cheering masses. As a variation of this fantasy, he sometimes envisioned leading his people in a successful battle against an enemy and establishing a peaceful society. Neubauer understood the fantasy as a defense against the patient's inner reality, covering up feelings of weakness and inadequacy, and his resulting rage. While in the daydream he is celebrated for imposing order and defeating the enemy, absent from the manifest content of the fantasy is the actual aggression toward the enemy. That takes place off camera, so to speak, and what remains is only the celebration of the peace that has followed.

The fantasy was a leitmotif in the patient's psyche, needed to reinforce his inhibition against his own aggression and to reverse his self-image from victim to charismatic leader. Beginning in his student days, when he had been punished and ridiculed for his poor performance in school, the daydream had assuaged his shameful feelings of powerlessness, comforting him and providing narcissistic gratification.

The daydream had also had an organizing effect on the way the patient lived his life, propelling him to position himself as a leader whose goals were high and noble. The need to rescue others, mobilized to cover over his fundamental fear of being a victim, had given his leadership a nonaggressive, benevolent quality, which won him widespread respect. In his life he had sought—and found—the greatness implicit in the daydream. Thus this daydream looked in two directions: While providing balm to the inner world, it was also a star for the patient to steer by in the external "real" world. But there were some negative effects, too; as a leader alone on a white horse, a rescuer of others, he could never regard anyone else as an equal. Thus it limited the intimacy and openness of his relationships.

GLOBAL FANTASIES

The psychoanalysts Morton Shane and Estelle Shane describe a self-fantasy they call a *global fantasy*. Global fantasies, in contrast to other kinds of fantasies, "involve the total self in relationship to its object milieu." They "define, and perhaps even determine, the life course of a given patient."[34] The final edition of the fantasy integrates a variety of drives and wishes, defenses against them, prohibitions of conscience, and reality considerations into one overarching whole.

One of my patients, Mr. Jacques, a successful married man, was a secret fetishistic masochist who frequented prostitutes in order to dress in rubber and be bound in chains. But his masochistic fantasies went beyond the masturbatory to the global. Although the enactments of his sexual fantasies produced great sexual pleasure, when the underlying masochism was acted out in nonsexual ways, as it often was, it caused him great personal turmoil. The most dramatic instance of his self-destructive propensity was his decision to cover up a major business mistake for a colleague; believed to be the errant employee, he took the blame and lost his job for a "crime" of which he was innocent. Gradually, I came to notice that Mr. Jacques kept using phrases like "being confined," "tied up in knots," and "locked up with the key thrown away" to describe everyday incidents in his life. I became acutely aware of his choice of phrases, understanding perhaps for the first time the pervasiveness of his fantasy preoccupation. Not just his sex life but every aspect of his experience was filtered through a masochistic lens.

All of us, like Mr. Jacques, tend to express our most important thematic fantasies in symbols or metaphors. Because these metaphorical expressions are potentially so revealing, their interpretation is often at the heart of an analysis, with much effort devoted to tracing their links to conscious and unconscious fantasies.[35] These same linguistic cues are probably the most frequent source of people's intuitions about each other outside the consulting room as well. However, we are each more alert to those cues that resonate with fantasies of our own, because we are primed to hear echoes of fantasies that have personal meanings or reverberations and tend to tune others out. Not only are we more alert; it is probably fair to say that we actively scan our environment for fantasy traces that are relevant to us (in the same way we are primed to hear our own names spoken, even if across a room). This is one mechanism by which we can unconsciously pick friends and lovers who have the same—or reciprocal—fantasy preoccupations.

Closely related to the global fantasy is the *personal myth,* first delineated by Ernst Kris in his work with a group of patients who regarded their personal histories as "a treasured possession." Kris attributed the unusual strength of this attachment to "the fact that the autobiographical self image has become heir to important early fantasies, which it preserves."[36] For such patients, Kris explained, the highly developed myth was a kind of "secret core," the hidden abode of many repressed fantasies, a pattern of life as well as a defense.[37] This characterization explains why these patients, though devoted to their respective myths, were also highly resistant to exploring them.[38] Because he believed that many aspects of their lives could best be interpreted through an examination of these autobiographical stories, Kris made a careful study of them.

One of Kris's patients, a woman who was a painter of some distinction, described her origins as undistinguished and totally lacking in refinement, and she blamed her current sense that her life was unsatisfactory and second rate on those unhappy beginnings. She reported a feeling of "sloppiness and contamination" that had existed in her childhood home, and Kris initially felt that these reports were supported by her sloppy appearance, although she clearly paid careful attention to cleanliness. But Kris also sensed that her life story was so contrived that something was missing from the history.

Analysis eventually recovered a more accurate history, which was at dramatic variance with her story; not only had her childhood home been distinguished, it had been the very center of an extended social life in the community.

What had so distorted her version of her family history? Frustrated by the apparent indifference of her mother (whom she very early in life suspected of having an extramarital affair), she turned to her father, only to feel rejected by him as well, whereupon she turned inward and created her own fantasy life. She invoked a family romance in which she was the child of the cook, whom she had sought out after being rebuffed by both parents. But the cook left the family. As it turned out, the cook had a last name that sounded like the word *slob.*

Kris believes that the patient had projected an identification with the cook into her life story and enacted it in life. In Kris's view, "The patient has eliminated from her awareness the longing for her mother but lived in her fantasy in union with the early substitute, the debased mother of her phallic conflicts."[39]

The personal myth is defensive inasmuch as it prevents certain experiences and groups of impulses from reaching consciousness.[40] It generally derives part of its power from a repressed, unconscious fantasy, which it replaces. Unlike other kinds of fantasy, however, the personal myth is not experienced as fantasy but is believed to be true. Thus, the painter truly believed her home had been "slobby."[41] (Like cultural myths, personal myths, are wrapped around a central fantasy, which is experienced as factual.)[42]

OTHER REPEATING FANTASIES

Prominent among other kinds of repeating fantasies is the suicide fantasy, what Robert J. Lifton has called a *suicide construct.* It is an internalized image or idea of oneself as a potential suicide.[43] While a suicide fantasy is often a one-time visitor triggered in response to a current crisis, it may also be a recurrence of a repeating fantasy that may recede or come to the fore depending on the individual's life situation. (One might question whether someone who has a genetic or physiological propensity to depression is experiencing a repeating fantasy. My answer would be yes, that the fantasy ought then to be understood as arising to contain, explain, or rationalize the depressive feelings.)

Some repeating suicide fantasies may be suppressed only to survive underground for many years and subsequently reappear, under circumstances that revive some unresolved issues. Such was the case with a patient described very early on in the psychoanalytic literature, the follow-up of which was just reported by the psychoanalyst Harold Blum.[44] A young girl had fantasized her own death, saying she wished she had never come into the world at all. Wishing that she could die, she sometimes actually pretended to die so that she could be reborn as an animal or a doll. "But if I do come back into the world as a doll, I know who I mean to belong to—a little girl that my nurse was with before, who is especially nice and good."[45] Looking at this case from a modern perspective, Blum has commented that she appears to have had a depressive illness that was overlooked and that stoked her suicidal fantasy. The patient's sad daydream proved to be predictive of her self-destructive tendencies and over forty years later, with the advent of renewed external conflicts, the woman killed herself.

Sometimes an ongoing depression and suicidal impulse can be sequestered out of awareness for many years, as they were for the writer William Styron. At a conference, Styron recounted how he had discovered, to his great surprise, that a serious bout of depression he had suffered turned out to have been anticipated and described many years beforehand in his various novels.[46] The depression and suicidal thoughts he attributed to his characters in *Lie Down in Darkness* and *Sophie's Choice* were like premonitions of what he himself would later suffer—and almost certainly expressions of his own innermost, but at that time unconscious, feelings and thoughts. This is an instance of the way artists in their work have access to ongoing fantasy material in the unconscious that they have yet to experience in life. If such a fantasy could be called a "repeating fantasy," it would be so only in the special sense of its having made repeat appearances in *other* people's minds: those of the author's characters. Obviously it had to have surfaced in the mind of the creator to allow him to describe it, but he was not yet ready to own it himself.

Our repeating fantasies are familiar friends (sometimes enemies) that have enormous impact on how we act and how we think about ourselves, and all of us have them. They are the disguised derivatives of unconscious fantasies, and they may be either normal, helpful resolutions of childhood conflicts or mal-adaptive, neurotic responses to those deep-seated conflicts.

Persisting from childhood into adulthood, repeating fantasies exert an impact on all aspects of mental life and everyday behavior, sometimes forming the basis of a character adaptation, as in the altruistic surrender described by Anna Freud. Because repeating fantasies invariably press for some form of actualization—direct or subliminated—they are always present in the direction our lives take.

When I first began to think about repeating fantasies and how to distinguish them from generative fantasies I made the overly simplistic assumption that repeating fantasies would have great relevance to the individual but less to the culture at large. In fact, the repeating fantasy, when shared and diffused through the culture as it sometimes is, can have important implications. Consider, for example, the widening or narrowing of the range of what is considered sexually acceptable. Works like the *Story of O* and the writings of the Marquis de Sade have become part of a cultural debate on the prevalence, meaning, and legitimacy of sadomasochistic fantasies and practices. But these works could never have achieved their popularity if they did not speak to deep-seated fantasies shared by large numbers of people. Probably their popularity helped legitimize such fantasies, which in turn helped to make them even more available to consciousness and therefore more widespread. In fact, because erotic fantasies are hard to suppress, they can eventually become a rallying point for a political or cultural movement. Hence, the protracted effort by one group of feminists—some of them lesbians—to legitimate sadomasochistic practices.

But perhaps the repeating fantasies that have most relevance to important cultural issues involve hatred, revenge, and rage.[47] Depending on the degree to which the culture sanctions them, the shape it allows them to take, and the scapegoats it designates, these are fantasies that often are organized into a cultural matrix and may have major consequences in political history. I will return to this topic in chapters 8 and 9, in a discussion of the social impact of fantasy shared by large groups of people.

5

GENERATIVE FANTASIES: REHEARSALS FOR LIFE

GENERATIVE FANTASIES, BY THEIR NATURE, VARY AND EVOLVE OVER TIME: Each new edition is a response to the fantasizer's age and life cycle preoccupations, current situation and realistic expectations, and to the values of the particular cultural milieu. Unlike repeating (durable, organizing) fantasies, which maintain current equilibrium by redressing the conflicts and traumas of the past, what I call *generative fantasies* or reveries focus on the future. Although, like repeating fantasies, generative fantasies draw on unconscious fantasy, they are one more step removed from it and therefore appear to be more rational and comprehensible. Often they relate in practical ways to current concerns and future desires. And while they have considerable durability, sometimes lasting many years in one edition or another, they are not lifelong.

Barring fixation on a specific unconscious fantasy, it is the very essence of fantasy to evolve, to search for alternate routes to realization. In Freud's aphorism, "Actually, we can never give anything up; we only exchange one thing for another."[1] The process of sequentially developing a fantasy to bring it into line with the dictates of reality is a major adaptive strategy of childhood. For example, when children realize that they cannot gratify their incestual longings toward a parent, they relinquish their Oedipally tinged wishes and daydreams, which later reappear in the more acceptable form of a series of crushes, or love affairs focusing on people who are, in different degrees, stand-ins for the desired parent.

One woman remembered, in the course of her analysis, the exact moment when, as a child passionately devoted to her somewhat seductive father, she first transferred her father longings onto someone else. She was in a tennis clinic, seven or eight years old, and her twentyish male instructor repositioned her serving stance, standing behind her and putting his left arm around her, extending her serving arm into the air with his own. She didn't experience his action as explicitly sexual, but she said the contact sparked an awareness of her, of him, and of some unnamed possibility. This presaged her utterly inexplicable adult crush on her exercise instructor—again triggered by an instructor's repositioning her body. Seemingly a body memory of contact revived an old emotional longing.

Such displacement from a parent to a surrogate is the usual course of events, and periodic regressions, like the one with the exercise instructor (in this case a stand-in for the tennis instructor), are also common. When there is no displacement—when the original Oedipal attachment is maintained—then we are in the realm of fixation. This generally only occurs if there is some parental complicity, some suggestion that Oedipal gratification is in fact possible, and the child is able to sense it. But in the normal developmental sequence, Oedipal longings metamorphose into other kinds of fantasies.

Similarly, a young boy relinquishes or significantly modifies a wish to give birth to a baby as he begins to perceive the limitations dictated by reality. However, remnants of this fantasy may appear in his adult dream life, often as a symbol of creativity.[2] The fantasy is extinguished (or suppressed) not only by the impossibility of enacting it but by severe superego or cultural prohibitions against its content. Thus, certain almost universal fantasies disappear or are transformed as the growing child discovers that those fantasies are dissonant with the cultural prescriptions for his or her gender. Conversely, other fantasies may be perpetuated and sometimes enacted insofar as others in the culture have already realized and affirmed a similar fantasy or its derivatives.

A generative fantasy, then, is not simply a substitute gratification. It provides a holding pattern for the short term, and its soothing quality may be an end unto itself, but it also holds out the promise of future fulfillment based on a modified form of the original fantasy.

Even if a fantasy is not destined to be enacted, it gains emotional power from the possibility that it *could* be enacted, which allows it to offer inspiration of a kind a purely fantastic daydream cannot. Consider, for example, the writer of novels who daydreams of winning the Nobel Prize in literature, until he abandons writing novels in favor of writing screenplays, at which time he shifts his daydreams to winning an Oscar. The desired narcissistic gratification and the wish for recognition remain, but the content shifts to move the daydream into the realm of possibility, however remote that possibility might seem to an observer.

Every one of us embraces a number of evolving, generative fantasies. All reverie-type fantasies are strung on a wish thread, and we ceaselessly shuttle back and forth along the length of that thread, which reaches back into our earliest life and propels us forward into the future, transforming longings born in childhood into possibilities for the here-and-now or the future. (In cases of fixation and of repeating fantasies, our daydreams are not so mobile but leave us stranded with more or less permanent compromises.) I have chosen several kinds of generative fantasies that are central to plotting a life to describe in depth. While I will focus on generative fantasies, each category contains a mix of generative, repeating, and fleeting fantasies.

THE FAMILY ROMANCE

The group of fantasies known as *family romances,* which originates in childhood, has a lifelong impact on our future relationships. Freud was the first to describe the family romance,[3] in which a child who is disillusioned with its own parents imagines or daydreams of a different mother and father, who are his or her "real" parents.

Children daydream, for example, that they have been adopted or abducted from these "real" parents, people who are infinitely superior to the everyday false parents with whom they unhappily find themselves. They believe that their real parents would love them fully and perfectly and in a way that would satisfy all their desires. Though the fantasized real parents are usually noble, rich, or famous, they may be more ordinary. The child may prefer to imagine lower-class parents, who presumably would more readily endorse sexuality, or make fewer demands for high achievement, or provide warmth that is otherwise lacking.[4]

Generally considered to be a universal fantasy, at least in modern Western culture, the family romance manifests itself in different plots at different stages of development, in response to specific problems and conflicts. The psychological impetus of the family romance lies in the inevitable frustrations of early life—children's sense of being slighted by their parents' preference (real or imagined) for a sibling or each other, their resentment of their parents' failure to gratify all their wishes, their increasing awareness of imperfections in the family itself, and so forth. Withdrawing idealization from these unsatisfactory parents and transferring it to the longed-for perfect parents of their imagination, children create for themselves a set of "real" parents who will love them unconditionally.

The fundamental function of the family romance is to restore a lost Eden (whether real or imagined) of unconditional love; this is the latent wish-thread on which the family romance is strung.[5] "Indeed, the whole effort at replacing the real father by a superior one is only an expression of the child's longing for the happy, vanished days when his father seemed to him the noblest and strongest of men and his mother the dearest and loveliest of women."[6]

Very young children's intense involvement with the family romance theme is readily apparent in their preferences for particular stories, for example, in their fascination with fairy tales in which unhappy, threatened children thrive under the protection of a powerful parent surrogate or fairy godmother. These fairy tales are useful adaptations in the present: By splitting the image of the mother, children can preserve an image of the good mother and direct their anger to the wicked stepmother—in a much safer, guilt-free form of anger. The fantasies also have implications for the future development of an individual identity. As Bettelheim says, "If the good mother did not for a time turn into an evil stepmother, there would be no impetus to develop a separate self, to discover the difference between good and evil, develop initiative and self-determination."[7]

Later on in childhood, Oedipal disappointments and narcissistic injuries are the main catalysts for the family romance. Stories involving alternate parents or parent substitutes may now serve an additional function—that of assuaging guilt feelings over sexual longings for a parent or a sibling. In a letter of 1898 written to Wilhelm Fliess, Freud pointed out, "If your sister is not your mother's child, you are relieved of guilt; the same applies if you yourself are the child of other parents."[8] In essence, if you are no relation to the object of sexual desire, then a sexual union is acceptable. Thus, in an almost paradoxical dynamic, incestuous longings start children on the imaginative journey away from the family, onto a path of their own.

These new Oedipally tinged versions of the family romance are embedded in some fairy tales, which we might view as crossovers between family-romance fantasies and full-fledged romance fantasies. Consider, for example, Cinderella and Snow White. Cinderella is the much abused stepchild in a family consisting of her wicked stepmother and her daughters, who torment her out of jealousy and spite. The prince, who recognizes her true merit, rescues her and makes her a princess. The "Snow White" story also centers on an evil stepmother, who is so jealous of Snow White that she orders her murder. Abandoned by her father in the forest, she is saved first by the Seven Dwarfs, then, like Cinderella, by a prince. Both Cinderella and Snow White live with a cruel stepmother; both are raised to an elevated status not by finding their real parents, but by being rescued by princes who recognize their intrinsic superiority and make them princesses. The male version of this story stars a young disinherited hero, but his role is proactive—that is, he vindicates his right to inherit the kingdom, often a kingdom that has fallen into disarray because of the death of the king, through a heroic feat. The theme is the same, however: a child deprived of what should (by right of inheritance or intrinsic merit) be his or hers ultimately regains it. Like the earlier pre-Oedipal family romances, these, too, have forward momentum as well as an idealized past, and that momentum may provide a tentative life plan ("I will look for my prince") and a kind of hopefulness.

The family romance longings many fairy tales express come out in yet another form in myth, an indication of their depth, intensity, and persistence. Many heroes of legends—Oedipus, Hercules, Moses—are also the protagonists of archetypal family romance dramas, having been adopted or given up by their true parents to prevent some catastrophe, their noble or royal birth thus obscured. So, too, are many comic book characters, among them Superman, Captain Marvel, and Batman.

The typical family romance fantasy acts as a balm to any current sense of narcissistic injury, and it also provides an imaginative step into the future, allowing the child to continue the work of psychically separating from the parents. This step is painful for both parents and children, but essential to establishing autonomy and achieving gratifying interactions with people outside the family. The family romance is also one of the child's first attempts to create an alternate world, within the context of the imagination. Originally a response to hurts and a way to restore self-esteem, the family romance allows the child to work out relationships in the family and points the way to future relationships and adaptations.

The story *The Secret Garden* depicts a girl's own role in working out her salvation and reconfiguring a family. Mary, the novel's protagonist, is an English girl living in India, a somewhat sour, disillusioned, and bitter child having been subjected to neglect by her socializing mother and career officer father. Her closest tie is to her devoted Ayah. When her parents and her Ayah die in a cholera epidemic, Mary is shipped back to England to live with her widowed uncle Archibald and his son, Colin. It is an icy environment, with her remote uncle still grieving over the premature death of his wife, her Aunt Lily, and distanced from his crippled and bedridden son. Through the ministrations of the nursemaid, Martha, and her brother, Dickon, a kind of nature boy, Mary begins to form a bond to them, and she discovers and revives her Aunt Lily's abandoned garden. Ultimately she is able to help her cousin Colin to heal and to create a loving and close-knit family with Archibald and Colin. Mary's is a tale of psychological rebirth and newly found emotional strength.

While the family romance fantasy may be gratifying in momentarily restoring or creating Eden, its long-term effects are felt in its links to the choices we make. Like Mary, we may be empowered to create for ourselves that for which we long.

However, the failure to generate a viable family romance fantasy may lead to the construction of the opposite kind of fantasy, the dysphoric or painful fantasy of abject dependence on one's parents or family for the duration of one's life. The "Remittance Man" is an adult child on the dole, sometimes a younger son who receives monthly checks to stay away. One man I know entertains an intermittent Remittance Man fantasy: In his fantasy, unable to live up to his family's expectations and feeling disgraced, he withdraws to a life in some remote part of the globe, living perhaps on a tropical island, where he is given to dissipation and anxiously awaits his monthly check from home. This fantasy serves multiple purposes: It wrests dependent gratification, though of a purely material kind, from a family perceived as emotionally unyielding. At the same time, being a Remittance Man preserves a fantasy bond with disparaging and disparaged parents. The fantasy also wallows in masochistic pleasures and is at the same time a fantasy of revenge against parents regarded as insufficient and unsympathetic. Like all fantasies, this one can provide a substitute pleasure or become the basis for a life choice. The man I know, who entertains periodic Remittance Man fantasies, became successful despite his best intentions. He enacts the Remittance Man fantasy vicariously by putting an assortment of unsuccessful friends on the dole. But while professionally successful, he has thus far been unable to create a happy family life for himself; in some way the idea of the happy family is still outside the range of imaginative possibilities.

The nature of the family romance fantasy, its primary purpose, and its potential for actualization differ at different stages. William, an only child, remembers a fantasy from age three or four that just falls short of being a full-fledged family romance:

> I was a very active, feisty, little kid, and I was always too much for my mother to handle. When I got into too much trouble, she would tell me that I was bad and that she would send me to the orphanage. Gradually I developed the following fantasy: My mother has sent me to the orphanage, and as I approach it, I see that it is filled with all kinds of kids, and I feel a lot of fear. But when I get closer, I see that it is very sunny, sort of like my grandmother's house. There are trees in the backyard, and when I go into the living room, there are a lot of kids at a long table, and they're eating bananas and sweet cream, which was one of the treats of my childhood. I don't feel so bad about being sent away from home.

In essence William solved the problem of his mother's threats by disarming them: If she sent him away, he would not suffer. However, this resolution reflected his growing estrangement from his mother. As a slightly older child, he began to feel ashamed of her and to withdraw from both his parents. He adopted his best friend's parents as surrogates, spending more time with them than in his own home. As an adult he often recounts with pride how he "divorced" his parents at an early age. (Like many adults who have rejected their parents, he is extremely attached to his wife and children.)

In latency, many children actualize their family romances and find substitutes for disappointing or absent parents. An extraordinary number of young people with traumatic backgrounds rescue themselves by partially realizing a family romance fantasy, when they induce someone—a teacher, employer, relative, or parent of a friend—to become a kind of surrogate parent.

Late adolescent and young adult fantasies continue to incorporate derivatives of the family romance. The persistent wish to be adopted by better parents may manifest itself by an intense attachment to an in-law or to an employer-mentor. An au pair or baby-sitter who wishes to be part of the employer's family sometimes fulfills that fantasy by marrying the father.

Young adults who work hands on, such as massage therapists, personal trainers, and hairdressers, frequently run the fantasy of being adopted by clients. The need arises from the young adult's uncertainty about the future and eagerness for guidance, and the physical contact promotes a sense of closeness that makes the idea seem possible. In fact, this fantasy is often actualized, when a young person gets professional advice or even backing from a client. One personal trainer, through his affluent clients, learned to aspire to a new way of life. His imaginative vision was, in a sense, enlarged by his contact with people of wealth, sophistication, and taste. The lineaments of his underlying fantasy appeared in small asides to his clients, as when a client would be talking about something she was doing for her daughter, and he would say, apparently jokingly, "Would you do that for me too?" Gradually, he transformed his longings for a patron/parent into a plan to use his connections to invest in a clinic for sports injuries—a very healthy actualization of the family romance fantasy.

Another adult form of the family romance is the young professional man's wish to find in his boss the hoped-for loving father who will elevate him and rescue him from obscurity and defeat, eventually designating him as a successor. Freud describes a classic family romance fantasy of young adulthood that combines the wish for a mentor with an amorous fantasy. The case involved a poor orphan boy, now grown, who had been given the address of a business where he might find employment. On the way to his interview, this young man fantasizes that he gets a job, finds favor with his new employer, makes himself indispensable to the business, is taken into his employer's family, marries the charming young daughter of the house, and then himself becomes a director of the business, first as his employer's partner and then as his successor. In his fantasy, the dreamer reclaims what he felt he must have possessed in his earliest childhood (before he was orphaned). Freud concludes, "You will see from this example the way in which the wish makes use of an occasion in the present to construct, on the pattern of the past, a picture of the future."[9]

Commenting on Freud's orphan, the distinguished Peruvian psychoanalyst Moisés Lemlij makes a point important to my thesis that cultural values shape and infuse the content of fantasy:

> I cannot help but think that if that orphan were one of the Peruvian poets that I know, he would have knocked on the employer's door not to ask for work but rather to renounce the inheritance and to inform his "father-in-law" that he was born to write and therefore that "Dad" should excuse him, but that his decision to divorce the [employer's] daughter is final.[10]

So many young adults actualize their fantasies that some aspect of those fantasies must mesh with the longings of the obliging surrogate as well. Often, people who take on the role of surrogate parents, or rescuers, are enacting a family romance vicariously: The rescuer identifies with the person being rescued. This observation is important in understanding the myriad ways in which a fantasy can be twisted and turned—even inverted—to achieve some form of actualization. (The interaction in the realized family romance in effect constitutes a shared fantasy.)

The following story traces the permutations of a family romance over a lifetime.[11] Mr. Jason, now in his midfifties, recalls the passionate family romance of his childhood and identifies derivatives of that fantasy in many areas of his adult life. As a young boy of about six, he came to believe that he was the son of a maharajah. Unhappy with his parents and their virtual adoration of his older brother, he lay awake at night, crying and praying for his true father to rescue him. Why he chose Indian royalty is unknown to him, but he is dark and might even be said to have a faintly Asian look. The maharajah fantasy receded, replaced at about age eleven by a related preoccupying fantasy. Feeling more and more an outsider in his own family, enraged to the point of rebelliousness, he imaginatively identified (in the opening years of World War II, when his father was in the service) with the Japanese enemy—their values, their life-style, and their hostility to Americans. As an adult this man appears the very paragon of equanimity, partly because he has managed to sublimate his childhood anger and rebelliousness constructively. Derivatives of those early fantasies survive in his profound intellectual and aesthetic interest in Japan. He has traveled there extensively, learned Japanese, has embraced one of the Asian religions, and is sexually attracted to Asians. He appears to compensate for a feeling of a lack of nurture as a child by passionate nurturance of his lovers (as already suggested, commonly the flip side of fantasies of being rescued and nurtured).

Derivatives of the family romance often persist into adulthood, infusing how we try to shape our newly created families. Thus we may be intent on creating the kind of interdependency depicted in "Little House on the Prairie," or we may fantasize some form of communal family life. One night at a dinner party, three of the four couples present confided they had fantasized and even planned creating some form of communal living arrangement. One couple and their friends had fantasized for over twenty years about buying a large tract of land on which each family could build a house; the various families involved would share the cost and upkeep of the joint property, including amenities such as a tennis court and a swimming pool. Socializing would be informal, and close ties of friendship could be more easily maintained. This fantasy projects an Edenic dream of nonconflictual, harmonious communal life, and is in part a retreat from the "isolation" of the conjugal couple, invoking a band of happy siblings. When the individuals in couples fantasize a "compound," they are also sometimes expressing or sublimating their complicated feelings of love and sexual attraction for one or the other of their friends. Another couple at the dinner party fantasized avoiding the indignities of aging by setting up with their friends their own retirement community, perhaps buying an abandoned camp or inn. (Their fantasies unraveled as soon as they turned to realities: "What if I wanted to have dinner alone?") To some degree, communal fantasies update the adolescent dream of a world in which the peer group reigns supreme and troublesome people—such as parents or children—have vanished.

A family romance fantasy can continue, in modified form, throughout adulthood and is often reinvoked in times of disappointment or even despondency. (The fantasy "What if I had a different spouse or different living arrangements?" is not so different from the fantasy "What if I had different parents?")

Some family romances are not cast as future fulfillment, but as revisions of the past. In casting family romance fantasies backward, one attempts to undo the past to create a stronger self in the present. To the degree that one might have had different advantages, or different experiences, the end product of the fantasy is an improved version of the current model of the self. One young woman, feeling outclassed her first year of college, spent a great deal of time fantasizing about different backgrounds, all of them involving wealthier and more sophisticated parents, which would have allowed her to become fluent in French, adept on the dance floor, and at ease in social situations. Alternatively, she fantasized that before college she had been a go-go dancer, and was thus more beautiful, sexy, and worldly-wise than her peers. These were seedling fantasies: "The-wishing-for-more-graces" fantasies pointed out her need to acquire new skills and assets (without the benefit of wealthier parents), while the go-go dancer fantasy promoted an adaption as a fledgling sophisticate. Her fantasy, then, was in fact forward-directed and transformative. Generally, however, revisionist, could-have-been fantasies, while consoling, often remain backward-thinking and regretful, rather than hopeful or adaptive. (If habitual and unchanging, they fall on the "repeating" end of the continuum between repeating fantasies and generative fantasies.)

What of the family romance when the fantasizer really is removed from her family—adopted, orphaned, or lacking one parent? *The Karate Kid* movies plays on the fantasy of finding a surrogate father. In the original, a young boy living with a single mother, and a devoted one at that, nonetheless feels the lack of a father. At school the other kids bully him, and he gets a reputation as a sissy. Through a friendship with an old Japanese man who works in his building, he learns karate and eventually enters a competition in which he is able to stand up to the other boys. The real heartstring at which this movie tugs, its emotional core, is the relationship he forms with his teacher, which fulfills his longing for a replacement father.

Eileen Simpson relates several of her own fantasies as an orphan. "To be what Mother Superior had called 'a poor little orphan' meant not to have a father to take one home from the Convent at Christmastime,"[12] she tells us by way of introducing one of her major fantasies, imagining that her father was still alive. This fantasy evolved into a search for father substitutes.[13] She also described the classic family romance fantasy of perfect parents, which in her case had the advantage of being unobstructed by real-life parents.

> It was true that no matter what difficulties Auntie and I had (and they increased, as, learning to be independent, I became more spirited), I suffered less from them psychically than my friends suffered from disputes with their parents. I could say to myself, and for the comfort it gave me frequently did, that Auntie was not my mother, or my father. If my parents were alive. . . . There followed a daydream of an idyllic home life, of perfect accord.[14]

Family romances may reinvoke a time when one's real family was united and happy. One woman who escaped to the United States from a war-torn country invoked a family romance fantasy by summoning up the visual image of the house in which she had lived as a child, secure in the bosom of her family. She invoked a mental picture of the house at dusk, just when the lights have been turned on, as a soothing fantasy to help her go to sleep.

Family romances often invoke actual parents who are absent as a result of death, divorce, or illness. The fantasy then takes the form of imagining the enormous happiness of the absent parent's miraculously returning. (The bitter irony of the child's idealizing an absent parent is, of course, not lost on the struggling parent who is left to raise the child.) Such fantasies can be very long-lived. In fact, the adult children of divorced parents commonly continue to hope that their parents will reunite even after decades, and even after third parties have irrevocably entered the picture. This ongoing fantasy can be very disruptive in stepfamilies; it can also be very harmful, when fantasizers become too preoccupied with changing a reality over which they have no control to attend to situations they can affect.

Natalie, a woman in her late teens whose mother abandoned her and whose father raised her, still wishes for redress. Her fantasies are reparative, and they often focus on undoing the past rather than on shaping the future.

> I fantasize that I was a love-child of parents who felt that the thing they most wanted in life was to have me. I daydream that, as I grew up, they were very involved with helping me grow and understand myself and sitting with me when I couldn't figure out my homework, and that somehow these two people would understand me in a way that no one else would and that I could totally depend on them. This is the fantasy . . . that I would have a mother who loved me and of whom I was proud—someone I felt I could look up to for her kind-

ness and for her steadfastness. I could trust that what she was saying was the right thing and that it would always be in my best interest and that she was a pillar who would be steadfast. But this will never be.

Her fantasies are cast backward, somewhat pleasurable, but only in an unrealizable form that leads nowhere and may even be counterproductive, in that Natalie has been unable to form a potentially positive relationship with her stepmother, who entered Natalie's life several years ago and has continually tried to befriend her. In a sense, Natalie cannot create a viable family romance, to transfer her longings onto a surrogate, who could conceivably offer her some of the love she didn't get from her mother.

Natalie suffers such a suffusion of guilt—relating to an unarticulated sense that she defeated her mother in competition for her father and thus drove her away—that she has become stuck in conscious longing for what can never be, thus punishing herself through her feelings of deprivation. Her version of the family romance veers toward being a repeating fantasy rather than a generative one in that it lacks both forward momentum and hope. Natalie's mother, too, is caught in a "what-if" mode, in her case, what might have been had she not run away with a ne'er-do-well and had instead taken advantage of her not inconsiderable gifts. For the time being, Natalie's negative identification with her mother's limitations helps lock her into a similar stasis. As stuck as she is in certain ways, Natalie nevertheless has been able to transfer her father longings onto a series of father surrogates and has had several long-term romantic relationships.

Family romance fantasies may go beyond the depressive effects that Natalie is suffering to the downright destructive: At the extreme, a florid version of family romance fantasies informs the lives of those impostors who make up fictitious autobiographies, which they then try to pass off as real and may half-believe themselves.[15] (When so extreme, they are no longer generative fantasies but well within the realm of a pathological form of the repeating fantasy.)

In general, however, family romance fantasies are more adaptive than harmful. As the young adult becomes better equipped to find gratification in the outside world in reality and not just in fantasy, family romances may be dissolved, sublimated, or co-opted to other life plots, in particular to romantic fantasies about a future mate.

ROMANTIC FANTASIES

Drawing on common if not universal fantasies that arise during developmental life, romantic love fantasies give new life to the dream of fulfilling half-forgotten, inevitably frustrated wishes for the perfect harmony and complete mutuality that were ours in infancy (whether in fact or fancy). Such fantasies are new editions of the buried fantasy of obtaining the perfect mother who would love unerringly and unceasingly,[16] and many other fantasies as well—for example, Oedipal fantasies. Romantic love is a creative synthesis precisely because it provides an overarching narrative that incorporates many subordinate fantasies. And as the generic name suggests, family romances of childhood are continuous with later amorous fantasies. Romantic fantasies cannibalize family romance fantasies, rejecting some elements while preserving others; rescue and nurturance are among the most important subtexts in these fantasies.

The psychoanalyst Leo Rangell reported a variant of a family romance that shaped the professional and romantic life of a woman patient. She grew up with a mother who constantly put down her kind father. The family lived modestly in an apartment that abutted on her father's tailor shop. The patient remembered that when she was about five, her mother, raging against her father, told her her real father was a doctor whom the mother had consulted for infertility and who helped her conceive by impregnating her! Thus her mother helped her daughter create a family romance, and the patient grew up with a split image of the father, part the kind "Papa" she loved and looked after, and part the tall, suave, good-looking doctor her mother described.

Though she never met her putative biological father, she fantasized situations in which she might find a husband very like him, and this would enable her to look after her Papa. Identifying with the elegance of the doctor, she stood tall and became a successful model. She never fulfilled a fantasy of marrying a tall doctor but, according to Rangell, came close by marrying a successful and prominent man in a comparable profession. Her dream finally came true when her son grew up to be a tall, good-looking doctor.[17]

People follow a long developmental course before arriving at full-blown romantic fantasies—or at the love that they anticipate. This developmental course involves the capacity for idealization and its transfer from the parents to a series of surrogates. As the child grows older, family romances weaken because they do not satisfy the more complex needs of someone striving for autonomy. No longer can the young adult find satisfaction in the fantasy of herself as dependent on better parents than her own; in her imagination she is now the protagonist of her own drama, striving to live up to the dictates of her own internalized *ego ideal* (that mental agency that is heir to the infantile wishes for perfection and that acts as a compass to ongoing aspirations).

At this stage, children people their world with new heroes and heroines, idols or icons who represent a projection of their own ego ideals. These heroes are not parent substitutes, but models for what the fantasists themselves hope to become. Moreover, they are not imaginary. While the heroic qualities with which their admirers endow them may be imaginary, the people are real, for at this stage translating fantasy preoccupations into everyday life is important.

As preadolescent children transfer their inner longings to the larger world, they begin to idealize teenagers or adults, most often of the same sex, frequently people they know and can relate to however marginally, and whom they can identify with and imitate, rather than the products of their own imagination. In some cases, the romance of the imaginary continues, in a fantasy preoccupation with fictional characters or famous people, for the ongoing process of self-creation cannibalizes creatures of the imagination as well as real people. But more commonly these fantasies glamorize the real by depicting the everyday as heroic.

The idealizers/fantasizers, who have put a friend or teacher or coach on a pedestal, often develop crushes on these newly exalted personages, whose lives they hope to emulate and whose paths they hope to follow. Although these same-sex crushes may be sexual, more often they are not. At this stage of life, the goal of idealization is usually identification alone, rather than any form of romantic union. But throughout the life cycle, idealization may act as a stimulus for envy and emulation or as the catalyst for love.

Though they may find a range of satisfactions in one-sided crushes, which are essentially fantasies, adolescents hunger even more for intense reciprocal relationships that hold out the promise of real intimacy. These are the years of progressively forming new identifications outside the nuclear family, and one major means of doing so is by taking one's own measure in a series of intense friendships.

Gradually the adolescent also begins to develop romantic, sexualized crushes, as derivatives of Oedipal urges and fantasies reemerge. When they form sexualized crushes, adolescents often choose family friends or relatives halfway between their age and that of their parents as objects of affection. Then they experience poignant episodes of infatuation, with its attendant fantasies. But they do not yet feel impelled to translate those feelings of romantic longing into real life, and certainly not into sexual expression. That is one of the reasons for the age difference between the young lover and the beloved. While it suggests the link with incestuous Oedipal fantasies, it also protects the fantasizer from a potentially real sexual encounter. Like the family romance that reveals (and conceals) a continuity between its dramatis personae and the beloved parents of one's earliest years, the romantic fantasy reveals (and conceals) a continuity between the current object of desire and the Oedipal parent.

The developmental sequence of love varies. Although crushes are particularly common in adolescence and young adulthood, they occur throughout life, and at whatever age we experience them, they provide valuable imaginative rehearsals for an experience that one is not quite ready to enter into in full. The "lover" is content with—in fact protected by—the ideality of the love. However, once past adolescence, most of us entertain fantasies of imaginary love relatively infrequently, primarily when we watch movies or read novels, for example, or in bouts of nostalgia for past love. Or we enjoy such crushes for what they are: imaginative excursions.

But in real life we eventually attempt to blend the imaginative with tangible gratification, in the context of an intimate relationship. To enjoy the intimacy, affection, and sexuality of "real" love, and not just the lesser pleasures of the crush, we must test our feelings, convert longing into action, attempt to bring about reciprocity between ourselves and the one whom we idealize. We make this possible when we allow ourselves to feel passion for someone who might actually be available to us—not Tom Cruise but the lab partner in biology class.

Nonetheless, the beginning of any love affair always resembles a crush, characterized by imaginative fantasy, mentally constructed possibilities of what may come to be—trial action with no potential for harm. The lover primes the interval between the first meeting and the reencounter with the beloved through imaginative play. Sometimes the imagination runs wild: One woman was so embarrassed by the elaborateness of the scenario she had concocted before her date with her new admirer that when he arrived at the door, she hesitated even to look him in the eye.

The narrative of a crush condenses, incorporates, and symbolizes important personality trends and conflicts of our lives that often presage the texts of our realized loves. Ms. Maxwell, now a thirty-five-year-old divorced woman and successful advertising executive, as a young adolescent, feeling unattractive to boys, fantasized a series of boyfriends so vividly that they served as imaginary companions. She loved to go on long solitary walks; in her mind she was never alone but always with a boyfriend. The imaginary beaus were boys she liked who had rejected her. On her walks she invoked a constant dialogue, a kind of verbal jousting between her and her "boyfriend." She imagined herself as hard to get, argumentative, and competitive in her cleverness—a showoff who possessed a quick wit. Her draw was her uproarious sense of humor, not her physical allure. Even so, she saw herself as a beauty, transformed so much that she did not even recognize her fantasied self. She persisted in keeping an imaginary companion on hand until she married, and she married someone she felt was contemptuous of her. Not surprisingly, the marriage did not last.

Once divorced, she found herself drawn only to married men, a predilection that kept alive her sense of being rejected. She relates both her readiness to feel rejected and her inclination to "steal" a man from another woman to her lifelong belief that her sister, five years older, was the beautiful one in the family, the one whom her father adored. For Ms. Maxwell, her sister's beauty and popularity acted to confirm her failure, and it is this negative comparison she believes she is constantly trying to overcome. Through her therapy, she has now changed her pattern and for the first time in her life is involved with an eligible, nonrejecting man.

Each imaginative excursion into love bears signature characteristics. One may dream of rescuing or being rescued by a lover, of surrendering to or dominating a lover, of achieving twinship or marrying one's opposite, of marrying up or marrying down, of retreating into a symbiotic world or becoming half of a glamorous public couple, and so on. For Ms. Morris, her signature theme was not one of love and redemption, but of reparation as a prerequisite to love. Ms. Morris has had a troubled relationship with her mother since adolescence. For her the dream of love depends on first making reparation to her mother, who has a chronic, and likely fatal, disease. Only then will she be free to fall in love or let love be reciprocated. She must assuage her guilt toward her mother to allow her to feel worthy, as the following fantasy sequence suggests.

Ms. Morris confides:

> I think about my mother's death daily, and when the phone rings late at night, I think it is my father or my brother calling to tell me my mother has died. I keep having this fantasy about how before she dies, I will finally be able to tell her for the first time, because I've never told her, that I love her and that I appreciate what she has given to me spiritually. We are going to have this very revealing conversation and for the first time I am going to realize that she knows who I am and that she has connected with me and she understands me but she has never been able to talk about it. I fantasize constantly about this conversation that I am going have with her before she dies.

She quickly moves to an apparently unrelated fantasy about Jack, a man whose mother died when he was eleven. Mostly they have a telephone relationship because he lives in another city. Yesterday, at the beach, she saw a man who looked like an older version of Jack, and this triggered a fantasy in which the man at the beach was the father of her potential beau. "I started to fantasize that as he waded out, he went too far and was about to drown. But I dove in and saved him and could not wait to get home to call Jack to tell him about how I had just saved his father's life." She wasn't even aware of this fantasy, she says, until it flitted through her mind after we had been talking about her fantasies about achieving some kind of understanding or intimacy with her mother.

The manifest purpose of her rescue fantasy is to satisfy her longing for praise and approval from her new beau and a deeper connection with him. But it is striking that she must make reparation to a parent (even if the parent is Jack's and not her own) before she can allow her as yet unrealized romance to flower.

FANTASIES OF HAVING A BABY AND FANTASIES OF BECOMING PARENTS

Why women choose to become pregnant or men and women choose to have children and what pregnancy and parenting mean to each of them are very complicated questions. Many of the feelings, fears, and motives involved are expressed in fantasy. Parental fantasies—fantasies about the prospect of becoming a mother or a father—take several forms: for women, fantasies about what pregnancy and childbirth will be like; for both sexes, the fantasy of who the child will be—the "imaginary child," as it were[18]—and accompanying scenarios of their relationship as parent and child.

Fantasies of being pregnant and parenting may be positive or negative. A woman may fear childbirth but not parenthood, or vice versa. Some women find fantasies of pregnancy and childbirth so frightening that they postpone pregnancy or decide not to have children. Mrs. Farber, described in chapter 4, whose major repeating fantasy was about a world of tiny people living in her gastrointestinal tract, was for many years afraid to have a child, imagining the fetus as an alien who would cannibalize her from within. Her many fearful fantasies centered on images of being torn apart during the pregnancy or delivery or of developing cancer during the pregnancy. The fantasy of the fetus as an alien cannibal emerged only gradually. These fantasies expressed the retaliation she anticipated in response to her own (unconscious) fantasies of cannibalistically attacking her mother.

The pregnancy itself is often rife with fantasies ranging from beatific, Madonna-like imagery to fears of losing one's husband interest or of damaging the baby (through sex, straining in the bathroom, or taking aspirin). Fantasies may involve getting bigger breasts or losing one's figure. And the father-to-be has comparable fantasies—about destroying the baby through the act of intercourse, about his wife's dying in childbirth or losing interest in him after the baby is born, and so on. These fantasies are stoked by underlying childhood fantasies of childbirth, often echoes of one's feelings about a mother's pregnancy. They also echo other early issues, in a subliminal awareness of setting up an Oedipal triangle more satisfying than the childhood triangle—that is, with oneself as the desired apex.

All who opt for parenthood also spawn myriad fantasies about the parent-child relationships they desire. Most prospective parents fantasize a new baby as a narcissistic extension of the self, but a new version with unlimited future possibilities. This was Freud's great insight into the nature of parental love:

> If we look at the attitude of affectionate parents towards their children, we have to recognize that it is a revival and reproduction of their own narcissism, which they have long since abandoned. . . . Thus they are under a compulsion to ascribe every perfection to the child—which sober observation would find no occasion to do—and to conceal and forget all his short-comings. Moreover, they are inclined to suspend in the child's favour the operation of all the cultural acquisitions which their own narcissism has been forced to respect, and to renew on his behalf the claims to privileges which were long ago given up by themselves. The child shall have a better time than his parents; he shall not be subject to the necessities which they have recognized as paramount in life. Illness, death, renunciation of enjoyment, restrictions on his own will, shall not touch him; the

laws of nature and of society shall be abrogated in his favour; he shall once more really be the centre and core of creation—"His Majesty, the Baby," as we once fancied ourselves. The child will fulfill those wishful dreams of the parents which they never carried out—the boy shall become a great man and a hero in his father's place, and the girl shall marry a prince as a tardy compensation for her mother. At the most touchy point in the narcissistic system, the immortality of the ego, which is so hard pressed by reality, security is achieved by taking refuge in the child. Parental love, which is so moving, and at bottom so childish, is nothing but the parent's narcissism born again, which, transformed into object-love, unmistakably reveals its former nature.[19]

During pregnancy (or even before conception), the prospective parents—particularly the mother—are already engaged with an image of the child. Susan Chira, when she was mourning a miscarriage that occurred when she was four months pregnant, wrote perhaps the most beautiful description of the imaginary child I have ever read.

> I was bewildered, torn by my physical and emotional experiences. I had no doubt that what was growing inside me was alive in some way. The very morning of the miscarriage, I had seen a sonogram. . . . Even more striking than the physical evidence of life was what many pregnant women feel: The fantasy about what that baby would be like, the sense of protectiveness toward that potential person I longed to know. . . . In time, I came to understand that, above all else, maternity for me is a matter of the mind; I was mourning what could have been more than what was. Pregnancy allows you to project life onto what is growing inside you, to overlay your dreams of what will be onto what is. Just because I could look forward to how this child would fit into our family, how we would rearrange the room the children would share, what her name would be—because I endowed her with a life in my imagination does not mean I thought of her as an actual living child, the same as the one in my house now. The child I needed to mourn was a combination of the one I carried in my body and the one I carried in my heart.[20]

People transfer many different emotional investments to the child-to-be. As Freud suggested, a predominant kind of fantasy investment endows the child with potential to realize our unfulfilled fantasies. I was recently struck by the responses to the birth of a child in my own extended family. Various relatives—four grandparents, the parents, and assorted aunts and uncles—competed to find a physical resemblance between themselves and the baby. Surely this longing is so compelling because a physical resemblance promotes the fantasy of a reborn self.

Feelings develop for an imaginary child in a process similar to the choice of a potential lover. Both involve a preexisting fantasy, with both conscious and unconscious components, about who one wants the other—lover or child—to be. While the child is most often invested as a newer, fresher version of one-self with still unlimited possibilities or as an extension of oneself, there are many possible versions. One whose self-concept is significantly damaged may make the child the repository of the hated self, rather than the idealized self. This, of course, has serious implications for the way the parents treat the child, even with the best of intentions. For example, the devoted mother who views herself as damaged or worthless tends to think, "How can anything good come out of someone [me] who is so bad?" Faced with the reality of a child, she may thwart any action by the child that reminds her of herself and insist strongly that the child takes after *only* the father. Her fantasy damages the potential for a healthy relationship from the start.

Sometimes, the imaginary child may not be an extension of one's self, but a replacement child (perhaps for one who has previously died) or the duplica-tion of a hated sibling. Or paradoxically, the child may be a substitute for the mother's mother. This fantasy text is often enacted when mother comes to lean on the child as early in his or her life as possible. (Examples are mothers who cultivate their daughters as their best friend and confide in them—even when they are in their preteens or early teens—material as inappropriate as their own adulterous affairs.)

However the unborn child is imagined, the fantasies affect the mother's perceptions of and responses to the child. Over time as the real child confronts the fantasy child (in the mind of the mother), the mother usually can integrate the two. If she cannot align the fantasy and the reality, at least to some degree, she may deinvest in the real child or actually come to hate it, viewing it as the clone of a hated husband, parent, or sibling, or as a disappointment, inferior to the imaginary child.

By most accounts, the mother begins to modify her attitude toward the imaginary child—to give it some autonomy—at about the seventh month of pregnancy.[21] In part this happens because the child begins to make itself felt in the mother's consciousness through its independent movements, as it wakes when she sleeps, sleeps when she wakes, kicks or doesn't, displaying a will of its own. The reality of the child asserts itself in ways that most mothers find undeniable. Nonetheless, characteristics of the imaginary child recede slowly and perhaps never completely, and we may assume that the features that char-acterize the imaginary child invariably color the interaction between mother and child from the beginning, for better or for worse.

Not only does the mother have an imaginary child, she has a fantasied rela-tionship with it, as does the father. Each woman enters into motherhood hop-ing that she will meet the challenges intrinsic to mothering (what has been called maternal practice)[22] and will derive satisfaction from it that will out-weigh the difficulties. Part of the anticipated gratification is her image of the specific pleasures of the relationship itself, the many moments of closeness and empathic attunement she experienced with her parents or has seen and envied in other families.

But the level of fulfillment depends both on the mother's fantasies and on who the child turns out to be. For mothers who dream of symbiosis or twin-ship, the only truly gratifying period may be early infancy, when the child expresses total dependency on her. Mothers who primarily enjoy the narcissis-tic rewards of being needed and who fantasize oneness and perfect accord may resent or impede any move toward independence by the child.

Fantasies (and expectations) of well-attuned mothers change over the child's life, in response to the child's age-specific needs and individual person-ality and endowments. The mother's fantasies change in relation not only to changes in the child, but to changes in her own needs. Problems may develop at different stages; for example, a woman who has totally supported her chil-dren's assertive inclinations up until adolescence may withdraw support from her daughter at that time if she feels threatened by her daughter's emerging sexuality, because it triggers competitiveness in her and a dread that her own attractiveness is waning. Mothers may also withdraw from sons at adoles-cence, feeling threatened by them as *men,* imagining them as developing into the same predatory, sexually aggressive males that they fear and that they imagine all men to be. Sometimes adolescence triggers problems because then the mother is forced to abandon the fantasy of herself as the center of her fam-ily, to acknowledge that her children are making separate lives, with new cen-ters of gravity—themselves. Since the image of the mother-centered constella-tion is for many women a sustaining fantasy, predating the family itself, the loss of that fantasy can be devastating. One fantasy shattered, the mother may then revive a fantasy that puts her at the center again—like the fantasy of an extramarital affair.

When the adult or adolescent child leaves home a major shift occurs in the real relationship, and this regrouping always impinges on the fantasized rela-tionship. The effect, much more profound than the expected sequela of the so-called empty nest syndrome, is to force the parents to relinquish some of their underlying wishes and fantasies. Here one can begin to see something of the impact of culture and ideology on the fate of fantasy, for children of the nine-teenth century, for example, did not always leave, nor was it automatically expected that they would. Children, particularly daughters, were to remain at home if their parents needed them there, renouncing marriage and parent-hood because of a sense of duty. The fact that such a choice was a cultural norm would of course dictate mother-daughter fantasies quite different from contemporary modes.

Some adults select a child unrelated by blood to serve as a "magic" child and begin a relationship with that child that is heavily invested with fantasy. Occa-sionally men in their sixties who have not been close to their own children attach to a magic child and infuse the relationship with caregiving, idealization, and concerns for the child's future. Often this is the child of a woman he loves—whether it is a consummated love affair or not. At the extreme, the magic child, who is in some ways the redeemed self, merges into a love object. This theme is immortalized in literature in Thomas Mann's *Death in Venice,* in which Gustave Aschenbach renounces his own life—family and career—to remain near Tadzio, whom he sees as embodying extraordinary beauty. Women, too, form intense connections with children not of their blood. To them the magic child may be an alter ego, someone to guide in the world almost in place of oneself. Relationships with the magic child are examples par excellence of heavily invested fantasy relationships that often yield great pleasure and fulfillment for both the adult and the child involved.

AUTONOMY AND ACHIEVEMENT/WORK AND AMBITION

Just as we grow up with dreams of love, of friendship, and of parenthood, so, too, do we have reveries about how we will make a living, gain recognition, express our desires for achievement and creative work, and so forth. We dream about money, power, and fame and about the reverse—failure, poverty, loss of status. These dreams may be mundane or exotic. In a society in transition, such as ours, these imaginative rehearsals are very time-consuming and may be very complicated, because they depend on both the current zeitgeist and unconscious fantasies and inner longings.

To some degree dreams are ordered by gender, though perhaps less than in the past (another instance of the way the cultural milieu affects our inner lives, allowing or disallowing certain kinds of fantasies). Childhood excursions into career-related fantasy are often based on same-sex identifications with our parents, with people we know, and with fictional characters.

Children act out these identifications in their play but also act out make-believe occupations that may have little relation to people they know, and in fact little relation to career choices, despite their surface content. For a little boy, the fantasy of being a firefighter is often related to urinary concerns and a fascination with arching streams of water. Similarly, the fantasy of being a police officer frequently involves the issue of aggression and its control. Very young children of both sexes play doctor to reassure themselves about medical examinations—turning passive into active. (Later in childhood, playing doctor is the pretext for sexual exploration.) Little girls playing at being mommy are as involved in mastering body functions—via the instructions they issue to their make-believe offspring—as in nurturing. Psychological issues that are age-specific, that express an unconscious phase-specific need or impulse, profoundly affect make-believe play.

Even when they issue from conflicts and preoccupations characteristic of childhood, however, some fantasies may transcend their origins and take on a life of their own, piquing intellectual interests and ultimately career choices.

Berta Bornstein reported on the analysis of a ten-year-old boy whose child-hood fantasies proved important to the genesis and perpetuation of an ongo-ing intellectual interest.[23] The boy had a complex relationship with both his brothers and his father, which many of his daydreams reflected. After Born-stein began to work with her patient on his competitiveness with them, he *con-sciously* tried to minimize it:

> At the beginning of his analysis, he openly played at being important men like generals and admirals; now, in his daydreams, he revealed a modification of these wishes. Motivated by the desire to please the analyst, he made a strong point of telling [her] that in his daydream he himself was a 10-year-old boy and that in reality he no longer sought to compete with his father but wanted to remain a boy of his own age.
>
> In his daydreams, however, young as he was, he was a famous brain surgeon, and had also discovered a cure for cancer. He attended school during the day, of course, but nevertheless, General Eisenhower had heard that [he] was a famous brain surgeon and ordered [him] night after night to the battlefield to perform his famous operations on outstanding generals. The brains of those generals were shattered by bullets or their lives were endangered by brain tumors. It was through his restoring the generals' mental capacity that the United States won the war.
>
> Up to this point his daydream emphasized that nobody at school knew about his fame as a brain surgeon. One day a variation of the dream occurred. A police-man entered the classroom and asked about a car that was not parked correctly. It turned out to be [the] patient's car; in this way everyone at school suddenly learned that he not only had, as he said, a "doctor's certificate," but in recogni-tion of his outstanding services, he had also been granted a driver's license.

Knowing that the boy tended to respond to slights with somewhat grandiose, compensatory fantasies, Bornstein asked him about what had hap-pened at school. He told her that a male teacher had reprimanded him for con-tinually yawning during class, and the incident triggered the exhibitionistic daydream. In the daydream, the patient is no longer a young helpless boy being scolded by his teacher but an important surgeon. In essence, he had reversed a shameful episode into a glorious one in his mind.

Even after the boy repudiated his grandiose daydreams, he maintained his interest in physiology and anatomy, associated with his fantasies about being a surgeon. The interests the fantasy provoked survived its dissolution. In fact, many adults incorporate the themes encoded in the make-believe play of early childhood and the daydreams of later childhood in their choices of pastimes and careers.

Though in adolescence the grandiosity of childhood diminishes somewhat as reality checks proliferate, it is not yet time for it to disappear. Reluctant to give up fantasies of glory, the typical adolescent may, however, temper them. Eric Klinger discusses one such typical fantasy as reported by an anonymous student.

> I was one of the top tennis players in the U.S. but was not ranked or anything. I just played for the fun of it and could beat about anybody. I lived in a big house in the mountains with my own private tennis courts beside them. I played tournaments now and then to earn money to live on but I didn't have everyone all after me to be in the papers and play for any teams. I kept going over certain plays in my mind and how good I was.[24]

This daydream may have been deliberately downgraded in grandiosity to keep alive the imaginative possibility that it might come true.

Because many early adolescent fantasies border on the grandiose, they cannot be sustained. A teenager inevitably notices the discrepancy between his or her fantasy life and the possibilities that are realistically available, in terms of his or her resources and talents. The psychologist Jerome Singer believes that part of the pain of adolescence arises because the discrepancy between what is wished for and what is possible becomes apparent within such a brief span.[25] "Between the ages of seventeen and twenty many of these dream balloons are likely to be punctured; in fact, the whole delicately balanced structure may collapse when commitments are made and a very different life appears in the offing."[26]

In adolescence other dream balloons are floated, too: fantasies that might be realized. This is all part of the process of developing personal autonomy and some sense of control over one's future, which is one of the key tasks of adolescence. So from adolescence to middle adulthood, many reveries center around relatively realistic plans for work and achievement.

While some of these fantasies are linear and transparent, others that appear to be obvious may actually be layered and complex, drawing on the wishes and fears of early childhood even as they address current concerns. Some fantasies of adolescent and adult life are still imbued with early life concerns and bodily preoccupations: For example, fantasies of making piles of money have a resonance with early life fantasies of anal retention and hoarding. This is readily apparent in the fantasy some very rich people have that unless they double their current net worth, they will lose everything.

Many work fantasies entail interpersonal wishes and longings. For example, a woman whose mother's erratic behavior tormented her during childhood and adolescence recognized that her mother was psychologically disturbed and always harbored the hope of making restitution to her in a way that would allow her to become stable. This never happened, but the woman's rescue fantasy fuels many of her feminist activities. What she could not do for her mother, she will do for women in general. Certain professions offer a vehicle for rationalizing and sublimating rescue fantasies, among them medicine, nursing, and teaching. (This is not to say that every doctor, nurse, or teacher harbors such fantasies, however.) A number of Wall Street people have told me that one of the pleasures of the work (and sometimes one of its terrible pains) is that there is a report card at the end of every day, in the form of a bottom line. The wish to be graded or marked on a day-to-day basis often resonates with insecurity in early life, and sometimes with lack of parental attention or encouragement. Alternately, the wish to be graded may arise from the childhood experience of feeling loved only for one's accomplishments. (There are of course many other reasons people wander into Wall Street, including a gift for mathematics, the desire to make money, and the love of risk.)

In midlife, as in adolescence, some people have a terrifying fear that certain cherished fantasies may not be fulfilled. Sensing that some real life options may be receding, the person may intensify work and ambition fantasies or express concern—via denial—over the perceived waning of possibilities. Ms. Vernon, a middle-aged painter, found herself daydreaming that she was pregnant. She believed her fantasy represented her wish to be pregnant, perhaps triggered by the fact that, just as she is passing through menopause she finds herself surrounded by little grandchildren. Although she did not want any more children, she believed the pregnancy fantasy was a product of her dislike of giving up anything at all, including the power of procreation, which had been so meaningful to her earlier in life. Ms. Vernon interjected the fact that the Bible describes how Sarah had a child when she was almost one hundred.

However, it eventually emerged that Ms. Vernon's manifest fantasy was concealing another fantasy just outside her awareness (because of her reluctance to address it)—the desire for greater commercial success as a painter. For weeks she had discussed her friends' view of her as a hack; they expected nothing new from her, and one of them had said—unaware of the hostility in the remark—how much she admired Vernon's ability to "grind it out." But because Ms. Vernon is frightened by her own ambitions and contemptuous of her wish to be famous, the fantasy of being famous appears to her less acceptable than the fantasy of becoming pregnant. The pregnancy fantasy disguises her wish to have a successful show. But the fantasy contains her assessment of her narrowing possibilities—just as having a child is no longer an option, neither is success. (She may well be wrong; therefore her fantasy may be maladaptive since it leads her to conclude her dreams and desires are in the realm of the fantastic. Nonetheless the Sarah association suggests that her ambition may not be dead; she just wants to protect it from critical eyes.)

Unlike Ms. Vernon, many people in our culture entertain undisguised and unadulterated dreams of glory, if only for the proverbial fifteen minutes of fame. Extremes of ambition—particularly among the middle class—are the very stuff of fantasy life, and while such fantasies may find no outlet in real life and may be dismissed as escapism by the practical-minded, sometimes they do find outlets—or create them—in unexpected and extraordinary places.

Anthony Storr, writing of Winston Churchill, proposes an interesting hypothesis about ambition:

> Extreme ambition, of the Churchillian variety, is not based upon sober appraisal of the reality of one's gifts and deficiencies. There is always an element of fantasy, unrelated to actual achievement. This may, as it did with Churchill, take the form of a conviction that one is being reserved for a special purpose, if not by the Deity, then at least by fate. One of the most remarkable features of Churchill's psychology is that this conviction persisted throughout the greater part of his life until, at the age of sixty-five, his fantasy found expression in reality.[27]

Storr goes on to say that one of Churchill's biographers, Lord Moran, believed that it was "the inner world of make-believe in which Winston found reality."[28] Storr himself suggests that England's very survival in 1940 may well have been due to Churchill's world of make-believe and to his "irrational conviction independent of factual reality."[29] (Perhaps the schoolboy dream of being a man of destiny is not uncommon among world leaders: DeGaulle in a sense was France.)

As Storr paints his portrait, Churchill's ambition and dreams of glory led the way out of periodic depression. Writing to his mother from India, Churchill says of himself: "What an awful thing it will be if I don't come off. It will break my heart for I have nothing else but ambition to cling to."[30] But ambition of this magnitude is not willed or even controllable. Storr quotes from Churchill's only novel, about Savonarola: "Ambition was the motive force and he was powerless to resist it."[31]

Of course, many factors predispose a person to intense ambition. Storr cites depression, which the anticipated achievement is expected to cure. Other factors include the sense of being special, bestowed from the outside (usually by one's family) or from within, for example, when a person invokes a self-generated fantasy to repair a sense of inner weakness. An identification with someone notable in the family can also promote a feeling of being special and consolidate ambition. Special gifts may also prepare the way for specific ambitions. As with all rehearsals for life, fantasies of work and ambition, while based on our longings and our dreams, are gradually shaped by our encounters with reality. Here, too, part of that reality is our familial and cultural milieu.

But fantasies about future life are not always specific. Future-oriented fantasies may sometimes be almost formless, interweaving wishes, longings, ambitions, and life plans so vague that they cannot be minutely articulated, even to oneself. In a recent interview, Robert Redford, talking about himself as a teenager in the San Fernando Valley, "a place of used car lots and appliance stores," conveys some of the amorphousness of the process, which draws on an odd assortment of sources, from books to travel posters.[32]

Redford remembers:

> When I read *On the Road* it struck me the way the movie *Rebel Without a Cause* did—like an arrow to the heart, to my own identity. That's what I felt about the Beats. I felt I was—like they were—on the edge of something, at the beginning of something, leading to something different.
>
> I began to develop a fascination for New York from about age 12. Baseball—sports—was part of that. There were no major-league teams in the West when I was growing up. New York had a mythological air to it. In high school I read Thomas Wolfe, *Only the Dead Know Brooklyn,* and Irwin Shaw's stories. I was working at the Standard Oil Refinery—that's how I made money for college and then for going to Europe—and I'd be dropped off from work on a corner of Hollywood Boulevard. There was a travel office with this poster of the New York skyline hanging in the window. It just killed me. All I wanted to do was be there.[33]

Dan Wakefield, the author of the Redford article, goes on to say: "So did many of our generation who sought more than the split-level 50's life style and a gold watch at retirement."[34] What exactly they saw is hard to articulate, other than the "more than" something else that New York somehow represented, even to people who had no particular career path in mind. But such fantasies were, for all their formlessness, *ambitious* fantasies that kept them going through hard times, until success began to be a realistic possibility. The fantasy of New York, or the romance of a particular job, admiration for someone we know—all these are elements we fit into a fantasy of how to order our work lives, our autonomous lives.

Salman Rushdie, in a wonderful meditation on *The Wizard of Oz,* touches a polarity that is at the root of two fundamentally different kinds of generative fantasies. Rushdie speaks of

> the human dream of *leaving*—a dream at least as powerful as its countervailing dream of roots. At the heart of *The Wizard of Oz* is a great tension between these two dreams; but, as the music swells and that big, clear voice flies into the anguished longings of the song, can anyone doubt which message is the stronger? In its most potent emotional moment, this is inarguably a film about the joys of going away, of leaving the grayness and entering the color, of making a new life in the "place where you won't get into any trouble." Over the rainbow is, or ought to be, the anthem of all the world's migrants, all those who go in search of the place where "the dreams that you dare to dream really do come true." It is a celebration of Escape, a Grand Paean to the Uprooted Self, Hymn—*the* Hymn—to Elsewhere.[35]

This is the great dream of *escaping* Kansas—our real-life, everyday drab family lives—for somewhere fantastical and exotic. It is the longing to put our families, our past, behind us and has its roots in our inner psyches.

Reflecting the culture's impact on fantasy life, people have always been impelled by psychologically reparative visions of adventure and rootlessness, excitement and freedom. Nonetheless the dream of elsewhere is more widespread in certain historical epochs than in others. In some periods in both American and European history economic pressures produced an exodus from the farm to the city. Similarly, poverty and hopelessness encouraged wave after wave of immigration to America. The pressures were not just negative. In the New World the streets were paved with gold, and "the dreams that you dare to dream really do come true." Such longings were the very fuel of steerage class, propelling millions from the old country to the United States. And many of us are the wanderlust children who have inherited those dreams or dreams of the open frontier.[36]

Dreams of "elsewhere" are related to the wish for new beginnings and are kin to what the psychoanalysts Stephen Rittenberg and L. Noah Shaw have described as fantasies of self-creation.[37] Self-creation fantasies are similar to family romances except that instead of improving their circumstances by conjuring up idealized parents, self-creators become their own makers, imaginatively annihilating their parents. Rittenberg and Shaw draw on F. Scott Fitzgerald's *The Great Gatsby* to illustrate fantasies of self-creation. Jay Gatsby was the self-invention of the seventeen-year-old boy James Gatz, the son of "shiftless and unsuccessful farm people—his imagination had never really accepted them as his parents at all. . . . His heart was in a constant, turbulent riot. The most grotesque and fantastic conceits haunted him in his bed at night."[38] By reinventing himself, Gatsby was able to "set out in pursuit of his dreams of glory, wealth and glamour."[39]

Tom, the narrator of Tennessee Williams's *Glass Menagerie* and alter ego for Williams himself, has a heart in similar riot, but, unlike Gatsby, Tom never quite succeeds in "annihilating" the mother and sister he leaves behind. In fact, the last words of that play are about the sister, about the impossibility of ever putting her behind him. As for Tom, dreams of new beginnings may appear to be fully realized on the surface, while the past continues to exert a never-ending tug within.

Rittenberg and Shaw believe that fantasies of self-creation, designed to stabilize a threatened sense of self, have become increasingly widespread in our contemporary culture.[40] As they point out, in *The Great Gatsby,* "Fitzgerald sought to portray not only an individual self-inventor [in the character of Gatsby] but also to delineate, in that portrait of a representative American character, the organizing fantasies that bind an entire culture together."[41] And it is true that in this respect, *The Great Gatsby* feels like a much more modern, specifically American work than *The Glass Menagerie*. We in America believe in the myth of self-creation, and belief in the myth has generated its own reality.

Fantasies of self-creation are an extreme example of the overall group of fantasies I have called "generative." Like make-believe and play in early childhood, which are also often dismissed as escapist, generative fantasy represents a creative effort to find our way in the real world. A complex product of the interaction of the inner world of the psyche and the external "real" world, generative fantasy allows us to create something that is wholly our own, and it influences the future course of our lives.

Both repeating and generative fantasies ultimately seek validation through actualization or through resonance with the fantasies of others. Such grounding gives the fantasies credence in the reality of the interpersonal world. The result is the formation of shared fantasy, which allows us to achieve our deepest bonds with others. The world of fantasy creates its own reality.

6

SHARED FANTASIES

BECAUSE EACH OF US EXPERIENCES OUR FANTASIES AS PRIVATE, IDIOSYN-
cratic, and revealing of us in particular, we generally assume that they are
strictly our own creation, personal products that do not depend on input from
the outside world. Analogously, we believe our emotional experiences are singular, distinct from everyone else's. For example, each of us generally experiences our own passionate love affair as unique, different from anything anyone else has ever experienced before. However, to the outside observer, all love
affairs have common features, from the imaginative act that sets them in
motion to the exaltation and expanded sense of self they create. Similarly, to an
observer our fantasies are much like other people's.

While some fantasies are more idiosyncratic than others, and every fantasy
bears the mark of its maker, I have never heard any fantasy that has not been
echoed—sometimes with variations—in others. A distinguished psychiatrist
relates a very telling story concerning dreams that applies equally to fantasies.
In a lecture, to preserve confidentiality, she hesitated to use any of her patients'
dreams to make a point. Instead, she related one of her own. After the lecture,
a former patient strode up to her in a rage and accused her of appropriating
his dream without permission. Therapist and patient had floated similar
dream images. This is not surprising, since what is true of fantasies is also true
of many dreams: They may be uncommon but they are seldom unique.

The plots of most fantasies are variations on familiar themes. Some fantasies are widely dispersed because all human beings share certain developmental paths with members of our species and other paths with those of our

sex. Because the narrative of fantasy draws on experience, to the degree that we share similar developmental crises and conflicts, our fantasies will be kin. Moreover, some psychoanalysts believe that certain fantasies may be inborn. These similarities, however engendered, allow us to empathize with and sometimes intuit one another's fantasies. We can "read" each other.

Some fantasies are literally shared—that is, one person communicates a fantasy to another, or two or more people jointly create it. Sometimes that sharing is conscious, as when someone tells his fantasy to someone else; at other times a fantasy is telegraphed out of awareness—preconsciously. In any intimate relationship, one individual's fantasy life inevitably impacts on or intersects the other's, thus becoming an integral part of their bond.[1] The interaction of the fantasy systems colors, or even decisively shapes, the relationship.

Shared fantasies are not unusual; they form part of the very ground of human relationships. We imbue all our significant relationships with fantasy, and intimate relationships provide the ideal medium in which shared fantasies can proliferate. Sharing fantasies intensifies the emotional and psychological connections between people. In fact, the deepest emotional ties generally occur between people who have congruent or complementary fantasies, whether explicitly shared or communicated through subliminal cues.

In the *congruent fantasy,* two people have the same wishes and impulses and construct a daydream as a joint venture, creating what Hanns Sachs calls a "community of two,"[2] and shared fantasies can form the basis of communities of three or four, or more. The implicit bonding between the fantasizers is grounded in appreciation of the shared wish; the sharing of the fantasy relieves the unpleasant feelings of guilt, shame, and anxiety that often accompany wishes. Congruent fantasies include joint revenge fantasies, death and rebirth fantasies (frequently seen in suicide pacts), and comrade-in-arms fantasies. Or two people may form a bond based on antisocial Bonnie and Clyde fantasies or us-against-the-world fantasies.

In the *complementary fantasy,* two individuals adopt (and sometimes act out) reciprocal roles—slave and master, student and mentor, rescuer and rescued, wild child and restraining parent, lover and beloved, and so on. A man whose underlying fantasy is based on the wish to be dominated may be drawn romantically only to powerful women who in turn need to enact the dominant role. In a complementary fantasy, the fantasizers may stick with their respective roles, or they may be flexible, shuttling back and forth between the two (as when children negotiate, "Now I get to be the mother and you be the baby, because I was the baby yesterday").

The process of sharing fantasy may be explicit; more often it is the product of preconscious communication, for example, when one person recruits another to enact his or her own fantasy. Parents do this all the time through the stories they tell their children. Stories told by a parent grouped around a particular theme may sound a note of approval and be correctly intuited by the child to embody a fantasy or a directive. Although the parents themselves may not be aware of the subtext of their stories, the children invariably pick up on it. One might say that the fantasy is transferred, with the parent's preconscious intent that it be enacted by proxy—in the process the psychoanalyst Martin Wangh has called an "evocation of a proxy," which allows the parent to enact a fantasy vicariously through the child.[3]

One young lawyer figured out in his therapy that his numerous and almost invariably unsuccessful and self-destructive excursions into entrepreneurial-ism were similar to—or borrowed from—the "pot-of-gold at the end of the rainbow" fantasy that his idealized father, a professional man who had spent a lifetime investing in failed Broadway shows and undeveloped land that was destined to remain undeveloped, had harbored.

One can also observe the intermingling of fantasies, sometimes in the form of memory, in family combinations other than parent and child. For example, one sister may remember her sister's experience as her own: "I thought *I* was the one who got lost at the bus stop, not *you*." Preconscious communication between family members—like explicit communication—leads to both con-gruent and complementary fantasy.

Shared fantasies also occur in the therapy setting. Transference by the patient onto the analyst is not just a displacement of feelings: It is also the patient's attempt to draw the analyst into a shared fantasy, often duplicating a bond from the patient's earlier life.[4]

Transference, however, is not restricted to the therapy situation (although it may be particularly intense there): It permeates all relationships. The play-wright Sam Shepard has it right when he says that his long-familiar theme of father and son, though apparently absent from his current work, nonetheless may infuse it.

> The odd thing to me is I think all of those relationships are inside other rela-tionships. . . . Those things aren't necessarily expressed by any external charac-ter. There are these territories inside all of us, like a child or a father or the whole man, and that's what interests me more than anything: where those territories lie.[5]

His fundamental intuition is about the pervasiveness of certain themes in life and in work.

Shared fantasies, directly and indirectly communicated, have different sig-nificance for adaptation at different points in the life cycle. Shared fantasies permit the emergence of impulses or wishes that might otherwise be sup-pressed by shame, fear, or humiliation. Sharing fantasies sometimes normal-izes those we might otherwise regard as eccentric, archaic, or crazy.[6] Shared fantasies promote bonding, and they are the catalyst for the formation of many groups.

Shared fantasy may serve the function of exorcism (that is, act as substitute wish-fulfillment) or may be a prelude to enactment. But once a fantasy is explicitly shared, for better or for worse it has a greater chance of being enacted than does a purely private fantasy. The very act of sharing removes the fantasy from its exclusive dominion in the subjective world of a single person's mind and propels it into the reality of a shared discourse. At that point, it may become a dress rehearsal rather than a substitute gratification, moving toward actualization or enactment.

While Freud introduced the idea of shared fantasy in the context of works of art,[7] Hanns Sachs emphasized its importance in everyday life. Noting that generally people do not reveal their daydreams to one another, Sachs described a few exceptions, in which the sharing of fantasy "marks the solemn beginning of a friendship [as] when two youngsters exchange their daydreams like hostages."[8] He contributed to the psychoanalytic literature two classic examples of shared fantasies he had observed in his practice, one of which I will recount here because of the light it sheds on the role of such fantasies in developmental life, with the potential for both positive and negative results.

This case involved a young man who entered analysis because he was depressed and had suicidal tendencies. His mother, widowed when he was only three and a half, was left alone to raise the patient, his older siblings, and one younger brother. During what proved to be a successful analysis, the patient told Sachs of an episode he had always half-remembered, but also half-forgotten.

At about the age of five, he had become close friends with a boy of his own age. During one of their play sessions, his friend suggested that they might go to India together, and they took up this joint fantasy, searching in vain for ways to get there. One day the friend developed a new idea: He claimed to know of a pond that was the starting point of a route to India. His proposal was that

> it was only necessary to jump into the water [of the pond] and to stay long enough at the bottom, and then one would get into a piece of machinery. This would cut one into very small bits, but this procedure would be pleasurable rather than painful, and, anyway, when it was over, one would be whole and hearty and in India.[9]

Sachs's patient approved the plan and the two boys located what they thought was the pond that led to India. The initiator of the fantasy then suggested that Sachs's patient jump into the water first; he did and very nearly drowned.

This, then, is a joint fantasy in which the originator of the fantasy persuades a surrogate to act out the fantasy for him. By transferring his fantasy to a proxy, he does not have to act it out himself but still gains the vicarious gratification of its enactment.

Sachs interpreted the India scheme as an elaborated (and partially enacted) fantasy involving a flight from home, and the descent into the pond as a "thinly veiled project of suicide," of birth and rebirth (after drowning), which he believed only children who felt rejected in some way and were consequently unhappy could have devised. He concluded that unconsciously his patient as a little boy must have wanted to leave his mother, to punish her for his feelings of jealousy, resentment, and anger, and at the same time to be resurrected and united with her. However, he surprised himself by arriving at this analysis, since the patient had always claimed that he and his mother had loved each other dearly, and Sachs had believed his characterization.

Yet, on reflection, Sachs realized that the boyhood episode might explain an apparent anomaly in the patient's history—the fact that as an adolescent he had felt no sorrow at his beloved mother's death and funeral. In contrast, he had experienced an enormous eruption of grief a year later, when he attended a play by Gerhart Hauptmann, *Little Joan's Ascension to Heaven*. In the play, a little girl who was herself unloved tried to drown herself and was subsequently rescued. The play depicted her fantasies while she was in a feverish delirium. Sachs believed that his patient had identified with the little girl because of their common suicidal ideation and sense of aloneness, and that the play had given his patient an opportunity for belated mourning. He concluded that the patient's earlier (shared) fantasy must have been related to a wish to leave home and must have resulted from a withdrawal from his mother, even though he no longer remembered those feelings. Sachs's conjectures subsequently seemed to be confirmed in the analysis when the patient's memories from that period began to emerge. These memories included episodes of jealousy of his mother's transient suitor, emotions that probably recapitulated his earlier response to the birth of his younger brother.

The two lost boys constructed a joint fantasy that allowed communion between them, a bond that ended their feelings of isolation. Sharing the fantasy allowed impulses that would probably have remained repressed to surface. Of course, acting out this shared fantasy might also have had a disastrous result, insofar as it involved a suicide-rebirth theme and an actual near-drowning. But the boys were lucky—Sachs's patient was saved—and the joint fantasy had no permanent negative effects.

At many junctures in the course of a life, people encounter situations that lend themselves to the mutual construction of a fantasy. The result may be a shared sense of pleasure, psychic ease, sexual excitement, or purpose. Or it may be the repetition of a significant relationship of early life, for good or ill.

Some shared daydreams are short-lived and ephemeral, serving only the most immediate of functions. Two women who shared a hostility to a third woman amused themselves (and grew closer) by thinking up ways to express that hostility. They invented fantasies about inviting their "friend" to a "B"-list party with all the other people they considered second-rate. They conjured up cruel put-downs to address to her at pivotal moments, and they fantasized elaborate scenarios they would stage to embarrass her.

Other shared fantasies persist over longer periods and serve more long-range purposes. Two sisters in their teens had a job as singers at a local club, the Moors in Provincetown. Carrying their guitars, they would try to hitch rides to work to save money. Whenever a car passed them by, they shook their fists at the driver and said, "I'll see you at the Moors." What this meant was "Okay, wait till you see our smashing triumph at the Moors. We're going to be a great success. Then you'll eat your heart out." This became a rallying cry that allowed them to express both the fantasy of enormous success and their anger and vengefulness at being slighted, literally passed by (this was especially helpful to one sister, who was very inhibited in expressing anger). Imagining their own success and the drivers' subsequent chagrin helped sustain their efforts through the struggles of the months and years that followed. The shared fantasy thus served the purpose of ambition, while helping to minimize competition between the sisters.

Shared fantasies often fall into an intermediate area between substitute gratification and trial action. Take a common example: Two lovers, one or both married to other people, are unable either to divorce their partners or to separate from one another. Trapped in an untenable position, they fantasize their future marriage, perhaps even perform a mock wedding, and celebrate subsequent "anniversaries." As an extension of their fantasy, they may exchange wedding rings or other tokens of their union to be worn only surreptitiously. Their joint fantasy may remain in the realm of make-believe, substituting for action, or it may be a prologue to action. Such shared fantasy and fantasy play resemble the make-believe play of childhood; the fantasies hover between pure fantasy and dress rehearsal as prologue to actualization. Often the play-acting lovers remain ambivalent about the way they want the play to go. Thus the adulterous lovers of John Updike's *Marry Me* fantasize a marriage but vacillate so incessantly that their creator himself does not seem to know whether their affair is the main act or a prelude and has therefore provided his lovers—and his readers—with several different endings.

Lovers, whether married or not, share fantasies at many different levels of articulation. They may express fantasies in such fleeting identifications as "Us against the world," permanent nicknames that reveal the underlying identification (e.g., "Tweet" and "Tweetie"), or in more structured role playing that enacts, say, mother-child relationships. Future-oriented fantasies relating to joint undertakings emerge, in "what-we-will-do-when" planning and plotting, as when newlyweds daydream about their unborn children—what they will look like, what they will become, and so on. Couples who are remarried and who are too old to have children together fantasize about the spectacular children they would have had had their gene pools merged (this in contrast to their actual children, who are tainted by other gene pools), thus consoling themselves with might-have-been fantasies.

Shared fantasies in couples are very common. In *Who's Afraid of Virginia Woolf?* George and Martha have an imaginary son. They agree to keep his existence secret. In the course of a horrendous sadomasochistic evening with another couple, they begin to talk about their fictitious child. Finally George, to Martha's horror, claims that the son, now a young man, has been killed in a car crash. The symbolic meaning of the imaginary child is not my concern here; the point is that the playwright, Edward Albee, can use such a symbol effectively because shared fantasies do exist, making the plot twist plausible enough to serve as part of the dénouement of the play.

Not just the bedroom but also the boardroom and the office provide settings for the formation and enactment of shared fantasy. Several shared fantasies may be running concurrently (just as in the family each of us plays out several shared scenarios simultaneously). For example, one president of a small company acts as a benevolent father to his women employees and an abusive father to his male employees, reenacting his father's demeanor (at home) and often evoking reciprocal feelings, fantasies, and behaviors from his staff.

The story of Mr. Timmons shows how an early sibling relationship (with all its attendant shared fantasies) can resonate throughout much of adulthood. Mr. Timmons was the second son of an Irish immigrant family. His older brother, a man who became successful and wealthy although he had never finished high school, served as his father surrogate and, on the surface, the much-loved partner in a mutually satisfying fraternal relationship. But it was predicated on the shared assumption that despite the younger brother's being the first in his extended family to acquire an education, he was to remain a vassal to his successful brother/businessman. The older brother was supportive insofar as he had contributed to the costs of Mr. Timmons's education, but he also deprecated his brother's professional accomplishments.

When Mr. Timmons was in school, he met the man who was to become his business partner, an elegant and erudite man—apparently the very opposite of his brother. Together Timmons and his new partner formed and worked in their own business for some forty years. Despite appearances, Mr. Timmons had duplicated the deferential, dependent sibling relationship that was in some ways the emotional center of his life with his partner. The partner, like the brother, experienced himself as the substantive one, as the caretaker of Mr. Timmons, whom he relegated to a subordinate role.

Both the brother and the partner needed to feel that combination of benevolence and contempt that the rescue of someone believed to be compromised and needy offered. This need was also fulfilled in their marriages. Both had married extremely neurotic women, and both had projected a picture of strong, competent, sacrificing, and providing husbands saddled with weak, compromised, and self-destructive wives.

Late in life, after both brother and partner had died, Timmons was able to look back at these pivotal relationships and to grasp the price of his fealty. His initial willingness to be "deferential" and act as the "spear carrier" for both these men had been the product of his traumatic intimidation by his drunken and violently inclined father, but its result was that his ability to express and assert himself was severely curtailed, long after deference had served a necessary function. Although his family and friends had feared that Mr. Timmons would enter a period of decline after losing the two pillars of his emotional life, exactly the opposite occurred. Their deaths signaled his liberation and renewal. The shared fantasy, in which he had viewed himself as the weaker next to the stronger, the passive next to the achieving, the dependent next to the self-starting, was no longer at the center of his feelings about himself. He came to intuit and renounce the rescued/rescuer fantasy (with its sado-masochistic element) in which he had participated for so many decades. Similar revisions in people's self-perception often occur after the death of a spouse, to the great surprise of friends and families who, like Mr. Timmons's, expect only the worst.

While shared fantasies imbue our friendships, our work relationships, our family connections, and our social lives, and exist at all levels of consciousness, perhaps the most common explicitly shared fantasies are sexual. Sharing of sexual fantasies may begin when one individual reveals a fantasy to a partner or when two people mutually construct a joint fantasy. For example, a middle-aged woman who had recently remarried loved to tell her new husband her sexual fantasies, mainly variations on one theme. In the central fantasy, she masturbated in the middle of a circle of enthralled men, all with erect penises. Elated by her boldness, her husband relished her ease of fantasizing and loved playing voyeur, thus joining the circle of enthralled men who surrounded her.

It turns out that *The Story of O,* one of the most frankly and astonishingly sexual books of the century, was first a fantasy that a woman set down in writing for the explicit purpose of inviting a man to share it. This was her strategy for reviving a waning love affair, for keeping her lover's interest in her alive. As "O" (now revealed to be Dominique Aury) explained to the writer John De St. Jorre: "'What could I do? I couldn't paint, I couldn't write poetry. What could I do to make him sit up?'"[10] Her solution to this age-old dilemma has a touch of Scheherazade.

> Because she knew he [her lover Paulhan] was an admirer of the Marquis de Sade and had written a learned introduction to his works, she began to draw upon her own sexual fantasies, which, she said, had begun during her lonely adolescence. The conjuncture of Paulhan's tastes and her fantasies gave her the idea of writing something.[11]

Her seduction strategy worked at both the real life and the literary level. Paulhan encouraged her to publish the stories, which proved an enduring, best-selling international sensation, and he continued his affair with her until his death.

Examples of acted out sexual scenarios are very common. Take the constructed playlets or scenarios in which the partners enact complementary roles, one partner pretending to be a prostitute, the other a john, or one partner acting out the role of sadist, the other of masochist. These joint fantasies can start simply, when one partner says, "I wonder what it would feel like to be tied up," and the other begins by merely holding her down, eventually ties her down, and so on. Shared sexual fantasies readily lend themselves to enactment in the private play zone shared by the lovers.

Prostitution is a special form of jointly enacted fantasy—in which one participant pays the other to realize a fantasy. In fact, the very concept of prostitution realizes the widespread male fantasy of having a woman on call at all times. One of the lures of visiting a prostitute is that it allows individuals to express fantasies they may be ashamed of in everyday life. Prostitution is a cultural institution designed as theater, in which prostitutes are rated on their skill at lovemaking, and perhaps more importantly on their ability to facilitate the client's fantasies, creating a kind of virtual reality. The best call girls—like the best psychotherapists—often have heightened insight into the needs and wishes of their clients. One intuitively gifted prostitute conceived the brilliant idea of tying up her paraplegic client, thereby providing a ready-made fantasy that normalized his disability.

One person may deliberately evoke a fantasy in another in order to serve his or her own purposes. Every successful confidence man or woman has an intuitive sense of the quarry's secret longings. Manipulators and scoundrels, as well as all the rest of us who succumb for brief moments to manipulative impulses, are either purposely or preconsciously acting in a way that will evoke fantasies in others to further our own ends. Ben Jonson's Volpone, a rich, childless Venetian, pretends he is dying to elicit gifts from all his potential heirs. He has a confederate, Mosca, who persuades each of the heirs apparent that he is to be the chosen one. The plot turns on the purposeful evocation of greed and the actions it breeds in the expectant "heirs." Consider another more current example: Rumors of scientific breakthroughs in, say, a biotech company may be leaked to cause a run on the stock. What is being manipulated is the extremely common get-rich-quick fantasy that makes such potential suckers of so many otherwise sensible people. One reads newspaper accounts of men who awaken fantasies of love in vulnerable, lonely women to swindle them. Some people would go so far as to argue that all advertising is a skillful manipulation of the population's widespread fantasies.

•   o   •

Intuitive or preconscious sharing of fantasies takes many forms and gives its participants a variety of satisfactions, and this holds true whether the fantasy remains in the mental arena or is acted out. One common form of fantasy gratification is achieved by the transmission of our own fantasy to someone we anticipate will live it out in our stead. This, of course, is a very common dynamic between parent and child. Consider the case of the 1950s woman, frustrated in her own ambitions to be a doctor, who raises her child to be one.

Alternately, fantasy may be gratified through bonding with someone who has already actualized one's own fantasy. This mechanism is particularly apparent among people with cross-gender disorders, as the following example illustrates. (Understanding the more dramatic fantasies and dynamics that are enacted by proxy alerts us to subtler examples in other relationships.)

I first met Ed, a married man with two grown daughters, over twenty-five years ago, when he was a participant in a research study Lionel Ovesey and I were conducting on cross-gender disorders,[12] and we have kept in touch intermittently ever since. When we met, he was a sixty-year-old transvestite, who had periodically considered undergoing a sex change operation in order to become a woman. But at that particular moment he was just recovering from the precipitous end of the first great love affair of his life in which he played a more distinctly male role than he had played in his marriage.

A year or so earlier, after having retired as captain of a tugboat, he had become the superintendent of a rental building in New York City and used that position to lease small apartments to others who, like him, had some kind of cross-gender disorder. He had fallen deeply in love with Claire, one of his tenants, who had already had transsexual surgery. Though they first met when Ed was cross-dressing full-time, self-identifying as Edna (his transvestitic identity), taking hormones to grow breasts, and contemplating sex reassignment, when he fell in love with Claire, he withdrew from hormones so he could regain his potency and become her lover. And love her he did.

The love affair changed him (at least temporarily) in a complex way: It firmly restabilized his desire to be a man and allowed him to project his fantasized female identity onto Claire and reincorporate it into himself through an (unconscious) identification with her.[13] Thus, in effect, Ed seemingly achieved the impossible—the vicarious enactment of his fantasy of becoming a woman who had been a man, which coexisted with, and assisted, his reassertion of his masculine identity in real life. These dynamics are, in a sense, an exaggeration of what occurs in the passionate phase of any romantic love affair, when unconscious and preconscious fantasies of merging are at their peak. What is particularly prominent in love is that the identification process allows us to enjoy our fantasies vicariously, that is, at one remove, without suffering guilt or anxiety. (Consider the phenomenon of dishonesty by proxy: the totally honest, upright partner whose spouse is a bit of a cheat—and who subconsciously likes it like that. And so on.)

But Ed's love affair was not destined to last. Claire ran off with a truck driver who she thought was a real he-man, and Ed staggered under the blow. Not
only was he unhappy as all spurned lovers are. Momentarily, he was unable to
sustain either aspect of his identity, male or female: the competitive defeat
undermined his masculine identity, while Claire's flight interrupted his projection of his female self onto her. Ed fell into a major depression. Gradually,
in order to stabilize himself, he reverted to hormones and began again to cross-
dress full-time, reassuming his predominantly female identity as Edna. To
bolster his female identity, he took on the role of "mother" to a lesbian couple
who also lived in his building. (In this tale of tangled fantasies, Claire's macho
truck driver lover turned out to be a closet transvestite, who spent his time in
Claire's bedroom not in lovemaking, but in trying to steal her nightgowns.
Their relationship ended on the rocks, with Claire disappointed that her truck
driver was not a *real* man after all—just another transvestite.)

Let me return to Ed, whose story is my main concern here. His childhood
had been filled with loss. In his very early years, his mother had died and then
his sister. When his father, too, died, he and his brother were taken in by an
uncle who was a shipyard rigger. The uncle and the two boys traveled around
the East Coast from shipyard to shipyard. The final tragedy in Ed's early life
was the death of his brother at the age of fifteen. This happened as the two
boys were walking across a railroad track on their way to go swimming, and
his brother was struck and killed by an oncoming train, leaving thirteen-year-
old Ed as the sole survivor in his immediate family. Disliking his uncle, he ran
away by bicycle from Pennsylvania to New York and moved in with his
maternal aunt, whose husband was a tugboat captain. So it was that Ed began
his own forty-five-year career as a tugboat captain.

Around the time that he went to live with his aunt he surreptitiously began
to wear some of her clothing, and this continued throughout his teens and
early twenties. Nonetheless, he married (when he was still a virgin), hoping
that his reliance on women's clothes, to achieve both sexual excitement and
psychological ease, would subside once he established sexual relations with his
wife. But the urge never disappeared. His wife disliked his fetishistic use of
women's clothes but learned to cope with it. Ed felt that she loved him and
that she tried to tolerate his then partial cross-dressing because she knew it
made him happy.

Growing up before cross-gender disorders became so well known to the
public, Ed was always puzzled as to what he was. He had never heard of
homosexuality, and he had no attraction to boys, only to girls. But neither had
he been a typical boy. He played with girls and did not seek out male friends
because he disliked sports and felt odd boy out. He became a loner, whose
greatest pleasure was reading.

It was through his reading that eventually—long after he married—he discovered the magazine *Sexology*. Studying that magazine, he learned that his

interest in cross-dressing was far from unique, and, shortly later, he became aware of another magazine, *Transvestia*. Only then did he discover what it meant to be a transvestite, and he had a kind of epiphany, realizing he had found the group to which he belonged. It was then that Edna was born.

Up until he read *Transvestia,* Ed wore items of female clothing surreptitiously, but never fully cross-dressed, though he did have a conscious fantasy of being a woman. Ed's is a fairly typical description of how learning about other transvestites' lives helps consolidate a tranvestitic identity: Ed was confused as to his "nature," until he accidentally came upon *Transvestia*. (Of course, it is probably impossible to grow up today with no awareness of cross-gender disorders, given the exposure to all degrees of gender-bending on national television.)

Ed also discovered through *Transvestia* that there were group gatherings of transvestites and their wives all over the country and he began to attend those "TV" parties (as they are called) once a month, fully cross-dressed. Insofar as the transvestites all respond to each other as women at such gatherings, they are participating in the enactment of a shared fantasy. Another shared fantasy often enacted at TV parties is that of "initiation" into femininity by a real woman. The woman, usually the wife of one of the transvestites, is stationed at the entrance door, where she greets the newcomer, then helps him (her) with makeup, attends to his (her) clothes, and acts in general as a kind of den mother. This "initiation" fantasy is a major theme in transvestitic pornography.[14] Underlying all transvestitic fantasies is the core fantasy of a world totally made up of women, some of whom happen to possess penises; the "lesbian" fantasy that permeates transvestites' imaginative life symbolizes the union between a woman and a man disguised as a woman. (This dynamic is the key to understanding the deepest meaning of the lesbian fantasy as it is invoked by heterosexual men who are not transvestites. At one level, the fantasizer feels powerful because he controls two women. But the defining feature of the fantasy is its virtual absence of men. The fantasizer has created a world of women, and thus found his way around threats of Oedipal rivalry. On the unconscious level, the fantasizer depicts himself as a "woman" with a penis. Because his penis is hidden, he is protected from competitive males, and he also achieves an intimacy with women denied most men. The lesbian fantasy so frequent among heterosexual men serves the same functions as the lesbian fantasy that permeates transvestitic life.)[15]

Through these meetings, Ed came to meet many transvestites, including a number who wanted to become transsexuals. Learning about transsexualism led him to flirt with the idea of a sex change for himself, though he was already in his midfifties. Here again, his fantasy was reedited via input from the outside world, for until Ed learned that others had jumped sexes, with the cooperation and sanction of the medical profession, he had never gone so far in his fantasy life as to imagine taking on some of the anatomical aspects of womanhood.

Even when Ed started to live as Edna full-time, which happened only after he started attending the TV parties, he never dreamed of leaving his wife. However, his wife tolerated his total cross-dressing less well than she had tolerated his occasional fetishistic use of female clothing, and for the first time friction entered their relationship. For business events or in the presence of his children, Ed still dressed as a man, but even clothed as a man, he now invariably wore a piece of female jewelry, generally a ring, to assert his female identity. It was at this juncture that he met Claire and their love affair unfolded, with its unhappy dénouement for Ed.

There were a dozen years when I didn't see Ed, though we corresponded. Last year, when he had just turned eighty-five, he came to see me again. It was then I learned what had happened to him after Claire. He had continued to work as a super, though in the person of Edna rather than of Ed. But once again he rented an apartment to a transsexual—this time a woman named Janet—and he soon fell in love with her. Again he gave up hormones, sent Edna packing, and resumed his life as Ed. Just before his fiftieth wedding anniversary Ed left his wife and went to live with Janet in a small town. Much to his amazement, Janet and his wife, who had been friends, remained so. (My suspicion is that his wife was relieved to have him in the male role again, even if it was as someone else's lover.) When his wife died, he married Janet. They were married by the mayor of his new little town, a source of particular pride to Ed, as was the fact that his youngest daughter and her husband stood up for him.

He was with Janet for ten years before she died. Married to her, Ed achieved one of the happier interludes of his life. The elaborate interlocking fantasy systems allowed both partners the luxury of realizing their fantasies (at least in part): Ed vicariously lived out the life of an operated transsexual, and Janet gained validation of her female identity through Ed's love—a man's love of a woman.

But Ed was not totally fulfilled. He confided to me,

I have thought of a question that may be asked. Do I have any regrets? I am going to be honest and reply, yes I do, that I did not get to be what I wanted to be. Even though I knew it would mean estrangement from my family, I believe I would have been very happy [as a woman]. The six years I was Edna were the happiest of my life. . . . The day I went with Janet was the end for Edna.

However, he has continued to live as Ed; Edna appears to have perished in the mayor's office.

Ed's early life has features common among many people with strong cross-gender identifications. They share a history of significant losses in early life with a resulting intense separation anxiety, or alternately, a history of early life illnesses also attended by high anxiety. But unlike other separation-anxious people, they bind their anxiety—or so I believe—in a fantasy of merging with their mother or a mother figure. (The underlying fantasy runs, If my mother is part of me I have her strength and I am never alone.) The fantasy of being a woman, based on an unconscious merger fantasy of being one with the mother, infuses both transvestism and transsexualism.

Ed's fantasy life is multilayered. By my understanding (based on in-depth research interviews), his basic fantasy is a merger fantasy—becoming the woman on whom he has always wanted to rely. Ed first enacted the fantasy in a small way by dressing in his aunt's clothes. (Most transvestites do not necessarily want to give up being male: they only want to imbibe the strength of the maternal figure through a kind of fantasied identification or merger with her.)

Ed's freedom to enact the fantasy of totally cross-dressing was first consolidated by exposure to the transvestite network, where it received validation. The parties that transvestites attend with their wives offer validation not just by other transvestites but by real women. Ed only began to fantasize actually becoming a woman after exposure to the possibility of sex change, particularly when he learned that the procedure was medically sanctioned—at least by one group of doctors. By making him aware that his fantasy was a literal possibility and weakening the sense of taboo attached to it, this knowledge tilted him toward enactment, but he stopped short of it.

Ed claims that he abandoned the idea of a sex change because of his age and the cost of surgery. (Underneath, he appears more tied to his male identity than he may care to admit.) But he found an indirect route to actualize the fantasy—by inverting it so that he could enjoy its actualization by someone else, first Claire and then Janet. Claire and Janet are who Ed might have become had he been younger, had he learned of transsexualism earlier, and had he been more willing to part with his masculinity. By loving a transsexual woman, he relieved himself of the necessity to enact the fantasy himself.

What happened to Ed's need for a symbiotic tie after his wife Janet's death? I believe her death probably made Ed want to touch base with me again. He has been very eager for me to make his story known, and I believe that, too, is part of his struggle to validate his quest. Just recently he sent me a New Year's card, with an illustration that may symbolize his unconscious fantasy. The card pictures a beautiful pink rose; attached to the stem of the rose and growing out from it is another perfectly formed, but smaller pink rose just beginning to unfold its petals.

Shared fantasy is ubiquitous and is essential to our development and all our ongoing relationships. Watching children in kindergarten or even in the nursery as they engage in make-believe play, storytelling, or story playing, one sometimes sees the actual social process of forming shared fantasies (or fantasy precursors) and observes their role in personality growth. One can also observe the bonding that sharing a fantasy facilitates.

Vivian Gussin Paley's *The Boy Who Would Be a Helicopter: The Uses of Storytelling in the Classroom* gives an excellent description of the sharing of childhood fantasies and the responses to that sharing. It conveys the ways shared childhood fantasies assuage individual anxieties and discontents while also promoting friendships among children.[16] In Paley's classroom, as each child tells his or her own imaginary story, the audience of other children is invited to contribute to it. Paley writes down the story and the children subsequently act it out: "Stories are not private affairs; the individual imagination plays host to all the stimulation in the environment and causes ripples of ideas to encircle the listeners."[17] Paley believes that such storytelling serves as a wider culture builder than make-believe play because it involves a larger number of participants.

Describing her class of three- and four-year-olds, Paley observes their ability to make up stories, and the wide range in the content of some of their fantasy themes:

> Amazingly, children appear to be born knowing how to put every thought and feeling into story form. If they worry about being lost, they become the parents who search; if angry, they find a hot-headed hippopotamus to impose his will upon the world. Even happiness has its plots and characters; "Pretend I'm the baby, and you only love me, and you don't talk on the telephone."[18]

Not only do the children's stories express their feelings and preoccupations (and suggest ways of handling them), but the character the child chooses as the protagonist tells us much about the self the child imagines or wishes himself or herself to be. Samantha is always a mother, Katie always stars a mother character in her stories; Simon is a squirrel who retreats to a squirrel hole whenever he feels anxious; Petey is often Mighty Mouse, and Alex a lion. Though the fantasized self-identifications in such play generally express wishes, they may be Janus-faced, looking in opposite directions, because fantasy constructs may express more than one wish or a wish *and* a defense against it. In the stories Dana tells, she is always a baby, but in make-believe play, she is always the big sister or the baby-sitter, just as Joseph is always a superhero in the block corner, but is invariably a bad guy in his stories.

While each individual child favors specific props and distinct themes—snakes, horses, imprisonment in jails or dungeons, trapdoors, monsters, princesses, danger, romance, and so forth—in joint play they incorporate one another's themes and fantasies. In Paley's classroom, once the snake had made an appearance in one child's story, it subsequently appeared in other children's stories; so, too, did the phrase "creeped downstairs," which always signified the discovery of a bad guy or monster. Paley sees this symbol sharing as a route leading to the development of a whole system of communal mythology. Over time in a nursery a culture with its own particular language and images develops, while still allowing each child to retain his or her signature style.

Paley posits play acting and storytelling as the primary reality for preschoolers and kindergartners, and their jointly authored stories as the vehicle for their bonding. Children invoke friendship and fantasy to avoid fear and loneliness, to find a comfortable relationship with people and events, and to address current concerns and future dreads. What is particularly significant is that children will relinquish part of their personal fantasies to other children's fantasies in deference to friendship (making a friend or nurturing a friendship). As Paley sees it, friendship forms in the process of shared fantasy play—play that begins with those magical words of early childhood: "Let's pretend that you're the daddy and I'm the mommy"; "You be the cop and I'll be the robber"; or "Let's play doctor." And the ability to reverse roles when necessary—"OK, I'll be the robber this time"—is often key to the ability to maintain friendships. (Similarly, the adult's facility at making preconscious adaptations to another's needs, as in "I'll be the lover today and you can be the beloved," may be critical to success in a wide range of mature relationships.)

Friendship and fantasy are the braided paths that lead children into an imaginative world of expanded possibilities. New voices and viewpoints, new ways of expressing ideas and feelings, and new techniques for solving problems overlap with their own and extend their range of responses. As Paley observes, the fantasies of any group form the basis of its culture, and "the classroom that does not create its own legends has not traveled beneath the surface to where the living takes place."[19]

In their make-believe play and storytelling, children have different gifts; some are limited to a particular fantasy, others are very inventive with story characters, others are responsive to cues. But make-believe play and storytelling provide a boost to all kinds of children—sociable, inarticulate, those who speak better than they play, those trapped in a single fantasy, and those who do not develop any one fantasy fully because they are involved in too many.

Charles, who initially appeared to Paley to be a troublemaker because of his insistent and domineering behavior with the other children, was nonetheless very popular among his peers. As Paley came to observe, one of Charles's skills was the ability to invent multiple plots and characters that his classmates could utilize. This gift can be analogized to the role of the artist in relation to the rest of the world—the fantasy producer who supplies a product to the consumer.

The case of Jason, the boy who loved helicopters, Paley's main protagonist, indicates that shared scripts are indeed routes to bonding, but that ability to share them depends on preexisting congruent or complementary fantasies. Jason, at the beginning of school, was locked into a cluster of fantasies around one single theme—pretending he was a helicopter or flying one or fixing its broken blades—which Paley characterizes as a story of "broken blades and power regained."[20] Jason seemed fixated on helicopters to the exclusion of any ability to interact with his peers.[21] But in fact the helicopters provided a partial way out of Jason's self-imposed isolation, because the image of the helicopter was very popular with the other children. In the process of borrowing it for their own stories, Jason's classmates became the instruments of the early stages of his socialization and acculturation.

One girl, Samantha, finally rescued Jason from his isolation; she chose him as her preferred "baby," almost bodily yanking him into joint play. She may have been able to do this because of the implication (in my reading if not explicitly in Paley's text) that Jason was preoccupied with a personal trauma—his relationship with his parents in the aftermath of the birth of his infant sister, Sarah. The first human he incorporated into one of his stories was a "she-baby." When he omitted her from the enacted version of his story and Paley asked why, he cried, "Sarah's not in my story." That was the first time Jason had ever mentioned the baby in school. One can only suppose that her birth and his subsequent feelings of displacement were part of his inner struggle and that Samantha gave him a way out by insisting that *he* be the baby.

Another instance of the way one child may construct a fantasy that can be borrowed and used to adaptive advantage by other children was observed by the psychoanalyst Roy Lilleskov while he was watching children in a nursery setting. There were three protagonists, a girl about one and a half years old, and a girl and a boy each about two years old. It was the birthday of one of the nursery children, but the mother who was to supply the cake was at least an hour late. The children became increasingly frustrated, hungry, and wild. The two-year-old girl had an ingenious adaptive response:

> [She] grabbed a doll, sat down at the table, and began to feed her doll. The eighteen-month-old girl, who was quite bright and reasonably well integrated, grabbed another doll, sat down next to the older girl and began to feed her doll. The two-year-old boy, who was quite disturbed and not as well advanced in his development, tried to take the doll away from one or other of them and, being prevented, accepted a substitute doll and sat down and pretended to feed himself.[22]

Lilleskov suggests that the first girl displayed creative adaptive function in her use of the doll play, which he considered a resolution fantasy. The second girl, in imitative identification, borrowed that adaptation, and, like the first girl, put it to good use, gaining considerable pleasure from her absorption in the fantasy. While the boy's behavior also had an adaptive aspect in the sense of maintaining his equilibrium, Lilleskov did not see his behavior as a comparably creative act.

The interpersonal dimension in fantasy formation is never lost. In adults, as in children, the capacity for creating adaptive fantasies (and enactments) differs from one individual to another, and within one individual over time. Some individuals are autonomously creative; others borrow the creative fantasy solutions of friends and family, using cues that emanate from interchanges with them or from their behavior. (While not exceptionally creative fantasists, the "borrowers" may be very creative in other areas.)

The fantasy co-construction and sharing that one easily observes in nursery or kindergarten between children occurs in virtually all parent-child interactions. Shared fantasies continue to form a basis of the child's adaptation as he or she grows to adulthood.

Parent-child fantasy sharing is universal, and indispensable to normal development. According to Anna Freud, the mother's feelings and fantasies about her child affect the child's psychic life so specifically that they create that child as the particular child of a particular mother[23] (as do the father's and those of other caregivers as well). Some sharing of fantasies within a family is necessary to ensure a familial "fit." The child's socialization and sense of belonging depend on the establishment of shared meaning, and one way to create shared meaning is through the process of communicating fantasy material.

Parental fantasies in the form of either subliminal or explicit communication favor some adaptations over others. For example, a parent's communication helps shape the child's sense of what is right and wrong, and therefore of what is acceptable. Adelaide Johnson's work shows how delinquency in children is most common when one parent has lapses in morality and conveys license to the child to engage in comparable lapses. The delinquent child appears to be acting out the parent's unconscious fantasy and/or directives.[24] The subliminal message (existing just below the level of consciousness) may be transmitted by a parent—even a parent trying to deliver a moral lesson—in animated anecdotes in which the protagonist is a thief or a wise guy. One father likes to tell the story of being caught stealing books when he was a teenager working in a bookstore. His manifest intention is to tell his children how frightened he was and warn them of the perils of crime. But his obvious excitement in telling the story communicates the rush he felt in the act of stealing. (As an adult, the father is honest to a fault, but some residue of his earlier preoccupation lingers.)

Very often fantasy communication occurs in the context of relating the family history—a history that always embodies the family mythology and inserts the child into it (for example, "You remind me of Uncle Dan. He always . . . "). The skeleton of the child's self-fantasy (the personal myth) may be formed by parental fantasy, such as the parent's wishful (or fearful) belief that the child is destined for greatness, crime, or ineptitude; that the child will grow up to be nurturant, polyperfect, or needy; or that the child will be exactly like—or unlike—the parent, parent's spouse, or parent's parent.

Frequently, an adult's ambitious (and sometimes grandiose) fantasies can be traced to parental inoculation. But the existence of the fantasies does not necessarily translate into their fulfillment. Among children who have been designated for great achievement, the parents' boundless indulgence, limitless admiration, and grandiose hopes may have different effects. One child may be so overwhelmed that he or she sinks under the weight of great expectations and retreats into passivity. Another may actively rebel against a perceived demand. Another child internalizes his parents' ambitions and may indeed succeed. But if the parents' expectations lead to fantasies that are too exaggerated, all accomplishment will fall short and disappointment will be inevitable. Thus a noted scientist's pleasure in his achievements may be spoiled because he did not win the Nobel Prize; the famous reporter still longs to write a critically acclaimed novel and despises journalism, and so forth. To the degree that parents require compensatory glory of their children, they put into play a series of fantasies that they cannot later rescind. Whether they become successful or not, grown children generally come to resent—and often distance themselves from—the parent from whom they acquired grandiose fantasies.

However, a parentally communicated fantasy cannot be elaborated—fleshed out—unless it corresponds to something of the child's own inner impulses, wishes, talents, and predispositions. Depending on the existence of a reciprocal need, impulse, or feeling in the child, certain parental fantasies will be rejected, others embraced. The degree to which parental fantasies can influence the child also depends on the child's feeling for its parents.[25]

An extremely common form of fantasy transmission from parent to child rests on emotional tone, for example, the contagion of anxiety and fearful fantasies. The anxiety itself may be contagious (the nervous mother begets an anxious child, whether through the gene pool or through her mode of mothering). And the anxiety binds to similar content. One patient describes herself as very like her mother in her propensity for fearful fantasies. As she remembers, her mother had always feared the worst for her, in matters large and small. For example, if she had the sniffles, her mother dreaded that she would get sick and therefore miss a special party, or flunk out of school, or perhaps even die. Her mother frequently kept her home before she was to go on a trip so there would be no possibility that she would contract a strep infection. On behalf of both herself and her daughter, she was fearful of airplane crashes or torrential rains while on holiday, and of financial disaster all the time—all vividly visualized and conveyed to her daughter. Fantasies such as these are often invoked in real life magically, to ward off the feared catastrophe: "If I think the worst it is less likely to happen." Whatever their purpose, these fearful fantasies are almost inevitably conveyed to a child. The daughter, in this case, attempted to avoid incorporating her mother's anxiety-ridden outlook, but nevertheless was still racked with anxiety and anxious fantasies well into adulthood. Even when attempting to generate a pleasant fantasy, she would feel terror creeping in: if she visualized traveling with her husband to Egypt, her initially happy visualizations of cruising down the Nile, admiring the temples, and enjoying the sunset would suddenly be interrupted by flash images of terrorist attacks—part guilt, part learning (from her mother), part identification, and part magical thinking.

Another woman was given to fantasizing her own early death often enough that she came to believe she would indeed die young. In part, this conviction was the outcome of a willed identification with her grandmother, who, though she constantly expressed hypochondriacal fantasies, lived to be ninety-five, in good health until the very end. Her adoption of her grandmother's fantasies was based on magical thinking: If she was like her grandmother, she could control fate by the same means that apparently worked for her grandmother.

Fantasy transmission is not a one-way street from parent to child. Children, reciprocally, influence their parents, though generally not to the same degree. The child is more susceptible to influence because he or she is totally dependent on the parent in early life and usually very impressed by the parent's power. Moreover, by the time the child can formulate and transmit a fantasy that might appeal to an adult, the parent's fantasy system, while still capable of ongoing evolution, is already fairly well defined. But parent-child fantasy systems do change over time, depending on what happens to both parent and child. Parents are often open to imbibing new fantasies as their children grow up and show them new ways of being in the world. Exposed to young love, seeing the new sexual freedoms and life possibilities that their children embrace, they may open the door to new possibilities for themselves.

Whatever the direction of influence, parent-child fantasy systems reverberate together. For example, fantasy systems undergo radical revision when roles are reversed and children become caregivers (parents really) for ill or aging parents. One beautiful woman, just operated on for uterine cancer, when she learned of her disease renounced her own well-developed romantic fantasies and ambitions and began to daydream that her adolescent daughter would marry an extremely wealthy man and live in a great estate, and that she, the mother, would have an elegant carriage house on her daughter's grounds. She seemed to impart to her daughter some urgency in finding a wealthy marriage partner, so that the daughter took on the task of finding a rich man (probably both to save the mother and to secure herself against the consequences of her mother's possible death). And she succeeded.

Shared fantasies extend far beyond two generations. Selma Fraiberg, in a beautiful passage, wrote: "In every nursery there are ghosts. These are the visitors from the unremembered pasts of the parents; the uninvited guests at the christening."[26] These ghosts carry the shared fantasy of an entire lineage.

•　　•　　•

Just as the scope and content of parental fantasies influence the child's fantasy constructions, the parent's own degree of ease with imaginative material and fantasy facilitate or inhibit the child's overall responsiveness to fantasy and ability to tap into unconscious material. Whether or not a child is read or told stories, for example, may affect her or his ease with preconscious fantasy material and with creative pursuits in general.[27] Encouragement or discouragement of fantasy play by the parent figure may also have profound significance in later life.

Hansi Kennedy and her colleagues[28] tell a charming story of James, a boy just short of four years old, observed at a moment of intense phallic competitiveness with his father accompanied by what are considered to be the usual fears of retaliation. He play-acted his preoccupation on a visit to his aunt, recounting to her the story of *Star Wars* and presenting a small stick that he claimed was his counterpart to Luke Skywalker's magic "life force." He required her participation by asking for reassurance that he had not inadvertently harmed himself: that is, he had not accidentally cut off his leg with the stick (that he believed he had to practice using blindfolded). Kennedy and her coworkers interpreted this vignette as an indication that the boy acquired vicarious strength through his identification with the very masculine Luke Skywalker and so overcame his sense of vulnerability. Yet his fear of losing a body part remained in his consciousness, even though he closed his eyes, trying to evade it.[29] Both the aunt and the father responded quite sensitively, the aunt by paying attention to the boy and reassuring him that both his legs were still attached, the father by refraining from interfering in the dialogue. In this instance, then, the family was able to assuage his anxiety and facilitate fantasy play.

Kennedy and her colleagues, looking at a whole range of mother-child interactions, noted that some were counterproductive to a child's immersion in fantasy play. After observing that some mothers interacted with their children in a resolutely unplayful manner, they considered several possible motives for such deficient behavior. First, some mothers did not view play as a joint activity but expected the child to play alone. Second, some mothers did not respect their child's preoccupation and pleasure in such fantasy play and interrupted. Third, some intruded and so forcefully directed the play that it was no longer fueled by the child's own fantasy material but by the mother's. Fourth, some objected to the content of the play as too childish, which I assume means too regressive or "primitive."

Kennedy and her coworkers concluded that any of these circumstances may inhibit the child's interest in fantasy play: Fantasy play that is not appropriately reinforced "becomes a source of disapproval, danger and shame."[30]

Along these same lines, Ilene Lefcourt has observed that in mother and child pairs, there is always a stage of fantasy play when the child pushes its mother to a point where she disengages from the interaction.[31] Though there is a wide range of what individual mothers consider acceptable, the mother will always set some limit, whether to regressive, sexual, or aggressive themes. Enlarging on Lefcourt's observation, one may say that a parent may err on the side of being too rigid to engage in fantasy play (as described by Hansi Kennedy), or, at the opposite extreme, too permissive, for example, by encouraging the child to engage in inappropriately sexualized play. For instance, one mother engaged in subliminally sexualized play with her six-year-old son, developing a go-to-bed mini-play in which her son sucked on her finger, while she played at pinning him down. Though it may seem a delicate balance to strike, most parents do the job quite adequately, in part by simply being attuned to the child's own wavelength. Since a child engaged in fantasy play presents a very charming picture, it can be surprisingly easy to join in.

Because shared fantasies are ubiquitous and essential to development, neurotic as well as adaptive patterns become embedded in them. Shared fantasies that are not brought to light in the course of a psychotherapy may have a deleterious effect on the outcome of that therapy unless they are explicitly recognized and introduced into the treatment process.

I first saw Andrea when she was a young woman, fresh out of graduate school and a newcomer to New York City. She felt isolated, somewhat depressed, lonely, and uncertain about what to do with her life. An attractive woman with many outstanding attributes, she had always been a good student and a good athlete (though never full-out), and she had a remarkable gift for friendship. She was charming and responsive and told a coherent story about her life. What was missing—the cause of her seeking therapy—was a sense of direction and purpose, the lack of which left her with a feeling that sometimes bordered on emptiness. While her graduate humanities program had been meaningful to her, she did not want an academic career.

She was the oldest of three children of an unusually successful father and a gifted but blatantly disturbed mother. From earliest life, she had been identified, both by herself and by her parents, as the good daughter, the one who looked out for her younger siblings, a sister Nancy and a brother Mark, and for her mother as well. As such she was gradually drawn into mediating in her parents' intense and sometimes violent quarrels. If there was anything remarkable in the family history, it was the combination of her father's passive demeanor (at home though not in business) and a major disturbance in her mother's maternal capacities. Her father, though preoccupied with his career, was intermittently very attentive and very loving, particularly to Andrea. Her mother, though a vivid and dramatic personality, had a chronic illness (ileitis) and when she was sick she had long periods during which she slept a good part of the day; these alternated with periods of overactivity concerning her children, particularly her daughters, when she very forcefully voiced her opinions about what they should and should not do, whom they should and should not see, what they should wear, eat, think, and so forth.

Despite her inhibitions, Andrea appeared to be so psychologically whole that I was inclined to believe her analysis would be straightforward and brief. And indeed we accomplished a great deal of work with apparent ease because, of course, Andrea's mode of adaptation—as the good daughter—made her a model patient. We analyzed her attachment to her emotionally seductive father as well as her almost saintlike devotion to her notoriously difficult mother. We began to understand her devotion in part as a compensation for the guilt she felt about her closeness to her father and her belief that she had stolen him from her mother.

However, after making what appeared to be very rapid analytic progress, she entered a period when no real change took place in her life. She went from promising job to promising job without any real traction that pointed her in a professional direction. Similarly, she went from promising man to promising man without any deepening of the relationship. We both began to suspect that forces other than those we had addressed were at play.

Her investment in keeping her parents' marriage intact was much deeper than any guilt about her attachment to her father could explain. She once awoke in a panic after a dream that the World Trade Center had toppled, the twin towers clearly symbolizing her parents, who loomed larger than life to her. Particularly resistant to any analysis was her utter devotion to her younger sister, Nancy, who was difficult like the mother—at best overbearing in her demands, at worst irrational in her expectations. Andrea was happy to propose that an analysis of sibling rivalry with her sister and her defense against it would be the end stage in the analytic game. But she blatantly failed to address the many ways in which she permitted her sister to take advantage of her. (She had no difficulties expounding on her overt sibling rivalry with her brother Mark.)

With the stalemate in the analysis, the patient began to experience increasing phobic symptoms. (She may have become more anxious because she was not "pleasing" me by getting "well"!) These symptoms included the outbreak of severe claustrophobia, often necessitating that the door to any room she was in, including my office, be kept open. In the course of exploring her phobias, she recovered memories of early childhood episodes in which she was overcome with the equivalent of an infantile panic attack. Yet as a child, awakening in terror, she was not free to reach out to her parents for comfort. Instead she sat outside their closed door, seeking comfort by being in the proximity of her parents' bedroom without daring to knock or call out to them. In fact, her parents had seemed utterly oblivious to the agony that she was enduring, even to this day not acknowledging that she had had a problem in her childhood. They persistently maintain the illusion of their golden, carefree, and untroubled daughter.

In contrast to the way her parents ignored her, they were unusually solicitous of her younger sister, Nancy. Her mother saw herself as almost cloned in Nancy, whom she perceived as high-strung, sensitive, potentially creative, and in need of being cared for and catered to just as she was. When as a child, Nancy became anxious and fearful of being alone, her mother was totally available to her. Andrea began to feel more and more cut off and left out. The only way she could obtain her mother's approval was through her kind behavior to Nancy, and to Mark as well, since he was an adored son.

Andrea's mother explicitly asked her to protect both Nancy and Mark from any sense of inadequacy; for example, Andrea was to shield them from any sense of being outclassed by her achievements. Her mother told Andrea that her sister was vulnerable and should not have to face the competitive threat of Andrea's being a high achiever, whether in school or horseback riding or field hockey. Both parents were also concerned that Mark's masculinity not be engulfed by his older sister's achievements. Again Andrea complied, though not consciously. What she was aware of experiencing was a loss of interest in whatever her current area of expertise happened to be. This pattern had continued into adulthood, producing a sensation of aimlessness in her professional life.

Tracing her past and current interactions with her mother, Andrea and I came to believe that her whole course of development was shaped by her assumption of the role her mother had assigned to her (with the consent of her father). Never really allowed to be a child, she played the role of her mother's mother—not her actual grandmother, who had been negligent, but the fantasied mother of her mother's desires. For example, her mother turned toward Andrea with all her problems, large and small, yet was impatient whenever Andrea mentioned concerns of her own. (Her mother's own needs stoked her demands of Andrea, and she appeared to have distinct preconscious fantasies about each of her daughters.)

As often happens in this kind of situation, Andrea began to generate a fan tasy that normalized, rationalized, and even endowed her necessary behavior with dignity: the fantasy was that the entire family's well-being depended on her nurturance and care giving. And her self-esteem—deprived of nourishment from other sources—became intertwined with her notion of herself as selfless. This was not just her own fantasy, however. It emanated from the rest of the family, from the mother in particular.

But why did Andrea comply? Andrea's compliance with her mother's demands was motivated by her Oedipal guilt, at least in part. But there was a more fundamental reason she did not rebel. In the course of exploring her infantile panic attacks, she had a flash fantasy that was a self-fantasy—what the Shanes call a global fantasy. And this self-fantasy underlies the more conscious shared fantasy. In the flash fantasy, Andrea saw herself impeded by a wall that totally surrounded her, waist-high, cutting her off from everyone else. Analyzing this image as a consolidation of many different events and conflicts in her life, she could use it to reach a new understanding of the forces that were driving her (and impeding her analysis). The wall represented the barrier between her and her parents, symbolically the closed bedroom door of her childhood.

The wall isolated her, but paradoxically it also provided safety. This image of being surrounded by a waist-high wall that locked her in and isolated her also protected her against her rage against her parents and her fear of their retaliation. This core fantasy of isolation and mutual rage, as it came more to the surface of her mind, infused her outbreak of claustrophobia. What emerged vis-à-vis discussion of the "wall" was her fear that if she were trapped in a room with someone else she would regress and become incontinent—or, alternately, lose control and express her repressed rage.

The self-fantasy, which encapsulated her sense of being cut off and abandoned, internalized as a sense of helplessness and isolation and deeply buried rage, explained why Andrea complied, why she did not rebel against her mother's demands that she submerge herself in goodness and service. By examining the global fantasy she recognized that her underlying sense of being emotionally and physically cut off had motivated her to participate in the shared fantasy, lest she be totally abandoned. Becoming the angel of the family, though it created a false sense of self, allowed her to feel connected. But being the angel was a devil's bargain. Andrea felt that she had the power to destroy by withholding nurturance from others but no power to create anything for herself. The price was that she felt cut off both from her surroundings and from her innermost self.

The shared fantasy of her as golden and giving (which protected her against the pain of the global fantasy of isolation) constituted the major resistance to progress in the analysis. Whenever she made analytic progress, Andrea felt she might have to set limits for her mother and sister and thereby risk being expelled from the magic circle of the family. Only when Andrea felt strong enough to confront her underlying fears of being cut off, unattended, isolated, and rageful, which were encoded in the global fantasy, could she gain a deeper understanding of the fantasy bonds that locked her into the crippling role assigned by her family.

What is the evidence that a shared fantasy actually existed? Was she, perhaps, alone in her view of herself as the angel of the family? I think not. It became clear from following this family for years that Andrea's family needed her to act out that role and reinforced it by giving her an esteem-boosting way to perceive it. Had there been any doubt about it, the events when Andrea eventually married, while still in treatment, illustrated the point quite clearly. As soon as she told her parents she had decided to marry, her mother—who had until then survived a tumultuous marital relationship—announced that she was divorcing.

Andrea's adaptation had worked moderately well as long as the nuclear family lived together and she played the role of the unambitious family peace-keeper. It faltered only when she began to live alone and start an independent life. Unraveling the nature of the shared fantasy—and the self-fantasy it protected her against—unshackled her, allowing Andrea to blossom professionally and to consider starting a family. Most important, it freed her to look at her family members with fewer distortions, and this, in turn, enabled her to love each of them more authentically, unencumbered by her need to be the angel of the household.

Although shared fantasies infuse every aspect of our lives, healthy as well as neurotic, psychoanalysts have given most attention to those associated with extreme pathological conditions—particularly the folie à deux. A tragic instance of the folie à deux is the relationship of the playwright Joe Orton and his lover, Kenneth Halliwell.[32] The two became lovers while students at the Royal Academy of Dramatic Arts (RADA) in 1951—"when Halliwell had everything Orton envied and lacked, his own flat, a car, a library, and education."[33] On his side, Halliwell's "possessiveness and desire to control were the result of the traumatic abandonments of his childhood."[34] So it was that they came together, Orton viewing Halliwell "as a teacher, a father and a friend. And Halliwell, an orphan, found in Orton someone willing to share his life and his dreams of glory. . . . And to educate Orton gave them both a mission and a bond. They were united in their desire to be special."[35]

Orton had first developed his drive to be outstanding as the standard-bearer of his mother Elise's vanished dreams of glory, but over time he had began to experience her as pretentious and suffocating and transferred his shared dream to Halliwell. In the beginning, Orton and Halliwell entertained the joint fantasy that they would become great actors. When this proved a dead end, they became writers instead. As Orton's biographer, John Lahr, described, "Cocooned in their room and their dream of literary success, they began to write and make a study of literature."[36] A traumatic interruption occurred when both were jailed for defacing library books; they were sent to two different prisons for six months, the longest separation they had endured since first coming together. Their responses to the separation were quite different. Halliwell was depressed and made a suicide attempt after his release, but Orton had changed in such a way that his writing was successful for the first time.

Both had believed that of the two, Halliwell was more likely to achieve fame. As Orton became the successful partner, their relationship underwent a major shift. Orton never abandoned Halliwell but tried to grasp for himself some little freedom within the relationship. When Orton began to withdraw from the increasingly unrealizable folie à deux of mutual, shared success, Halliwell became angrier and angrier, and even more disconsolate and depressed.

Orton started to keep a diary, which became a source of discord, for it included details of Orton's many sexual encounters. The diary was kept in full sight of Halliwell, who "read their punishing contents"[37] as proof that he was less and less the center of Orton's world. On August 9, 1967, Halliwell killed Orton, beating his head to a pulp, and then swallowed enough Nembutal to kill himself. As Lahr sums it up: "For fifteen years, they lived and often wrote together. They wore each other's clothes. Their wills each named the other as sole beneficiary. They shared everything except success. But on August 9, 1967, murder made them equal again."[38] Lahr makes the interesting observation that Orton had flirted with death in two ways, through his dangerous sexual encounters in public bathrooms, and more riskily in his use of his diaries to provoke Halliwell. This is not sheer speculation: Halliwell placed his suicide note on top of Orton's diary, stating that the cause of his act resided within. One might make the case that to some degree the deaths were jointly orchestrated.

Ironically, or perhaps predictably, Orton and Halliwell had jointly fantasized their violent deaths long before. In 1959 and 1960 they had collaborated on a novel, *The Boy Hairdresser* (later a play by Orton). In that book Donelly, who is the stand-in for Halliwell, fantasized that "if Peterson [the stand-in for Orton] were dead he could end it now."[39] But while "in their novel the revenge is botched," it was not botched in their real lives.[40]

Lahr suggests, referring to *The Boy Hairdresser,* "Murder was the perverse solution Halliwell had predicted for himself in fantasy."[41] This fictional anticipation of what is yet to come in the author's life is fairly common[42] and confirms the role fantasies play in our construction of our lives.[43]

A classic fictional example of the folie à deux is one of the subplots in *Sunset Boulevard.* The focus of the drama is the relationship between the aging silent film star Norma Desmond and Joe Gillis, the struggling young writer she takes to bed, tries to possess, and eventually kills when he tries to leave her. One reviewer describes them as an odd but repulsive pair: "If she's a spider, he's a leech."[44] But the relationship between Norma Desmond and her butler, Max von Mayerling, is perhaps the more interesting one. Desmond has for years been able to deceive herself about her waning popularity—she believes she is still the world's reigning star—because Max sends her fan letters to perpetuate the illusion of her ongoing fame. Each evening, they ritualistically screen one of her famous silent films. Together they are the keepers of the flame, cherishing her brilliant career as a silent film star. In an extremely chilling dénouement, it emerges that Max, Desmond's "butler," had once upon a time been both her first husband and the director of her early films; both now live to preserve the vanished glory of her reign as the great dramatic actress and femme fatale of the silent screen. Their profoundly symbiotic relationship crystalizes around their shared fantasy of immortality, based on Desmond's "immortal" star status.

•   •   •

Shared fantasy infuses our lived lives because it permeates all our important relationships. Fantasy serves both as a mode of communication between people and a significant component of the adhesive that binds them. But shared fantasy is not restricted to our personal relationships; it also links us to small groups, and ultimately, in the more expansive form of the "culturally shared" fantasy, to the larger world. Fantasies, then, are private *and* shared, connected to both our inner world and our familial, social, and cultural milieu. They link our inner reality to the world of culturally shared fantasy; in so doing, they create the "reality" in which we live.

7

GENDER AND SEX: PSYCHOLOGICAL AND CULTURAL SCRIPTS

As children mature, fantasy envelops or narratives permeate their environment, not only through their immediate contact with relatives, friends, and peers, but also through their exposure to fairy tales, novels, films, television, pop versions of history, and other cultural sources.[1] They are exposed to, and participate in, the same conscious and preconscious fantasies as others in the world around them and become acculturated to that world, just as in their early years participation in shared fantasy and fantasy play, as described by Vivian Paley, link them to the worlds of the family and the nursery school. Some of that culture-based fantasy reflects mainstream values, but some of it, particularly when the culture is in flux, subtly subverts those values. Thus depending on the specifics of time and circumstances, fantasy can play either a conservative or an evolutionary role.

The culture expresses its mythic themes in many forms and communicates them in many ways. Those that resonate on more than one level are more likely to become part of the child's world view, available for incorporation into fantasy. Bruno Bettelheim has written an entire book, *The Uses of Enchantment,* on the way in which one kind of cultural product—fairy tales—speaks to the preconscious and unconscious minds of children.[2] Because fairy tales carry messages from which children can garner solutions to their conflicts and shape scenarios for the future, they are powerful enough to become culturewide transcripts for dreams and fantasies.

The tendency to look to cultural products for our self-images, to use them to express our personal myths, may continue throughout life. Take a typical example of how an underlying need or wish finds narrative expression through an identification with the protagonist of a novel or fairy tale. I call a friend. I tell her that I am writing about fantasies and that I want her to tell me one of hers. She says she is absolutely sure that the first thing that comes to her mind will be her deepest fantasy. Suddenly she says:

> Do you remember that Come-as-a-Fantasy party? Do you remember I came as Rima the Bird Girl? It makes me blush now. Rima the Bird Girl was a character in, I believe, a Judson novel. This story has always haunted me, felt familiar to me. Rima the Bird Girl goes and lives in the forest and learns a special language to talk to the animals; I don't know why, perhaps her parents reject her. Only after she is a grown woman does a man-boy come into the forest. She cannot talk to him because she only speaks the animal language. But through his patience and understanding he learns to speak her language and takes her back into the world.

Listening to her retelling of this fictional work, I remember how later, some years into her marriage, my friend—whom I will call "Rima"—gave a birthday party for her husband and he showed off the birthday message she had written to him, penned on a postcard that depicted a man rescuing a beautiful young woman from drowning. It stuck in my memory because Rima appeared to me such an earth mother that it seemed ludicrous for her to think she needed rescuing. But the postcard and the Rima-the-Bird-Girl fantasy expressed her inner truth—her wish to be made whole through an outside agency. This is an example of how a central feeling state gets expressed in a work of popular fiction that the fantasizer sees as the story of her life. In her case, the Rima-the-Bird-Girl identification and fantasy found expression in a love affair and marriage structured around the longing to be rescued and subsequently dependent—a fantasy that was in the 1960s (and to some degree still is) common to many women. Such a fantasy would not, however, appeal to most men, at least not at the conscious level.

INFLUENCES AND PRESSURES ON GENDER DICHOTOMY

From earliest life, different scripts are provided for girls and boys, for women and men. And the two sexes generally grow up dreaming different dreams, incubating different fantasies. While girls have traditionally dreamed of romantic love, marriage, motherhood, and other outlets for bonding and for delivering tender, nurturant care, boys have fantasized quest missions, either feats of individual derring-do or group exploits, on the playing field or the battlefield. Just as "Cinderella" and "Sleeping Beauty" speak to female dreamers about their hopes for the future, so "Jack and the Bean Stalk" and "Sindbad the Sailor" speak to male dreamers.

While some fantasies are common to both sexes, in general, the fantasy scripts call for Ulysses to go forth and have adventures, Penelope to wait faithfully behind. Both psychologists and psychoanalysts have been reporting on these gender dichotomies for decades. By 1904 Theodate Smith had already published work on the psychology of daydreams that noted the sex differences that occurred at different ages.[3] He observed that young children often used fairy tales as the narrative spine of their fantasies, and that even when both sexes used the same stories to frame their fantasies, girls and boys differed in their use of the original material. Responding to the story of Aladdin, for example, nearly all the girls retained the original materials in their fantasies, preserving the magic carpet qua carpet, whereas boys transformed the carpet into flying machines or balloons. According to Smith, as children grew older and began to develop independent interests, boys' fantasies revolved around their exploits as athletes, explorers, or cowboys. Girls might fantasize travel, but only if it were comfortable and deluxe, not adventurous and exploratory. In general, girls were less daring.

In adolescence, future-oriented daydreams—generative fantasies—revealed comparable gender differences. Boys dreamed of achieving honors in military or naval service, law, medicine, politics, music, acting, and so on. Girls, on the other hand, dreamed of "useful womanhood," a term that encompassed their future duties as wives and mothers or their roles in other nurturant endeavors (teaching and nursing). And just as fairy tales had provided raw material for the child fantasist, so, too, were teenagers' books frequent sources of plot material for the adolescent fantasizer. Implicitly if not explicitly, Smith's work presents us with a model for the incorporation of cultural narratives into daydreams.

Smith's observations about gender differences are similar to those of Freud made in 1908.[4] In a passage that telescopes extensive information about daydreaming, Freud noted:

> These motivating wishes vary according to the sex, character and circumstances of the person who is having the phantasy; but they fall naturally into two main groups. They are either ambitious wishes, which serve to elevate the subject's personality; or they are erotic ones. In young women the erotic wishes predominate almost exclusively, for their ambition is as a rule absorbed by erotic trends. In young men egoistic and ambitious wishes come to the fore clearly enough alongside of erotic ones.[5]

Freud believed these differences to be innate, not cultural. But it has turned out that he was wrong.

Nonetheless, Freud did appreciate that conscious fantasies were malleable, responding to the subject's shifting impressions of life and changes in situation,[6] and that many fantasies can evolve or adapt over time. In Freud's model a fantasy does not necessarily repeat itself unchanged; it is subject to modification in response to changes in either the inner life of the individual or external circumstances.

As it turns out, fantasies evolve not just over the life of one individual, but from era to era. And knowledge of this characteristic allows us to examine the impact of history on the psyche. To determine the influence of the surrounding culture on fantasy, it is useful to watch for any shift in fantasy content that might correspond to a significant cultural change. The women's movement, dating from the 1970s, presents a natural experiment, so to speak. By drawing on various contemporary sources, we can explore the nature and extent of the influence of feminism—if any—on the content of gender-related fantasy. Do men and women today entertain fantasies that differ from those of earlier generations?

Some theorists had anticipated that the women's movement would produce an almost global change in women's fantasy life, whereas others assumed that any change would await a radical reconstitution of the family. In fact, some fantasies have undergone relatively rapid and profound transformation, while others—and not necessarily those one might expect—have been almost completely resistant to change.

It came as an unwelcome surprise to some feminist theorists, for example, that "politically incorrect" fantasies—those incorporating such themes as masochism and rape—remained unchanged, even in the minds of those who disapproved of and hated their own fantasies. What are the possibilities for social change, they worried, if certain "retrograde" fantasies persist, even when the fantasizer herself wishes to repudiate them? What does it mean when many women (and men too) continue to be aroused by sexual fantasies whose content is intellectually repellent to them?

At first glance, the persistence of these retrofantasies appears incompatible with contemporary gender theory, which posits that gender is a cultural construct rather than a biological given. Since wishes that have been constructed should be amenable to reconstruction, sexual fantasies ought to be changeable. Instead, it appears that the construction of gender—at least as regards many fantasies—produces "a pattern of development . . . which seems to fix things forever."[7]

Yet gender *is* to a great extent a cultural construct. Culture impacts on fantasy formation at the deepest levels of the psyche. It plays a critical role in fantasy formation during that period in earliest childhood when gender identifications as male and female, masculine and feminine, are formed. In fact, our basic gender identifications appear to be almost completely culturally mandated. And through these identifications we become socialized to our gender role. But while gender is scripted in early life (rather than inborn), only certain gender fantasies can be rescripted. This means that strong conservative forces come into play once fantasies are formed.

Before we can explore how some gender fantasies are rescripted in response to cultural changes, we need to examine our core fantasies as they are related to, and are informed by, issues of gender and sexuality. Only then can we begin to explore the reasons why certain gender fantasies either *are* or *are not* mutable, and how culture acts to rescript those that are.

FORMATION OF GENDER IDENTITY

In the past, health professionals and theorists held that the female sex was the emotionally and physically weaker of the two sexes. The female, an 1827 report explained, "is far more sensitive and susceptible than the male and extremely liable to those distressing afflictions which for want of some better term have been determined nervous." This vulnerability to emotional distress resulted from the female's anatomy and reproductive biological processes, which, according to the theorists of the time, made her genetically susceptible to mental stresses and "weak" personality traits. The origins and development of femininity and masculinity received little attention, because they were assumed to be biological, despite the fact that the characteristics that defined femininity and masculinity were not the same across cultures or in different historical epochs.

The idea that the existence of personality differences between the sexes was something that required a psychological explanation was a major intellectual leap, and Freud must get the credit for it. But, brilliant though he was, he was no more free of his era's biases than his contemporaries, and his explanations were limited accordingly. He believed that masculine personality traits were the norm. Women, he hypothesized, "retreat" into their feminine personality traits when they discover at a very early age that they cannot be the men he believed they would naturally want to be. His explanation of female psychology was based on his theory of "penis envy," in which he hypothesized that as soon as a little girl discovers she lacks a penis, she naturally and normally retreats into a dependent, passive, masochistic, and childish personality pattern. Freud believed that this personality pattern was normal, inevitable, unchangeable, quintessentially feminine, appropriate, and desirable for all women.[8] He made exceptions for his female disciples, whose "unresolved masculinity complexes"—he believed—allowed them to excel in the field.[9]

Both Juliet Mitchell[10] and Nancy Chodorow[11] have pointed out that Freud's theory, which essentially posits that man is born while woman is made, is not only incorrect and sexist but inconsistent because it fails to treat masculinity and femininity as parallel constructs. And decades earlier, predating all the feminist critiques of Freud, Freud's contemporaries, Karen Horney and Ernest Jones, had noted early differences in the behavior of boys and girls which manifested themselves long before the children would have been able to conceptualize the anatomic distinction, and they came to a different conclusion from Freud's. They asserted that both men and women were born, not made: that is, that masculinity and femininity were both biologically innate. This analysis was based on their belief that both males and females were intrinsically heterosexual.[12]

Subsequent observations have confirmed Horney's and Jones's remarks about early behavioral differences in females and males, which appear as early as the end of the first year. But their explanations, like Freud's, have ultimately proved incorrect, and for similar reasons: They, too, gave too much priority to biology, to anatomy, and to perceptions of genitals and genital sensations as the primary determinants of gender development and sexual object choice. The preponderance of current research suggests that sexual object choice is acquired, not innate.[13] While they were right in giving the same weight to "primary" femininity as to "primary" masculinity, correctly perceiving them as parallel constructs, designating them as innate or biological obscures the complexity of gender development.

For every person, the sense of oneself as female or as male erects the scaffolding around which personality develops and behavior takes shape. Not only do little girls and little boys go their separate psychological ways before they are old enough to recognize that they have different sexual organs, as both Jones and Horney observed, but the differences may originate months before birth. After a certain point in fetal life, male and female brains develop somewhat differently, apparently leading to some of the differences we see in behavior, including greater male aggressiveness and perhaps such female tendencies as the nurturing behavior little girls demonstrate in doll play. Nonetheless, these differences are relatively modest, and most of what society considers masculine or feminine behaviors are not inborn.

John Money and his colleagues demonstrated that the first and the most crucial step in gender development is the child's self-designation (in accordance with labeling by the parents) as male or female. This self-designation (core gender identity) arises in agreement with the sex of assignment; core gender is the child's resulting sense, unconscious as well as conscious, of belonging to one or the other sex.[14] Gender differentiation is observable by the end of the first year of life and, under normal circumstances, immutable by the third.[15] Studies of children whose biological sex is ambiguous or unclear at birth because of abnormal prenatal development show that as these children grow up, they by and large develop the traits and identities of the sex in which they are raised—the sex of assignment—even when the assigned sex is opposite from the genetic sex.

Consequently, *core gender* is believed to be primarily socially constructed, derived from learning experiences, and it is a profound part of one's identity by the third year of life. Once core gender is established, the child locates the "appropriate" same-sex objects for imitation and identification and develops along lines that the surrounding society recognizes as either masculine or feminine.[16]

Gender identity, however, is different from core gender; it refers not to the distinction between male and female, but to that between masculinity and femininity. Gender identity encompasses such culturally determined attributes as interests, mannerisms, emotional responsiveness, and to some degree aggressiveness (though the level of aggressiveness may be tied to a hormonal component). In addition to such outward manifestations of role, the feminine-masculine polarity also organizes the individual's self-image, the belief that one is feminine or masculine, as measured against the prevailing cultural norm. Consequently, gender identity is a very important part of self-identity.

Although its roots are established in the first years of life, gender identity is not a static self-representation; it develops and fluctuates well into adulthood. It is a dynamic, functional self-representation, modified by sexual development, psychic conflict, and self-evaluation of gender performance, and varying with each individual's motivation and capacity to adhere to the societally prescribed gender role at any given time.[17] (And here there is considerable room for complexity and for cultural input and change.)

Depending on gender attribution, different basic fantasies develop. Some of these fantasies are rooted in the asymmetrical patterns of the relationships of early life; for example, the basic fact of having a primary caregiver who is either of the same sex or the opposite sex. Others arise from the distinct Oedipal configurations of girls and boys. The two sexes experience differently configured conflicts, rivalries, and longings, with resulting differences in unconscious and conscious fantasy.

Self (or core) fantasies that are distinctive for males and females are set into motion.[18] Young children form a mental image (representation) of themselves and of the people most important to them as gendered; they also form representations of the interactions between them, their relationships, and even their dialogues. These mental representations of role relationships are a major component in the fantasies that children eventually form.[19] The gendered story line that is most fully developed takes shape during the Oedipal phase, its key components depending on how the child identifies with, competes against, and loves and hates each of its parents, issues that in turn depend on the sex and sexual preference of the child.[20]

Another important reason that so many of us opt for the dreams "appropriate" to our sex has to do with the nature of fantasy. Hoping to realize our fantasies, we scan our environment from earliest childhood on to see which ones have the best chances of being actualized. We come to recognize that the successful realization of a fantasy is more likely insofar as it is gender consonant.

Oedipally tinged and structured self-fantasies are essentially unchangeable. But other gender fantasies also tend to be immutable, for at least three reasons.

First, many gender-dichotomous fantasies use imagery rooted in different bodily experiences and body parts. Second, some fantasies may be stoked by hormonal fuel. Third, the culture exerts a major pressure to gender conformity, in fantasy as in life.

THE INFLUENCE OF BODY IMAGE AND FUNCTION

To the degree that fantasy is expressed in body parts and functions, there is a conservative bias to fantasy: That is, it is harder to change. Consider the following fictional fantasy, culled from a novel, which shows how body functions provide gender-distinct envelopes, even for impulses, feelings, and wishes that are universal. No man could fantasize as did the fictional woman character who, upon getting her menstrual period during a service in an Orthodox synagogue, muses:

> I was directed to a bathroom with a bare light-bulb, slung on a chain above a green toilet. I looked down at the dark blood gathering in heavy drops at the vaginal opening. As these drops splashed into the bowl below, the water streaked pink like a sunset, then darkened further into a deep maroon. Dark red like my mother's lipstick and fingernails, like Eve's apple, dangerous but delicious and fascinating. I looked around for toilet paper but there was none. Damn them all, I thought. What if I walk calmly upstairs onto the first floor, past the men. . . . What if I go quickly past them before they can spot me and where the white satin covers the Ark, where the Torah is waiting—what if I climb into the Ark and sit on the Torah and bleed and bleed away, letting my blood seep into the sacred pages, soil away, bleed out the letters, left to right, marking the rhythms of the year? I bleed and I bleed and the other women behind the curtains hear the commotion and dare to peek. Then they come, come, all the unclean ones, quickly down the stairs, and sit with me. And the white satin of the Ark turns to red, "murderers" the man screams and the rabbi faints in his chair.[21]

What seems to invoke the character's fantasy is her anger, first, at being sequestered in the synagogue in the balcony with the other women and, second, at finding no toilet paper. That is, she is designated as second-class and, furthermore, provided for inadequately. (Were this a real person, one would look for some earlier experience that primed her to feel second-class and neglected.)

The envelope of this fantasy is quintessentially female, drawn from the memories and images of a cyclical female experience, even though its underlying feelings and impulses—resentment, envy, murderous rage, revenge, and restitution—are, of course, universal and could be expressed in alternative ways, some of them sexual. For example, a man feeling slighted or passed over might invoke a rape fantasy—with himself as rapist—as restitution for his deflated narcissism. While culture may play a role in the punishment-through-menstruation fantasy (insofar as the character's resentment in the above scene stems from her being put in a kind of purdah), nonetheless body experiences and personal relationships determine the form the fantasy takes.

The fantasy of havoc-through-menstruation is not common, however, primarily because it is "fantastic"—that is, it has little real possibility of enactment and thereby loses some of its power. In contrast, a man's rape fantasy is more potentially realizable, and thus more widespread, even among those to whom enacting that fantasy would be completely anathema. (Another factor in the relative prevalence of these fantasies is that the penis can be invested as an instrument to express rage early in life, whereas menstruation does not begin until a girl has already acquired a whole repertoire of other expressions of anger.) And yet, I do know of a variant of the menstruation fantasy that was not only entertained but enacted. A young woman with an Orthodox Jewish background visited the Lower East Side every month during her period. Her mission was to touch each shop owner, knowing he would be horrified to be touched by an "unclean" woman, were he aware of it. She felt powerful, and her thirst for revenge was quenched by the knowledge that she, a menstruating woman, considered an untouchable, was "tainting" extremely religious Jewish men.[22]

Like the menstruation and rape examples, many fantasies are sex-specific because they invoke female or male genital and reproductive organs in their scripts even when they express universal feelings and underlying motives. Such gender-dichotomous fantasies may seem to address issues unique to each sex, but in fact their motives are nonsexual and common to both sexes. In essence, males and females have "different modes of mastery" (to use Doris Bernstein's apt phrase)[23] to assuage similar problems and gratify virtually identical desires, and these biologically dictated modes of mastery are incorporated in fantasy narratives.

THE INFLUENCE OF HORMONES

In childhood, boys engage in aggressive fantasies much more frequently than girls, as evidenced in their make-believe play. As one mother, a reporter, tells the story:

> I was nursing our new baby the other day when guilt—the amphetamine of the working-mom—prodded me to turn to my attention-starved four-year-old son with an offer. "Tell ya what, hon," I said, my voice a little too eager, "When the baby is finished eating, we'll read a book. OK?" . . . "Nah," Taylor responded with that boyish shrug, the swaggering shuffle passed on like a bad suit from one generation of pre-school boys to the next. "I have a better idea. . . . *Let's fight bad guys!*"

The mother goes on to reflect: "Bad Guys. They entered our lives about a year ago, and I'd venture a calculation that they will be with us in one form or another for close to another decade—as will the guns, grenades, swords and rocket launchers needed to defend against their onslaught."[24]

Male aggressive fantasies may be the result not just of purely cultural or psychological phenomena ("the swaggering shuffle passed on . . . from one generation . . . to the next") but of hormonal influences as well. In boys, a high level of assertive aggressive play is seen cross-culturally. This is also true in other mammalian species. General opinion has it that this assertion/aggression may well be due to prenatal exposure to the male hormones known as androgens. For males, aggressive sexual fantasies may serve to bind and rationalize free-floating, hormonally primed aggression.[25]

Heeding the advice that the games of aggression so beloved by boys may be normal and healthy for children, the mother in the vignette just cited worked out her qualms by moving from realistic-looking toy guns to Ninja Turtle swords and Power-Rangers. But whether the child deploys a plastic machine gun or, as one little gun-deprived boy was observed doing recently, a banana, boys do seem to require toys that allow them to express their aggressions. A therapist in a school for troubled children describes the adaptive purpose these toys may serve. Recounting a recent conversation with a thirteen-year-old boy in which he asked the child why he liked playing with X-men, he quoted the child as answering, "Wolverine is wild and he needs Cyclops and Professor X to get him under control." Asked which character he resembled, the boy responded "Wolverine," but when asked which character he wanted to be like, he replied, "Cyclops, I want to be under control too."[26]

Later in childhood and in early adolescence, cops and robbers, cowboys and Indians, and war are frequent fantasy preoccupations in make-believe play. Remember in the film *Born on the Fourth of July* the passion with which the Tom Cruise character (as a boy) participated in war games, so poignant because we know he later becomes paraplegic due to war injuries sustained in Vietnam. These "Let's fight the bad guy" fantasies are not necessarily dress rehearsals, but it is probably safe to say that they can be reinvoked as antidotes to fear and feelings of depression and helplessness later on in life.

Comparable fantasies, and the behaviors that go with them, can be observed in girls with the adrenal genital syndrome (AGS), in whom the adrenal cortex does not synthesize cortisol but releases too much androgen, the hormone believed to account for masculine sexuality. These girls are born with genital masculinization, including an enlarged clitoris that may be mistaken for a penis (at least in the days before genetic sex typing). Even when operated on at birth (surgically feminized), girls with AGS are different from other girls in specific ways: They display higher physical energy, prefer rough play, live as tomboys, are career oriented, and engage in few maternal rehearsals (doll play). In other words, a hormonal effect appears to influence some of the behaviors that comprise gender identity and gender fantasies as well. Nonetheless these girls by and large grow up to assume "normal" female roles.

Hormones also seem to influence sexual behavior, as evidenced by the sexuality of late-treated women with AGS. These women tend toward a sexuality more typically masculine than feminine in terms of its formal characteristics: They have more erotic dreams resulting in orgasm than other females, they are more responsive to visual stimuli, and they display what investigators have portrayed as high sex drive (more like the male profile).

However, these women, who are raised as females from birth, do not view themselves as masculine in either gender or sexuality. In their ultimate consolidation of gender identity they adapt to "feminine" norms, substituting more "appropriately" feminine pursuits and fantasies. And their erotic fantasy preoccupations correspond more to feminine than masculine models. In fact, the women before treatment were disturbed by—and, after treatment, glad to be rid of—those manifestations of typically masculine sexuality that they themselves viewed as masculine—their clitoral hypersensitivity and tendency to initiate sexual encounters very frequently.[27] According to the sex researcher John Money, "The imagery of the erotic thoughts and desires is all suitably feminine in keeping with the sex of rearing and the psychosexual identity." More recently, however, Money reported that one group of AGS women had a higher incidence of homosexuality than a control group.[28]

Thus, while the studies on pseudohermaphroditic or intersexed patients establish the primacy of endocrines in shaping certain formal characteristics of sexuality and of personality traits and interests as well, they also establish the primacy of socialization in shaping the overall content and direction of gender identity, eroticism, fantasies, and life plans. In other words, socialization most often seems to override hormonal predisposition.

THE CULTURAL PRESSURE TO GENDER CONFORMITY

The third, perhaps most profound, factor that preserves gender differences in conscious fantasy life is the cultural pressure to gender conformity. For most of us, the psychology of gender is in part, the psychology of conformity. Even when men and women experience the same underlying conflicts or wishes, they form different fantasies, mobilizing gender-specific scripts that maintain gender role identity. The surrounding culture plays a dual role in this process: It indicates what is acceptable—and thus more likely to be achievable—and it provides raw materials for depicting these aims in fantasy form.

By providing narrative content that can link up with preconscious wishes and shape story line accordingly, the culture influences both the scripting and the rescripting of fantasies. The familial interactions of early life reinforce a person's access to or suppression of fantasy material and dictate which material is suppressed. To the degree that a person's fantasies are dissonant with the culture's prescriptions and injunctions, and that conformity or conventionality is important to the fantasizer, he or she may suppress fantasies or at least redraft them into more acceptable story lines.

Sometimes parental pressure is explicit. One of my friends, a natural-born fantasist if ever there was one, longed to be an actress. Here is her memory of how one of her dreams was squashed:

> I was born acting. It was the only escape from the dreary prison of my limited life. Inescapable boundaries were everywhere—the hills, the church, Mother's fears, Daddy's grimy job, poverty. Very early I learned to speak with accents befitting my character of the day—imaginary British was my best. With a blink of the eye I could dress in glorious outfits and deck any room with garlands of roses and baskets of lilies. Play-acting, I could be almost anyone, travel anywhere. I could be a great lady or terribly naughty without fear of punishment for either.
>
> And if I could become an actress, perhaps I could truly escape to somewhere where the world was. I was thirteen when I noticed a small announcement in the regional newspaper for the national search for a young girl between thirteen and eighteen years old to play Joan of Arc in a new film. Auditions were to be held in Memphis. I counted my savings, fifteen dollars. It was six weeks off and I figured I could increase my cache by another five dollars. With Daddy's railroad pass travel would be free, so surely it would be enough.
>
> The school library had nothing, no Joan, but the town reading room produced a biography and an obscure play. I read, I memorized, I wrapped my braids around my head and I dreamed of suffering for the betterment of my countrymen and the salvation of their souls.
>
> Two weeks before the most important day of my life, I risked telling my mother about my plan. She didn't cry, she howled, she screamed, she took to her bed yelling "Oh, my God, what did I do to deserve this?" She went on "Acting is a dirty business. Men do awful things to young girls. I won't let you go, because I will lose you to that evil world—and then what will become of us?"
>
> My mother was so certain of the catastrophe that would befall me that I began to feel that Joan had turned into real life and that if I got the part I would be tortured and burned. That inhibition that she put into me about acting has lasted my whole life so I had to find another way to go.

As a courtroom lawyer, she eventually did find a way to incorporate her theatricality into her life's work.

This is a straightforward account of how external pressures act upon our self-fantasies. It contains a small gender component: The girl's mother is motivated in part by her fear of what "awful things [men do] to young girls." Generally speaking, the way in which external pressures affect our gender-related fantasies is a much more complex matter. Parents, of course, play a role in this, because they do treat children somewhat differently according to sex. But children are very sensitive to the culture at large and generally engage in much more stringent sex stereotyping than they ever encounter in their homes; in fact, they become veritable gender police when it comes to monitoring their own behavior and that of their peers. Effeminate boys especially are teased, ostracized, and humiliated. While taunting and teasing may not suppress effeminacy in an extremely effeminate boy, the fear of being called a sissy certainly acts as a powerful deterrent in all other boys. To a lesser degree, the young gender police also monitor conformity in girls.

The psychoanalysts Joseph Sandler and Anne-Marie Sandler have described in general how suppression and, consequently, conformity is mediated:

> As the child develops the increasing capacity to anticipate the shaming and humiliating reactions of others . . . so he will become *his own* disapproving audience and will continually internalize the social situation in the form of . . . censorship. Only content that is acceptable will be permitted through to consciousness. It must be *plausible* and not ridiculous or "silly." In a way [this censorship] is . . . a narcissistic censorship. . . . The narcissism involved often tends to center around fears about being laughed at, being thought to be silly, crazy, ridiculous or childish—essentially fears of being humiliated.[29]

Consequently, the potential pleasure of realizing a gender dissonant fantasy is greatly diminished. Thus, as the growing child or adolescent discovers that his or her fantasy is at odds with the gender prescriptions of family culture, suppression or transformation of certain virtually universal fantasies takes place.

And yet, despite all these pressures toward gender conformity in everyday life, there still exists in the preconscious and unconscious ranges of the mind a complicated, multilayered interplay of wishes, impulses, and fantasies that derive from each individual's specific psychobiography and multiple identifications.[30] Thus, against what appears to be a powerfully "dichotomous, categorical expression of gender," each individual has a countertendency that may allow for more creative possibilities than are at first apparent.[31] This diversity, this lack of unity, in the unconscious and preconscious—in contrast to the conformity at the surface—is a potential locus of change, as I shall argue later. In essence, then, the pressure toward gender conformity leads to the suppression of many fantasies, but not necessarily to their eradication.

FEMALE FANTASIES

In conjuring up images of the lives they want to live, women, like men, have always entertained numerous fantasies, but these were generally restricted to traditionally "feminine" areas. For example, in her memoirs, Madame de La Tour du Pin, born in 1770, writes:

> From my earliest days I had a feeling that adventures lay in store for me. My imagination was continuously inventing changes of fortune. I visualised myself in the most unlikely situations. I wanted to know everything that might be useful in any imaginable circumstance. My maid went to visit her mother two or three times each summer, and I made her tell me everything that went on in her small village. For several days on end, I would think of nothing but what I would have to do if I were a peasant, and I envied the lot of those I often visited in the village. They were not forced, as I was, to hide their tastes and ideas.[32]

She goes on to say that she had no taste for sentimental novels but was herself enamored of Abbé Prévost's romance *Cleveland,* which described acts of great devotion. During her mother's illness she "was so anxious to practice it [the devotion] that [she] longed to give [her] mother daily proofs of it."[33] Like Madame Du Pin, most women in earlier eras have fantasized "adventures" more limited than men's, typically having to do with love (the "erotic" fantasies described by Freud), acts of devotion (as quoted above), or social advancement. Fantasies of individual achievement, however, were for the most part beyond their ken.

Until recently those women who might aspire to high levels of achievement found their daydreams of glory counterbalanced by fearful fantasies in which their accomplishments caused them to be rejected or passed over by men. Their fears were quite realistic. Women had little or no power or socioeconomic independence, and their welfare and security in life depended entirely on their marriageability and their ability to accept and submit to the authority of their husbands. In Victorian culture, for example, unmarried middle-class women were viewed as a "surplus of women," constituting a social and economic problem that was frequently alluded to in the press. The woman who was psychologically dependent on men, who did not assert herself, and who was reluctant to voice her own interests if they conflicted with the needs or demands of her husband was expressing a feminine adaptation to the realities of her life that men found very attractive. Women gave up ambitious fantasies because of fear of losing the opportunity for *female* fulfillment. For a woman to hold on to ambitious wishes in those years would have been counterproductive. Such wishes could only end in frustration, humiliation, and despair. This is one of the major mechanisms by which cultural conformity was—and still is—reinforced.

But as times have changed, the scope of fantasy content has broadened. Because some career paths were open to them earlier than others, women engaged in fantasies pertaining to *those* occupations first. For example, women dreamed of being nurses, teachers, actresses, singers, or even glamorous figures in the demimonde, long before they were able to dream about being

doctors, lawyers, entrepreneurs, or managers. Nowadays even a fairly traditional female fantasy—that of being a fashion model, for example—incorporates broader aspirations. Thus models who were once idolized only for their
beauty and allure are now fantasy figures for girls who aspire not just to their
looks but to their independence, their travel opportunities, and their ability to
use their assets to launch careers as entrepreneurs.

Not too surprisingly, generative fantasies relating to work and career ambitions are the ones that have changed the most in response to economic reality—
the fact that more women are in the workplace—and to the newly emerging
values and beliefs of feminism. ("Not too surprisingly" because these fantasies
do not depend for their imagery or their inspiration on body parts, early developmental processes, or hormones.) Now women too fantasize about professional triumphs, accolades, and awards. Thus, no one today would support
Freud's contention that women's ambitions are generally expressed through
erotic longings. His observation of 1908 that women fail to generate ambitious
fantasies had relevance to his culture, but not to ours.

In fact, even in eras when such fantasies were unrealizable, they did exist in
some women, flickering briefly into consciousness, only to be quickly suppressed out of fear of ridicule or an inner sense of violating the dictates of femininity. But sometimes a residue of the fantasy material persisted in a more
acceptable form. For example, one woman, now in her late forties, remembers
that as a prepubescent girl she fantasized with equal frequency about being a
heroic soldier and a sought-after sweetheart. As she entered the teen years, she
condensed the soldiering fantasy with the sweetheart fantasy to create a femme
fatale fantasy in which she wielded power vicariously through her seduction
of a ruler or magnate, a man over whom she had sexual and romantic control.
Her fantasy incorporated the wishes that underlay her heroic soldier fantasy—
wishes for narcissistic aggrandizement, power, and aggression—and expressed
them more consonantly with prevailing feminine gender stereotypes, which
meant that all the aggressive content of her longings had to be channeled
through a man. The remnants of the soldier fantasy are perhaps to be found
in the martial music that always plays in her mind (unaccompanied by any
narrative) at moments when she is about to assert herself with another person.

Today women can float the heroic soldier fantasy or a derivative (for example, an astronaut fantasy) with less need to disguise the heroic motive in an
erotic jacket, because there is less fear of reprisal.

In response to changes in cultural mores, many women now in their fifties
and older first formulated work aspirations relatively late in life, modifying or
reviving old and often buried fantasies. In the younger generation the gender
difference in achievement fantasies has diminished dramatically. Now that a
critical mass of working women has come into existence, even more con-
formist women can incorporate explicitly ambitious and competitive wishes
into their dream scenarios. In fact, if one were to examine the achievement

fantasies of a typical group of contemporary men and women, it would be hard to differentiate them by sex.

Women are now being drawn not just to scripts of hard work and advancement, but to more adventurous story lines as well. Witness the popularity of such books as Beryl Markham's *West with the Night,* which poetically describes the author's life as a pioneer aviator in the 1930s. Originally published in 1942, Markham's memoir was reissued a few years ago and quickly shot onto the best-seller lists—a book whose time had finally come. Accounts of such lives over different decades are the best evidence that change does not occur all at once, but that certain free and rebellious spirits lead the way—some taking new directions out of natural inclination, others out of necessity or opportunity. Think of Rosie the Riveter in World War II. (But because the major risk of nonconformity was the loss of marriageability, it ought come as no surprise that many—though by no means all—of the pioneer professional women were gay or had given up the idea of marrying for other reasons.)

Fantasies pertaining to procreation, both to the raising of children and to the acts of begetting and birthing them, have also responded to changes in cultural mores and expectations with respect to both men's and women's roles. Given a wider range of options, women (and men) are now freer to fantasize a life *without* children. Just as one may now fantasize (and have) a spouse and no children, one may have children with no spouse, or with a lesbian or gay partner. (For many years, "straights" typically assumed that homosexuals did not want children!)

Sometimes the increased range of fantasies is aided and abetted by other changes. Fantasies about procreation (and about the freedom to forgo it), for example, draw on the new reproductive and birth control technologies as well as cultural changes. The long existing "Adam" fantasy of being the last man in the world who has viable sperm and who de facto is the only one who can repopulate the earth drew on a man's potential to produce large numbers of sperm. This is a *cosmogonic* fantasy, a godlike fantasy of begetting a new world. Now that multiple eggs can be generated in one menstrual cycle and be harvested for future use, some women are entertaining Eve fantasies, which express the same narcissistic wishes the Adam fantasy expresses. One woman fantasizes donating twenty eggs to be fertilized by twenty different men of different racial and ethnic backgrounds, the fertilized eggs all to be carried to term by surrogates, with the idea that her children will repopulate the world. Another expresses her love of (and perhaps also her competitive rivalry with) her infertile daughter by fantasizing donating an egg to her, and so on. And there's even the fantasy of a man carrying a child in his own body. But the box-office failure of the Arnold Schwarzenegger movie *Junior,* which has this plot, suggests that procreative fantasies still tend to be gender-dichotomous. The anatomical differences of the sexes limit our ability to be completely flexible in this area of our fantasy life.

Sexual fantasies are also conservative, in the sense of being stubbornly unchangeable. In general, they show remarkable durability either in essentially unmodified form or in gradually evolving new editions, regardless of current dictates from the surrounding culture. But some sexual fantasies have proved malleable in response to input from the culture, and they reflect the changing cultural climate of the past thirty years. Or perhaps it would be more accurate to say that we are now better able to access certain kinds of fantasy material. It is not so much a question of fantasy being rescripted as it is of our having greater conscious access to it.

Many more women, for example, are now in touch with their sexual fantasies courtesy of the women's movement, sexual liberation, and the proliferation of written depictions of female sexual fantasy, such as *My Secret Garden,* a write-in collection of female sexual fantasies.[34] Another reason for the increased range of female sexual fantasies is that women have more to fantasize about. Along with changes in sexual rhetoric, there have been real changes in sexual practices that have offered women new material for fantasies, and new pleasures.[35]

The sea change in the manifest content of women's fantasies includes more focus on seducing rather than being seduced, forcing rather than being forced. This may be the result of greater access to the preconscious or to reversals of preexisting fantasies rather than new fantasies. Few fantasies are created de novo, unless they have had an already existing precursor script in the preconscious. But once a fantasy is formed, the fantasizer may rotate roles, for example, alternating masochistic and sadistic roles in a relationship.[36] From this perspective, reversals of plot, of seducing rather than being seduced, are less surprising than totally new narratives. Women may also be more tolerant of their fantasies: Many have accepted "forbidden" fantasies, concluding that what gives pleasure need not negatively influence the rest of life.[37]

MALE FANTASIES

Since men and women live in the same society, it would be strange if radical changes in the fantasy life of women had no counterpart in the fantasy life of men. One possible manifestation of that change is the increasing emphasis on the theme of nurturant fathers, as movies and television series depicting single-father households abound. Whether this trend genuinely reflects male fantasy life, the wishful thinking of women, or the fantasies of a small cultural elite of men and women is hard to say. In fact, although male fantasies are regularly recounted in the consulting room, they have been the focus of fewer culture-wide studies. Perhaps our relative ignorance of possible changes in male fantasy reflect the minimal scholarly and practical attention male psychology in general has received in recent years, compared to the vast outpouring of material about women. Perhaps, too, we are fearful of what we will see if we look too closely, for the changes in men's lives and in the fantasies that encode those changes may not carry the optimism and excitement associated with changes for women.

If women now imagine themselves as "running with the wolves," some men may feel threatened. Increasing opportunities for women have challenged the traditional sphere of men, at home and in the workplace. Many men feel that their prerogatives are being eroded by the increasing power of women (and of teenage children), and in recent decades men have faced an overall diminution of their opportunities for economic advancement. It was much easier for a male to meet the culturally mandated expectations of economic performance in the halcyon days of the 1950s economy, when the prevailing tide was toward upward mobility. Nowadays, if there is a drift, it is a downward one. Some have argued, too, that male hegemony has been negatively impacted in the United States by the loss of the war in Vietnam, and the loss in our collective mythology of the prototype of the invincible hero-warrior.[38] My own reading is that the women's movement, the trend to downward mobility, and the effect of Vietnam are fairly late influences in an ongoing redistribution of power between the sexes.[39]

Men's escalating anger at women, and fear of them, goes back at least half a century. For example, Philip Wylie's hugely successful 1942 book, *Generation of Vipers,* accused mothers of emasculating their husbands and sons and so severely as to render them incapable of functioning as men. The sense of male disenfranchisement also found ample comedic expression in the sitcoms of the fifties and sixties. Jackie Gleason's Ralph Kramden character in the now classic "Honeymooners" was a lovable if irascible buffoon, always embarking on grandiose schemes against the advice of his sane, competent wife and always having to concede her superiority at the end with the signature line, "Alice, you're the greatest."

A variety of cultural evidence suggests that the women's movement of the 1970s crystallized a social movement already in play: Women were already becoming more empowered, men perhaps less so. Over the course of the century, men have been losing their traditional male prerogatives while finding fewer and fewer opportunities for proving themselves as men—a devastating blow because masculinity has always been viewed as an achievement, not a state of being. "In fact what outlets are then left for the achievement of the masculine prowess depicted in fairy tale, myth, and fiction? Though he may have been raised to be a giant killer, a hero, 'What does a boy do in his adult years?'" This question is raised in *The Courage to Raise Good Men,* whose authors, Olga Silverstein and Beth Rashbaum, use John Updike's Rabbit series to depict the plight of the modern male: "What Updike is telling us is that there is no suitable arena in which a grown-up Rabbit can continue to prove himself a hero. Once off the basketball courts of youth, he's lost, always pining for the place 'where they remembered him when,' the crowds, the glory, the adulation."[40] This is resonant of the plight of many of John O'Hara's protagonists, the high point of whose lives also took place on the playing field in high school or in college. So what the adult American male does, is "at night he lights up a good cigar . . . and shoots out home. He mows the lawn, or sneaks in some practice putting, and then he's ready for dinner."[41]

The dislocation the modern American male is experiencing has inspired a small rash of books and group workshops purporting to enrich the life of the male, the most prominent among them Robert Bly's *Iron John* and the weekend retreats he sponsors. Bly's offering to men is a new mythic self-image incorporating the "hairy man," who empowers them to regain their masculine selves by stealing the key to their freedom from a woman/mother figure (who has deprived them of something). But group leaders of the Bly persuasion tell me that the heyday of such groups was in 1990 and 1991 and that interest in them has slackened, suggesting that this mythic reformulation of male psychology may have had a limited appeal.[42]

Many men seem to have found their own remedies—whether personal or cultural—to narcissistic injuries. Collectively and individually, men have traditionally coped with sexual and social anxieties by submerging their fear in an overestimation of male sexuality and autonomy. Observers from diverse disciplines now suggest that macho sexuality has gained increasing sanction as the cultural ideal. The psychologist Robert May believes that in addition to the cultural directive for males to be assertive in general, "the popular prescription for male sexuality is also heavily invested with assertion and activity. The man is supposed to be constantly on the move and on the make. The image of the tireless seducer differs only in style and degree from that of the rapist."[43] The only question is whether the male attracts and seduces the female or overpowers and forces her.[44] According to Kate Millett, the euphemism and idealism of the descriptions of sex in earlier eras have given way to the explicitness and antisocial character of pornography.[45] My own questionnaire study of a nonpatient population of male university students (and therefore relatively advantaged men) indicated that 44 percent entertained fantasies of sexual domination.[46]

The cultural stereotype of male sexuality depicts phallic omnipotence and supremacy and invests the phallus with the power of mastery. At the very least, this view of male sexuality depicts a large, powerful, and untiring phallus attached to a man who is long on self-control, experienced, competent, and knowledgeable enough to make women crazy with desire. As the psychologist Bernard Zilbergeld has described it, "It's two feet long, hard as steel, and can go all night."[47] In the shared cultural fantasy, even the normally reticent female is utterly powerless and receptive when she confronts pure macho sexuality. Yet this fantasy conceals and reverses male anxieties.

Short of violence, many men embrace some version of macho sexuality (especially the belief that *other* men are truly in possession of it). On one level, "macho" fantasies are adaptive, counteracting underlying fears and resentments and simultaneously incorporating and neutralizing hostile impulses. At the same time they may aggravate a preexisting sexual anxiety, since many men literally believe other men are doing better, "getting more," and so forth.

The increasing pervasiveness of the dominant and aggressive theme of male fantasies, sexual and nonsexual, and of the macho image in general, may well be related to current cultural stresses. Though basic developmental characteristics often infuse male sexuality with hostility to, and fear of, the female, the increasingly explicit representation of this hostility in fiction and film gives men greater conscious access to fantasies of aggressive sexuality.[48] And once raised into consciousness and expressed culturally, those themes are validated. Therefore, we are seeing a cultural accentuation of preexisting fantasies—or, as with the proliferation of female sexual fantasy, a decreased repression of those fantasies.

Overall, the diminution in the male's sphere of influence appears to have caused a shift not only to more intensely aggressive fantasies of sexual mastery but to vigilante and paramilitary fantasies as well. (Chapter 8 explores the mushrooming of these aggressive fantasies.)

What seems to many of us to be a crisis in the sense of masculinity may have been obscured by the focus on positive changes in female adaptations. For example, for all the rhetoric about the move toward more male involvement in nurturance and coparenting, in fact there is an epidemic of absentee fathers today, as men flee their families in greater numbers than ever before. And the "new" male who was so briefly fashionable, at least in the media, seems to be in the process of being supplanted by the macho, even violent male depicted by Hollywood.

TOWARD CHANGE

Up to this point my main focus has been the scripting and rescripting of the individual's fantasy life in response to cultural prescriptions and cultural change. But fantasy does not just *reflect* change. Through the sensibilities of the culture's poets and prophets, its novelists and moviemakers, fantasy also prepares the way *for* change. Thus, some feminist theorists argue that exposure to fiction promotes changes in fantasy themes, and ultimately in life. Such changes are not likely to result from message-oriented, didactic works, however; more likely they arise from the reader's preconscious perception of the subversive themes embedded in superficially conventional scripts, themes that speak to the reader's own repressed yearnings.

Noting the power of the novel *Jane Eyre* on many readers, Jean Wyatt observes,

> Charlotte Brontë's *Jane Eyre* is in fact rich in fantasies that address the pleasures and frustrations of growing up in a patriarchal nuclear family structure: Fantasies of heroic rebellion against tyrannical parents, fantasies based on a split between good mother (Miss Temple) and bad mother (Mrs. Reed), and fantasies

of revenge on more powerful brothers and prettier sisters (John and Georgiana Reed). Perhaps most appealing, Rochester offers Jane the excitement combined with frustration and enigma that characterize father-daughter interactions in a traditionally structured nuclear family. Against the pull of its Oedipal love fantasy, *Jane Eyre* presents an equally passionate protest against patriarchal authority.[49]

The fantasies embedded in the novel are divided, perhaps even polarized; that division probably accounts for much of its appeal, allowing it to speak simultaneously to many levels of female need and longing, fear and anger.

Wyatt's explanation of why many women—even today—have considered the novel a revolutionary force in their lives rests heavily on the notion of our ability to entertain and enjoy multiple and sometimes conflicting fantasies. On the one hand, *Jane Eyre* gratifies the wish for a close father-daughter relationship by depicting Jane's romantic attachment to Rochester, a man twice her age who is powerful, authoritative, and distant. Their union after he has been blinded is ambiguous; even though she now takes care of him, he is still a strong oak. Wyatt believes that the popularity of the book rests on the female reader's ambivalence toward her own father. But to the degree that this is a radical novel, one that predisposes to change, its appeal may rest on the way Jane defines herself. According to Adrienne Rich, "As a child, she [Jane] rejects the sacredness of adult authority; as a woman, she insists on regulating her conduct by the pulse of her own integrity."[50]

Another aspect of the novel's enduring appeal is that it incorporates a very common female fantasy—nursing a man back to health. And in this respect, too, there is thematic ambivalence, or even outright polarization, because the fantasy relates both to father longing and to fear of rejection. At another level, it allows a recapitulation of the closeness of the mother-daughter interaction— the experience of intense nurturance—but now this closeness appears in the context of a relationship between a man and a woman, and the daughter figure is now herself in the nurturant role and therefore in the more powerful position. To the extent that women are fearful of men and their phallic aggression, this is a profoundly reassuring fantasy, because the male's illness or incapacity defangs him, disarms him. (In some such fantasies, the male may even be symbolically castrated. In *Jane Eyre* he is blinded.) In a culture in which men are still deemed the powerful ones, the nursing fantasy provides not just a sense of safety, but a sexually acceptable form of egalitarianism.

Movies also provide material that the viewer can use to mold amorphous preconscious fantasies and yearnings into daydreams and life dreams. And movies can also be ambiguous, delivering subliminal messages that contradict what we see on the surface. The film critic Molly Haskell suggests that

> movies, being basically conservative, generally hold up traditional and officially sanctioned notions of maleness and femaleness, but if that was all there was to it, i.e., if these models were mutually exclusive and rigidly defined, movies would

soon lose their audiences. The ones that have held up are precisely those in which there is an inner tension between surface acceptability and subversive challenge . . . those which challenge the gender conventions of their time and toy with (rather than simply compensating for or satisfying) even such basic Freudian immutables as castration anxiety and penis envy.[51]

The subliminal fantasy opens up new ways of being in the world, and it does so without being too threatening. This can happen because the multilayered complexity of the viewer's preconscious/unconscious responds to the multiple (often conflicting) layers of meaning in the movie.

Haskell cites a wonderful example, the Lauren Bacall character in the movie *To Have and Have Not*. It is 1940 in a crowded hotel bar in Martinique when Bacall first meets the Humphrey Bogart character, a self-sufficient loner, a man who supports himself by hiring out his boat. Bacall pickpockets a man who's buying her drinks, the very man who was trying to cheat Bogart out of money he owed him for the boat. According to Haskell, "The wallet is clearly a phallic commodity, especially when one considers that its owner, in not paying Bogart the money he owes him, is withholding some remnant of the manhood he has lost as an incompetent fisherman in the eyes of his superior [Bogart]."[52] Haskell suggests that this opening scene establishes the fact that the phallus as symbolized by the wallet is migratory (not permanently attached to any one person) and the power it stands for consequently unstable: "The act of laying claim to it underlines the aggressiveness Bacall is permitted, as a resourceful and unfettered spirit, sexually freer than was the custom in the heavily censored films of the 40s."[53] When Bacall says to Bogart, "If you want me, just whistle," although you might, Haskell suggests, read this invitation as abject surrender, the visual impact of the delivery is exactly the opposite.

> [Bacall's] head, shining blonde and bullet-like, is cocked forward, so the eyes are always peering skeptically over an invisible obstruction, like someone looking over reading glasses as if to say "Who's kidding whom?" and the voice, because the mouth has been thrust back from the camera by the position of the head, becomes deeper and throatier.[54]

The Bacall character may be emotionally needy, but what comes through more strongly is that she is sexually desirous, in a most presumptive, un-old-fashioned way.

Art creates the conduit through which the creative writer or artist's preconscious—in all its ambivalence and ambiguity—speaks to the same qualities in the preconscious of the consumer. That is why books and movies can simultaneously signal social changes and help shape them. The subliminal, often subversive fantasy allows both women and men to feel comfortably in conformity with traditional expectations, even as it opens them to the possibility of radical change.

• • •

The course of life dictates that all of us face certain universal developmental dilemmas and, in the course of resolving them, take our places in the cycle of generations. Though all of our species share the tools we bring to the task, gender shapes the specific strategies we employ. In fact, gender identity, the sense of femininity or masculinity, produces differences in adaptive strategies that begin in the first year of life and continue to its end.

One of the tasks of the preconscious is to fashion fantasies that assuage discomfort and incorporate hope. To this end, fantasy must be consonant with unconscious fantasy *and* acceptable to internalized "rules," including notions of what is gender-appropriate. To the extent that our fantasies themselves become the source of conflict or the fear of humiliation or rejection they are modified, disguised, or suppressed.[55]

Because the narrative content of fantasy is to some degree incorporated from the fantasizer's world, some theorists have misconstrued fantasy as an almost exclusively conservative force, both individually and culturally, characterizing it as a mere replication of early familial arrangements. This is the interpretation of some object-relations theories, which view society as reconstituting or reduplicating itself psychologically in the psyche of the individual.[56] In such accounts, any unconscious fantasy formed under the influence of the culture's pattern of family structure would inevitably predispose individuals to repeat the early patterns of their own lives, including the enactment of sex-stereotypical roles. And, to some degree, this does happen. But this viewpoint underestimates both the complexity of unconscious and preconscious fantasies and their radical potential. (The very content of some fantasy will dictate that some individuals live out their lives as rebels.) It also fails to acknowledge the differences in our inborn capacity for adaptation and change. At their best, our fantasies are so designed that they make us feel good about ourselves, and they contain the possibility of being realized.

Constitutional as well as experiential and conflictual factors determine whether one greets life with a fistful of commandments or a pocketful of dreams. Our fantasies may reinforce the former, or herald the latter.

8

BORROWED FANTASY: ART, ICONS, AND MYTHS

CULTURALLY MEDIATED FANTASY COMES TO US NOT JUST PASSIVELY, THROUGH our families and through culturewide myths, but through our active exploration of cultural materials. Each of us processes the raw materials of the culture to see what we can cobble together for use in scripting our own wishes and needs, our preconscious and unconscious fantasies. We might call the material we choose from the culture at large *borrowed fantasy* or *shared cultural fantasy,* to distinguish it from the *shared fantasy* communicated explicitly or subliminally in exchanges with people we know. Our ability to borrow fantasy is thus analogous to the power of our distance receptors, hearing and sight, in that it gives us access to experiences beyond our immediate surroundings. Sharing fantasy interpersonally, on the other hand, is more like using the senses of taste, touch, and smell in our contacts with the surrounding environment.

The scope of possibilities that we can imagine always depends on our exposure to the world in which we live, whether that exposure is as a participant or as an observer. In constructing our personal daydreams, we employ—both in and out of awareness—what we know of our real selves and what we fantasize as our possible selves. Studying the lives of people we know (whose inner world we imagine), reading and watching fictional depictions, and assessing cultural icons, we gauge the culture's range of our alternatives and select those that suit us, which we then modify through our own creative synthesis.[1]

As we concoct our fantasies, choosing from menus that contain selections from art as well as from life, we can make identifications not just with fictional characters or with real-life people, but with cultural icons who are both.[2] For those of us who are conformists by bent, fearful of straying beyond the range of what mainstream culture endorses or tolerates, icons who are innovators and rebels—a Madame Curie, a Jackie Robinson, an Oscar Wilde—are particularly liberating, helping us to conceive of possibilities beyond our customary limits.

What we borrow draws heavily on fictional stories, and we have considerable testimony about its impact on us. Carlos Fuentes puts it graphically: "You are what you eat. You are also the comics you peruse as a child."[3] Referring to her convent education, Eileen Simpson observes: "As girls who are read fairy tales daydream about becoming princesses, we who were read the lives of the saints daydreamed of becoming saints."[4] Because who would know better than writers themselves, novels contain numerous depictions of fictional characters being influenced by what they read and living out their most treasured stories: Cervantes's Don Quixote is acting out the tales of medieval chivalry consumed in his youth; Catherine Moreland, in Jane Austen's *Northanger Abbey,* is under the sway of Mrs. Radcliffe's *Mysteries of Udolfo,* and sees mystery and horror everywhere; Emma in Gustave Flaubert's *Madame Bovary* believes in the romances she reads and acts on them, to her detriment.[5] Writers understand that fantasy, like art, is a two-way street, the flow of information and sensation shuttling ceaselessly back and forth between the internal and external worlds we inhabit.

Borrowed fantasies provide material for vicarious wish-fulfillment and for scripting individual fantasies. But what we borrow does not always stay in the realm of fantasy and may affect the real world. As we observe fantasies enacted by others, we are freer to act out comparable fantasies of our own. Moreover, as we discover that some of our peers share our fantasized identifications, we can use that commonality to foster intimate ties with them. Freud was the first to observe that we use our mutual identifications to join in groups, where our ties are based on our idealization of, and corresponding imaginative identification with, the same icon, leader, or hero.[6] Such groups may promote the enactment of the shared fantasy.

Culturally transmitted fantasy in the form of borrowed fantasy draws on a complex mix of real life and art, firsthand and vicarious experience, all mobilized at the behest of our preexisting desires, impulses, and unconscious fantasies. I will try to get at something of the psychology of borrowed fantasy by addressing how we use cultural icons to give shape to our own longings. And because the effect of exposure to imaginative works has received extensive attention in relation to two specific kinds of behavior—suicide and violence—I will use those topics to exemplify the complex interactions of individual fantasy and culturally mediated fantasy, borrowed and shared.

ICONS AND IDENTIFICATIONS

Growing up, each of us invokes icons, heroes of our imagination, real or imagined, as figures to idealize and imitate, as templates for our fantasies. An icon speaks to a devotée's deepest feelings and longings, dreams and hope—or hopelessness. Iconiclike fantasies are common among children, as illustrated by their almost apostolic identification with Batman, Superman, Wonder Woman, and all the superheroes. These fantasies are exaggerations of the child's vision of the powerful adult he or she will be. Vampires and monsters reflect another aspect of the child's inner reality, the expression of the evil self.

Out of our deep need for models, almost every one of us, adults as well as children, cherishes one or another icon: saints or sinners, mad or bad, political hero, religious martyr, or narcissistic darling. Often we pick as our icons those with whom we can genuinely identify, some of whose characteristics we can at least hope to incorporate. Icons serve as frames on which to hang our fantasies, vessels for our imagination, ships to launch our dream voyages.

By dint of some extraordinary correspondences between the public imagination and their own inner lives, certain real people become icons for vast numbers around the globe, capturing and expressing the dream of the moment. The Beatles, for example, became iconic on more than the strength of their music, exciting as it was, and on more than the strength of their success. They combined the drama of upward mobility, as those four down-to-earth young men made their rapid rise from the lower class to celebrity status, with all the irreverence, energy, buoyancy, and cheekiness of youth—qualities that many people could readily identify with, and aspire to, regardless of the celebrity status that might seem to keep them at a vast distance from their idols.

Fictional characters can also be icons: In *Gone with the Wind* the tempestuous Scarlett O'Hara, as opposed to the good, sweet Melanie, was the character women—particularly women of an earlier era—identified with. Willful and assertive at a time when women were supposed to be neither, Scarlett became a liberating force many women used in devising their own life scripts. In a certain way she is a protofeminist hero. (Like identification with real-life characters, mutual identification with fictional characters may lead to group formation; consider, for example, the Baker Street Irregulars and the Trekkies.)

Sometimes we may become preoccupied in fantasy with an icon whom we admire and even identify with, but whose admired characteristics cannot become—at least not self-evidently—part of our "real" self. Thus, an icon can condense and express the desires of a devotée's innermost psyche—whether or not those desires can ever be fulfilled.

Gay men can tell us a lot about the uses of icons, in part, because some of them are extremely vocal and flamboyant in declaring their choices. And these choices are at first glance improbable, since many gay men and almost all "queens" select as their icons not sports heroes or power brokers, but female celebrities, often stars of stage and screen, and sometimes royalty. Several different groups of female icons are favored.

Wayne Koestenbaum, chronicler of Jacqueline Onassis's iconic status, describes how "every moment you imitate Jackie, or stage your own emergence into imaginary limelight or into the clarity of self-knowledge, then the Jackie moment rebegins."[7] Koestenbaum, whose icons include not just Jacqueline Onassis but Maria Callas, writes eloquently, amusingly, and passionately of "opera queens" (among whom he includes himself), gay men deeply involved with, and identified with, one or another diva:

> We consider the opera queen to be a pre-Stonewall throwback. . . . I am an anachronism. After sexual liberation, who needs opera? But this logic would also have us renounce our fetishes, would deny us lace or leather, and would deny a taste's inevitability (those intertwining roots which determine and bind the heart).[8]

The phenomenon of the opera queen survives, called into being and sustained by icons whose appeal goes beyond the simply musical. It is their power to invoke emotion through their voice, their passion, their glamour, and their grandeur that beckon to the fan. And each diva is special in her own way; a Maria Callas follower will not have the same all-out response to, say, Anna Moffo. Koestenbaum describes in part what the Callas devotée is responding to when he chooses her as icon: "She was Callas long before she died, but she would be a little less Callas if she were still living. Untimely death assists her legend and connects her to themes that have shadowed gay culture: premature mortality, evanescence, solitude."[9]

Another group iconized by gay men comprises grand and commanding movie stars such as Joan Crawford, Marlene Dietrich, Mae West, Bette Davis, and Tallulah Bankhead. All are perceived as erotically dominant women who exert power through their physical attractiveness and personal magnetism. In the fantasizer's imagination, the icon is able at will to erotically control any powerful man whom she desires. These women are a peculiar mix of "masculine" and "feminine" that speaks eloquently to many gay men. Because their glamour is exaggerated and extreme, they also represent a sort of lampoon of the straight world, a joke on conventional sex roles—camp of the highest order. "Drag queens," mistresses of a sort of "camp-garbage aesthetic," often favor them as icons and as fantasized self-representations.[10]

Iconic status is also often conferred on those glamorous child-women perceived as helpless waifs or as tragically self-destructive rather than as powerful and dominant. This category includes such figures as Judy Garland, Marilyn Monroe, and Billie Holiday. They, too, control men through sexuality and personal magnetism, but their special appeal lies in their sensitivity, vulnerability, suffering, and intense passions.[11]

The taste for suffering or masochistic icons is certainly not restricted to gay men. Whether we are male or female, straight or gay, many of our icons, interestingly enough, are devoted to self-destructive pursuits. The poet Sylvia Plath is among those glamorous icons of violent death (death effected either through suicide or through progressively more serious acts of self-destruction) who include Anne Sexton, Marilyn Monroe, Judy Garland, James Dean, Elvis Presley, Jim Morrison, Jimi Hendrix, Janis Joplin, and Kurt Cobain. The literary critic Jacqueline Rose refers to Plath as the Marilyn Monroe of the literati, a characterization that captures some of the glamour that has come to be associated with Plath.[12] According to Rose, "Sylvia Plath haunts our culture. She is—for many—a shadowy figure whose presence draws on and compels. . . . Above all she stirs things up."[13] Her iconic status illuminates many of the psychological complexities involved in icon worship—beginning with the indisputable fact that much of that status stems from her self-destruction.[14] What that reveals about the meaning of icon worship and its uses is by no means straightforward. Many psychic twists and turns are embodied in this form of worship.

Plath's life, anguished and meteoric, creative and destructive, has been read as case history, cautionary tale, feminist parable, and sometimes as a story of demonic possession. Born in 1932, Plath saw her childhood happiness destroyed when she was eight and her father died from complications of diabetes, and her life was further dislocated by a move soon afterward to a new town.[15] Immersing herself during adolescence in academic and extracurricular achievements, she created a frenzy of activity that some have interpreted as a manic defense against an inner void.

Extremely ambitious, she brooked no deviation from her early goal of becoming a writer and persisted through forty-five rejections before her first story was published in *Seventeen* magazine. In 1950 she was attending Smith College, where she continued her twin pursuits of writing and prize collecting. The summer following her junior year, having won a *Mademoiselle* magazine competition, she spent a month in New York as a guest editor, and it was then that many internal stresses began to surface and she became depressed.

Returning home from her *Mademoiselle* job, Plath found not only a sick mother and grandmother but a rejection from the Harvard summer creative writing course, all of which served to plunge her into an even deeper depression. Unresponsive to a brief and apparently inadequate psychiatric intervention, she took a massive overdose of sleeping pills and was found on the verge of death only by the sheerest luck. She was revived, hospitalized, and given shock therapy and insulin treatments, after which she made what appeared to be a remarkable recovery, which she romanticized as a rebirth. Eventually she returned to college, graduated, and continued her studies. Whatever the anguish of her inner life, Plath had resumed her habitual coloration as polite and obliging, a red-lipsticked, polyperfect adherent to the conventions of the 1950s.

Plath wrote and traveled and won a fellowship to Cambridge, where she met and married the striking and talented poet Ted Hughes (now poet laureate of England), whom she came to idolize. Elaine Showalter evokes Plath's fantasy of life as half of a literary couple: "They launch . . . the hard labour of poetic careers, supporting themselves on writing prizes and intermittent teaching jobs. She dreams that they will divide the kingdom of poetic fame; she will be 'the Poetess of America,' as he will be 'The Poet of England and her dominions.'"[16] This manifestly glamorous marriage is a cornerstone of the Plath myth.

Nonetheless, tied down to two children, success ever elusive, the couple gradually found their marriage eroding, and Plath soon discovered that Hughes was having an affair with a beautiful aspiring writer, Assia Wevill. Plath and Hughes separated. Plath, in a frenzy, wrote what are considered the greatest and angriest poems of her life, but they were rejected.[17]

In 1963, at the age of thirty, with her two young children in the room upstairs, Plath put her head into the oven and gassed herself to death. She became famous posthumously as a poet, especially as author of the *Ariel* poems, and as the author of the autobiographical novel *The Bell Jar.*

Whether her intent was to die we cannot ever know with any certainty. Neither can we determine the essential nature of her depression, whether it was biological or psychological, whether it centered on the early-life loss of her father, the domination by her mother, or the betrayal by her husband. My interest here is not in Sylvia Plath herself—not in the sources of her depression or in the links between her creativity and her neurosis—but in Sylvia Plath as cultural icon, the artist as the nexus between the individual psyche and the surrounding culture.

Plath's life, as imagined by her admirers, lends itself to sometimes contradictory fantasy identifications. Part of her significance is as a death poet, an icon of suicide. But there are other layers as well: In both her life and her writing, Plath evokes complicated feelings about the way men and women parse sex and power. So Plath has become not only an icon of death but also of sexual poetics, be it as feminist hero or as betrayer of feminism. And even as death poet Plath has an iconic status that is more complicated than at first meets the eye, resting on two different and opposing mechanisms: identification with her as depressive, and identification with her as heroic, defiant, and rageful. In each of these roles, she has her defenders and detractors.

Those who themselves harbor feelings of depression and isolation may identify primarily with Plath's depressive feelings, vulnerability, and sensitivity, and her suicidal propensities. But icons of suicide, while they are the locus for identification, do not generally inspire suicide in those who identify with them. Many people identify with a death poet and to some degree feel comforted by the identification, if for no other reason than that the suicidal impulse may come to seem less crazy, less bizarre, when known to exist in someone who is very accomplished. The identification may also allow the devotée to feel less alone—and thereby defuse any suicidal propensities. It may also lead to bonds with others who have made a similar identification, further mitigating the depressed person's feelings of isolation.

In her novel *Sleepwalking,* Meg Wolitzer catches the romantic depressive's fascination with famous real-life suicides and illustrates how that identification can be the basis of a friendship.[18] Wolitzer's protagonists, three young college students—known on campus as the death girls—form strong bonds based on their individual identifications with three different "death" poets who have killed themselves—one identifying with Sylvia Plath, one with Anne Sexton, and the third with Lucy Ascher (a poet of Wolitzer's invention). Each expresses her identification with her special poet by imitating that poet's dress and life-style. They stay up all night reading aloud to one another from the work of their chosen poets, thus overcoming the isolation that contributed to their feelings of sadness. Through identification, each can rationalize her sadness by elevating it into something romantic, enlightened, and superior to the drabness of the surrounding college drones. The focus of the novel is on the recovery from depression of the Lucy Ascher devotée, but the ultimate fate of one of the girls is unclear.

In real life, Plath has not inspired copycat suicides among the public at large. To the best of my knowledge, there is in fact only one documented suicide that can be connected to Plath, that of Assia Wevill—the woman whose affair with Ted Hughes precipitated the couple's separation.[19] While Hughes and Wevill never married, they had a child, born in 1967. Two years later, Wevill, like Plath, gassed herself in the kitchen oven. And she gassed her daughter as well. According to one report, the oven stood alongside "a trunk that contained the unpublished manuscripts of Sylvia Plath."[20] Whether the account is accurate or not, it is difficult not to speculate on the many levels of shared fantasy and the diverse motives that must have been at work in Wevill.

However, many devotées of a self-destructive icon are not necessarily drawn to the suicide per se but to the struggle the life entails. The identification many admirers make with Plath rests not so much on her self-destructive side as on a perception of her suicide as heroic, defiant, and rageful. In part, Plath haunts our culture in her emblematic role as victim of the repressive 1950s, of the stranglehold of the feminine mystique, and of an implied death struggle with men.[21] Plath embodied a violent cultural conflict and is alternately seen as the victim *of* or liberator *from* cultural bias or political repression. Here lurks the basis of another potential for identification, another kind of fantasy of a nonsuicidal nature.[22]

The internal split that Plath exemplifies is that between victimhood and self-affirmation. Plath's major influence may be that her embrace, explication, and poetic depiction of victimhood *and* her struggle against it have entered the cultural storehouse of fantasies on which we feed, and paradoxically she is seen as a survivor—despite her suicide. Plath was either the first or one of the first to employ Holocaust imagery to convey personal feelings. In the poem "Daddy," claiming she "may be a bit of a Jew," she evokes the masochistic image "Every woman adores a fascist/The boot in the face, the brute/Brute heart of a brute like you." But "Daddy" is far from being a poem just about victimhood; there is a line of development in it from victimhood to self-assertion and revenge.[23] It is about rising up and destroying her father and probably Hughes as well.[24]

Plath, then, is more than a creature we might predictably think of as a female victim of some combination of men, motherhood, and madness: She is also or alternately construed as a hero, a larger than life figure, a mythic self-creation, with much of the aggression, rage, sexuality, and forcefulness that we traditionally associated with men. She is not (in her role as symbol, regardless of what she was in life) woman-as-victim in her suicide; she is woman-as-heroic figure, seizing control of her own destiny by committing suicide. She is asserting, not submitting—or that is how we construe her.[25]

The ambiguity in Plath's life mirrors a similar, highly visible conflict in modern culture—the dual allegiances to victimhood and self-determination.[26] Although many literary and social critics have denounced Plath for her Holocaust imagery, on the grounds that the torture and attempted extermination of a whole people becomes trivialized when they are equated with the personal suffering of one individual, clearly her metaphor speaks to our time. Everyday, on television and in print, and in the many twelve-step programs spawned by the culture, we hear people referring to themselves as "victims" and "survivors."

Whatever impels it, a sense of victimhood—and a corresponding aspiration to be a survivor—is abroad in the land.[27] Hal Foster, professor of art history and comparative literature, observes,

> From high theory in the Academy to television talk shows, a celebration of trauma rules the day; from the halls of Yale to the set of "Oprah" the motto is "enjoy your symptom!", confess your sin, bare your stain. In this way, the cult of abjection may be a new version of an old American religion. Stand up, testify, be saved.[28]

In a society where these feelings are so often expressed, it is not surprising that one of the favored icons should be a gifted, self-destructive yet struggling artist, who appears to be eternally battling both her inner demons and her external adversaries (among them, father and husband).

Yet even while embodying so many conflicts in her own life and work, Plath seems somehow to assuage them in others. The conflict she wrote about, and our sense of the conflict she lived seem to help people exorcise rather than enact the corresponding conflicts in their own lives. Despite its tendency in many cases to tip the balance toward enactment, iconic identification can sometimes ameliorate internal conflict, stabilizing and strengthening the self, freeing devotées from the need to act out.

THE CULTURALLY MEDIATED SUICIDE FANTASY

Many who harbor suicidal fantasies explicitly share them with others or seek out in literature and biography stories of those who were likewise suicidal. Why should this be so? It seems almost counterintuitive that a fantasy explicitly designed to eliminate oneself from this world should seek endorsement, or even companionship, in it. Part of the reason for this apparent paradox lies in the nature of depression. The profound feelings of isolation associated with depression often lead the person to make a restitutive emotional connection with another depressive (as did the boys in the Hanns Sachs vignette and the girls in the Wolitzer novel).

Separated from real relationships by depression, or, conversely, depressed by their isolation, depressives are primed to form an imaginative identification with someone, flesh-and-blood or fictive, who is depressed or suicidal or who has committed suicide. Often the icon they select is a well-known and admired suicide. The psychological benefit of imaginative identification with an icon is solidarity with a fellow depressive ("I'm not so crazy"), as well as narcissistic gratification ("Look at the company I keep"). This narcissistic identification may stabilize the self, sometimes enough to avert the suicidal impulse. (One way to stabilize a barely recognized suicidal fantasy is to bond with someone more overtly suicidal, in the same way that Ed stabilized his cross-gender fantasy by falling in love with a transsexual.)

Sylvia Plath, for example, made liberal use of icons in charting her own life. She seems to have formed an identification with Virginia Woolf that was based on both literature and depression. The literary critics Sandra Gilbert and Susan Gubar argue persuasively that the influences of Virginia Woolf (as well as William Butler Yeats) liberated Plath to seize the powerful voice of her masterwork *Ariel*.[29] They also track kinship in Plath's work to Woolf's,[30] but they do not refer to their other kinship. In a journal entry of 1957, Plath writes of Woolf, "I feel my life linked to her, somehow. I love her from reading Mrs. Dalloway . . . but her suicide, I felt I was reduplicating in that black summer of 1953. Only I couldn't drown."[31]

Anne Sexton, also a poet and an eventual suicide, attended Robert Lowell's weekly poetry seminar at Boston University with Plath and with the poet George Starbuck; afterward the three went on to the Ritz bar, where they drank martinis and talked suicide. After Plath's death, Anne Sexton remembered, "Often, very often, Sylvia and I would talk at length about our first suicides; at length, in detail and in depth between the free potato chips. . . . We talked death, with burned-up intensity, both of us drawn to it like moths to an electric light bulb. Sucking on it! She told the story of her first suicide in sweet and loving detail and her description in *The Bell Jar* is just the same story."[32] Sexton goes on to wonder that they didn't depress George but thought instead that "we three were stimulated by it, even George, as if death made each of us a little more real at the moment. . . . We talked death and this was life for us, lasting in spite of us."[33] Here Sexton describes the pure pleasure of fantasy sharing, and the pleasure is palpable, almost erotic. After Plath's death, Sexton described how it acted as a clarion call to her. Speaking to her psychiatrist, Dr. Orne, of the suicide, Sexton said, "Sylvia Plath's death disturbs me. . . . Makes me want it too. She took something that was mine, *that* death was mine!"[34]

The suicide fantasy and impulse are contagious, often contracted through exposure to the suicidal ideas—or acts—of others. The imaginative possibility of killing oneself may crystallize through exposure to suicidal ideation or acts in one's own family, to fictional portrayals of suicide, or to actual reported suicides. However, exposure alone does not create a suicidal longing; the most one can argue is that it allows a preexisting feeling of sadness, depression, or despair to crystallize as a suicide fantasy. Each suicide or suicidal fantasy needs to be understood individually, as the product of a complex interplay of variables, only one of them the borrowed or shared fantasy. The most important variables are the intensity of an individual's depression and the depth of his or her despair. When the feelings of despair and depression are deep, exposure to the idea of suicide provides a script that can give shape to those feelings, even when they are as yet unexpressed. Moreover, such precedents, by destigmatizing or even glamorizing suicide, can trigger those who are susceptible to act out a preexisting fantasy. One reason fantasy contagion works this way is that it creates a sense of community. Within the close-knit web of family life, the fantasy may be particularly virulent.

How is the legacy of suicide passed on? Describing his suicide attempt in a coda to *The Savage God,* the literary critic and author A. Alvarez confesses,

> I see now that I had been incubating this death far longer than I recognized at the time. When I was a child, both my parents had half-heartedly put their heads in the gas-oven. Or so they claim. It seemed to me then a rather splendid gesture, though shrouded in mystery, a little area of veiled intensity, revealed only by hints and unexplained, swiftly suppressed outbursts. It was something hidden, attractive and not for the children, like sex. But it was also something that undoubtedly did happen to grown-ups. However hysterical or comic the behavior involved—and to a child it seemed more ludicrous than tragic to lay your head in the greasy gas-oven like the Sunday joint—suicide was a fact, a subject that couldn't be denied; it was something, however awful, that people did. When my own time came, I did not have to discover it for myself.[35]

Mental health professionals and psychoanalysts have long known about the potential for transmission of suicidal thoughts and fantasies within families: Commonly the history of a person who has attempted or committed suicide reveals that other family members have made similar threats or gestures or engaged in failed or realized attempts. Every first-year psychiatric resident confronting a potentially suicidal patient in the emergency room knows how important it is to ask for the family history as an indication of the person's level of risk.

Biological psychiatrists have made a strong case for a biological propensity to depression and a genetic component to suicide, specifically that among depressives a low serotonin level acts as a predisposing factor to the drive to kill oneself.[36] I believe that there are biologically driven propensities to mood disorder, to depression, and to impulsivity, but not to a gene that shouts "kill yourself." The proposed hereditary nature of suicide may be as much cultural as genetic. As Alvarez suggests, the knowledge of real-life suicide can become part of one's reality, so that suicide no longer seems to be beyond the pale.

Emotional contagion and shared fantasy are often observed among people who are not related by blood and for whom there is no possibility of genetic continuity. When I was a psychiatric resident in training, a young woman hospitalized on the ward where I was working, apparently recovering, threw herself off the George Washington Bridge, exactly one year after her boyfriend, who had also been a patient, killed himself in the same way and in the same spot. The anniversary suicide, extremely common, loudly proclaims the symbolic meaning attached to the act—whether identification, guilt, or *Liebestod* ("We will be together forever") fantasy.

Suicide contagion is not restricted to fantasy communicated or shared among people who know each other. An extreme example of fantasy *borrowed* through the medium of fiction is the eighteenth-century epidemic of suicide among the young romantic readers of Johann Goethe's loosely autobiographical novel *The Sorrows of Young Werther,* which depicts the suicide of a young man of exquisite sensibility tormented by unrequited love.

The borrowed suicide fantasy can provide substitute gratification or lead to enactment. For Goethe himself, writing *Werther* appeared to exorcise something. He lived to be eighty-three years old and died still wishing for life. But as a young man, he had been an admirer of the Emperor Otto, who had stabbed himself, and he had decided that he too must die in this way—or else not seek death at all:

> By this conviction, I saved myself from the purpose, or indeed more properly speaking, from the whim of suicide. Among a considerable collection of arms, I possessed a costly well-ground dagger. This I laid down nightly by my side, and, before extinguishing the light, I tried whether I could succeed in sending the sharp point an inch or two deep into my heart. But as I truly never could succeed, I at last took to laughing at myself, threw away these hypochondriacal crotchets, and determined to live.[37]

But for many readers of the novel, *The Sorrows of Young Werther* was a call to action. The novel was highly acclaimed and widely read, and young men across the continent began to imitate Werther—in dress, in speech, and even in the act of suicide. It seems clear that something more than a death wish characterized these suicides. Those who identified with Werther were probably responding in part to the idea of a New Man in old Europe, where most lives were imprisoned in conventionality.[38] The identification of one's self as a rebellious spirit, the hope of being a creative person and an agent of change, and the narcissistic gratification of identifying as an artistic genius, even a stifled one, may all have been factors in the Werther suicides. It became a mark of stature and romantic sensibility "to suffer for one's genius, to struggle for art's sake, and to die young—a hero mourned by all the world."[39]

Alvarez points out,

> Werther was no longer a character in a novel, he was a model for living who set a whole style of high feeling and despair. The rationalists of the previous generations had vindicated the act of suicide, they had helped to change the laws and moderate the primitive churchly taboos, but it was Werther who made the act seem positively desirable to the young Romantics all over Europe.[40]

Thus Goethe through his novel created a veritable epidemic of romantic suicides throughout Europe.

However, the Werther fantasy acted differently on different readers. One of the novel's most enthusiastic readers was Napoleon, who read it seven times— in Egypt, St. Helena, everywhere!—and who had quite a different response to it. Goethe believed,

> Napoleon's predilection for *Werther* was founded on the great contrast between the two natures. Napoleon liked melancholy, sweet music and the sad, moonlit laments of Ossian and *Werther*. The effect that *Werther* had on Napoleon was to dissolve what was too rigid in him, to ease what was too tense and highly strung. *Werther* brought him the comfort of relaxing, mitigating, softening—precisely what a man of heroic temper needs. . . . Napoleon himself often remarked what a vast influence a poem may exert on a receptive nature; and he had that receptive quality. His nature was attuned to poetry.[41]

The critic Fritz Strich suggests that through Napoleon *Werther* had real significance in the creation of a new Europe. He indicates that *Werther* did

> perhaps open his [Napoleon's] eyes to the falsity and inadequacy of existence in Europe, in which the latent power of a young man would be stifled by prejudices, traditions and conventions. . . . The grief that drove *Werther* to his death drove Napoleon to act, to change the static world, to break down the narrowness of existence. And the German poetic dream called on him to create a political reality.[42]

Among those who were touched by the Romantic preoccupation with suicide was Gustave Flaubert. He wrote in his letters that as a youth he had dreamed of suicide, noting that he and his friends "lived in a strange world. . . . We swung between madness and suicide; some of them killed themselves. . . . Another strangled himself with his tie, several died of debauchery in order to escape boredom; it was beautiful!"[43] And surely it is no accident that although Flaubert did not act on any suicidal longings, his greatest novel, *Madame Bovary,* deals with a suicide, one who is explicitly influenced in her fantasy life by her readings of romantic novels. "Madame Bovary, c'est moi," Flaubert said of his fictional creation. Like Goethe, Flaubert and many other writers have used the characters in their novels to work out their own fantasies and impulses and thus spare themselves the necessity of enactment.

Suicidal contagion—borrowed fantasy—so flamboyant as the Werther epidemic is rare. But it remains a constant in our culture. We have all been witness, via ever recurring news reports, to accounts of miniepidemics of suicide among teenagers whose classmates have committed suicide, a kind of copycat suicide. In assessing this phenomenon, the question always arises whether the suicides would have occurred anyway, sooner or later. Madelyn S. Gould, an epidemiologist of suicide, has studied suicide clusters that seem to occur in response to media coverage of other suicides and has concluded that this is a genuine phenomenon.[44] She bases this conclusion on a statistical analysis that indicates that some suicides that take place in epidemics might not otherwise occur, as indicated by the fact that the suicide rate does not decline after the epidemic, whereas if the epidemic comprised *only* people preordained to kill themselves, the rate *should decline* afterward because some of the anticipated suicides would already be dead.[45] That the rate remains the same demonstrates that suicides occur among imitators and adherents who might otherwise have resisted the suicidal urge. The total number of suicides in an epidemic represents a significant *excess* of suicides. Since cluster suicides account for approximately 1 to 5 percent of all teenage suicides,[46] this finding suggests the powerful role of identification—and of borrowed fantasy—as a risk factor in suicide.[47]

There is no comparable epidemiological research on the impact of fictional stories, but Gould's research "suggests that an increase in teenage suicides in the greater New York area followed fictional films featuring suicidal behavior that were broadcast on television in the fall and winter of 1984–1985."[48] Her results have been replicated, and a quick perusal of history indicates that suicide epidemics do occur in response to fiction, notably the *Werther* suicides discussed previously. Gould's working hypothesis is very similar to the psychoanalytic proposition that the transmission of a suicide fantasy via stories of real people or fictional characters depends on preexisting longings—both depressive feelings and suicidal urges—but can spur enactment that might otherwise not take place.

The suicide fantasy is such a hardy and poisonous plant in part because it is so constructed that many subsidiary fantasies can become attached to it and thereby be gratified. These subsidiary fantasies include revenge fantasies ("how so-and-so will suffer"), death and rebirth fantasies, and Liebestod fantasies.[49] Robert Lifton observes that "there is . . . the quest for a future in suicide, the desire to make a statement in a way that the person could not in life."[50] He believes that the novelist Yukio Mishima regarded death as somehow erotic, and surely this was true of Sexton and Plath as well. The writer Janet Malcom attributes some of the charisma of suicide to the paradoxical notion that "to take one's life is to behave in a more active, assertive, 'erotic' way than to helplessly watch as one's life is *taken away* from one by inevitable mortality. . . . On some level, perhaps, we may envy the suicide even as we pity him.[51] Suicide seems less deathlike than the death of old age; it is an act of will, providing a sense of control over death—possession of godlike powers. There are also suicides that gratify another kind of search for meaning and transcendence—those rooted in the culturally shared fantasy of dying for a cause. Kamikaze-type suicides and cult suicides are excellent examples of the immense power of a culturally mediated and sanctioned shared fantasy.

"SEDUCED BY DEATH": THE ROLE OF FANTASY IN SOCIAL POLICY[52]

The psychiatrist Herbert Hendin, a major researcher into suicide, believes that hidden, shared fantasies about suicide play a major role in the movement advocating physician assisted suicide. In a study of "assisted" suicides, Hendin discusses, among other cases, a report in which Timothy Quill, an associate professor at the University of Rochester School of Medicine, made what seemed to be a reasonable case for assisting in the suicide of Diane, his patient of eight years, whose situation he described as essentially "unbearable." Diane had suffered from both depression and alcoholism for much of her adult life. After a diagnosis of acute leukemia when she was told that she had only a 25 percent chance of surviving what was anticipated to be painful chemotherapy and radiation, Diane told Quill that she was going to decline treatment and wanted him to help her die. According to Hendin, when Diane went to say good-bye to Quill before taking her own life (Quill had prescribed the requisite amount of barbiturates), she promised him a future reunion "at her favorite spot on the edge of Lake Geneva, with dragons shining in the sunset."[53] Quill ended his case report wondering whether he would in fact eventually see Diane again on the shore of Lake Geneva at sunset.[54] Quill's echoing of his patient's fantasy led Hendin to suspect that a shared fantasy might be at work. Observing that death can be a metaphor for reunion in a magical netherworld, Hendin's concern was that because both doctor and patient shared that fantasy, neither had "come to grips with the fact of death."[55]

Hendin describes another physician who considers death as a liberation for patients who are suffering but is also drawn to euthanasia "by a special bonding or closeness that he developed with a dying patient whose life he would end that seemed unlike anything else he had encountered."[56] The possibility Hendin raises (particularly in cases of depressives, who are not otherwise ill) is that a patient seeks and finds someone to play the role of his or her executioner, and that both patient and doctor may feel a particular closeness in the moment of death.

Though each assisted suicide may start as a shared fantasy between two people, the publicity surrounding such suicides has attracted advocates to the cause. Thus a personally shared fantasy has fueled cultural fantasies, and groups dedicated to the right-to-suicide are proliferating.

Hendin believes that the debate about assisted suicide and euthanasia demands an understanding of the shared fantasies to which both doctor and patient may be prone. From the physician's side, Hendin fears that

> by deciding when patients die, by making death a medical decision, the physician has the illusion of mastery over the disease and the accompanying feelings of helplessness. The physician, not the illness, is responsible for the death. Assisting suicide in euthanasia becomes a way of dealing with the frustration of being unable to cure the disease.[57]

Policy issues concerning assisted suicide and euthanasia are, of necessity, infused with fantasy. The challenge is how best to engage in as objective a discourse as possible on a subject that is inevitably fantasy-laden for patients seeking death and doctors seeking to help them, and now increasingly sanctioned by large support groups. The assisted suicide debate is, of course, but one example of the way that fantasy influences the climate of opinion about many social and political issues.

THE CULTURALLY SHARED AGGRESSIVE FANTASY

In any discussion of how fiction and media reports impact on us, the first question generally asked is, What about violence? There are two opposing hypotheses about the impact of viewing violence. The more traditional view postulates that the viewer's catharsis of his or her angry feelings and hostile impulses through participation in a violent fictional work relieves the pressure toward any enactment. The opposing view suggests that violent and aggressive stories act to colonize the psyche, inculcating the idea that violence is adaptive—even heroic—and sometimes leading to the formation of destructive myths.[58] In fact, most of the commissions set up to investigate the connections between spectatorship and exposure to violent images and stories (whether fictional or real-life) have not definitively established whether spectatorship leads to substitute gratification or to action. The lack of conclusive findings relates to the fact that the many variables involved make designing a study of the phenomenon very difficult. For many people, especially those who are not aware of their own violent fantasies, watching violent movies or reading violent books *is* cathartic even as it allows those fantasies to remain sequestered in the unconscious. There is no doubt, however, that in some people, spectatorship does weaken a repressive boundary; we need only consider the many instances of copycat crimes.

A major impediment to gauging the impact of viewing violence on behavior is that the nature of the violence being studied may not be specified. Individual anarchic violence such as many of us now fear on our streets is generally linked to early life determinants, including characteristics of the perpetrators (learning disabilities, behavior problems, physical anomalies, and so on) and characteristics of the perpetrator's family (poor parenting practices including child abuse, rejection, lack of supervision or involvement, or family criminality). Shared fantasy, as exemplified in family history, is undoubtedly a factor. Child abusers beget child abusers. Violent fictional depictions may also act to release this kind of aggressive behavior. But anarchic aggression appears to be predominantly a default mechanism; that is, a behavior that is triggered by extreme and unrelieved frustration.[59] In contrast, culturally sanctioned aggressions organized against a common enemy are always consolidated around some form of widely shared fantasy or myth.[60] This kind of aggression also draws on early life determinants, but in conjunction with an overarching cultural set that often emphasizes the transcendent function of violence. It is the culturally shared aggressive fantasy on which I will focus more here.

Aggressive fantasies may be enjoyed vicariously, expressed, or acted out. However they are experienced, they often seek rationalization and grounding in the group's sanctioned modes of expressing aggression—lawful or unlawful—and they frequently draw on cultural sources in their very formation. Aggressive fantasies often thrive in situations where there is a confluence between personal disenfranchisement and a cultural crisis, in conjunction with a widely sanctioned "enemy." Since aggressive fantasies are virtually universal, they are generally organized into a cultural matrix, whose specific features depend on how the culture validates, limits, and directs the expression and disposition of aggression.

One of my patients, a born-again Christian and a successful executive, sought treatment because of sexual problems precipitated by a marital crisis. He was a gun collector who engaged in both target shooting and hunting, attended a self-defense school, and fantasized about attending a paramilitary function he had learned about through one of his gun magazines. He carried a weapon "just in case," he explained, because of the anarchic turn he felt New York had taken— all the while running violent, but ultimately self-protective fantasies in which he administered vigilante justice to drug addicts, rapists, murderers, and so forth. (Like one of my other patients, at my request, he checked the gun he kept on his person in an outside closet before entering the consulting room.) He did not appear to be a violent threat to anyone in his personal life, and I never felt threatened by him in the treatment situation. If there was any risk of his acting out his violent fantasies, it would have been in the context of an encounter with a threatening stranger, and his life was organized in such a way that this was a very unlikely occurrence.

What was significant to our successful work together was the discovery that his underlying conflict was related to self-destructive urges, specifically the struggle against suicide, rather than aggressive impulses toward other people. He mobilized self-defense and militaristic fantasies as a psychological defense against a profound sense of vulnerability caused by losses he had experienced early in life.

His vigilante fantasies did not appear with predictable regularity but were triggered by specific moments of crisis. The triggers included any incidents that he experienced as rejections or competitive defeats, such as a marital quarrel or a conflict with an employee. Though not consciously processed, remembered, or acted upon, such incidents were immediate triggers to the vigilante fantasy. That fantasy achieved for him what shooting up achieves for a drug addict—nullification of anxiety. Thus the fantasy of taking the law into his own hands was reparative, bolstering his self-esteem and allowing him to feel strong at moments of vulnerability. This man restricted his violent fantasies to the realm of the fantastic. However, others with the same dynamics may act on the violent fantasy in an effort to maintain their defenses against underlying feelings of being weak and unprotected.

Just as there are specific real-life triggers to the appearance of aggressive fantasies, so too do cultural triggers predispose large numbers of people to form aggressive fantasies. They may be particularly persuasive when the inner needs and conflicts of the individual converge with the shared fantasies and myths of the group to which he or she belongs. Klaus Theweleit's remarkable book about the Freikorps—that part of the German army that never demobilized after the 1918 Armistice[61]—describes the intersection of the personal and the cultural, the fantasies that emerge from that mix and the eventual enactment of those fantasies. Theweleit quotes the novelist and Freikorps member Ernst Junger's description of himself and his fellow warriors: "We were asked to believe that the war was now ended. We laughed—for we were the war. Its flame burned on within us and gathered all our actions under the glowing and mysterious spell of destruction."[62] Many thousands strong, the soldiers of the Freikorps, believing Germany had been stabbed in the back (through what they viewed as unfair terms of the Armistice), fought against the Communist and worker uprisings after World War I and some went on to become the core of Hitler's *Sturm Ableilung* (SA), known to us as storm troopers, and key figures in the Third Reich.[63]

Examining their shared fantasy life, Theweleit proposes that a widely dispersed cultural fantasy ultimately produced a violent, fascist reality that gave a sense of protection to those who participated in it. Theweleit uses the memoirs, diaries, letters, and fiction of the men of the Freikorps, as well as comic books, lewd cartoons, and photographs and drawings from Nazi publications to illustrate what he considers to be male desire turned fascistic. The fantasies he uncovers are not fantastic fantasies designed to provide substitute gratification, but rehearsal fantasies that are eventually acted out. At their heart is frustrated desire, which, through the destruction of whatever provoked the desire, is somehow converted into deep pleasure. The writings of the Freikorps have been described as "ripe with dreamy scenes of brutality and the familiar male text-passions (a quest-mission, a beloved commander, hallucinated vision-queen-women without cunts.)"[64]

Women in the minds of these men of the Freikorps belong to three categories: the wives and mothers left behind (that is, the absent women); the white nurses who inhabit both the imagination and the battlefield, and who are chaste and well-bred German women; and the red women, class enemies, who are wantonly sexual whores and evil temptresses. Of the pure woman, Theweleit writes, "Anything beyond her is uncharted, dangerous territory, yet she herself is taboo."[65] The men of the Freikorps allude to the red women as a flood or a tide against whom a man must stand firm and upright or be drowned—"sucked into" an impure sea. The link of the red women to communism associates a sexual threat with a political threat as well. Just as the warrior may find death in the embrace of the red woman, so, too, may he be drowned in an undifferentiated sea of communism. The warrior's goal is to stay erect and powerful, to avoid liquefaction in either the sexual situation or the political one.

The warrior has few sexual options, forced to choose between pure women or dangerous, engulfing lascivious ones. Thus sexual intimacy is denied to him and his quest for intimacy is corrupted into murderous penetration of his adversary:

> The nearest thing this man will enjoy to the utopian encounter of the lover and the beloved is at the same time the most distant from it: a collision between the unbending wills of two people, embodied in two men in armed confrontation. They meet to kill; and the only one to "flow" is the man who dies. The holes bored in him are a signal of the murderer's own transcendence of self. His self dissipates as he melts into the blood of the man of his own kind.[66]

The victor experiences a perverted sense of merger with the vanquished, and thus he incorporates the power of his felled adversary. The reward for the actual destruction of one's evil enemies is not only enhanced power but a fictive world of mythic grandeur, composed of hero warriors and pure women.

Like suicide fantasies, aggressive fantasies are so powerful because they act as an umbrella for many subsidiary fantasies. Like suicidal fantasies, they produce an illusory sense of strength, of participation in the Godhead, since they assume the power of life and death and therefore relieve sexual conflicts, unavenged hurts, individual insults to self-esteem and safety, and group uncertainties and insecurities.

These men of the Freikorps came by their fantasies honestly, first, through their individual histories, which generally involved a stern and often violent upbringing; second, through their collective national history, which drove them to seek relief for the humiliating defeat of the warrior culture they had embraced and the killing inflation that tore the German national fabric apart. Theweleit begins his search into the fascistic imagination with a personal image, touching and terrifying:

> A photo of Hindenburg, one of my earliest heroes, hung above the desk of my father, the railroad man, with a facsimile signature I long considered genuine. . . . My father . . . was primarily a railroad man (body and soul, as he put it) and only secondarily a man. He was a good man, too, and a pretty good fascist. The blows he brutally lavished . . . were the first lessons I would one day come to recognize as lessons in fascism. The instances of ambivalence in my mother— she considered the beatings necessary but tempered them—were the second.[67]

War not only provided the direct expression of the bottled-up rage evoked in a sometimes brutalized childhood, but presented a convoluted solution to psychosexual conflicts.

Theweleit does more than depict the morbid psychology of the men of the Freikorps. Titling his book *Male Fantasies,* it is male psychology—not just fascistic psychology—he sets out to explore, roaming the centuries for fantasies similar to those of the Freikorps man. He invites the male reader into his search for the fantasy basis of fascism by declaring, "Any male reading the texts of these soldier males—and not taking immediate refuge in repression— might find in them a whole series of traits he recognizes from his own past or present behavior, from his own fantasies."[68]

A more recent example of a phenomenon embodying many of the same themes as the Freikorps SA movement is provided by J. William Gibson, who traces the escalation in what he calls paramilitary fantasy culture in the United States.[69] In an analysis similar to Theweleit's Gibson relates the growth of this subculture to a national threat to the male ego—or at least to many men in our culture. He observes that after the Americans were defeated in Vietnam in the 1970s—the country's first major military defeat—a new image of the heroic male warrior as an invincible avenger began to emerge. This fantasy was exemplified, in part, through a new kind of movie—*Death Wish, Death Before Dishonor, The Terminator,* and *Rambo.*

In the post-Vietnam era, Gibson sees a huge, almost exponential resurgence of war and warrior stories, including action-adventure films and, perhaps more importantly, the male counterpart to women's romance novels, a "novel series for men featuring commandos, vigilantes and mercenaries who have left normal society and made battle their way of life."[70] (Many of the protagonists are Vietnam veterans or former Green Berets or SEALS. They, too, like the men of the Freikorps, divide women into those who are absent or sometimes dead and those who are dangerous and deadly, black-widow-spider women.) Gibson points out that by 1986 the magazine *Soldiers of Fortune: The Journal of Professional Adventures,* first published in 1975, was printing up to a quarter of a million magazines and now had several competitors as well. Clearly there is an expanding audience for paramilitary fantasy material. And for many in the audience the films and stories serve a cathartic function—they allow the fantasy impulse to be discharged vicariously.

But at the same time, the boundary between fantasy qua fantasy and fantasy as precursor to some form of enactment may be weakening. Tellingly enough, the rising interest in paramilitary and vigilante fictional material has been paralleled by an increase in sales of rifles. Gibson notes the growing popularity of the annual week-long *Soldier of Fortune* magazine convention in Las Vegas, of war games, special combat weapons, and training schools for self-defense. Among a significant minority of aggressive-minded people, the individual fantasy is seeking grounding, rationalization, and organization in culturally mediated fantasy and in group make-believe.

Looking at a whole array of evidence, Gibson believes we have spawned a "paramilitary culture," a new edition of a traditional war culture. But it is a new edition with an important difference: The new warrior hero no longer belongs to a conventional military or law enforcement unit. He fights alone or with a small band of like-minded fellow warriors. As Gibson points out, by existing outside the official power structure and bureaucracy, the warrior hero is freed of those legal and political restraints normally exerted on soldiers or subordinates.[71] This evolution marks an important shift, from a vision of the warrior as part of a larger social whole, to a vision of the warrior outside and sometimes opposed to the prevailing social order. Consider, for example, the popular belief that World War II was fought to make the world safe for democracy. Today the struggle is only for personal justice: "Struggles in the primeval chaos are no longer connected to the establishment of a sacred social order. In neither the films, the novels, the magazines, nor the war games, is there any vision of the world beyond war."[72] In Gibson's cultural analysis, the defeat in Vietnam created a crisis, because it destroyed earlier warrior dreams that were part of the legitimate concerns of the state. In his view, post Vietnam, the very concept of heroic manhood was shattered. He believes, however, that the defeat in Vietnam was intensified by other social shifts, including the eroding powers of the white race and of the male sex. If so, then the emerging paramilitary fantasy culture stabilizes both the individual's self-esteem and the group's sense of security in a world where many men feel that their traditional prerogatives are disappearing.

That the paramilitary fantasy is shared, even at the level of small subgroups of society, lends validity to the individual's fantasies. Still and all, it is extremely important to note that this fantasy gratification, even when it involves the acquiring and bearing of real arms, may remain at the level of wish-fulfillment and not be converted into actual violence. (And when it does leave the realm of fantasy, it is more likely to be converted into Far Right political preferences and groups than into violence. But violent enactment *is* a possible outcome.) The props, the guns, and the games shared at paramilitary and self-defense schools increase a sense of power and invulnerability, but generally the real power is the validation they provide through shared fantasy.

In a recent article on the National Rifle Association (NRA), the reporter Philip Weiss found apparent confirmation of the appeal of that shared power fantasy.[73] One of his hosts told Weiss, "No one even knows when I am carrying a firearm. As a matter of fact, I have been carrying my .38 here all the time."[74] He goes on to say, "This is great for walking in the woods. Because if anyone disturbs you, they're in for a little bit of a surprise."[75] Describing the advantages of a five-shot .22 Magnum that can be held with only two fingers, he explained that it was the perfect gun to have if he ever encountered trouble, say in a parking lot:

> This is belly to belly. . . . It's a last-ditch self-defense. If I want to I can stick this in my watch pocket and slip my belt over it. My kids call this my nasal decongestant. This is absolutely secret stuff. If I find myself in a threatening position or perceive that the environment is such, I will quietly retrieve it from the case and I know that if I have to, I can deal with the situation.[76]

The fantasies implicit in this exposition are right at the surface, as is the almost childlike delight in the fantasy of having "secret stuff." Weiss concludes that despite all the rhetoric about freedom and personal sovereignty, Gunnies are frightened: "Once you get past all their talk about birth rights and nerve gas, [they] are plain paranoid."[77] You don't have to agree with Weiss's conclusion to get some sense of the imaginative world of at least some of the Gunnies.

On the shooting range, Weiss observed, they

> traded stories of real encounters with enemies—of people with blunderbusses subduing Nazis, of someone pulling a gun on you while you were taking a walk in the woods—to give the fantasy greater verisimilitude. But they really wanted to avoid the reality at all costs. A real encounter would be both uglier and richer than the fantasy. It was much easier to live in a never-bloody belief about their powers and put off engagement. The Gunnies' dream about subduing endless

enemies was like a pornographic illusion: Your sexual powers cause scores of people to succumb to you at your will. No wonder the Gunnies were so attached to ugly guns. Asking a Gunnie to go back to a less sophisticated firearm was like asking a devotee of pornography to go from videos back to still photographs: The level of actuality, the degree to which the thing simulates a primal experience, was greatly diminished.[78]

Wisely, Weiss is quick to say that shooting does not have these particular fantasy connotations for all sportsmen. Nor, I would add, does the connection between guns and fantasy necessarily invalidate the Gunnies' arguments against gun control. The point here is not to promote or abolish gun control, but rather to illustrate how a fantasy of power based on guns receives validation in a culturally shared group fantasy.

If sufficiently widespread, intense feelings of fear, rage, and disenfranchisement can sometimes promote the formation of a sect. Self-styled militias have been reported in at least twenty of our states. A number of current media reports suggest that in some of the new militia groups a shared fantasy may be in the process of evolving into a belief system with potentially important political ramifications—and the communications technology to take their messages to a much larger audience. According to one news account, the Michigan Militia, a group that claims membership of twelve thousand, holds meetings to practice paramilitary techniques in preparation for defending itself against the United States government.[79] As described by the reporter, Keith Schneider, "What they [the members] have in common is opposition to gun control. But most of them also harbor conspiracy theories that the federal government wants to utterly control the lives of citizens and will crush those who resist, by means up to and including United Nations troops with old Soviet military equipment." The leader of the group, a forty-eight-year-old gun shop owner and pastor of the Calvary Baptist Church, told him: "When we started the militia, I thought it might get big very fast. . . . I'd been seeing the uneasiness that people have about their Government. It is not a Government by the people anymore. . . . When people sense danger, they will come together to defend themselves." Schneider observes that the rallying cry of many in the militia is to invoke the memory of the federal siege of the Branch Davidian compound in Waco, Texas, on April 19, 1993, as an event that demonstrates our government's threat to the individual's autonomy and freedom. To the degree that a group of militia members come to feel extremely endangered, and by their government at that, their potential for violent enactment escalates.

A study on fanaticism, and on the foundation of sects, jointly authored by a psychoanalyst, a historian, and a historian/political scientist describes the process by which disciples flock to a leader who holds out the promise of accomplishing a mission of transcendent value. The lead fanatic possesses the power to authorize the followers/disciples to overcome their superego inhibitions in the interest of rejecting or reforming the established society. Although a sect does not necessarily lead to fanaticism, it often provides a framework— a belief system evolving within a closed universe—wherein whatever "pathological" traits do exist in the members can emerge and flourish. "And, as a world outside the world, distinct from if not opposed to society, it is a ferment of deviation, fostering an atmosphere of vindictiveness toward those who condemn or fail to recognize its laws."[80]

Fanaticism rests on an ideal, the search for the lost Eden as restitution for current dissatisfactions. The fanatic invokes a pathological and omnipotent fantasy as an antidote to feelings of impotence and despair.

> During great popular movements—whether messianic, millenarian, or of mystical renewal—prophets come forth who stir the enthusiasm of the crowds by promising them the advent of an ideal world of happiness. Indeed, it seems as if each time a civilization gives off a reflection of degradation and despair, movements are born that allow people to have a glimmer of a world unlike the real one. Sometimes, these illusions collapse in self-destruction, but other times they succeed in giving a new impetus to the society; their success can be said to depend on their realism. In other words, if the optimistic image of a future world takes factors of reality sufficiently into account, it can lead to something, at least partially. If, on the other hand, it is completely utopian and unreal, the result of a purely paranoid projection distorting the projection of reality, it runs the risk of actually contributing to the destruction of the society.[81]

A detailed discussion of the psychology of fanaticism is beyond my scope here, but even a superficial examination indicates that fantasy plays a key role in it. For better or for worse, the "ideal world of happiness" that sects promote, the "optimistic image," whatever form it happens to take, is the very engine of the enterprise of fanaticism.

Plato argued that the work of poets and tragedians would best be banned in the ideal state, because stories had a profound and generally deleterious effect on their audiences, leading them to bad actions. His argument was that stories had the power to suggest too wide a range of imaginative possibilities—what I would call fantasy—and thereby to turn morality on its head. Obviously Plato viewed fantasy as prelude to enactment. Plato's argument is still used in one or another guise in support of censorship. (And, certainly, some of the ways we use our culture's storehouse of myth and story—of borrowed fantasy—give us reason for pause. Irrespective of our politics, many of the vigilante fantasies abroad in the culture right now are disquieting.)

The opposing view is that the very essence of humanity depends on active use of the imagination, which requires the cultural granary of stories as its nourishment. Both points of view suggest that we are strongly influenced by, if not constituted of, the stories of the surrounding culture.

Unlike the daydream, which is egocentric and can be shared with only a few others, both myth and art can reach a huge audience. As such, they have great potential not just for evil, but for good. As Hanns Sachs said of poetry, and by implication of art in general:

> Poetry . . . is a social phenomenon in the fullest sense. Produced by one mind, it proceeds to touch and move thousands of others; it binds together in a common emotion the most divergent personalities, which in almost in every other respect are widely separated by space, time, and cultural level.[82]

Sometimes an inchoate fantasy gets crystallized and expressed by the work of one mind—poet or playwright, myth maker, novelist, or prophet. Once crystallized the fantasy may speak so powerfully to the conscious and unconscious aspirations of a very large group that an entire culture is shifted. This happens only at times of great flux, when change is inevitable. But the specific content of the change is not inevitable; it is the product of a rare confluence of circumstance and sensibility, in which there is extraordinary correspondence between the minds of one or a few creative spirits and vast numbers of receptive, reactive people. Having examined some of the fantasies mobilized around the issues of suicide and violence, I will now consider a different kind of cultural material.

9

FANTASY AND
CULTURAL CHANGE

SHARED AND BORROWED FANTASIES PLAY AN IMPORTANT ROLE IN THE INDI-
vidual adaptations we make in life, in the cementing of personal relationships,
and in the forging of ties within large groups. They also influence the way a
whole culture is shaped and its myths begotten. The cultural myth is a special
form of shared fantasy; like the personal myth it is generally regarded as a
reality and is not recognized as being laced with wishes and creative imaginative material. A culture's myths, taken together, form what I call *the cultural
unconscious*.[1] By cultural unconscious, I do not mean a collective unconscious
or any universal cultural content; quite the contrary, I refer to those shared
fantasies and narratives specific to a particular culture that become part of the
individual's real world. These cultural myths constitute a major means by
which a group's members become socialized.

The psychoanalyst Jacob Arlow illustrates a culturewide myth, and the acting out of that myth, with the case of a little girl in a religious society who is
socialized to imitate the ideal qualities of purity, virtue, and love associated
with the Madonna (what might be construed as the myth of—or the ideal of—
pure and saintly womanhood). To take hold and flourish, to be disseminated
throughout a culture, such myths have to work on a number of different levels, providing channels for multiple and sometimes conflicting needs and
longings. Thus, as the child's identification with the Madonna socializes her,
enabling her to fulfill her society's expectations, it also gives her a culturally
sanctioned mode of gratifying an unconscious, unacceptable, incestuous wish.[2]

197

That the Madonna identification affords such gratification we can infer from the passion with which many nuns give themselves as brides to Christ.

Our myths primarily have an acculturating effect; that is, they act to preserve the status quo. However, under extraordinary circumstances they may also lead to profound cultural change. Michel Tournier writes:

> Man is nothing but a mythical animal. He becomes man—he acquires a human being's sexuality and heart and imagination—only by virtue of the murmur of stories and kaleidoscope of images that surround him in the cradle and accompany him all the way to the grave. . . . That being the case, it becomes easy to describe the social—one might even say the biological—function of the creative artist. The artist's ambition is to add to or at any rate modify the "murmur" of myth that surrounds the child, the pool of images in which his contemporaries move—in short, the oxygen of the soul. In general the artist affects this form of myth in only barely perceptible ways.[3]

What better description of the indispensable role of the artist, the poet, the prophet in gently reshaping the stories we live by.

A few gifted creators capture and modify the dream, not just of the moment, but of the future. From time to time, we are the beneficiaries of a great creative artist or innovator who pushes the envelope, introducing into the culture the possibility of significant change. Change of that magnitude cannot be accounted for, however, by any great-man theory of history that characterizes it as the consequence of one person acting in solitude. Jacob Arlow describes the true prophet as one "who correctly divines and expresses the emergent but still inarticulate dreams and aspirations of his people," the "midwife of humanity's dreams."[4]

Our myths undergo a sea change—and sometimes radical change—as the outcome of a shift in "collective imagining,"[5] the product of almost imperceptible imaginative changes that occur among many people simultaneously, in response to altered circumstances and a changing milieu. The coalescence of these changes into one overarching creative insight is the province of the artist/creator. The result may be scripts geared not just to anxiety-free or guilt-free indulgence of fantasy or to acculturation, but to authentically new modes of gratification, hence to social transformation.

There are a few detailed accounts of the artist-prophets who through their own creative insights almost singlehandedly ignite a flame that changes the historical course of a people. For Theodor Herzl, who was destined to effect a seismic shift in the aspirations and fate of the Jews,[6] the revised edition of one of his conscious fantasies appears to have been a critical factor in the creation of Zionism as a real nationalist political movement rather than a vague cultural agenda. Herzl provides a a rare in-depth glimpse into the process by which a fantasy became the stuff of history in the diary he began in 1895. There he set down a detailed record of his political aspirations as well as his active fantasy life.[7]

Born in Budapest in 1860, Theodor L. E. Herzl was the son of a Europeanized, assimilated, middle-class Jewish banker. But his paternal grandfather was an observant Jew, follower of a Sephardic rabbi who preached the ideal of the return of the Jews to Palestine.[8] Herzl's mother, to whom he was devoted all his life, has been described as "a type familiar in the history of every Mid-European Jewish family. . . . A woman . . . who strove most ardently for [German] cultural identification."[9] She was a passionate admirer of Ludwig Börne and Henrich Heine, two German Jews who at that time, and for several generations, symbolized the potential for full intellectual and artistic participation of those Jews who chose to assimilate.[10] In 1878, after Theodor's older sister, Paulina, died of typhoid fever, the grieving family moved to Vienna.

A brilliant young man, amply supported by his parents, Herzl was an outstanding student whose ambitions incorporated his parents' hopes and dreams for him. (He appears to have absorbed his mother's extravagant expectations of him.) In Vienna, he matriculated in the university's faculty of law. But the zeal and forcefulness that are crucial to courtroom lawyers and that later came to characterize Herzl's commitment to the Zionist movement took different forms in his young manhood. At first, Herzl had literary hopes and wanted desperately to achieve fame as a playwright; his chief ambition was that one of his plays be produced in Vienna's Burgtheater. Disappointed by the lack of success of his plays, none of which he could sell, he dreamed for a while of becoming a famous poet. He worked briefly in the law courts of Vienna and Salzburg, but ultimately it did turn out to be his writing gifts that brought him renown.

Herzl achieved recognition as a major journalistic talent. As Paris correspondent and later feuilletonist of the *Neue Freie Presse,* he was much admired by the Viennese public. (A brief essay or sketch, the feuilleton was highly prized in Vienna when brought off in suitably witty and urbane style.)

During this period of his life Herzl appeared to be, if anything, an assimilationist, like many Jews of his class, education, and background in Austria. Despite his apparent assimilationist bent, however, Herzl had always understood that the situation of the Jews in German culture was ambiguous, and from early on he had been imaginatively involved with the fate of the Jewish people.

As an adult he recorded in his diary a dream he had had when he was twelve:

The King-Messiah came, a glorious and majestical old man, took me in his arms, and swept off with me on the wings of the wind. On one of the iridescent clouds we encountered the figure of Moses. The features were those familiar to me out of my childhood in the Statue by Michelangelo. The Messiah called to Moses: "It is for this child that I have prayed." But to me he said: "Go, declare to the Jews that I shall come soon and perform great wonders and great deeds for my people and for the whole world."[11]

The Moses fantasy—to be savior of his people—is already apparent in this dream.

In Vienna, in 1881, Herzl had a brush with anti-Semitism. When his dueling fraternity chose to take part in an anti-Semitic commemoration of the death of Richard Wagner, he decided to resign as a point of honor. He took his revenge in his imagination—in fantasies of challenging various leading Austrian anti-Semites to duel. In these fantasies he played out what would happen if he lost—he would claim to be a victim of an unjust cause—and if he won—he would offer his regrets about the lives lost and deliver an oration about the Jewish question that would change the hearts and minds of all those who heard it.

In 1895, he recorded in his diary a seminal fantasy, this one dating from 1883, designed around the theme of saving the Jews (and establishing his own greatness). Austrian Jewry was to heal the schism with Christianity by means of a mass baptism. Herzl had imagined to himself how on a Sunday, in broad daylight, in a festive procession with bells ringing, he would lead the Jews of Austria to the Cathedral of St. Stephen, there to be converted to Christianity.[12] But in his fantasy he and all the other leaders were to remain outside, unbaptized, by way of signaling that they were not acting for personal gain—a characteristic Herzl gesture, since it incorporates his highly developed sense of honor. (According to the psychohistorian Peter Loewenberg, this decision to remain outside is an identification with the aggressor, since it draws on a Teutonic code of honor.)

Herzl was soon to abandon this fantasy-plan, acknowledging it as highly unlikely, after which he turned back to his preoccupation with writing, presumably leaving aside the Jewish question. Nonetheless, his desire to overcome anti-Semitism found its way into his work and, in 1894, into his play *The New Ghetto*, which he hoped would be so powerful that it would bring about a rapprochement between Jews and Gentiles. The hero, a young Jewish lawyer, prizes gentlemanly conduct and says to his friend: "I have learned from you how to honor a man without crawling at his feet, how to be proud without being arrogant."[13] But the lawyer has learned this lesson all too well and is killed in a duel. As a dying statement, he proclaims: "Jews, my brothers, there will come a time when they will let you live again—when you know how to die."[14] Peter Loewenberg believes that by this time Herzl had perfected the vision of the "new" Jew—a man who knew how to die like a cavalier—that would later be incorporated into his aspirations for a Jewish state.[15]

During his time as Paris correspondent for the *Neue Freie Presse,* Herzl experienced a trauma that led to the next step in his thinking about how to ensure the welfare of the Jewish people and the role he himself might yet play in forging that destiny. In late 1894, he was witness to the public degradation of Alfred Dreyfus; he saw the ceremony in which the epaulets of Dreyfus's uniform were torn off and his sword was broken, even while Dreyfus cried out his innocence.[16] At that moment, Herzl became convinced that Dreyfus, an Alsatian Jew, was in fact innocent and was being persecuted as a traitor only because he was a Jew. The Parisian mob's shouts of "Death to the Jews!"—not "Death to the Traitor!"—seared his soul. Zweig has called it "one of those hours that change an entire existence."[17]

The Dreyfus case became an important turning point in Jewish consciousness, and not just for Herzl, because it took place in France, home of the Revolution and the Enlightenment (both of which promulgated the ideal of the universal brotherhood of man), and because Dreyfus, a professional soldier who had risen to the rank of a captain attached to the French general staff, was the very symbol of the potential for successful assimilation. If *he* could be singled out for anti-Semitism, anyone could. Moreover, for Herzl, Dreyfus's degradation reverberated symbolically with the event that had awakened Moses to the plight of his people: When Moses saw an Egyptian task master strike a Jew he killed the slave master and escaped to the desert to lead his people to the safety of the promised land. Given his preexisting identification with Moses, it seems inevitable that Herzl would have a powerful response to the public humiliation of Dreyfus.

Herzl now realized that he had to conceive a political solution to the problem of anti-Semitism. He began the confessional diary that comprises a record of his emerging political vision interspersed with many grandiose, often compensatory fantasies. The *Diaries* of 1895 describe the feverish work leading up to his pamphlet "The Jewish State." Herzl had "been laboring for some time on a work of infinite magnitude. . . . Even now I don't know whether I will be able to carry it through. . . . It appears like a mighty dream." He experienced himself as finding release through the unconscious. Obsessed with the creation of the Jewish state, he compares himself to Moses, to Otto von Bismarck, to Napoleon Bonaparte, and to Helmuth von Moltke. Walking in the gardens of the Tuileries, fantasizing his success, he sees a statue of Léon-Michel Gambetta and thinks, "I hope the Jews put up a more artistic one to me."[18] He visualizes a new Jewish state, on the model of the Venetian state, with himself as doge. He sees himself as inspired by God. He experiences a volcanic eruption of creativity. Of his own work, Herzl writes:

> Artists will understand why I, who otherwise reason clearly, have allowed extravagances in dreams to grow wildly among my practical, political, and legislative ideas—as green grass sprouts between the paving stones. I could not permit

myself to be tied down purely to sober fact. This light intoxication was necessary. Yes, artists will understand this fully. But there are so few artists.[19]

And he was right. The fantasies were necessary handmaidens, first to his political perceptions and then to his political solutions. And they were indeed comparable to those that fuel the creative process of the artist.

In February 1886, Herzl published "The Jewish State," the pamphlet in which he proclaimed that since all attempts at creating tolerance had failed and true assimilation was impossible, the Jews had to create for themselves a new homeland—and not just a homeland but a state—by returning to their old homeland in Palestine. This pamphlet broke the long-standing impasse that held that there were only two paths open to the Jews: the ghetto practice of separateness, in which the unity of the Jewish people was affirmed but their hopes for a decent life, free of persecution, were deferred until the coming of the Messiah; and assimilation, in which the unity of the Jewish people was denied but individuals might achieve full rights as citizens. It was Herzl's genius to identify a third way. He declared that the Jews were one people and that the time had come for political, nationalist action.

The pamphlet created a hostile uproar in Viennese Jewish circles where hope for cultural coexistence or assimilation still flourished. Though hardly the first man to voice Zionist aspirations, Herzl was perhaps the most prominent one to do so and the one with the most fully articulated plan for making the Zionist dream a political and practical reality. As such, he brought down on himself a denunciation by the rabbis, and the opprobrium of Karl Kraus, perhaps the leading Viennese intellectual of his day, and of most of German-identified Jewry. In part, they were offended by his declaration of the Jews as *one* people, since assimilationist, Western European Jewry had done its best to distinguish itself from the badly educated, sometimes primitive shtetl Jews of Eastern Europe. At first Herzl felt hurt and misunderstood. In Vienna, where his articles had been a great success and he had thought himself securely loved, the Jewish population had turned on him with mockery and contempt. People accused him of wanting to become king of the Jews, and when he entered public places whispered that His Majesty had arrived. Their accusations of megalomania were not totally misplaced; his diaries bear ample witness to the grandiosity of his fantasies.

In revising his mass conversion fantasy into a dream of a mass exodus, Herzl had tapped into an old dream of the Jewish people—the return to the homeland. The Jews of Western Europe were not desperate enough to long for an empty, arid homeland few of them had ever seen. But Jews elsewhere responded to Herzl's pamphlet "with such force and such ecstasy that he was almost frightened to see how mighty a movement, already growing beyond his control, he had brought into being with his few dozen pages."[20] Rather than coming from the well-off, somewhat assimilationist German-speaking Jews to whom Herzl felt ties, this many-voiced hallelujah was sounded by the peoples of the East, the millions of oppressed Jews in Galicia, Poland, and Russia.

> Without realizing it, Herzl with his pamphlet had brought to flame the glowing coal of Judaism, long smoldering in the ashes, the thousand-year-old messianic dream confirmed in the Holy Books, of the return to the Promised Land.... Whenever anyone—prophet or deceiver—throughout the two thousand years of exile plucked this string, the entire soul of the people was brought into vibration, but never as forcefully as upon this occasion, never with such a roaring and rushing echo. By means of a few dozen pages, a single person had united a dispersed and confused mass.[21]

The old dream of a Jewish homeland had been transformed in Herzl's vision into a politician's demand for a Jewish nation based on international guarantees. By mounting a viable plan for the salvation of the Jews, Herzl had finally been able to transform his conscious fantasies—and his people's two-thousand-year-old dream—into something that could become a reality. As Loewenberg says, he had "the capacity to pass from the unreal to the real, to mix the spheres of dream and politics, to transfer the enchantment of make-believe staging to the world of diplomacy and political power."[22] Herzl was not content with the gratification his fantasies qua fantasies gave him; he was able to convert them into action, and it appears he was also shrewd enough to know the important role that theatricality played in the real world, for he used his dramatic flair to draw Jews and non-Jews alike to his cause.

I leave aside here the many psychological insights offered into Herzl and the many studies published on the relationship of his fantasies to his erotic and familial life. Some of these studies are reductivist insofar as they collapse *all* his fantasy life into sexual concerns. My focus here is not to relate Herzl's fantasies to his early life experiences—though some explanations given for his grandiosity and his identification with Moses are compelling—but rather to indicate that whatever his unconscious fantasies, it was his *conscious* fantasies, in which he totally identified with the Jewish people, which were essential to his plans for the salvation of the Jews and which ultimately were enacted.[23]

Once formed, Herzl's exodus dream was transmitted to a receptive audience, one which had been primed for such a dream for millennia. The result was a shared fantasy/political plan with major and still continuing implications for the future. By 1904, when he died at the premature age of forty-four, Herzl had in place those institutions that would lead to the founding of the Jewish state in Palestine. But, like Moses, he was not destined to live in the promised land.

Some prophetic fantasies do little more than promote substitute wish-fulfillment, as exemplified in Eastern Jewry's perennially hopeful responses to the successive proclamations of one or another false messiah. But sometimes such fantasies point the way to new ways of being in the world, new ways of channeling desire, or reawaken buried dreams whose moment has come. Herzl was able to convert his fantasies into reality because, by evoking the ancient dream of a homeland for the Jews, a dream that still lived in the collective imaginings of Eastern European Jewry, a dream that had long served as a salve to the persecuted millions, he struck a responsive chord.

I turn now to a different kind of evidence, which shows how changes in preconscious fantasies that are disseminated among a large group of people may ultimately produce major political change. The historian Lynn Hunt, whose work I will be citing, is interested "in the ways that people collectively imagine—that is, think unconsciously about—the operation of power, and the ways in which this imagination shapes and is in turn shaped by political and social processes."[24] In her study of the French Revolution, Hunt proposes that a major shift in the French family romance infused the revolutionary politics of the time.

Freud's formulation of the family romance referred to the child's fantasy that its "real" parents were more elevated than the impostor parents with whom it lived. While Freud's idea describes a certain stage in human development, when the child's inevitable dissatisfaction with the imperfections of family life result in dreams of a more perfect world, the concept of the family romance is also relevant to individuals' fantasies about improving their position in the social order. According to Hunt, the French Revolution enacted this family romance (rather than the one Freud describes). Thus, the revolutionaries did not imagine replacing their symbolic parents, the king and queen, with anyone of higher standing; quite the contrary, they imagined a totally different kind of family, one with no parents. Stripped to its bare bones, the achievement of the French revolutionaries was the removal of their king and queen—who might be imagined as the parents—in favor of a band of brothers.

Hunt argues that formulating the French Revolution as a family romance is apropos because "the French had a kind of collective political unconscious that was structured by narratives of family relations."[25] She does not claim that this phenomenon is universal; other peoples at other times might well perceive politics in other terms. "But most Europeans in the eighteenth century thought of their rulers as fathers and of their nations as family writ large. This familial grid operated on both the conscious and the unconscious level of experience."[26]

It was self-evident to most observers that the killing of the king, which was the most important political act of the revolution, had symbolic significance. The kingship had been based on what was considered to be a natural hierarchical order. Just as wives deferred to their husbands and children to their parents, so too did peasants defer to their landlords and great magnates to their king. A royal declaration of 1639 had stated, "The natural reverence of children for their parents is linked to the legitimate obedience of subjects to their sovereign."[27]

Hunt makes the point that just as

> traditionalists in European history have long pointed to the family as the first experience of power and consequently as a sure model of its working; just as the father was "naturally" the head of the family, so too the king was naturally the head of the body politic. . . . Under the Old Regime in France, the "mystic" fiction had it that the sacred was located quite precisely in the king's body, and as a consequence, the ceremonial and political life of the country revolved around that body. The French Revolution attacked this notion and replaced it with another, in which charisma was displaced and dispersed, to be located in language, symbols, and the new ceremonies of power, that is, in the collective representations of revolutionary fraternity.[28]

By evoking the Freudian concept of the family romance, Hunt has no intention of implying that the revolutionaries were acting out of neurosis. She views their actions not as pathological reactions to personal experiences, but "creative efforts to reimagine the political world, to imagine a polity unhinged from patriarchal authority."[29] Once that retelling of the traditional narrative was set into motion, not just the revolutionaries, but the counterrevolutionaries' opposition had to continue the process. They, too, had to confront issues that were germane to any reordering of the family romance—questions related to paternal authority, the rights of women, and fraternal bonds. They had to summon into existence a new form of government, the republic—headed by a new kind of leadership, a band of equal brothers—for the forces of the revolution demanded a basis for political consent that was different from the deference implicit in the paternal model of authority. The stories that encoded these changes had to deal with family conflict and resolution.[30]

Hunt attempts to substantiate her claims through a study of these stories, embodied by the literature and iconography of the prerevolutionary and revolutionary periods. There she has found the psychological underpinnings to the revolution, which can be observed for a number of years preceding it.

Hunt's thesis is that a new family romance of politics, quite different from kingship, was only possible if "the romance of patriarchal kingship and that of the king as good father were destroyed."[31] Part of her analysis centers on evidence that people's faith in the "good" father in whom authority and love were to be vested had been steadily eroding for years.

What is the evidence that such a shift preceded the execution of the king in 1789? Prerequisite to the fall of the king as "good" father was the rise of the idea of the good father as the head of the family—a transformation that was indeed taking place in the collective imagination. The rise of this good father, as opposed to the authoritarian father, appears to have had several antecedents. Among them was the increasing perception of children as different from adults, with different psychological, emotional, and intellectual needs, deserving affection and an educational curriculum designed specifically for them. Jean-Jacques Rousseau and other philosophers called for a limit to paternal power, which they believed should ideally conclude as soon as the child no longer needed help. According to Rousseau, "The father is only the master of the child as long as his help is necessary to him; beyond that moment, they become equals and then the son, perfectly independent of the father, owes him only respect and not obedience."[32] This widespread change in the ideology of the father-son relationship was already explicitly mirrored in the Parliament in 1732, in which magistrates asked Louis XV to prove that he was "more a father than our master."[33]

By 1770, another kind of attack on paternalistic power, with ramifications in both the practical and the familial sphere, had been mounted. This one involved the *lettres de cachet,* which gave the king unlimited power to imprison or exile anyone deemed a threat to the public order. Without any kind of hearing, the *lettres de cachet* could also be solicited by parents against their children, if the children were declared a threat to the rest of the family. Honoré-Gabriel Mirabeau's denunciation of the *lettres de cachet*—written while he was himself imprisoned as a result of a letter his father had written against him—was published in 1782. Other prisoners published memoirs depicting their denunciation by *lettres de cachet,* and public opinion was transformed. Subsequently, the king's officials tried to put a stop to this misuse of power, hoping that such a concession to the public would enable them to refashion the king's image into that of a good father, concerned about and responsive to the needs of his children (subjects).

With the rise of the ideal of the ruler as good father in political life, novels began to depict the good father qua father in family life. The Baron d'Etange, father of Julie in Rousseau's novel *Julie, Ou La Nouvelle Heloise,* of 1791, is often considered to be a transitional figure in this regard. Vacillating between loving and harsh, authoritarian behavior, he is part old-fashioned patriarchal father, part modern "good" father. According to Hunt, literary critics concur that novels in the last half of the eighteenth century began to portray new-model fathers who earned the respect and obedience of their children through affection and concern rather than unquestioned authority—when they depicted fathers at all, for "real biological fathers began to disappear altogether from [these] novels." Such changes constituted "a major shift in the representation of fatherhood and in the meaning of all authority relations."[34]

Another, related change pertained to the depiction of children. At first fiction had relegated them to a sentimental role on the sidelines; they did not figure in the plot. But this began to change, as books were published specifically for children. And, in 1788, with the publication of Bernardin de Saint-Pierre's

Paul et Virginie, children begin to appear as protagonists. Indeed, after *Paul et Virginie,* there was a veritable vogue of popular books about orphans and abandoned children. While many of the plots hinge on problems set in motion by a lost or abandoning father, the father himself is in fact absent from these works. This increasing emphasis on children, and children as individuals operating in an independent sphere of action, coincided with the undermining of the father in his traditional authoritarian role (and sometimes his complete disappearance). Hunt remarks that the absence of the father is also to be noted in the reminiscences of revolutionary politicians about their own childhoods—although many include vivid accounts of their mothers.[35]

Hunt believes,

> The literary transformations of repressive fathers into good and generous ones and the seeming effacement of the father in contrast to the more emotive mother and the increasingly interesting child all suggest that the novel as it developed in eighteenth-century France was inherently antipatriarchal.[36]

Marthe Robert, author of the *Origins of the Novel,* on whose work Hunt in part relies, suggests that the very existence of the novel, in the form it assumed at its beginnings in the eighteenth century, itself heralds the public appearance of the Freudian family romance, its move out of the sequestered realm of personal daydream and into the public world of literature. She views the typical eighteenth-century novel, with its many plots about foundlings and bastards, as a genre whose main subject is the individual finding a place in the social world. Thus, the individual's personal family romance fantasy of a higher birth is transformed into "the literary trope of social ascension." Robert argues that the novel became possible only because political and economic changes then taking place meant that actualizing the family romance daydream was now conceivable. Once the daydream of social ascension moved into the realm of the plausible, it could become the basis for the plot of a novel.

Hunt identifies connections among the appearance of the novel, the increasing potential for social mobility, and the decline of patriarchal culture and of patriarchal fathers in particular, right up to and including the king:

> In a sense, then, the eighteenth-century French novel predicts the fate of the king; it might even be argued that the novel produces the fate of the king in that the spread of the ideal of the good father and the father's subsequent abasement fatally undermined the absolutist foundations of the monarchical regime.[37]

The same erosion of the father appeared in the paintings and engravings of the prerevolutionary period. Hunt argues, and very persuasively, that the new capacity to imagine a world without fathers made revolution possible.

Hunt serves us well by projecting a chain of interconnected social phenomena that lead to a conceptual erosion of patriarchal power. The political and

social themes of the Enlightenment, particularly the ideal of universal brotherhood along with the reality of social mobility, impacted on and weakened
the long-existing idea of patriarchy in both social and political life. Major
changes in the external world almost mandate that personal fantasies take new
shapes, devise new scripts. If Marthe Roberts is correct, the novel itself reflects
the new reality of what had up until that time been a fantastic fantasy—
upward mobility. Changes in fantasy are not the defining features of the
French Revolution, which are in the end political. Surely the French Revolution was a "bread" revolution in which economics and exploitation played the
major role. But the ability to imagine and fantasize change is prerequisite to
profound political change.

The family romance played a crucial role in the direction the Revolution
took. As Hunt points out, in the American Revolution, the "revolutionary sons
of liberty" transferred power to the "founding fathers." This is very unlike the
French Revolution in which the ascendancy of the "band of brothers" followed the beheading of the king.

Hunt's analysis of the psychological underpinnings of the French Revolution
presents a modern historical enactment of Freud's original family romance,
that of *Totem and Taboo*.[38] In Freud's fantasy reconstruction, the first great act
of sacrifice in human history occurred when the sons banded together to kill
the father and eat him. Killing and eating him, they identified with him and
won the precious females. But once they had done the deed, feeling guilty, they
undid it with the creation of two taboos: a taboo against killing the totem animal (the substitute for the father) and the incest taboo, which restricts access to
those women liberated from the father's control. Out of the band of brothers a
new social order arose. Fanciful although Freud appeared to be in *Totem and
Taboo,* he grasped the profound interpenetration of fantasies about the self in
the family and the self in the political order. This major insight Hunt ably doc-
uments in her political and cultural exegesis of the French Revolution.

The rise of romantic love in the West is another illustration of the profound
effect of a change in collective imagining on personal life. It is an excellent
example of the intersection between the personal (universal) unconscious and
the cultural (contingent) unconscious.

As a large-scale phenomenon, romantic love is a product primarily of the
West, a cultural construct or innovation that first appeared in eleventh-century
Provence, according to most historical analyses of the concept.[39] Recounting
the history of the phenomenon, C. S. Lewis explains:

> French poets ... were the first to express ... that romantic species of passion
> which English poets were still writing about in the nineteenth century. They
> effected a change which has left no corner of our ethics, our imagination, or our
> daily life untouched, and they erected impassible barriers between us and the

classical past or the Oriental present. Compared with this revolution the Renaissance is a mere ripple in the surface of literature.[40]

Lewis argues that the phenomenon of romantic love was extremely rare, if not unknown, in classical antiquity and in the Dark Ages.

Romantic passion, mythic in its power over contemporary lives, draws on a shared fantasy of attaining bliss and transcendence through possession of, or union with, a specially endowed, irreplaceable, and unique Other.[41] While the individual imagination acting on early life experience decisively influences the lover's choice of the beloved, the underlying impulse to fall in love is shaped by the culture's love stories, fairy tales, and lyrics, and by its fundamental values.

Subjectively, nothing seems more real or important to lovers than their passion. In fact, however, such a seemingly primordial emotion is not universal but is specific to individual cultures. While one may plausibly argue that affectionate bonding is nearly universal—indeed some classifications name it as a primary affect—romantic love, for all its intensity of emotion, is decidedly not primary, not one of those universal affects depicted by Charles Darwin,[42] Charles Izard,[43] and others as bound up with the survival of the species and therefore central to the human condition.

The best evidence that romantic love is not hard-wired into the emotional repertoire of humanity is its virtual absence from many cultures.[44] The sociologist William Goode suggests that romantic love occurs on a continuum: At one end of the continuum, romantic love receives negative social sanction and is regarded as a comic or tragic abnormality (as it may still be in Japan and China); at the other, it is considered disgraceful to marry without love (as in much of contemporary Western society).[45] As Goode points out, these facts are consonant with two different but not inconsistent hypotheses about the nature of love: Either love is "a universal psychosocial possibility,"[46] the flowering of which largely depends on positive sanction, or it depends entirely on specific structural factors (I take this to mean certain cultural configurations including the culture's value system and the presence or absence of romantic role models). However, we do know that even in cultures and situations that negatively sanction love, there are frequent examples of full-blown, and on occasion death-defying, love, for example, that of Abelard and Héloise, whose passionate sexual love flew in the face of the precepts of the church. Such examples support Goode's first hypothesis: Love, if not a hard-wired emotion, is certainly a universal psychological possibility, a potential that may be cultivated (as in our society) or largely suppressed (as in most tribal cultures) but may sometimes, even against great odds, appear spontaneously, revealing its roots in some universal aspect of the human condition.

Not a primary affect, then, but a powerful compound passion in which emotions and thoughts are intertwined, romantic love is an act of the imagination, a creative synthesis in which many diverse fantasies, wishes, feelings, and impulses crystallize to focus on one person alone, the idealized beloved.

Romantic passion, sanctioned (and in large part generated) by cultural prescription, unites those fantasies, wishes, feelings, and needs that in other cultures find alternate modes of expression and are dispersed among different
objects. For example, in another culture, sex might be shared with a spouse,
intimacy with a friend; idealization reserved for God; and meaning derived
through religion.

Love stories, the narratives that bind these impulses and wishes and voice a
culture's attitudes toward love, are for the most part a product of the West, and
through them many in the West have learned to seek romantic love. Without
both the example and the endorsement—expressed through such stories—
romantic love is very rare.

Through its sanction of particular modes of gratification and its provision of
a storehouse of meaningful narratives and myths with which to organize emotional and instinctual life, the cultural milieu variously encourages, ignores, or
suppresses the potential for romantic love. The Duc de Rochefoucauld's much-
quoted maxim that people would not love had they never heard of love has
some merit. It does not, however, discredit love; rather it highlights the fact
that the expression (and content) of our dearest longings depends not only on
instinctual life and individual development but on the cherished myths and
goals around which a culture coheres.

Romantic love today in the West is prelude (and often prerequisite) to marriage. Within our own culture romantic love is almost universally sanctioned,
but that is a relatively recent development. The history of romantic love in
Western culture as revealed in the prototypical love stories of each era illustrates that popular conceptions and expectations of love have changed greatly
over the centuries.[47]

Until the Middle Ages, there were relatively few love stories: the Song of
Songs (although some rabbis have claimed that the love expressed in that wonderful poetry was for the Hebrew people, not the queen of Sheba); Greek and
Roman myths centered around the gods and goddesses, which depict love as
capricious and for the most part destructive; and the *Iliad,* which, although not
about love is set in motion *by* love—the adulterous love of Paris for Helen,
which precipitated the Trojan War. While these works suggest that romantic
love did exist in earlier epochs, it was not an important cultural (and literary)
concern until the Middle Ages.

The innovative product of the medieval imagination, the first love stories
flourished in the troubadour culture of southern France in the eleventh
through fourteenth centuries, though not in the form with which most of us
are familiar today. The troubadour tradition promulgated a romantic love,
religious in its intensity, in which the love relationship was to be kept in the
realm of the ideal, leading neither to carnal knowledge nor to marriage.

Believed to draw its inspiration in part from the Crusaders' exposure to the
Sufi tradition of mystical eroticism, and in part from the increasing emphasis

on Madonna worship, the source of the troubadour tradition has yet to be fully explained. Whatever impelled its origin, by circumscribing love's expression and its effects so carefully, the tradition managed to celebrate individual passion without sanctioning a breach of the social order.

In the literature of the age of chivalry, the beloved woman is *always* married to someone other than the would-be lover, her devoted knight.[48] However adulterous the longings expressed in the prototypical love songs of the medieval troubadours, the love they described remained chaste. Although the knight might long intensely for the lady, he respected his commitment to his lord (generally the lady's husband) and would not violate that bond. Consequently, the knight had no thought of expressing his love in the flesh, for doing so would compromise his allegiance to his liege lord, who was, within the hierarchical order of medieval society, his symbolic father.

Nonetheless, in setting up their own courts of love and establishing their own rules of conduct, the troubadours and their ladies reflect the West's abandonment of absolute authority and its growing romance with autonomy. The Church, sensing some defection, marked the courtly lovers for extermination in the Albigensian Crusade but with limited success, since, as we know, the ideology of ideal love survived.

Even in the Middle Ages, however, the theme of love that is adulterous not just in longing but in actuality began to surface; in fact, it was frequently invoked, but in a manifestly admonitory mode. In the popular Arthurian legends, Guinevere, in betraying her husband, King Arthur, with Sir Lancelot, fell outside the morality of her day and had to end her life in a nunnery, as Lancelot ended his in a hermitage. Even more of a cautionary but perhaps also a subversively inspirational tale is that of Tristan, the nephew of King Mark of Cornwall, who was sent to Ireland to accompany his uncle's bride, Isolde, to Cornwall, but fell in love with her instead. These two illicit lovers defiantly found release only in death, in the *Liebestod*.

Romantic love continues to appear mainly in the guise of adulterous love in the literature of successive generations, generally portrayed as something more to be cautioned against than celebrated, a force at odds with the social order. Even Shakespeare, one of the great love poets of all time, made adultery and its earth-shattering consequences one of his major themes. And even when he portrayed love in other guises—the pure love of Romeo and Juliet, for example—it was often as a force that could destroy lives.

Adultery was a major theme in virtually all Restoration drama but seemingly fell from favor as a topic of interest to the rationalists of the eighteenth century.

Adultery reappeared as a major theme in many of the great nineteenth-century novels, for example, *The Red and the Black, Madame Bovary, Anna Karenina,* and *The Ambassadors.* The manifest content of these works was still cautionary, as the adulterous lovers pay a great price (sometimes death) for flouting the social order. The novels suggest sympathy for their suffering, however, and if only because of the frequency and intensity with which adulterous longings are evoked in the nineteenth century, one senses something subversive in the air: a major assault on the rules of possession both in the private and public spheres—on the control of women and property. Adultery appears to be emblematic of a larger issue: the extent to which the flowering of the cult of individuality, with its legitimatization of individual desire, would preempt the claims of society, the prerogatives of the "father."

And soon enough, a momentous change did occur in the way Westerners regarded romantic love. A new emphasis on union and a transformation of love from a violent, subversive force into a tamer, domesticated vision the culture could deem respectable and institutionalize redefined romantic love and overturned the premises of courtly love and its emphasis on longing for but not possessing the beloved. Now marriage became the natural culmination and institutionalization of love, a sacrament between two individuals rather than a social contract, and love was the birthright of all. This new concept is a remarkable transformation of the former perception of romantic yearning as idealized and chaste, with no consequences in the outer world, or adulterous and impure, with disastrous consequences. What had been the anomalous experiences of a chosen—or, alternately—cursed few was now acknowledged to be a universal experience, devoutly to be wished for, and, moreover, the only proper basis for entering into marriage.

According to the historian Lawrence Stone, this shift arose out of the Romantic movement that began in the late eighteenth century, was consolidated with the flowering of that movement in the nineteenth century, and won general acceptance only in the twentieth.[49] By the late nineteenth century, then, romance had become a "sentimental love religion," its rise paralleling the erosion of the values of communality as the valuation of the individual increased. Only in a society inclined to celebrate the autonomy and self-assertion of the individual, it would appear, could the ideal of realized romantic love flourish.

The dissemination of this new ideology of love depended on the unprecedented availability of the written word in the nineteenth century, courtesy of the institution of the lending library as well as the greater affordability of books and periodicals. Love stories then constituted much of what was written about in both the novel and the popular press. For a long time, the tone remained cautionary, as adultery and its dire consequences were still central to literary depictions of love. But love became the pursuit of Everyman and Everywoman—in fiction, then in life. Once again, life imitated art.

Not just historians, but artists have acknowledged love's debt to love stories. According to Dante Alighieri, the adulterous lovers Paolo and Francesca, whom he encounters in the second circle of hell, are descendants of a direct literary line from Lancelot and Guinevere, for in reading together about those earlier transgressors they themselves came to feel the spark of love.[50]

Gustave Flaubert too was aware that the longing for love can be catalyzed by reading about it. In *Madame Bovary,* Emma's desire for romance, her taste for "Sighs in the moonlight, long embraces, hands bathed in lovers' tears—all the fevers of the flesh and the languors of love,"[51] appears to have arisen from her devouring of novels, specifically those of Honoré de Balzac and George Sand, and her sensuality in general to be a direct result of her convent-girl immersion in the mystic languors of the Catholic Church. Thus, a particular cultural construct, the popular love story, itself a product of important but not fully articulated cultural aims, comes to shape the expression of an individual's hopes, wishful fantasies, and behaviors.

As the story of Emma Bovary makes clear, love itself is in part a cultural construct: a learned phenomenon transmitted through the oral and written culture of the times. But as it was for Emma, it is far more than that. As Flaubert describes Emma,

> she was waiting for something to happen. Like a sailor in distress, she kept casting desperate glances over the solitary waste of her life, seeking some white sail in the distant mists of the horizon. She had no idea by what wind it would reach her, toward what shore it would bear her, or what kind of craft it would be—tiny boat or towering vessel, laden with heartbreaks or filled to the gunwales with rapture.[52]

Secondhand though Emma's passion may be, we sense in her those impulses toward radical change, specifically toward self-transformation and the amelioration of the solitariness of the self, that are among the factors that motivate all lovers, however unworthy the object.

It has been said that "the noble lover loves love stories."[53] It seems equally true that love stories create lovers. The longing for romantic love most often crystallizes in the context of emulation and envy of other lovers, in real life, in books, or in film, in short, our prevailing cultural narratives encourage the individual to believe that his or her ideal self will be achieved through the agency of romantic love.

However, cultural narratives (or prescriptions) only take root when they present an opportunity to gratify the deepest wishes and needs, those that originate in instinctual and emotional life, with ramifications throughout the course of psychological development.

What psychic needs does love satisfy? It can gratify the needs for sex and attachment, but so can affectionate bonding. Romantic love achieves many aims (such as needs for sex or intimacy), but the lover's quest for union with the idealized beloved is the specific need that romantic love fulfills. This longing has its roots in the universal fantasies that arise in the earliest days of developmental life. Love revives the dream of fulfilling the half-forgotten, inevitably frustrated wishes for perfect harmony and complete mutuality—wishes that originated in the now-buried fantasy of obtaining the perfect mother to love one unerringly and unceasingly.

Although some claim that one's own happiness is the goal (and motivator) of love, this claim does not take into account those lovers who sacrifice all hope of conventional happiness for the sake of their love and may even be prepared to die for it. Love is better understood as the pursuit not of happiness but of the beloved, whose possession guarantees self-esteem.[54]

Through union with the idealized beloved, the lover gains a sense that his or her grander self, a self experienced as both more perfect and more powerful than at any time since infancy, has been restored.[55] And here Plato's and Freud's views of love flow together, as both believe that the impetus to love grows out of an awareness of one's own insufficiency and a wishful (fantasied) move to narcissistic restitution.[56] The notion of romantic love as narcissistic repair explains the sense of peace, of rightness, that is so prominent a feature of requited love. Contemporary theorists explicitly posit what is only implied by Freud: namely, that lovers attempt to undo the unhappy past.[57]

If, as Freud suggested, the "motive forces of phantasies are unsatisfied wishes, and every single phantasy is the fulfillment of a wish, a correction of unsatisfying reality,"[58] then love, which is an imaginative act, a "phantasy," is a means of reversing the disappointments of early life, of gratifying unfulfilled and forbidden childhood wishes, and of restoring narcissism—all at the unconscious level, of course.

Thus far, I have given a brief history of the way love has evolved in the West and an even briefer description of the psychic roots of love in the individual's developmental history. What remains to be explored is the role of the imagination—of fantasy—in the selection of the beloved. Toward the end of his life, H. G. Wells (who was a noted Don Juan) tried to come to grips with the question of why we love whom we love and in so doing gave a brilliant account of how each of us forms an unconscious image of an idealized Other:

> I think that in every human mind, possibly from an extremely early age, there exists a continually growing and continually more subtle complex of expectation and hope: an aggregation of lovely and exciting thoughts; conceptions of encounter and reaction picked up from observation, descriptions, drama; reveries of understanding and reciprocity: which I will call the Lover-Shadow. . . . I think it is almost as essential in our lives as our self-consciousness. It is *other* consciousness. . . .
>
> When we make love, we are trying to make another human being concentrate for us an impersonation or at least a symbol of the Lover-Shadow in our minds; and when we are in love it means we have found in someone the presentation of the promise of some, at least, of the main qualities of our Lover-Shadow.[59]

Wells is clear that our choice of lovers is related to our internal psychic processes—to imagination, in short. In love the imaginative valuation and idealization of an Other, who in turn loves us, lead to many gratifications, among them enhanced self-esteem and a sense that life has meaning.

This dynamic is not, of course, limited to romantic love. The same psychic stratagem is at work in religion, in the passionate love of God; a similar mechanism is at play in any passionate devotion to a person or cause, whether political, religious, or artistic.

Insofar as different cultures may generate different needs in the individual and propose different methods of assuaging them, we would expect them to construct different narratives and idealized pursuits. Though there are great similarities between religion and romantic love, there are equally important differences. What is celebrated in religion are obedience and conformity. The religious narrative proposes a God who is divine; devotion and closeness to God allow one to establish a sense of goodness, of rightness, of self-esteem, and of meaning. The ideal self is achieved through dedication to and worship of God, about whose divine attributes there is generally a consensus. In contrast, romantic love celebrates uniqueness, individuality, the propensity for self-will, for the choice of a particular love object is very much a matter of individual, idiosyncratic taste.

The historical appearance of romantic love marks the beginning of a shift from an authoritarian, traditional, God-oriented society to an individual-centered one. Joseph Campbell goes so far as to suggest that "of all the modes of experience by which the individual might be carried away from the safety of well-trodden grounds to the danger of the unknown . . . the erotic (mode of feeling) was the first to waken Gothic man from his childhood slumber in authority."[60]

In Western culture, in which religion had been so long on the wane and the cult of radical individuality correspondingly on the rise, love more and more came to be invoked as the major route to happiness, as well as one of the principal solutions to the problem of meaning. Romantic love, then, as we know it in the West, is related to the rise of individuality; it is an instrument of self-will and self-transformation—and a product of those psychic forces. Without self-will (self-assertion) there is no capacity for psychological separation from a preexisting tie and therefore no possibility for establishing a new preeminent relationship.[61] (But so much autonomy creates its own conflicts, and we now see a revival of religion among many groups.)

Fantasy-based, romantic love appears to be a cultural innovation of the medieval world, which borrowed both from the world of Islam and a Marian revival (Mary worship) within the Catholic Church. Romantic love—at least that experienced between men and women—depends, as Stendhal knew, on some ability of men to admire women. For this reason Mary worship was undoubtedly a prerequisite to the wholesale development of romantic love. Redefined in the nineteenth century, romantic love has continued to exert a major influence on imaginative life and behavior in the West. What is powerful about the cultural innovation of romantic love is that it merges in one story

line—the plot of idealized mutual love—possibilities for simultaneously fulfilling many disparate fantasies, wishes, and needs.[62]

Though the historical forces that allowed the medieval imagination to create romantic love are not entirely clear, that creative synthesis has proved deci-
sive to the psychological development of individuals in Western culture.
Romantic love, then, is a cultural creation, developed in tandem with the
West's romance with autonomy. As a cultural construct, it has as much influence on the resolution of issues of authority and personal autonomy as on narcissistic repair and psychosexual development.

Romantic love, as it draws on the fantasies and narratives that permeate the
surrounding culture, resists reductive theorizing that explains it exclusively in
terms of instinct or psychosexual development. But it similarly resists interpretation as a cultural artifact, in its occasional appearances in cultures in
which the quest for romantic love is either unknown or anathema.

The variable status of love in different cultural milieus and historical epochs
is not an impediment to theorizing; it is itself relevant to the way we think
because it points to the influence of the cultural unconscious—the stamp of a
culture on expressions of fantasy and emotion. Romantic love provides a premier case study of the intersection of the cultural unconscious with the fantasies and needs of the individual psyche in the creation of new stories, and
corollary shifts in the ways the individual construes the self and seeks adaptations and gratifications.

Fantasies are mediators between the inner and outer worlds; they are fueled
by both the fantasizer's biological and emotional needs, as shaped by his or her
personal history, and by circumstances. But the story lines of fantasy cast a
wider net; they borrow their narrative content from the cultural surround.
Some fantasies are communal at their inception: That is, they borrow narrative content, consciously or unconsciously, from the fantasy content of significant others, of families and small groups. Individuals are integrated into the
mores and customs of the culture at least in part through shared fantasies and
the myths, art, and popular culture that embody them. Borrowed cultural narratives provide story lines that the fantasizer may not be able to create independently but can adopt as an umbrella for many different wishes and needs.

We are acculturated through the myths and fantasies that surround us; so,
too, the culture changes through the influence of certain creative individuals
and through sea changes in the fantasy life of its members. While most people
may believe that the imaginative and mythic changes wrought by Herzl, by
the French Revolution, and by the rise of the ideal of romantic love may be all
to the good, nevertheless many fantasy-based change-moments are at best
problematic and sometimes disastrous, such as the Aryan fantasy of the
Superman that infused Nazism. I call these cultural and political transforma-

tions *change-moments* because they appear to be turning points, and they sometimes seem to appear in a flash. But this is illusory. These change-moments have a long prehistory either in the individual psyche or in the collective imagining. Moments that reorganize our collective imagining may expand our human possibilities, but some such moments are cultural dead ends or even lethal threats to the species. It is for this reason that I have analogized instances of cultural change to mutations: Fantasy is to cultural evolution as mutation is to biological evolution, and cultural mutations, like biological mutations, may benefit us, but they may also kill us.

NOTES

Introduction

1. As Robert Stoller commented, ". . . our mental life is experienced in the form of fantasies." In *Sexual Excitement: Dynamics of Erotic Life* (New York: Pantheon Books, 1979), p. xiv.

2. See H. G. Wells, *H. G. Wells in Love: Postscript to an Experiment in Autobiography,* ed. G. P. Wells (Boston: Little, Brown, 1984), pp. 53–55.

3. In Henry James, *The Altar of the Dead; the Beast in the Jungle; the Birthplace; and Other Tales* (New York: Scribner, 1909).

4. Charles Laughton, "The Barber's Tale of His Fifth Brother," in *Tell Me a Story* (New York: McGraw-Hill, 1957).

5. One version of this story appears in W. W. Jacobs, *The Monkey's Paw: A Story in Three Scenes,* dramatized by Louis N. Parker (New York: Samuel French, 1910).

6. Teresa of Avila, quoted as epigraph in Truman Capote, *Answered Prayers: The Unfinished Novel* (New York: Random House, 1987).

Chapter 1

1. Laplanche and Pontalis describe the function of fantasy as providing a setting for desire. They refer to this as a "mise èn scene" of desire. See Jean Laplanche and Jean-Bertrand Pontalis, *The Language of Psycho-Analysis,* trans. Donald Nicholson-Smith (New York: W. W. Norton, 1973).

2. Sigmund Freud, "Creative Writers and Day-Dreaming" (1908[1907]), *The*

Standard Edition of the Complete Psychological Works of Sigmund Freud (hereafter *S.E.*), ed. and trans. James Strachey (London: Hogarth Press, 1953–1974; New York: Basic Books, 1981), vol. 9, p. 145.

Hanns Sachs made an observation similar to Freud's, suggesting that "every man wants to keep his daydreams secret, even the perfectly harmless ones, and considers his friends as outsiders when they approach this most sacred precinct of his private life. It is a proof of great confidence and intimacy when this barrier is let down." See Hanns Sachs, "The Community of Daydreams" [1920], *The Creative Unconscious* (Cambridge, Mass.: Sci-Art Publishers, 1942), p. 24.

3.   Harold Blum, "Chairman's Opening Remarks," presented at the panel "Clinical Value and Utilization of the Daydream," Scientific Meetings of the American Psychoanalytic Association, New York City, December 19, 1993.

4.   Robert Stoller, *Sexual Excitement: Dynamics of Erotic Life* (New York: Pantheon, 1979), p. 93.

5.   Ibid., p. 111.

6.   Sometimes, too, the patient is troubled by his or her need for an obligatory fantasy in order to achieve arousal and may intuit how central to his or her innermost self the fantasy cuts.

7.   As regards sexual fantasies, some therapists may be hesitant to ask about them too early, for fear of frightening skittish patients.

The relative neglect of conscious fantasy is an intellectual bias that inheres in psychoanalytic theory and has been characteristic of psychoanalysis for decades. Unlike unconscious fantasy, which has been extensively explored, conscious fantasies, except for sexual and perverse ones, have received relatively scant attention since Freud's pioneering and revolutionary insights. Analysts may have eschewed an interest in conscious fantasy because of the fear that no distinction would be maintained between the concept of fantasy (or daydream) and unconscious fantasy.

8.   Robert D. Gillman reported essentially the same fantasy in an eight-year-old boy whom he was evaluating. See Gillman "Rescue Fantasies and the Secret Benefactor" in *The Psychoanalytic Study of the Child,* vol. 47, ed. A. J. Solnit, Peter B. Neubauer, S. Abrams, and A. Scott Dowling (New Haven: Yale University Press, 1992), pp. 279–298.

9.   Why her fantasies were about maimed males rather than females is beyond the scope of this presentation, but had to do with a gender-related conception of power, with penis envy, and with castration fantasies toward males originating in part from her unconscious rage at her father's desertion of her mother, and with many other issues, ultimately implicating the patient's own self-identity and sense of bodily integrity.

10.   See Jay Martin, *Who Am I This Time? Uncovering the Fictive Personality* (New York: W. W. Norton, 1988), pp. 102–106.

11.   The story of Fowler's psychological testing of MacDonald is reported both by Jay Martin and by Eric Klinger. See Martin, *Who Am I This Time?* pp. 102–106, and Klinger, *Daydreaming: Using Waking Fantasy and Imagery for Self-Knowledge and Creativity* (Los Angeles: Jeremy P. Tarcher, 1990), pp. 158–161.

12. Martin, *Who Am I This Time?*; Klinger, *Daydreaming*.

13. Quoted in Martin, *Who Am I This Time?* pp. 105–106.

14. Martin, *Who Am I This Time?* p. 106.

15. Freud, "Creative Writers and Day-Dreaming" (1908 [1907]), *S.E.*, vol. 9, p. 153.

16. Italo Calvino, "A Cinema-Goer's Autobiography," in *The Road to San Giovanni* (New York: Pantheon, 1993), p. 60.

17. Hanna Segal remarked,

each dreamer has a favourite style in his dream language, and the style itself often reveals their personality. "Le style, c'est l'homme," said Buffon. It applies to dreams as well as to art. The very style of the dream, like the style of the personality, reflects the broad combination of object relationships, anxieties, and defenses that moulds one's personality.

See Hanna Segal, *Dream, Phantasy and Art* (London: Routledge, 1991), p. 11. The same may be said of the fantasies of waking life, but I would include variations in addition to those Segal invokes, such as those referred to in my text.

18. See Oliver Sacks, "An Anthropologist on Mars," *The New Yorker* (December 27, 1993–January 3, 1994), 106–125; quote on p. 115.

19. Ibid., p. 121.

20. David Lodge, *The Art of Fiction* (New York: Viking, 1992), pp. 50–51.

21. William James, author of the term *stream of consciousness* and its preeminent explorer, should be required reading for psychologists and psychoanalysts.

Chapter 2

1. See Jerome L. Singer, *Daydreaming: An Introduction to the Experimental Study of Inner Experience* (New York: Random House, 1966), p. 57.

2. Sylvan Tomkins, from the foreword to Singer, *Daydreaming*, p. xii.

3. Almost all authors agree that daydreaming is an imaginative activity accompanied by the fantasizer's withdrawal of attention from the immediate demands of the external world, particularly away from sensory input, fantasy being a state in which the fantasizer's gaze is allowed to drift inward. Jerome Singer, one of the most creative and prolific psychologists writing about fantasy, suggests that the term *daydreaming*

is used to mean a shift of attention away from an ongoing physical or mental task or from a perceptual response to external stimulation towards a response to some internal stimulus. . . . While wish-fulfillment is a frequent feature of the content of waking fantasy, common usage and the sparse scientific literature have also noted daydreaming's planful or constructful aspects, as well as its anxiety-ridden or obsessional character in particular individuals or in different periods for a given person. (Singer, *Daydreaming*, pp. 4–5)

As common an activity as fantasy is—as indicated by the fact that virtually everyone studied by researchers knew what was meant by the term *daydream* and could describe material from their own experience—*fantasy* is hard to define because it applies to a diverse range of imagined material. Thus, most nonpsychoanalytic definitions of fantasy are largely descriptive, and little attempt is made to get beyond the phenomenology of the experience to an understanding of its major functions.

4. Technically speaking, the remembered past is also in part construction. That is, the shape of the past as we recall it is imbued with current needs, feelings, and so forth.

5. Anthony Storr, *Churchill's Black Dog, Kafka's Mice and Other Phenomena of the Human Mind* (New York: Grove Press, 1988), p. viii.

6. The distinction between directed thinking on the one hand and dreaming or fantasizing on the other was first made by Carl Jung in "Concerning the Two Kinds of Thinking," a paper which appears as Chapter 1 in his *Psychology of the Unconscious* (New York: Dodd, Mead, 1957[1916]). Nonetheless there is a continuum between goal-directed abstract thinking and daydreaming, rather than a sharp divide.

David Rapaport points out:

> Daydreams—reveries, fantasies—are not a homogeneous group of phenomena, though all share the involuntary-effortless character and a form in which imagery, visual and acoustic, predominates. They range from planning to wish-fulfillment, from the realistic to the fantastic, and the usual laws of logic may or may not hold in them. Preconscious thinking also includes all these variants, as evidenced in preconscious fantasies of patients brought to daylight by psychoanalysis, and by thoughts and problem-solutions that arise ready-made in our minds. Even most complex, ordered thought-processes take place without the participation of consciousness. Though there are obvious differences between their extremes, there is no sharp dividing-line between daydreams and ordered thinking.

From "Toward a Theory of Thinking," in *Organization and Pathology of Thought: Selected Sources* (New York: Columbia University Press, 1951), p. 718.

7. Margaret Atwood, *The Handmaid's Tale* (Boston: Houghton Mifflin, 1986), p. 104.

8. Ibid, p. 105.

9. Ibid.

10. Singer, among others, has observed that affect can invoke fantasy. "In psychotherapy one often deals with the extensive reactions persons have to a state of affective arousal, which evokes a chain of speculation of recrimination that may lead to even further persisting arousal and despair." Singer, *Daydreaming*, p. 33.

11. Dominique Aury (pen name, Pauline Réage) quoted in John De St. Jorre, "The Unmasking of O," *The New Yorker*, 70 (August 1, 1994), p. 45.

12. Ibid.

13. Freud, "Creative Writers and Day-dreaming" (1908 [1907]), *S.E.*, vol. 9, p. 146.

14. Robert Stoller, *Sexual Excitement: Dynamics of Erotic Life* (New York: Pantheon, 1979), p. xi.

15. Quoted in Jaffa Elich, *Hasidic Tales of the Holocaust* (New York: Vintage, 1988), p. xxxi.

16. Socrates put it: "It is not drink he desires, but replenishment by drink, which is a change of state."

17. Most classifications focus primarily on the distinction between unconscious fantasies and conscious fantasies. For example, Edward D. Joseph distinguishes different meanings of fantasy by differentiating between basic fantasies, which are unconscious, pervade the whole character, and influence both the development and final form of the ego, and those more conscious, daydreamlike products that are derivatives of the basic fantasy. But this conceptualization tends to minimize the impact of conscious fantasy on the lived life. See E. D. Joseph, "An Unusual Fantasy in a Twin with an Inquiry into the Nature of Fantasy," *Psychoanalytic Quarterly,* 28 (1959): 189–190.

18. Peter Neubauer refers to repeating, organizing fantasies as "conscious fantasies," to distinguish them from fleeting fantasies, and so do many other psychoanalysts. But in this restricted sense the term can be confused with the sense in which it is used to differentiate the whole class of conscious fantasies from unconscious fantasies. I have chosen to use the term *repeating fantasy* in order to delimit one subset of *conscious fantasy*.

Peter Neubauer makes this distinction in his paper "The Clinical Use of the Daydream," presented at the panel "Clinical Value and Utilization of the Daydream," at the Scientific Meetings of the American Psychoanalytic Association, New York City, December 19, 1993.

Chapter 3

1. See, for example, Jerome L. Singer, *Daydreaming: An Introduction to the Experimental Study of Inner Experience* (New York: Random House, 1966); and Eric Klinger, *Structure and Functions of Fantasy* (New York: Wiley Inter-Science, 1971).

2. Sigmund Freud, "The Aetiology of Hysteria" (1896), *S.E.*, vol. 3, p. 203. One simple example of a troublesome (if not classically traumatic) memory that served as the source of a symbolic symptom is to be found in Freud's case of Frau Cäcilie M., whose presenting complaint was a severe facial neuralgia. In a conversation with her husband, Frau Cäcilie M. felt one of his remarks as a stinging insult. Recounting the impact of that insult in session, "suddenly she put her hand to her cheek, gave a loud cry of pain and said: 'It was like a slap in the face.'" Freud's interpretation was that the patient felt as though she had been slapped in the face and the symptom symbolically represented that slap. Although a metaphoric

transformation of the traumatic memory took place, there was no wish fulfillment involved. Sigmund Freud and Josef Breuer, "Studies on Hysteria" (1893–1895), *S.E.,* vol. 2, p. 178.

3.   Sigmund Freud, Letter 69 of September 21, 1987, to Wilhelm Fliess in Marie Bonaparte, Anna Freud, and Ernst Kris, eds., *Origins of Psychoanalysis: Letters to Wilhelm Fliess, Drafts and Notes: 1887–1902* (New York: Basic Books, 1954), p. 215.

4.   The quote continues: "Our observations no longer leave any room for doubt that such fantasies may be unconscious just as well as conscious; and as soon as the latter become unconscious they may also become pathogenic. . . . In favorable circumstances, the subject can still capture an unconscious fantasy of this sort in consciousness." Sigmund Freud, "On Hysterical Phantasies and Their Relation to Bisexuality" (1908), *S.E.,* vol. 9, p. 160.

5.   Sigmund Freud, "Introductory Lectures on Psychoanalysis, Part III" (1916), *S.E.,* vol. 16, p. 368. The assumption that material reality cannot be totally apprehended has bedeviled clinical attempts to distinguish pathogenic trauma from repressed fantasy. Freud's formulation, crucial though it is, had the unhappy result of drawing attention away from the role of traumatic events in patients' symptoms, and away from the different ways fantasies and memories are sometimes stored.

6.   Schimek, for example, says:

The majority of [Freud's] female patients did not report conscious memories of seduction, but merely memories, thoughts and symptoms that Freud interpreted as the disguised and indirect manifestation of an infantile sexual trauma. In other words, we are dealing with inferred, unconscious repressed memories of seduction that are related to the patient's conscious production, much as the latent is to the manifest content of a dream.

See Jean G. Schimek, "The Interpretations of the Past: Childhood Trauma, Psychical Reality, and Historical Truth," *Journal of the American Psychoanalytic Association,* 23 (1975): 846.

7.   See Jeffrey Moussaieff Masson, *The Assault on Truth: Freud's Suppression of the Seduction Theory* (New York: Farrar, Straus and Giroux, 1984). Masson came to believe that Freud's abandonment of the seduction hypothesis was not the result of new insight so much as a failure of Freud's courage.

8.   Freud's abandonment of the seduction theory opened up the way to his discovery of infantile sexual activity, viewed as innate and subject to a preordained developmental sequence, culminating in the development and resolution of the Oedipus complex. But this reversal in Freud's thinking skewed the field toward an almost exclusive focus on the role of the developing stages of sexuality and their accompanying wishes and fantasies both in the formation of neurosis and in healthy adaptation.

9.   Sigmund Freud, Letter 62 of May 16, 1897, to Wilhelm Fliess, in Bonaparte et al., eds., *Origins of Psychoanalysis,* pp. 200–202.

10. In regard to nocturnal dreams, Freud remarked,

At night there ... arise in us wishes of which we are ashamed; these we must conceal from ourselves, and they have consequently been repressed, pushed into the unconscious. Repressed wishes of this sort and their derivatives are only allowed to come to expression in very distorted form ... night dreams are wish-fulfillments in just the same way as day-dreams—the phantasies which we all know so well.

See Sigmund Freud, "Creative Writers and Day-Dreaming," (1908[1907]), *S.E.,* vol. 9, pp. 148–149.

11. Eric Klinger, *Daydreaming: Using Waking Fantasy and Imagery for Self-Knowledge and Creativity* (Los Angeles: Jeremy P. Tarcher, 1990), p. 25.

12. Ibid.

13. Ibid.

14. Sigmund Freud, "The Interpretation of Dreams" (1900), *S.E.,* vol. 4, p. 1.

15. It is also because daydreams serve as rehearsals for life that they have drawn negative attention. Fantasies can serve as the breeding ground of a rebellion against authority or as an opposition to convention and morality. The Catholic Church has understood full well the potential power of daydreaming; this is the reason that evil thoughts are often considered on a par with evil deeds.

16. See Norman MacKenzie, *Dreams and Dreaming* (New York: Vanguard Press, 1965), pp. 26–56.

17. An extraordinarily long-lived book, widely read in many different countries over the centuries, Artemidorus's *Oneirocriticon* (The Interpretation of Dreams) is considered the most complete work on dream interpretation that has survived from the ancient world. Because Artemidorus draws on so many earlier works, including Greek, Assyrian, and Egyptian dream books, it is readily apparent that his fascination with dreams was not merely his own preoccupation but the culmination of a long tradition. MacKenzie, *Dreams and Dreaming,* p. 55.

18. Ibid., p. 153.

19. Ibid.

20. Freud, "The Interpretation of Dreams," p. 396.

21. Ibid., p. 310.

22. For a very sophisticated discussion of the way symbolism is used in psychoanalysis, see the chapter on symbolism in Hanna Segal, *Dream, Phantasy and Art* (London: Routledge, 1991), pp. 31–48.

23. See Segal, *Dream, Phantasy and Art,* p. 9.

24. Freud, "The Interpretation of Dreams," p. 99, n. 1; see also MacKenzie, *Dreams and Dreaming,* p. 153.

25. Freud, "The Interpretation of Dreams," p. 621.

26. Hanna Segal makes the same point but in reference only to *unconscious* fantasy: "Unlike his theory of dreams, Freud never worked out in full a theory of unconscious phantasy." Segal, *Dream, Phantasy and Art,* p. 16.

27. Many German philosophers and intellectuals of the nineteenth century

had alluded to an unconscious mind, and the concept had already been used in Germany as early as 1776 and by Wordsworth. But the Germans were much more aware than the English that the dream might be a clue to the underside of personality. MacKenzie, *Dreams and Dreaming,* p. 89.

28. Freud, "The Interpretation of Dreams," p. 492.

29. Sigmund Freud, "Formulations on the Two Principles of Mental Functioning" (1911), *S.E.,* vol. 12, pp. 215–226.

30. Sigmund Freud, "Paths to the Formation of Symptoms" (1917), *S.E.,* vol. 15, p. 372.

31. Nonetheless there are now known to be important signs and symptoms that would point to trauma rather than to fantasy as the etiology in any particular case of psychological disturbance. These signs and symptoms often make the discrimination between memory and fantasy fairly certain. See, for example, Ethel S. Person and Howard Klar, "Establishing Trauma: The Difficulty Distinguishing Between Memories and Fantasies," *Journal of the American Psychoanalytic Association,* 42 (1994): 1055–1081.

32. Sigmund Freud, "Hysterical Phantasies and Their Relation to Bisexuality" (1908), *S.E.,* vol. 9, p. 161.

33. This position is close to that which Melanie Klein came to take. Kleinian psychoanalysts, proponents of the idea that unconscious fantasies are inborn, distinguish between conscious fantasies (with an *f*), and unconscious phantasies (with a *ph*). The latter are believed to be the primary content of unconscious mental processes, which are essentially coexistent with drive. While it is hard to prove the existence of inborn fantasies, the proposition that they exist is also difficult to disprove, and there may be some distinct theoretical advantages to assuming inborn fantasies beyond my discussion here.

In contrast to the Kleinians, Freudians view unconscious fantasies as relating to drive as it is filtered through ego. In other words, for Freudians, unconscious fantasies are constructs incorporating aspects of experience.

34. See Sigmund Freud, "From the History of an Infantile Neurosis" (1918[1914]), *S.E.,* vol. 17, pp. 3–122, esp. pp. 48–60 and 95–97. He also raises the possibility of retrospective fantasies: *"Zurückphantasieren,"* mediated through deferred action: *"Nachträglichkeit."*

35. Most North American ego psychologists no longer view unconscious fantasy as coexistent with drive. Instead it is understood as essentially the same thing as unconscious conflict. (This shift in theory mandates a shift in the theory of technique. No longer is the goal of psychoanalytic therapy to make the unconscious conscious; rather, it is to resolve unconscious conflict into its component elements.) See, for example, Jacob Arlow, "Conflict, Regression and Symptom Formation," *International Journal of Psycho-Analysis,* 44 (1963):12–22; and Jacob Arlow, "Unconscious Fantasy and Disturbances of Conscious Experience," *Psychoanalytic Quarterly,* 38 (1969): 1–27.

36. Harry Trosman, "Transformations of Unconscious Fantasy in Art," *Journal of the American Psychoanalytic Association,* 38, 1 (1990): 47–48.

37. Jean Laplanche and Jean-Bertrand Pontalis, "Fantasy and the Origins of Sexuality," *International Journal of Psycho-Analysis,* 49 (1968): 11.

38. Scott Dowling, "Fantasy Formation: A Child Analyst's Perspective," *Journal of the American Psychoanalytic Association,* 38, 1 (1990): 95.

39. Ibid.

40. Ibid.

41. Dowling too raises the possibility that while many fantasies derive from conscious fantasies which have been repressed, still others are primal in the sense that they were never explicitly conscious and were probably not originally verbal in form. He gives the example of oral cannibalistic tendencies that "may be described in fantasy form though they are completely inaccessible to verbal memory." See Dowling, "Fantasy Formation," p. 96.

42. See Lili Peller, "Daydreams and Children's Favorite Books: Psychoanalytic Comments," *The Psychoanalytic Study of the Child,* 14 (1959): 414–433. See also Martin E. Widzer, "The Comic-Book Superhero: A Study of the Family Romance Fantasy," *The Psychoanalytic Study of the Child,* 32 (1977): 600–601.

43. See Lawrence B. Inderbitzen and Steven T. Levy, "Unconscious Fantasy: A Reconsideration of the Concept," *Journal of the American Psychoanalytic Association,* 38 (1990): 113–130.

44. See Jacob Arlow, "Unconscious Fantasy and Disturbances of Conscious Experience," p. 9. Because Arlow's example is so much referred to, it might seem that illusion or misperception of this sort is uncommon. Nothing is further from the truth. One has only to think of the young child on the edge of sleep, seeing monsters and all kinds of other threatening creatures in the shadows that fall across his room. Such misperceptions as these are closely linked to fear and fearful fantasies.

45. The phrase is Fred Weinstein's, quoted in Robert Wallerstein, "The Continuum of Reality, Inner and Outer" in *Fantasy, Myth, and Reality,* ed. Harold Blum et al., p. 317. Weinstein's statement is that "there are no immaculate perceptions of reality, no perceptions unmediated by memory and experience, and by the need to demonstrate loyalty to some group or principle."

46. Robert Emde gives a brilliant discussion of the adaptive function of play and the future orientation of fantasy in "Fantasy and Beyond: A Current Developmental Perspective on Freud's 'Creative Writers and Day-Dreaming'" in *On Freud's "Creative Writers and Day-Dreaming,"* ed. Ethel S. Person, Peter Fonagy, and Sérvulo Figueira (New Haven: Yale University Press, 1995), pp. 133–163.

47. Freud, "Creative Writers and Day-Dreaming," pp. 143–153; Freud, "Formulations on the Two Principles of Mental Functioning," p. 222.

In his paper Freud suggested that "the child at play behaves like a creative writer in that he creates a world of his own" (p. 143). Play is not frivolous because the child regards his play with a certain seriousness. As Freud put it, "the opposite of play is not what is serious but what is real" (p. 144)—which might equally be said about creative writing. Both the child at play and the creative writer at work are engaged in "phantasying," an exertion of the imaginative capacity. And while both take their respective activities very seriously, they are both able to separate the product of their imaginative lives from reality.

48. Sigmund Freud, "Beyond the Pleasure Principle" (1920), *S.E.,* vol. 18, pp. 14–15.

49. See Klinger, *Structure and Functions of Fantasy*, p. 49.

50. One of the real-life girls on whose lives the movie is based grew up to be Anne Perry, a prominent mystery writer. See Pam Lambert and Ellen Stein, "Blood Memory: Writer Anne Perry Once Took Part in a Murder," *People*, September 26, 1994, pp. 57–60.

51. This point of view is a staple in both the psychological and the psychoanalytic literature. See, for example, Robert A. King, "Cookies for the Emperor: The Multiple Functions of Play in the Analysis of an Early Adolescent Boy," in *The Many Meanings of Play*, ed. Albert J. Solnit, Donald J. Cohen, and Peter B. Neubauer (New Haven: Yale University Press, 1993); and Jerome Singer, *The Inner World of Daydreaming* (New York: Harper and Row, 1979), pp. 149–179.

52. See Joseph Sandler, "Dreams, Unconscious Fantasies and 'Identity of Perception,'" *International Review of Psychoanalysis*, 3 (1976): 33–42.

53. Ibid. I am using the term *centripetal* in a different sense from Sandler. He restricts it to our perception in reverse of the process of fantasy formation.

54. Freud, "Creative Writers and Day-Dreaming," pp. 147–148.

55. Jerome Bruner, *Acts of Meaning* (Cambridge, Mass.: Harvard University Press, 1990), p. 34.

56. Arnold M. Cooper, "Infant Research and Adult Psychoanalysis," in *The Significance of Infant Observational Research for Clinical Work with Children, Adolescents, and Adults*, ed. Scott Dowling and Arnold Rothstein (Madison, Conn.: International Universities Press, 1989), pp. 79–89.

57. Nancy Chodorow has popularized this point—encoded in the object relations point of view—in the United States.

58. See, for example, Jean Wyatt, *Reconstructing Desire: The Role of the Unconscious in Women's Reading and Writing* (Chapel Hill, NC: University of North Carolina Press, 1990), p. 7.

59. Ibid.

60. Ibid., p. 17.

61. Ibid.

62. Ethel S. Person, *Dreams of Love and Fateful Encounters: The Power of Romantic Passion* (New York: W. W. Norton, 1988), pp. 351–353.

63. Walter B. Cannon, "The Role of Hunches in Scientific Thought" in *The Creativity Question* ed. Albert Rothenberg and Carl R. Housman (Durham, NC: Duke University Press, 1976), pp. 63–69.

Chapter 4

1. See Jacob Arlow, "Unconscious Fantasy and Disturbances of Conscious Experience," *Psychoanalytic Quarterly*, 38 (1969): 1–17; and Jacob Arlow, "Fantasy, Memory, and Reality Testing," *Psychoanalytic Quarterly*, 38 (1969): 143–153.

2. *Global fantasy* is a term used by the Shanes; the personal myth was described by Ernst Kris. See Morton Shane and Estelle Shane, "Unconscious Fantasy: Developmental and Self-Psychological Considerations," *Journal of the American Psychoanalytic Association*, 38 (1990): 75–92; and Ernst Kris, "The Personal Myth:

A Problem in Psychoanalytic Technique," *Journal of the American Psychoanalytic Association,* 4 (1956): 653–674.

3. Harold Blum, "The Clinical Value of Daydreams and a Note on Their Role in Character Analysis," in *On Freud's "Creative Writers and Day-Dreaming,"* ed. Ethel S. Person, Peter Fonagy, and Sérvulo Figueira (New Haven: Yale University Press, 1995), p. 45.

Among those analysts who have early recognized the impact of the conscious fantasy per se are Harold Blum, "The Clinical Value of Daydreams and a Note," and Peter B. Neubauer, "The Clinical Value of the Daydream" (unpublished manuscript presented at a panel of the American Psychoanalytic Association, New York City, December 19, 1993). My own work has also pointed in the same direction, to the multiplicity of ways in which the fantasies that perfuse the cross gender disorders are enacted in both the sexual and nonsexual arenas. See, for example, Ethel S. Person, "Discussion of 'Initiation Fantasies and Transvestism,'" *Journal of the American Psychoanalytic Association,* 24 (1976): 547–551.

Person et al. show that sexual fantasies are not compensations for a lack of sexual encounters. Quite the contrary, there is a positive correlation between the two domains of sexual fantasies and sexual behaviors. See Ethel Person, Nettie Terestman, Wayne Myers, Eugene Goldberg, and Michael Borenstein, "Associations Between Sexual Experiences and Fantasies in a Non-Patient Population: A Preliminary Study," *Journal of the American Academy of Psychoanalysis,* 20, 1 (1992): 75–90.

4. See Ethel S. Person, "Sexuality as a Mainstay of Identity" in *Women—Sex and Sexuality,* ed. Catherine R. Stimpson and Ethel S. Person (Chicago: University of Chicago Press, 1980).

5. The unity of our sexual fantasies with our everyday personalities—or their divergence—is not by itself a predictor of mental health. An angry hostile individual whose sadistic fantasy life is consonant with his character may nonetheless have a neurotic problem that often enough he himself recognizes as problematic.

6. The study analyzed data from questionnaire responses of 193 university students in the years 1982–1983. See Ethel S. Person, Nettie Terestman, Wayne A. Myers, Eugene L. Goldberg, and Carol Salvadori, "Gender Differences in Sexual Behaviors and Fantasies in a College Population," *Journal of Sex and Marital Therapy,* 15 (1989): 197.

7. There is a divergence of opinion among therapists as to the general question of whether the obligatory use of sexual fantasy with one's partner ought be viewed primarily as a pilot light (a stimulant to excitement) or as a Rosetta stone (a clue to a patient's psychological life). Analysts tend to use a sexual fantasy as a Rosetta stone. Sex therapists tend to utilize fantasy as a pilot light, particularly because they so often see patients inhibited to such a degree that they suppress much of their sexual fantasies. Consequently, many sex therapists take the appropriately therapeutic tack of introducing the patient to sexual pornography. (The limits to this approach appear when one is dealing with a fantasy of a harmful nature and a patient with a personality structure so constituted that he or she might well act out. Consider, for example, a man who relies heavily on pedophiliac fantasies for sexual stimulation.)

The question as to whether sexual fantasy is deleterious—or in what circumstances it is deleterious—probably must be answered on a case by case basis, although many people routinely make use of sexual fantasy in order to achieve sexual arousal. To the best of my knowledge there are no comprehensive contemporary studies on how often fantasy is invoked as an erotic aid during interpersonal sex. This would certainly be a fruitful line of inquiry.

8. Moses Laufer, "The Central Masturbation Fantasy, the Final Sexual Organization in Adolescence," *Psychoanalytic Study of the Child,* vol. 31 (Madison, Conn.: International Universities Press, 1976), pp. 297–316.

9. Sigmund Freud, "Dynamics of Transference," *S.E.,* vol. 12, p. 99.

10. For an extended case history of the way in which elements of traumatic experiences are incorporated into sexual fantasy, see Ethel S. Person and Howard Klar, "Establishing Trauma: The Difficulty Distinguishing Between Memories and Fantasies," *Journal of the American Psychoanalytic Association,* 42 (1994): 1055–1081.

11. Heinz Lichtenstein, "Identity and Sexuality," in *The Dilemma of Human Identity* (New York: Jason Aronson, 1977), pp. 49–122.

12. See for example Renée Spitz, "Hospitalism: An Inquiry into the Genesis of Psychiatric Conditions in Early Childhood," in *The Psychoanalytic Study of the Child,* vol. 1 (New York: International Universities Press, 1945), pp. 53–74; Renée Spitz, "Hospitalism: A Follow-up Report on Investigation Described in Vol. 1," in *The Psychoanalytic Study of the Child,* vol. 2 (New York: International Universities Press, 1946), pp. 113–117; See also I. Dowling, *Attachment and Love* (New York: Basic Books, 1969). For a speculative essay on these issues, see Nathaniel Ross, "On the Significance of Infantile Sexuality" in *On Sexuality: Psychoanalytic Observations,* ed. Toksov B. Karasu and Charles Socarides (New York: International Universities Press, 1979), pp. 47–59.

13. See Renée Spitz and Katherine Wolff, "Autoeroticism: Some Empirical Findings and Hypotheses on Three of Its Manifestations in the First Year of Life," in *Psychoanalytic Study of the Child,* vol. 3/4 (New York: International Universities Press, 1949), pp. 85–120.

14. Charles Sarnoff, "Narcissism, Adolescent Masturbation Fantasies, and the Search for Reality," in *Masturbation from Infancy to Senescence,* ed. Irwin Marcus and John J. Francis (New York: International Universities Press, 1975), p. 281.

15. Mother absence is counteracted in other ways, too. For example, a shoe may sometimes symbolically represent the absent mother, sometimes her imaginary phallus, and it may be incorporated into a masturbatory fantasy as a shoe fetish.

16. See Stephen A. Mitchell, *Relational Concepts in Psychoanalysis* (Cambridge, Mass.: Harvard University Press, 1988), p. 102. Drawing on contributions from many different psychoanalysts, Mitchell gives an excellent overview of those attributes that make sexuality a premier arena for expressing other fantasies.

17. Karen Horney, "The Dread of Women: Observations on a Specific Difference in the Dread Felt by Men and Women Respectively for the Opposite Sex," *International Journal of Psychoanalysis,* 13 (1932): 348–360.

18. Person, "Sexuality as the Mainstay of Identity."

19. As the psychoanalyst Janine Chasseguet-Smirgel points out, interpersonal fantasies can also be invoked to counter "the infant's feeling of hopelessness when he is flooded by painful sensations in relation to which he is totally powerless." For the child, fantasizing an internal enemy that can be expelled is more comforting than acknowledging that the pain comes from one's own body. See J. Chasseguet-Smirgel, "Creative Writers and Day-Dreaming: A Commentary," in *On Freud's "Creative Writers and Day-Dreaming,"* p. 112.

20. Mitchell, *Relational Concepts in Psychoanalysis,* p. 103.

21. Ibid.

22. Lionel Ovesey, *Homosexuality and Pseudohomosexuality* (New York: Science House, 1969).

23. Anna Freud, "Beating Fantasies and Daydreams," in *The Writings of Anna Freud, vol. 1, 1922–1935* (Madison, Conn.: International Universities Press, 1974).

24. Elisabeth Young-Bruehl, *Anna Freud: A Biography* (New York: Summit Books, 1988), p. 104.

25. Ibid.

26. Anna Freud, "Beating Fantasies and Daydreams," p. 152.

27. Ibid., p. 149.

28. Young-Bruehl, *Anna Freud,* p. 107.

29. But Anna Freud paid a price, perhaps giving up something of her sexuality. She had little in the way of a personal life other than her relationship with her father and psychoanalysis. The closest intimate friend of her adult life was Dorothy Burlingham, also the daughter of a very powerful man, Louis Tiffany. Burlingham also became an analyst.

30. Anna Freud, "Denial in Fantasy" in *The Writings of Anna Freud, vol. 2: The Ego and Mechanisms of Defense* (New York: International Universities Press, 1966 [1936]), pp. 69–82.

31. W. Shapiro. "One Went Right: Woes From Wall Street to the Gulf—But a Happy Ending in Texas," *Time,* 130 (1987), p. 30.

32. I described this case very briefly in my paper "Plagiarism and Parallel Process" in *Psychoanalysis: Toward the Second Century,* ed. Arnold M. Cooper, Otto F. Kernberg, and Ethel S. Person (New Haven: Yale University Press, 1989), pp. 57–59.

33. Neubauer, "Clinical Value of the Daydream."

34. Shane and Shane, "Unconscious Fantasy," p. 75.

35. Jacob Arlow makes the point that the analysis of a patient's characteristic metaphors leads to understanding that patient's important unconscious phantasies. One of his patients misperceived a delivery man as "attempting forced entry." He frequently entertained fantasies of becoming rich by robbing or taking over from powerful authorities. One specific fantasy pictures him submitting to anal penetration by a powerful authority. The subtext of the fantasy was that the patient would use the opportunity of the anal encounter to castrate the father figure and acquire his sexual prowess. (This is essentially the same dynamic Lionel Ovesey described as pseudohomosexual. See Ovesey, *Homosexuality* and *Pseudohomosexuality*.) Arlow believes the childhood event that predisposed his patient to the fantasy was the experience of having frequently been given suppositories and

cathartics, which he experienced as forced entries. See Jacob Arlow, "Metaphor and the Psychoanalytic Situation," *Psychoanalytic Quarterly,* 58 (1979): 374.

36. Kris, "The Personal Myth," p. 654.

37. Ibid.

38. Ibid., p. 655.

39. Ibid., p. 671.

40. Major life history distortions of a fantasied nature are quite common. One of my patients who always prided herself on her fierce independence from her family turned out to be invoking a myth of voluntary separation from her family in order to cloak her all-pervasive anguish about having been abandoned—an anguish that had left her with a persistent sense of separation anxiety. But these distortions, which are reversals in fantasy, fall short of the full-blown personal myth.

41. As an extreme pathological extension of the self fantasy, consider those persons who devote many hours of each day to fantasy or fantasy derivatives, and for whom the fantasy relates either to an altered self or to an alter ego. Transvestites—by definition cross-dressing heterosexual males—have fantasies that involve the creation of an entirely altered self, one not visible to the external world. For many transvestites the belief is that they have two personalities, male and female, which are alternating.

I have never seen a full-fledged example of transvestism in a woman, but there are a number of patients who appear to have developed strong male identifications that are projected onto a male alter ego. Their fantasy lives—based on the adventures of someone other than the self—are the center of their attention, their serial fantasies so consuming that they almost supplant any interest in the real world. Over the years, I have seen in therapy one woman with a fantasy life in which the central character was a homosexual or crippled man and have had extended consultations with two other women with very similar fantasy profiles. Yet these fantasies stop short of psychotic or delusional beliefs about being someone else, insofar as reality testing is preserved. Though they are preoccupied with an alter ego, the identification is preconscious or unconscious. Their experience resembles total preoccupation with a novel—in this case a novel of one's own composition—the individual fantasy episodes corresponding to chapters.

42. Jacob Arlow, "Ego Psychology and the Study of Mythology," *Journal of the American Psychoanalytic Association,* 9 (1961): 371—391.

43. Robert J. Lifton, presentation at the conference "Waiting to Die: Suicide in American Literature," organized by the American Suicide Foundation, New York City, November 11, 1994.

44. Blum has referred to this case in "The Clinical Value of Daydreams and a Note."

45. Ibid.

46. William Styron, presentation at the conference "Waiting to Die: Suicide in American Literature," organized by the American Suicide Foundation, New York City, November 11, 1994.

47. Aggressive daydreams, too, may be either situational or repeating. Repeating aggressive daydreams are perhaps more common than one would imagine,

insofar as many people, fearful of what the response would be, are reluctant to share them. But the capacity to repeatedly fantasize the death of our friends, acquaintances, or lovers, when not specifically situation-oriented is usually the product of an ongoing, repeating fantasy that has been invoked to contain our rage, whatever generated it in the first place.

One man who broke an unspoken taboo about revealing repeating aggressive fantasies has caused an uproar in the press, landing on front pages all over the globe. Sir Kenneth Dover, a renowned classicist and a former president of Corpus Christi College, Oxford, reports in his recently published memoirs that he became preoccupied with wishing for the death of a member of his faculty. A manic depressive as well as an alcoholic, Trevor Aston was a constant troublemaker and disruptive presence in the college. In his memoir, as reported by the *New York Times,* Dover wrote: "It was clear to me by now that Trevor and the college must somehow be separated. My problem, the one which I felt compelled to define with brutal candor: how to kill him without getting into trouble." According to the *Times,* Dover reported fantasizing about Aston's death, consulting a lawyer to see if he would be legally at risk if he ignored a suicide call, and not investigating Aston's room at the college after a colleague expressed concern the night Aston died. Dover also admits to a disturbing sense of relish the day after Aston killed himself: "The next day I got up from a long, sound sleep and looked out of the window across the Fellow's Garden. . . . I cannot say for sure that the sun was shining, but I certainly felt it was. I said to myself, slowly, 'Day One of the Year One of the Post-Astonian Era.' For a little while, I even regretted my decision to retire the following year." A singular confession for a memoir but not such an unusual fantasy.

Dover, according to the newspaper account, "uses the word 'conscience' only when he is fantasizing about what would happen if he rejected a plea for help from Mr. Aston in the throes of an overdose and in wondering what he would tell the authorities. 'I had no qualms about causing the death of a fellow from whose nonexistence the college would benefit, but I balked at the prospect of misleading a coroner's jury.'" Dover's colleagues appear to be divided as to the appropriateness of Dover's response and memoir. Dover himself professed to be amazed to discover how shocked people were, even though his aggressive thoughts took such an extreme form. See John Darnton, "A Scholar's Memoirs Raise Some Ghosts at Oxford," *New York Times,* November 18, 1994, A1.

Chapter 5

1. Sigmund Freud, "Creative Writers and Day-Dreaming" (1908[1907]), *S.E.,* vol. 9, p. 145.

2. See Gilbert Rose, "Pre-Genital Aspects of Pregnancy Fantasies," *International Journal of Psycho-Analysis,* 42 (1961): 544–549.

3. Sigmund Freud, "Family Romances" (1909[1908]), *S.E.,* vol. 9, pp. 235–241.

4. See the vignette of Kris's patient presented in Chapter 4; Ernst Kris, "The Personal Myth: A Problem in Psychoanalytic Technique" *Journal of the American*

Psychoanalytic Association, 4 (1956): 653–681. See also Helene Deutsch quoted in Linda Joan Kaplan, "The Concept of the Family Romance," *The Psychoanalytic Review,* 61 (1974): 178.

5. Linda Joan Kaplan elaborates nicely on Freud's metaphor of the wish-thread. See Kaplan, "The Concept of Family Romance."

6. Freud, "Family Romances," pp. 240–241.

7. Bruno Bettelheim, *The Uses of Enchantment: The Meaning and Importance of Fairy Tales* (New York: Alfred A. Knopf, 1976), p. 274.

8. Sigmund Freud, Letter 91 of June 20, 1898, to Wilhelm Fliess, in Marie Bonaparte, Anna Freud, and Ernst Kris, eds., *The Origins of Psychoanalysis: Letters to Wilhelm Fliess, Drafts and Notes, 1887–1902* (New York: Basic Books, 1954), p. 256.

9. Freud, "Creative Writers and Day-Dreaming," p. 148.

10. Moisés Lemlij, "Creative Writers and Day-Dreaming: A Parochial View," in *On Freud's "Creative Writers and Day-Dreaming,"* ed. Ethel Person, Peter Fonagy, and Sérvulo Figueira (New Haven: Yale University Press, 1995), p. 168.

11. I have written about this fantasy previously, in my book *Dreams of Love and Fateful Encounters: The Power of Romantic Passion* (New York: W. W. Norton, 1988; Penguin, 1989), p. 96.

12. Eileen Simpson, *Orphans: Real and Imaginary* (New York: New American Library, 1987), p. 9.

13. Ibid.

14. Ibid., p. 120.

15. See for example Phyllis Greenacre, "The Imposter," in *Emotional Growth: Psychoanalytic Studies of the Gifted and a Great Variety of Other Individuals,* vol. 1 (New York: International Universities Press, 1971), pp. 93–112.

16. Despite the generic kinds of fantasy fulfilled in love, specific fantasies always enter into love in one way or another. Among these are the fantasy of the perfect mother. See Nancy Chodorow and Susan Contratto, "The Fantasy of the Perfect Mother" in Nancy Chodorow, *Feminism and Psychoanalytic Theory* (New Haven: Yale University Press, 1989), pp. 79–96.

17. Leo Rangell, "Roots and Derivatives of Unconscious Fantasy" in *Fantasy, Myth and Reality,* ed. Harold Blum, Yale Kramer, Arlene Richards, and Arnold Richards (Madison, Conn.: International Universities Press, 1988), p. 71.

18. The phrase *imaginary child* was coined by Serge Lebovici. It is also translated from the French as the "phantasmatic baby," a passive being who is the object of its mother's desire. The maternal phantasm influences the subsequent mother-baby interactions. See Serge Lebovici, "Le Nourrisson, la Mére a te le Psychanalyste." *Les Interactions Prècoces* (Paris: Le Centurion, 1983).

See also Serge Lebovici, "On Intergenerational Transmission: From Filiation to Affiliation," *Infant Mental Health Journal,* 14 (1993): 260–272.

19. Sigmund Freud, "On Narcissism," (1914) *S.E.,* vol. 14, pp. 90–91.

20. Susan Chira, "When Hope Died," *New York Times Magazine* (June 6, 1994), p. 20.

21. Massimo Ammaniti, E. Baumgartner, C. Candelori, M. Pola, R. Tambelli, and F. Zampino, "Rappresentazioni materne in gravidanza: Contributi prelimi-

nari," *Rivista di Psicologia Clinica,* 1 (1990): 36–50. Massimo Ammaniti, "Maternal Representations During Pregnancy and Early Infant-Mother Interactions," *Infant Mental Health Journal,* 12 (1991): 246–255.

See also Massimo Ammaniti and Daniel Stern, eds., *Psychoanalysis and Development: Representation and Narratives* (New York: New York University Press, 1994).

22. See Sarah Ruddick, *Maternal Thinking: Toward a Politics of Peace* (New York: Ballantine, 1990).

23. Berta Bornstein, "On Latency," in *The Psychoanalytic Study of the Child,* vol. 6 (New York: International Universities Press, 1951), pp. 279–285.

24. Eric Klinger, *Daydreaming: Using Waking Fantasy and Imagery for Self-Knowledge and Creativity* (Los Angeles: Jeremy P. Tarcher, 1990), p. 28.

25. Jerome Singer, *The Inner World of Daydreaming* (New York: Harper and Row, 1979), p. 159.

26. Ibid.

27. See Anthony Storr, *Churchill's Black Dog, Kafka's Mice and Other Phenomena of the Human Mind* (New York: Grove Press, 1988), p. 26.

28. Ibid., p. 27.

29. Ibid.

30. Ibid., p. 25.

31. Ibid.

32. Dan Wakefield, "His 50's Then and Now: Robert Redford," *The New York Times Magazine* (August 21, 1994): 26–29.

33. Ibid., p. 28.

34. Ibid.

35. Salman Rushdie, "A Critic at Large: Out of Kansas," *The New Yorker* (May 11, 1992), p. 97.

36. There are still other groupings of generative fantasies, including fantasies of self-sacrifice for the good of others, whether these are fantasies of social or political reform or of healing the sick and the underprivileged. These impulses find expression in a variety of settings and at different moments. In the movie *Alice,* the affluent Mia Farrow character, despairing of both her marriage and her affair, goes off to cleanse her spirit by working with Mother Teresa. In addition to self-purification, the dream of doing good may involve self-sacrifice for an ideal, for a family member, or for passion. Doing-good fantasies, of course, have many root causes. In young adults they often represent an impulse in part motivated by a rebellion against the materialistic and self-interested values of one's parents, hence the frequency of these idealistic fantasies in adolescence and younger adulthood.

Some other fantasies focus not on happy future possibilities but rather on the possibility of failure, loss, or disaster, and they run the gamut from self-blame for erroneous judgment, to fear of the loss of loved ones, to a sense that one will fall prey to cruelty, misfortune, or even madness.

37. See Stephen Rittenberg and L. Noah Shaw, "On Fantasies of Self-Creation" in *The Psychoanalytic Study of the Child,* vol. 46 (Madison, Conn.: International Universities Press, 1991), pp. 217–236.

38. Ibid., p. 222. The authors are quoting from *The Great Gatsby.*

39. Ibid., pp. 222–223.

40. Ibid., pp. 225–228. Rittenberg and Shaw present the case of a man in whom fantasies of self-creation took on pathological proportions. Mr. B., a forty-two-year-old business man, had been sent into analysis by a male mentor in order to learn more about himself. While manifestly successful, this man was, as the authors tell us, the "victim" of an early Oedipal triumph, by virtue of having been left alone with an intrusive and adoring mother: "She wiped my behind until I was five or six years old and when I went to school, I didn't know how to tie my shoes because she kept doing it for me and never taught me how." At the same time she imparted to him fantasies of the glory and greatness he would achieve—but only on the condition that he be loyal to her and trust no one else. His dilemma was not an uncommon one—how to free himself from his mother while holding on to the dream she had imparted to him. He did this in an ingenious way, creating his own fantasy kingdom, which he ruled totally. He identified with all those heroic stories of Superman and Batman in which Clark Kent and Bruce Wayne were able to create themselves over and over again.

41. Ibid., p. 224.

Chapter 6

1. I have benefited in this chapter from Dr. Roger L. Shapiro's discussion of a talk on shared fantasies that I gave to the Washington Psychoanalytic Society, January 13, 1995.

2. Hanns Sachs, "Community of Daydreams" [1920], in *The Creative Unconscious* (Cambridge, Mass.: Sci-Art Publishers, 1942).

3. See Martin Wangh, "The 'Evocation of a Proxy': A Psychological Maneuver, Its Use as a Defense, Its Purpose and Genesis," *The Psychoanalytic Study of the Child,* vol. 17 (Madison, Conn.: International Universities Press, 1968), pp. 451–472.
A fantasy is shared insofar as the child's fantasy would have taken a different shape without the communication of a specific parental fantasy. Harold Blum suggests the parent's communication is "an invitation toward identification, shared living out, or defense intrinsic to the fantasy." See Harold P. Blum, "Shared Fantasy and Reciprocal Identification, and Their Role in Gender Disorders" in *Fantasy, Myth and Reality,* ed. Harold P. Blum, Yale Kramer, Arlene K. Richards, and Arnold D. Richards (Madison, Conn.: International Universities Press, 1988), p. 323.

4. Sometimes the therapist is drawn in, leading to a rich literature on transference/countertransference enactment. This has become a major interest in the psychoanalytic literature over the past five to ten years. But it is generally referred to as "transference/countertransference" and seldom as "shared fantasy." In the Kleinian frame of reference this transaction would likely be referred to as "projective identification." The focus on what I call shared fantasy has not been explored to the same degree outside the consulting room as in it.

5. Sam Shepard quoted in Ben Brantley, "Sam Shepard, Storyteller," *New York Times* (November 13, 1994), p. B-1.

6. Freud makes this point in "Creative Writers and Day-Dreaming" (1908[1907]), *S.E.,* vol. 9, when he suggests that the communication of fantasy in art alleviates guilt and avoids anxiety, bribing us "by the purely formal, that is, aesthetic, yield of pleasure which he offers us in the presentation of his phantasies" (p. 153).

7. Ibid., pp. 141–153.

8. Hanns Sachs, "Community of Daydreams," p. 24.

9. Ibid., pp. 25–26.

10. Dominique Aury quoted in John De St. Jorre, "The Unmasking of O," *The New Yorker,* 70 (August 1, 1994), p. 43.

11. Ibid., p. 45.

12. Lionel Ovesey and Ethel S. Person, "Transvestism: A Disorder of Sense of Self," *International Journal of Psychoanalytic Psychotherapy,* 5 (1976): 219–235. In that article, Ed was called Mr. S.

13. Ibid.

14. See Milton E. Jucovy, "Initiation Fantasies and Transvestitism," *Journal of the American Psychoanalytic Association,* 24 (1976): 525–546; and Ethel S. Person, "Discussion of 'Initiation Fantasies and Transvestitism,'" *Journal of the American Psychoanalytic Association,* 24 (1976): 547–551.

15. See Ethel S. Person, "The Omni-Available Woman and Lesbian Sex: Two Fantasy Themes and Their Relationship to the Developmental Experience," in *The Psychology of Men: New Psychoanalytic Perspectives*, ed. Gerald Fogel, Frederick M. Lane, and Robert S. Gilbert (New York: Basic Books, 1986), pp. 236–259.

16. Vivian G. Paley, *The Boy Who Would Be a Helicopter: The Uses of Storytelling in the Classroom* (Cambridge, Mass.: Harvard University Press, 1990). A child in a dreamlike state may verbalize his fantasy aloud to himself, but will become embarrassed if anyone overhears and repeats the fantasy. In contrast, in make-believe play, children vocalize and combine their fantasies; there is more openness, a dialogue going on throughout, and an attempt to structure the material.

17. Ibid., p. 21.

18. Ibid., p. 4.

19. Ibid.

20. Ibid., p. 32.

21. Two adult men reminiscing about childhood fantasies have told me of similar exclusive fantasy themes. One man fancied an airplane like an exoskeleton or second skin which he always donned at bedtime and which enlarged in size as he grew. Functionally, it was more like Simon's squirrel hole than like Jason's helicopter. He grew up to be a pilot. In neither man was the fantasy a fixation or evidence of any hardcore isolation.

22. Roy Lilleskov quoted in "The Proceedings of the International Scientific Colloquium on the Role of Fantasy in the Adaptive Process," *Bulletin of the Hampstead Clinic,* 7 (1984): 184.

23. Anna Freud, *Normality and Pathology in Childhood: Assessment of Development* (New York: International Universities Press, 1965), p. 86.

24. Adelaide M. Johnson, "Factors in the Etiology of Fixations and Symptom Choice," *Psychoanalytic Quarterly,* 22 (1953): 475–496; see also Adelaide Johnson

and S. A. Szurek, "The Genesis of Antisocial Acting Out in Children and Adults," *Psychoanalytic Quarterly,* 21 (1952): 323–343.

25. See Blum, "Shared Fantasy and Reciprocal Identification," p. 324.

26. Selma Fraiberg, Edna Adelson, and Vivian Shapiro. "Ghosts in the Nursery: A Psychoanalytic Approach to the Problems of Impaired Infant-Mother Relationships," *Journal of the American Academy of Child Psychoanalysis,* 14 (1975): 387.

27. Ellen Handler Spitz writes that some children's picture books "affirm the need for regressive fantasy while generally moving in the direction of more adaptive, integrative function." Using the psychoanalyst Winnicott's theoretical frame of reference, she views picture books as providing a transitional space between fantasy and reality that allows children of three to five to move back and forth between the two realms. Ellen Handler Spitz, "Picturing the Child's Inner World of Fantasy: On the Dialectic Between Image and Word," in *The Psychoanalytic Study of the Child,* vol. 43 (New York: International Universities Press, 1988), pp. 433–447.

28. Hansi Kennedy, George Moran, Stanley Wiseberg, and Clifford York. "Both Sides of the Barrier," in *The Psychoanalytic Study of the Child,* vol. 40 (Madison, Conn.: International Universities Press, 1985).

29. Ibid., p. 279.

30. Ibid., p. 282.

31. Ilene Lefcourt, personal communication, 1994.

32. See John Lahr, ed., *Prick Up Your Ears: The Biography of Joe Orton* (New York: Limelight Editions, 1978); and John Lahr, ed., *The Orton Diaries* (New York: Harper and Row, 1986).

33. Lahr, *Orton Diaries,* p. 24.

34. Ibid.

35. Ibid., p. 25.

36. Ibid., p. 27.

37. Ibid., p. 21.

38. Lahr, *Prick Up Your Ears,* p. 3.

39. Ibid., p. 121.

40. Lahr, *Orton Diaries,* p. 23.

41. Lahr, *Prick Up Your Ears,* p. 270.

42. See the parallel to William Styron's experience, described in Chapter 4.

43. Jacqueline Rose pointed out the anticipation in Ted Hughes's fiction of events he was to live out with Sylvia Plath. Jacqueline Rose, *The Haunting of Sylvia Plath* (Cambridge, Mass.: Harvard University Press, 1993), p. 127.

44. David Richards, "Boulevard of Broken Dreams," *New York Times* (November 18, 1994), p. C-1.

Chapter 7

1. Hanns Sachs, "The Community of Daydreams" [1920], in *The Creative Unconscious* (Cambridge, Mass.: Sci-Art Publishers, 1942).

2. Bruno Bettelheim, *The Uses of Enchantment: The Meaning and Importance of Fairy Tales* (New York: Alfred A. Knopf, 1976).

3. Theodate Smith, "The Psychology of Daydreams," *The American Journal of Psychology,* 15 (1904): 465–488.

4. Sigmund Freud, "Creative Writers and Day-Dreaming" (1908[1907]), *S.E.,* vol. 9, pp. 141–153.

5. Ibid., pp. 146–147.

6. Ibid., p. 147.

7. Stephen Heath, "Joan Riviere and the Masquerade," in *Formations of Fantasy,* ed. Victor Burgin, James Donald, and Cora Kaplan (New York: Methuen, 1986), p. 56.

8. Sigmund Freud, "The Dissolution of the Oedipus Complex" (1924), *S.E.,* vol. 19, pp. 173–179; "Some Psychical Consequences of the Anatomical Distinction Between the Sexes" (1925), *S.E.,* vol. 19, pp. 241–258; "Female Sexuality" (1931), *S.E.,* vol. 21, pp. 222–243; "Femininity" (1933), *S.E.,* vol. 22, pp. 112–135.

9. Only later would psychoanalysts and other theorists realize that Freud's theories about female psychology were mired in nineteenth-century cultural attitudes toward women, and reinforced by observations of the behaviors that resulted from those attitudes. With few approved avenues for self-assertion outside the nursery and the kitchen, little authority over the course of their lives, and numerous cultural admonitions to curtail their sexuality, many women may well have experienced acute psychological distress, hence the "nervous afflictions" that were apparently so common among women of the time.

10. Juliet Mitchell, *Psychoanalysis and Feminism* (New York: Pantheon Books, 1974).

11. Nancy Chodorow, *The Reproduction of Mothering: Psychoanalysis and the Sociology of Gender* (Berkeley: University of California Press, 1978).

12. See Ernest Jones, "The Early Development of Female Sexuality," *International Journal of Psycho-Analysis,* 8 (1927): 459–472; "The Phallic Phase," *International Journal of Psycho-Analysis,* 14 (1933): 1–33; "Early Female Sexuality," *International Journal of Psycho-Analysis,* 16 (1935): 263–275. See also Karen Horney, "On the Genesis of the Castration Complex in Women," *International Journal of Psycho-Analysis,* 5 (1924): 50–65; "The Flight from Womanhood: The Masculinity-Complex in Women as Viewed by Men and Women," *International Journal of Psycho-Analysis,* 7 (1926): 324–339; "The Dread of Women: Observations on a Specific Difference in the Dread Felt by Men and by Women Respectively for the Opposite Sex," *International Journal of Psycho-Analysis,* 13 (1932): 348–360; "The Denial of the Vagina. A Contribution to the Problem of the Genital Anxiety Specific to Women," *International Journal of Psycho-Analysis,* 14 (1933): 57–70.

13. Susan Baker, "Biological Influences on Human Sex and Gender," in *Women—Sex and Sexuality,* ed. Catharine R. Stimpson and Ethel S. Person. (Chicago: University of Chicago Press, 1980), pp. 175–191. But just recently, the debate about the nature of sexual object choice has been reopened in the context of claims that there may be a biological component to homosexuality.

14. John Money, ed., *Sex Research: New Developments* (New York: Holt, Rinehart and Winston, 1965); John Money, "Gender Role, Gender Identity, Core Gender Identity: Usage and Definition of Terms" *Journal of the American Academy of Psychoanalysis,* 1 (1974): 397–404; see also Ethel Person and Lionel Ovesey, "Psy-

choanalytic Theories of Gender Identity," *Journal of the American Academy of Psychoanalysis,* 11 (1983): 203–226.

15. For example, a genetic male—perhaps a male child with a severe hypospadia, a deformity of the penis that makes it look more like a vulva—mistakenly assessed at birth as female and labeled as such will develop along feminine lines. That is, if we have made a mistake and designated a genetic male as female or vice versa, we are unable to reassign the child after the third year of life without causing a major psychological upheaval.

For an exception, see J. Imperato-McGinley, R. E. Peterson, T. Gautier, and E. Sturla, "Androgens and the Evolution of Male Gender Identity Among Male Pseudohermaphrodites with 5a-Reductase Deficiency," *New England Journal of Medicine,* 300 (1979): 1233–1237.

16. Lionel Ovesey and Ethel S. Person, "Gender Identity and Sexual Psychopathology in Men," *Journal of the American Academy of Psychoanalysis,* 1 (1973): 53–72; see also Person and Ovesey, "Psychoanalytic Theories of Gender Identity," *Journal of the American Academy of Psychoanalysis,* 11 (1983): 203–227.

17. Person and Ovesey, ibid.

18. As the sociologists John Gagnon and William Simon put it:

Once a parent or doctor has identified a child, always by the anatomic confirmation of his genitals (perhaps this is the meaning of "anatomy becomes destiny," anatomy in conjunction with social attribution) as male or female, there are released the separate cultural syndromes that are related to the rearing of male or female children.

See John H. Gagnon and William Simon, *Sexual Conduct: The Social Sources of Human Sexuality* (Chicago: Aldine Publishing, 1973).

19. According to the Sandlers:

Not only do the concepts of object choice and object relationship come together if we think in terms of the individual seeking particular role relationships (in the transference or outside in his everyday life) but the traditional distinction between the search for objects on the one hand and the search for wish-fulfillment or need-satisfaction on the other fades into insignificance. *The two can be regarded as being essentially the same.*

See Joseph Sandler and Anne-Marie Sandler, "On the Development of Object Relationships and Affects," *International Journal of Psycho-Analysis,* 59 (1978): 277–296.

20. Classical formulations of heterosexual female development focused almost exclusively on the girl's putative penis envy and on her father-longing as a route to achieve the penis. In contrast, in my view, the fact that the girl relinquishes her first object—her mother—in favor of her father has several important ramifications. My formulation emphasizes the uncertainty of the girl's relationship with her father and also the girl's special vulnerability to the threats of the Oedipal

complex, when her rival is also still her much-needed caretaker. (The Oedipal rival is condensed with the bad mother of early childhood and she is a formidable threat.) But in the classical formulation, the girl, already "castrated," is said to bypass Oedipal competition comparable to what the boy experiences. I believe girls are more vulnerable, not less, because at risk is their very sustenance, hence their frequent preoccupation with, and fantasies about, eating.

The girl's difficulty (fear of competition at the threshold of the Oedipal period) is complicated by the consequences of her renunciation of her mother and simultaneous turn to her father. She feels she has abandoned her mother for an uncertain substitute and fears retaliation. Further, the renunciation of her mother is felt as a loss. One could therefore say that all heterosexual women have experienced the loss of their first love object, whereas the same cannot be said for men.

The classical formulation of male psychology focused on the boy's struggle to achieve phallic strength and power vis-à-vis other men, based on his competition with his father for his mother's favor. Oedipal themes and fears—particularly castration anxieties—are explicit in male fantasy life; they are copiously revealed in conscious fantasies, dreams, and analytic associations.

But beginning with Karen Horney, analysts have added to Freud's formulation to include the impact on the boy of the characteristics of the mother-son relationship at different developmental stages. During the Oedipal phase, not only is the boy fearful of his father, but he also feels inadequate to the father in his ability to secure his mother's sexual love. While he may desire the Oedipal mother, he senses that his mother will reject him in favor of his father, because, as he comes to believe, his penis is too small. Many men never recover from this literal sense of genital inadequacy. It appears that many men are therefore destined to suffer lifelong penis envy. But the male's fear of the female, his anxiety over his inability to please her, and his anger at her stem from different developmental levels: fear of the pre-Oedipal mother who abandons/engulfs, of the anal mother who intrudes/indulges, of the phallic/narcissistic mother who falsely seduces/denigrates masculinity, of the Oedipal mother who cannot be fulfilled, rejects, and falsely seduces. Out of the amalgam of potential fears arises the male tendency to compensate through sexual fantasies of power and control of the woman and through denial of his dependency on females.

21. Anne Roiphe, *Torch Song* (New York: Farrar, Straus and Giroux, 1977), pp. 177–178.

22. My thanks to Dr. Marion Hart for sharing this story with me.

23. Doris Bernstein, *Female Identity Conflict in Clinical Practice,* ed. Norbert Freedman and Betsy Distler (New York: Jason Aronson, 1993).

24. Nina J. Easton, "So You Think War Toys Are Bad? Well, Tell That to the Mother of a Four-Year-Old Ninja Turtle Who Longs to Fight the Bad Guys," *Los Angeles Times* (July 5, 1994), p. E-1.

25. For a summary statement, see Richard C. Friedman and Jennifer I. Downey, "Biology and the Oedipus Complex," *Psychoanalytic Quarterly*, 64 (1995): 234–264.

26. Douglas Martin, "The X-Men Vanquish America," *New York Times* (August 21, 1994), p. B-27.

27. John Money, "Sex Hormones and Other Variables in Human Eroticism," in *Sex and Internal Secretions,* 3rd ed., vol. 2, ed. W. C. Young and G. W. Corner (Baltimore: Williams and Wilkins, 1961), pp. 1383–1400. For a good summary statement, see Donald Symons, *The Evolution of Human Sexuality* (New York: Oxford University Press, 1979).

28. John Money, *Sex Research: New Developments* (New York: Holt, Rinehart and Winston, 1965), p. 9. In later work, however, Money suggests that there is some increase in homosexuality among AGS-treated women. See John Money, Mark Schwartz, and Viola G. Davis, "Adult Erotosexual Status and Female Hormonal Masculinization and De-Masculinization: 46, XX Congenital Virilizing Adrenal Hyperplasia and 46, XY Androgen-Insensitivity Syndrome Compared," *Psychoneuroendochrinology*, 9 (1984): 405–414. My thanks to Dr. Martha Kirkpatrick for calling this article to my attention.

29. See Joseph Sandler and Anne-Marie Sandler, "The Past Unconscious, the Present Unconscious, and the Vicissitudes of Guilt," *International Journal of Psycho-Analysis,* 68 (1987): 337.

30. See Nancy Chodorow, *Femininities, Masculinities, Sexualities: Freud and Beyond* (Great Britain: Free Association Books, 1994).

31. E. Kirsten Dahl, "Play and the Construction of Gender in the Oedipal Child," in *The Many Meanings of Play: A Psychoanalytic Perspective,* ed. Albert J. Solnit, Donald J. Cohen, and Peter B. Neubauer (New Haven: Yale University Press, 1993), p. 117.

32. *Memoirs of Madame de La Tour du Pin,* trans. Felice Harcourt with an introduction by Peter Gay (New York: McCall, 1971), p. 22.

33. Ibid., p. 24.

34. Nancy Friday, *My Secret Garden* (New York: Pocket Books, 1974).

35. Female sexuality was liberated in at least two ways by virtue of the sexual revolution. First, it was freed from ignorance. The recognition that maximum sexual pleasure and orgasm depended on adequate clitoral stimulation and that it was not an automatic outcome of heterosexual intercourse was a crucial insight that permitted more women to find sexual fulfillment than ever before. Second, female sexuality was separated from an almost exclusive focus on male preferences and from the traditional idea of female submissiveness in relationships. Female sexual inhibition was often based on deference to the male and included a repertoire of behaviors such as faking orgasm, failing to insist on adequate stimulation, assuming that male orgasm determined the nature of the sexual encounter, and paying more attention to giving than to receiving pleasure. When these sexual strictures were resolved, women achieved a greater assertiveness and sense of autonomy. Sexual fantasy also flowered.

36. We generally think of fantasy as built around a kind of narrative, with a subject, an action, an object, and sometimes a context or a scene. In these narratives it is usually easy to identify the fantasizer. But some theorists envision fantasy as providing "a setting for desire." As Laplanche and Pontalis put it:

Fantasy is not the object of desire, but its setting. In fantasy the subject does not pursue the object or its sign: he appears caught up himself in the sequence of

images. He forms no representation of the desired object, but is himself represented as participating in the scene although, in the earliest form of fantasy, he
cannot be assigned any fixed place in it.

Jean Laplanche and Jean-Bertrand Pontalis, "Fantasy and the Origins of Sexuality," *International Journal of Psycho-Analysis,* 49 (1968): 17.

37. The literary critic Jacqueline Rose gives a persuasive argument as to why
such fantasies ought not be so frowned upon:

It has never been part of feminism's argument that because an image of femininity can be identified as male fantasy, it is any less intensely lived by women.
Conversely, the fact that the woman discovers something as a component of her
own self-imagining does not mean that it cannot also be the object, or even product, of the wildest male projection, repulsion or desire. Who owns what? Who
gives what to whom?

Because fantasy plays with gender arrangements, the masochistic fantasy may
tame, reverse, or edit the perceived reality. Jacqueline Rose, *The Haunting of Sylvia
Plath* (Cambridge, Mass.: Harvard University Press, 1993), pp. 128–129.

38. J. William Gibson, "Paramilitary Fantasy Culture and the Cosmogonic
Mythology of Primeval Chaos and Order" *Vietnam Generation,* 1, 3/4
(Summer/Fall 1989). This volume was a special edition entitled "Gender and the
War: Men Women and Vietnam," ed. Jacqueline Lawson.

39. The crisis in masculinity goes back at least to the early part of this century.
In their three-volume study in literary criticism of the twentieth century, Sandra
Gilbert and Susan Gubar use this crisis as an organizing principle. They describe
"the relationship between female dreams of a powerful Herland and male fears of
a debilitating no-man's land, showing that the rise of the New Woman was not
matched by the coming of a New Man but instead was identified (in the imagina-
tions of both men and women) with a crisis of masculinity that we have imaged
through the figure of the no-man." See Gilbert and Gubar, *No Man's Land: The
Place of the Woman Writer in the Twentieth Century,* vol. 2 (New Haven: Yale University Press, 1989), p. xii.

40. Olga Silverstein and Beth Rashbaum, *The Courage to Raise Good Men*
(New York: Viking, 1994), p. 184.

41. John Updike, *Rabbit Is Rich,* quoted in Silverstein and Rashbaum, *The
Courage to Raise Good Men,* p. 183.

42. My first inkling of this change came up in a discussion following a talk I
gave at a meeting cosponsored by the Southern California Psychoanalytic Institute
and Division 39 of the American Psychological Association in February 1995.

43. Robert May, *Sex and Fantasy: Patterns of Male and Female Development*
(New York: W. W. Norton, 1980), p. 131.

44. May's view echoes that of Susan Brownmiller. She declares: "Throughout
history no theme grips the masculine imagination with greater constancy and less
honor than the myth of the heroic rapist. As man conquered the world, so too he
conquers the female. Down through the ages, imperial conquest, exploits of valor

and expressions of love have gone hand in hand with violence to women in thought and deed." Susan Brownmiller, *Against Our Will: Men, Women and Rape* (New York: Bantam Books, 1976), p. 320.

45. Kate Millett, *Sexual Politics* (Garden City, N.Y.: Doubleday, 1976), p. 46.

46. Ethel S. Person, Nettie Terestman, Wayne A. Myers, Eugene L. Goldberg, and Carol Salvadori, "Gender Differences in Sexual Behaviors and Fantasies in a College Population," *Journal of Sex and Marital Therapy,* 15 (1989): 187–198.

47. Bernard Zilbergeld, *Male Sexuality* (New York: Bantam Books, 1978), p. 23.

48. For the developmental fault line in males, see Karen Horney, "The Dread of Women: Observations on a Specific Difference in the Dread Felt by Men and Women Respectively for the Opposite Sex," *International Journal of Psycho-analysis,* 13 (1932): 348–360. See also Ethel S. Person, "The Omni-Available Woman in Lesbian Sex: Two Fantasy Themes and Their Relationship to the Male Developmental Experience," in *The Psychology of Men: New Psychoanalytic Perspectives,* ed. Gerald Fogel, Frederick M. Lane, and Robert S. Liebert (New York: Basic Books, 1986), pp. 236–259; and Ethel S. Person, "Male Sexuality and Power," *Psychoanalytic Inquiry,* 6 (1986): 3–25.

49. Jean Wyatt, *Reconstructing Desire: The Role of the Unconscious in Women's Reading and Writing* (Chapel Hill, NC: The University of North Carolina Press, 1990), p. 23.

50. Adrienne Rich, "Jane Eyre: The Temptations of a Motherless Woman," in *On Lies, Secrets, and Silence* (New York: W. W. Norton, 1979), p. 106.

51. Molly Haskell, "To Have and Have Not; The Paradox of the Female Star," *American Imago,* 50, 4 (1993): 405.

52. Ibid., p. 402.

53. Ibid.

54. Ibid., p. 403.

55. The psychoanalysts Joseph and Anne-Marie Sandler have described this mode of suppression as the result of a second repression barrier (as distinguished from the repression barrier that pushes material into the unconscious) located at the junction of consciousness and preconsciousness and having as its fundamental motivation "the avoidance of conscious feelings of shame, embarrassment and humiliation." See Joseph Sandler and Anne-Marie Sandler, "The Past Unconscious," p. 336.

From the developmental point of view, they trace this censorship to the point at which the child relinquishes play in favor of conscious fantasizing, and feels the need to keep some fantasies secret.

56. Nancy Chodorow, *The Reproduction of Mothering,* p. 50.

Chapter 8

1. The language of possible selves and alternate selves runs through the psychological literature. I first became aware that this was the precise language to

convey an important aspect of fantasy through the very title of Jerome Bruner's *Actual Minds, Possible Worlds* (Cambridge, Mass.: Harvard University Press, 1986).

2. Psychoanalysts have long been aware of the role of art in both eliciting and gratifying fantasy. In this respect, art, particularly fiction—kin to dreams, daydreams, and play—is known to embody fantasies. In his "Creative Writers and Day-Dreaming," Freud noted that artistic works on some level express the artists' daydreams, and serve to elicit similar fantasies in the reader by facilitating his or her identification. Creator and consumer of the work, without knowing one another, are connected by fantasy material. See Sigmund Freud, "Creative Writers and Day-Dreaming" (1908[1907]), *S.E.,* vol. 9, pp. 143–153.

3. Carlos Fuentes, *My Self With Others* (New York: The Noon Day Press, 1990), p. 4.

4. Eileen Simpson, *Orphans: Real and Imagined* (New York: New American Library, 1987), pp. 30–31.

5. Fuentes, *My Self With Others,* p. 17. Fuentes alludes to these four authors.

6. Sigmund Freud, "Group Psychology and the Analysis of the Ego" (1921), *S.E.,* vol. 18, pp. 69–143.

7. Wayne Koestenbaum, "Jacqueline Kennedy Onassis: Her Bouffant Magnificence," *The New York Times Magazine* (January 1, 1995): 40.

8. Wayne Koestenbaum, *The Queen's Throat: Opera, Homosexuality, and the Mystery of Desire* (New York: Vintage Books, 1993), p. 31.

9. Ibid., p. 134.

10. Ethel S. Person and Lionel Ovesey, "Homosexual Cross-Dressers," *Journal of the American Academy of Psychoanalysis,* 12 (1984): 178–179.

11. Ibid., p. 179.

12. Marilyn Monroe, as icon, serves different functions in different contexts. For a segment of the gay male culture, she is someone who controlled men through her sensuality and personal magnetism, but her special appeal lies in her sensitivity, vulnerability, and suffering, feelings which the devotee shares and in some way rationalizes through his imaginative identification with her. Marilyn Monroe can also be invoked as a symbol of how women can be abandoned and/or destroyed by men. Thus she is quite different from Madonna—that icon of apparent sexual emancipation and in-your-face confrontation.

My interest in Sylvia Plath began in 1993 with an invitation from Herbert Hendin to participate in the conference "Waiting to Die: Suicide in American Literature," organized by the American Suicide Foundation, New York City, November 11, 1994. Of all the scholarship on Plath, I have found Jacqueline Rose's *The Haunting of Sylvia Plath* (Cambridge, Mass.: Harvard University Press, 1993) most useful in portraying and exploring her iconic status.

See also Sandra Gilbert and Susan Gunbar's "In Yeats's House: The Death and Resurrection of Sylvia Plath" in *No Man's Land: The Place of the Woman Writer in the Twentieth Century, vol. 3: Letters from the Front* (New Haven: Yale University Press, 1994).

13. See Rose, *Haunting of Sylvia Plath,* p. 1.

14. Ibid., p. 23.

15. For biographical background, see Edward Butscher, *Sylvia Plath: The*

Woman and the Work (New York: Dodd, Mead, 1977); and the prologue to A. Alvarez's *The Savage God* (New York: W. W. Norton, 1990), pp. 15–56.

16. Elaine Showalter, "Slick Chick," *London Review of Books* (July 11, 1991), p. 6.

17. Ibid. For Elaine Showalter "the double story of Sylvia Plath and Ted Hughes is material for an Emily Brontë or a Henry James, a great ghost story with the roles of haunter and haunted, villain and victim, hopelessly entwined." She agrees with Rose that this story "seems to have the power to draw everybody who approaches it into its orbit, to make you feel that somehow you belong."

18. Meg Wolitzer, *Sleepwalking* (New York: Random House, 1982).

19. See the account by Showalter, "Slick Chick."

20. Paul Alexander, *Rough Magic: A Biography of Sylvia Plath* (New York: Penguin, 1991), p. 346. Quoted in Devoney Looser, "Heroine of the Peripheral," *Auto/Biography Studies,* 5 (Fall 1993): 195.

21. Speaking of Plath and Hughes as a couple, Rose asks, "What could be the outcome of such a contract if what she fears in him, she also desires; if what he seeks to repair in her, he most fears?" Those who have acted out in response to the Plath legend have been feminists who do not self-destruct but who, resenting Plath being memorialized as Sylvia Plath Hughes, have symbolically tried to protect Plath from Hughes by effacing the name of Hughes from her tombstone. See Rose, *Haunting of Sylvia Plath,* p. 128.

22. For still others, Plath is not an admired icon at all but emblem of the woman as victim or, alternately, the woman as a feared and powerful force of nature, a kind of avatar of the horrors of feminism.

23. Rose, *Haunting of Sylvia Plath,* pp. 205–238.

24. This is depicted in the last two stanzas:

> *If I've killed one man I've killed two—*
> *The vampire who said he was you*
> *And drank my blood for a year—*
> *Seven years, if you want to know.*
> *Daddy, you can lie back now.*
> *There's a stake in your fat black heart*
> *And the villagers never liked you.*
> *They are dancing and stamping on you.*
> *They always knew it was you.*
> *Daddy, daddy, you bastard, I'm through.*

See Sylvia Plath, *Ariel* (New York: Harper and Row, 1966). According to Jacqueline Rose, this is the poem that launched the Sylvia Plath mystique.

25. If the literary critics Gilbert and Gubar are correct, "As both an icon and an articulator of the new . . . Plath had more positive meanings for her contemporaries and descendants"—more positive than as a suicide is what is implied here. See Gilbert and Gubar, *No Man's Land,* vol. 3, p. 305.

Plath, as icon, exerts her power in many ways, in part through the enactment of rage. (Suicide is, after all, self-murder.) Sylvia Plath was aware of a violence in herself that could be turned either inward or outward. In a journal entry of 1958 she writes, "I have a violence in me that is hot as death-blood. I can kill myself or—I know it now—even kill another. I could kill a woman, or wound a man. I think I could." See Frances McCullough and Ted Hughes, eds., *The Journals of Sylvia Plath* (New York: Dial Press, 1982), pp. 237–238.

26. Our current cultural emphasis on sexual abuse, wife battering, rape, and harassment may be a necessary corrective to our previous collective inability to see and curb a variety of abuses perpetrated against women and children. However, the idea of strength as embodied in being a survivor—whether of divorce or disease or something else—must be seen as a transitional stage, not the last stop, on the way to empowering women.

27. See, among other recent works, Katie Roiphe, *The Morning After: Sex, Fear and Feminism on Campus* (Boston: Little, Brown, 1993).

28. Hal Foster, "Cult of Despair," *New York Times* (December 30, 1994), p. A-31.

29. Gilbert and Gubar, *No Man's Land,* vol. 3, pp. 286–288. Plath was delighted to find an apartment in the house where Yeats had once lived and Gilbert and Gubar believe she was able to absorb his vision of the subversive strength of the woman poet.

30. Ibid., p. 284.

31. McCullough and Hughes, eds., *Journals of Sylvia Plath,* p. 152.

32. Anne Sexton, "The Bar Fly Ought to Sing," in *The Art of Sylvia Plath,* ed. Charles Newman (Bloomington: Indiana University Press, 1971), p. 175.

33. Ibid., p. 135.

34. Quoted in Diane Wood Middlebrook, *Anne Sexton: A Biography* (Boston: Houghton Mifflin, 1991), p. 200.

35. A. Alvarez, *The Savage God, a Study of Suicide* (New York: W. W. Norton, 1990[1971]), pp. 291–292.

36. See, for example, Marie Asbery, Peter Nordstrom, Lil Traskman-Bendz, "Biological Factors in Suicide," in *Suicide,* ed. Alec Roy (Baltimore, Md.: Williams and Wilkens, 1986), pp. 47–71; see also E. F. Coccaro, L. J. Siever, and H. M. Klar, et al., "Serotonergic Studies in Patients with Affective and Personality Disorders: Correlates with Suicidal and Impulsive Aggressive Behavior," *Archives of General Psychiatry,* 46 (1989): 587–599.

37. Quoted in Alvarez, *The Savage God,* p. 231, attributed to Forbes Winslow, *The Anatomy of Suicide* (London, 1840), p. 118.

38. Fritz Strich, *Goethe and World Literature* (Westport, Conn.: Greenwood Press, 1971 [1945]).

39. Glen Evans and Norman Fanberow, *The Encyclopedia of Suicide* (New York: Facts on File, 1988), p. 139.

Sympathetic suicides have been documented in other contexts among teenagers, for example, in response to publicized suicides of celebrities, the punk rock songwriter and singer Kurt Cobain being one of the latest instances. After the discovery of Cobain's death, the Seattle Crisis Clinic received 100 more calls a day than usual. At least two people were reported to have killed themselves in response to Cobain's death. Chris Mundy, "The Life of Kurt Cobain: The Lost Boy," *Rolling Stone* (June 2, 1994), pp. 51–53. See also Neil Strauss, "The Downward Spiral," *Rolling Stone* (June 2, 1994).

40. Alvarez, *The Savage God,* p. 230.

41. Strich, *Goethe and World Literature,* p. 167.

42. Ibid., p. 164.

43. Quoted in Alvarez, *The Savage God,* p. 233. *Flaubert correspondence, Paris, 1887–1893,* vol. 2, pp. 191, 58.

44. Madelyn Gould, "Suicide Clusters and Media Exposure," in *Suicide Over the Life-Cycle,* ed. Susan J. Blumenthal and Donald J. Kupfer (Washington, D.C.: American Psychiatric Press, 1990), pp. 517–532.

45. Ibid. Gould reports: "Increasing concern about the role of imitation and contagion as risk factors for suicide has been associated with a number of highly publicized suicide outbreaks in teenagers and young adults and with evidence that an increased number of suicides appear to be associated with suicide stories in the mass media" (p. 517).

While many studies of suicide clusters are methodologically flawed, Gould tried to conduct her studies using methods to "establish clustering by demonstrating an excess frequency of suicide in certain times and places or a significant relationship between the time and space differences between pairs of suicides" (p. 521). She found that "suicide clusters occur predominantly among teenagers and young adults" (p. 521).

Certain epidemics suggest that contagion must certainly be part of the etiology; for example, clusters in which the suicides choose almost identical methods of killing themselves.

46. Ibid., p. 521.

47. Ibid., p. 522. Gould points out that "prominent newspaper coverage of a suicide has the effect of increasing suicide behavior within the readership area of the newspaper. The magnitude of the increase is related to the 'attractiveness' of the individual whose death is being reported and the amount of publicity given to the story."

48. Ibid., p. 523.

49. Plath viewed her recovery from her depression and suicide attempt in 1953 as a poetic rebirth. She described it in her journals as "Waking to a new world, with no name, being born again, and not of woman." McCullough and Hughes, eds., *Journals of Sylvia Plath,* p. 318.

For an in-depth exploration of *Liebestod* fantasies, see Helen Gediman, "On Love, Dying Together and *Liebestod* Fantasies," *Journal of the American Psychoanalytic Association,* 29 (1981): 607–630.

50. Robert Jay Lifton, presentation at the conference "Waiting to Die: Suicide in American Literature," organized by the American Suicide Foundation, New York City, November 11, 1994.

51. Janet Malcom, "The Silent Woman," *The New Yorker* (August 23, 1993), p. 107.

52. I take the phase "Seduced by Death" from an article by Herbert Hendin, "Seduced by Death: Doctors, Patients, and the Dutch Cure," *Issues in Law and Medicine,* 10, 2 (1994): 123–168.

53. Quoted in ibid., p. 127.

54. Quoted in ibid.

55. Ibid., p. 128.

56. Ibid., p. 139.

57. Ibid., p. 129.

58. As suggested by Slotkin, "a mythology is a complex of narratives that dramatizes the world vision and historical sense of a people or culture, reducing centuries of experience into a constellation of compelling metaphors." Richard Slotkin, *Regeneration through Violence: The Mythology of the American Frontier, 1600–1860* (Middletown, Conn.: Wesleyan University Press, 1973), p. 6.

59. For antecedents of violent behavior in antisocial people, see Stephen Buka and Felton Earls, "Early Determinants of Delinquency and Violence," *Health Affairs,* 12, 4 (Winter 1993): 46–64.

Media violence *can* teach adolescents violent behavior, according to the American Psychological Association Commission on Violence and Youth, *Violence and Youth: Psychology's Response, vol. 1: Summary Report* (APA, 1993). The report summarized findings from a six-year review of influences of the mass media. The conclusion: "There is absolutely no doubt that higher levels of human violence on television are correlated with increasing acceptance of aggressive attitudes and increased aggressive behavior."

60. For a poetic approach to the formation of culturally sanctioned aggression, see William Butler Yeats, "The Stare's Nest by My Window," *The Collected Poems* (New York: Macmillan, 1933). Musing on the civil war in Ireland, Yeats wrote: "We had fed the heart on fantasies, / The heart's grown brutal from the fare / More substance in our enmities; / Than in our love; O honey bees, / Come build in the empty house of the stare."

61. Klaus Theweleit, *Male Fantasies,* vol. 1: *Women, Floods, Bodies, History;* vol. 2: *Male Bodies: Psychoanalyzing the White Terror* (Minneapolis: University of Minnesota Press, 1987).

62. Ibid., vol. 2, p. 353.

63. See Barbara Ehrenreich's foreword to Theweleit, *Male Fantasies,* vol. 1.

64. Robert Gregory, "Tactic of Evasion: A Review of *Male Fantasies,*" *American Book Review* (March/April 1990): 6.

65. Theweleit, *Male Fantasies,* vol. 2, p. 125.

66. Ibid., vol. 2, p. 276.

67. Ibid., vol. 1, pp. xiv–xx.

68. Ibid., vol. 1, p. 89.

69. James William Gibson, "Paramilitary Fantasy Culture and the Cosmogonic Mythology of Primeval Chaos and Order," *Vietnam Generation,* 1, 3/4 (Summer/Fall 1989): 12–32. See also, James William Gibson, *Warrior Dreams* (New York: Hill and Wang, 1994). My thanks to Vicki Goldberg for introducing me to the work of Gibson.

70. Gibson, "Paramilitary Fantasy Culture," p. 12.

71. Ibid., p. 13.

72. Ibid., p. 30.

73. Philip Weiss, "A Hoplophobe Among the Gunnies," *The New York Times Magazine* (September 11, 1994), pp. 65–100.

74. Ibid., p. 100.
75. Ibid.
76. Ibid.
77. Ibid.
78. Ibid.
79. See Keith Schneider, "Fearing a Conspiracy, Some Heed a Call to Arms," *New York Times* (November 14, 1994), p. A-1.
80. André Haynal, Miklos Molnar, and Gérard de Puymàge, *Fanaticism: A Historical and Psychoanalytic Study* (New York: Schocken Books, 1983).
81. Ibid., pp. 68–69.
82. See Hanns Sachs, "The Community of Daydreams" (1920), in *The Creative Unconscious* (Cambridge, Mass.: Sci-Art Publishers, 1942), pp. 14–15.

Chapter 9

1. I coined the term *cultural unconscious* in 1988 and it appears in my paper "Romantic Love: At the Intersection of the Psyche and the Cultural Unconscious," *Journal of the American Psychoanalytic Association,* 39 (1991): 383–411. Others have independently used the same term, probably because it so vividly captures a quality of unconscious that thus far has not been explicitly addressed. Jacqueline Rose uses the term in a throwaway line in the introduction to her *Haunting of Sylvia Plath* (Cambridge, Mass.: Harvard University Press, 1993). She writes of Plath's use of fascistic and Holocaust imagery, "It . . . appears like the return of the repressed—a fragment of the cultural unconscious that will not go away" (p. 8). And Edith Kurzweil refers to the cultural unconscious affecting psychoanalytic theories in different geographical areas in her book *The Freudians: A Comparative Perspective* (New Haven: Yale University Press, 1989).
2. Jacob Arlow, "The Consecration of the Prophet" *Psychoanalytic Quarterly,* 20 (1951): 374–397.
3. Michel Tournier, *The Wind Spirit* (Boston: Beacon Press, 1988), pp. 159–160.
4. Arlow, "The Consecration of the Prophet," p. 397.
5. *Collective imagining* is the term used by Lynn Hunt to describe what she calls the "political unconscious" in her book *The Family Romance in the French Revolution* (Berkeley: University of California Press, 1992). She borrows that term from Fredric Jameson, who elaborated it in *The Political Unconscious: Narrative as a Socially Symbolic Act* (Ithaca, N.Y.: Cornell University Press, 1981). It is similar to my term *cultural unconscious;* see note 1.
6. My thanks to Caroline Stoessinger, one of whose avocations is the study of eighteenth- and nineteenth-century European literary and cultural history, who pointed me to Herzl. My account of Herzl is based on the following sources: Peter Loewenberg, "Theodor Herzl: A Psychoanalytic Study in Charismatic Political Leadership," in *The Psychoanalytic Interpretation of History,* ed. Benjamin B. Wolman (New York: Harper Torch Books, 1971); Avner Falk, *Herzl: King of the Jews: A Psychoanalytic Biography of Theodor Herzl* (New York: University Press of America, 1993); Stefan Zweig, *The World of Yesterday* (Lincoln: University of Nebraska Press,

1964 [1943]); and Ludwig Lewisohn, ed., *Theodor Herzl: A Portrait for This Age,* preface by David Ben-Gurion (New York: World Publishing, 1955).

7. See, for example, Loewenberg, "Theodor Herzl," p. 150.

8. Loewenberg, "Theodor Herzl," p. 151. Whether or not Herzl specifically spoke to his grandfather about his views is unknown, but Loewenberg believes it unlikely that he could have avoided knowing what his grandfather's ideas were.

9. Lewisohn, *Theodor Herzl,* pp. 34–35.

10. Ibid., p. 35.

11. Quoted in Loewenberg, "Theodor Herzl," pp. 151–152.

12. Falk, *Herzl,* p. 158.

13. Quoted in Loewenberg, "Theodor Herzl," p. 161.

14. Quoted in ibid.

15. Ibid.

16. Zweig, *The World of Yesterday,* p. 102; Lewisohn, *Theodor Herzl,* pp. 52–54.

17. Zweig, *The World of Yesterday,* p. 102. Whether or not Herzl actually witnessed the public degradation of Dreyfus is a matter of debate, Zweig and Lewisohn contending that he did, Falk disputing that version of events. But regardless of whether Herzl was actually present there is no doubt that the Dreyfus case made an enormous impression upon him. At about the same time as the accusation against Dreyfus and his public humiliation, a prominent anti-Semite named Lueger was elected burgomaster of Vienna. Herzl is said to have asked a French Jewish friend: "Why were you overcome by Lueger's election and I by Dreyfus' degradation if you are a Frenchman and I am an Austrian?" See Lewisohn, *Theodor Herzl,* p. 52.

Dreyfus was assimilationist, signified by the fact that he had chosen the military as his profession and against all odds had become a captain attached to the French General Staff. What was more unsettling to the Jews than the degradation of Dreyfus was the fact that the cry of the French mob was "Death to the Jews" and not "Death to this traitor."

18. Quoted in Loewenberg, "Theodor Herzl," p. 163.

19. Ibid., p. 164.

20. Zweig, *The World of Yesterday,* p. 104.

21. Ibid.

22. Loewenberg, "Theodor Herzl," p. 166.

23. The creativity implicit in fantasy is invariably missed if one sees fantasy solely as a compromise solution to unconscious conflict. In fact, fantasy is often the means of becoming aware of what ails one not just in one's personal life but in one's public life. What happened in Herzl's mind is called a *tesuva* (illumination), which in his case marked the end of a repression not in his internal life but in his political life.

24. Hunt, *The Family Romance,* p. 8.

25. Ibid., p. xiii.

26. Ibid., p. xiv.

27. Quoted in ibid., p. 3.

28. Ibid., pp. 196–198.

29. Ibid., p. xiv.

30. Ibid., p. xv.

31. Ibid., p. 50.

32. Quoted in ibid., p. 18.

33. Ibid.

34. Ibid., p. 25.

35. Ibid., p. 28.

36. Ibid.

37. Ibid., p. 34.

38. Sigmund Freud, "Totem and Taboo" [1912–1913], *S.E.,* vol. 13, pp. ix–99.

39. This section draws on material I have published elsewhere. See Person, "Romantic Love: At the Intersection of the Psyche and the Cultural Unconscious." See also Joseph Campbell, *Creative Mythology: The Masks of God* (New York: Penguin Books, 1968); Denis de Rougemont, *Love in the Western World* (New York: Pantheon Books, 1956); C. S. Lewis, *The Allegory of Love: A Study in Medieval Tradition* (New York: Oxford University Press, 1936).

40. Lewis, *Allegory of Love,* p. 4.

41. See Francesco Alberoni, *Falling in Love,* trans. Lawrence Venuti (New York: Random House, 1983); and Ethel S. Person, *Dreams of Love and Fateful Encounters* (New York: W. W. Norton, 1988).

42. Charles R. Darwin, *The Expression in Man and Animals* (London: John Murray, 1872).

43. Charles E. Izard, *Human Emotions* (New York: Plenum Press, 1977).

44. Some argue that it is not absent, but rare. See, for example, William R. Jankowiak and Edward F. Fisher, "A Cross-Cultural Perspective on Romantic Love" *Ethnology* 31, 2 (1992): 149–155. My thanks to Dr. George Pollack for calling this article to my attention.

45. William J. Goode, "The Theoretical Importance of Love," *American Sociological Review,* 24 (1959): 34–47. Professor Cynthia Epstein was very helpful in pointing me to sociological references on romantic love.

46. Ibid., p. 41.

47. The material on the evolution of love stories, in addition to my own reading, draws on analyses by Leslie Fiedler and Toby Tanner. See Leslie Fiedler, *Love and Death in the American Novel* (New York: Stein and Day, 1966); and Toby Tanner, *Adultery in the Novel: Contract and Transgression* (Baltimore: John Hopkins University Press, 1979).

For changes in the practice and expression of love in different decades, see Stephen Kern, *The Culture of Love: Victorians to Moderns* (Cambridge, Mass.: Harvard University Press, 1992). See also Ellen K. Rothman, *Hands and Hearts: A History of Courtship in America* (New York: Basic Books, 1984).

48. This is the observation crucial to the thesis on the politico-social meaning of the development of romantic love.

49. Lawrence Stone, "Passionate Attachments in the West in Historical Perspective," in *Passionate Attachments: Thinking About Love,* ed. Willard Gaylin and Ethel S. Person (New York: The Free Press, 1988), pp. 15–26.

50. Dante Alighieri, "Inferno: Canto V," *The Divine Comedy,* trans. John Ciardi (New York: W. W. Norton, 1977).

51. Gustave Flaubert, *Madame Bovary,* trans. Francis Steegmuller (New York: Random House, 1957), p. 66.

52. Ibid., pp. 69–70.

53. The poet Gottfried, quoted by Campbell in *Creative Mythology,* p. 42.

54. Person, *Dreams of Love and Fateful Encounters.*

55. Sigmund Freud, "On Narcissism," *S.E.* vol. 14, pp. 69–102.

56. This has been pointed out by Martin Bergmann in *The Anatomy of Loving: The Story of Man's Quest to Know What Love Is* (New York: Columbia University Press, 1987).

57. Yet if this were all there is to love—new gratifications for old urges, new solutions to old problems—then love would be, as many claim, no more than narcissism à deux and Freud correct in his contention that the so-called selflessness of love is no more than the disguise under the cover of which Eros and Narcissus seek their own gratifications. However love is not merely a closed loop, as is sometimes postulated even within the framework of ego psychology. We know that the lover's sense of well-being is something more than a transient instinctual gratification or narcissistic exaltation, because psychic change (transformation) may endure even when a love affair ends. Certainly it is true that love is a process born of psychic need. But as an act of the imagination, it transcends need and may sometimes culminate in inner change.

58. Sigmund Freud, "Creative Writers and Day-Dreaming," *S.E.,* vol. 9, p. 146.

59. H. G. Wells, *H. G. Wells in Love: Postscript to an Experiment in Autobiography,* ed. G. P. Wells (Boston: Little, Brown, 1984), pp. 53–55.

60. Campbell, *Creative Mythology,* p. 2.

61. There are many cultures in which the self (if indeed there exists in those cultures anything like what we regard as the self) is not so problematic a construct as it is in our own. These are cultures in which all members fit into predetermined and externally defined roles, that automatically provide strong bonds with group or tribe or God and through which they can realize themselves and achieve meaning. See Hans Morgenthau and Ethel S. Person, "The Roots of Narcissism," *Partisan Review,* 45 (1978): 337–347.

Romantic love cannot be so important in such cultures. In Japan, for example, conformity and identification with the group are valued above all, and romantic love is a rare occurrence, disapproved of and feared. However, the Japanese do celebrate one highly romantic convention: Lovers who cannot be together in life join each other in death—by suicide. For the Japanese, self-will, because of its potential for social disruptiveness, cannot easily exist within the cultural framework. Consequently, the only acceptable outlet for love (one of the ultimate manifestations of self-will) is doomed love, in which the lovers, by dying for their love, simultaneously assert and extinguish the self, thus insuring the primacy of the group over selfish claims of the lover. The Japanese weep at stories of doomed lovers' suicides and thereby vicariously indulge, romanticize, and exorcise those impulses within themselves.

This means of channeling illicit desires is not so different from the celebration of chaste, doomed love that was the defining feature of troubadour culture, or the punishment of adulterous love which was the stuff of Arthurian romance. During the Middle Ages, when the valuation of autonomy was coming into its ascendancy but the individual's behavior was still bound by strict laws of fealty and obligation, it made perfect sense for the culture to have arrived at a means of acknowledging the peremptoriness of love, and, through the literary convention of the *Liebestod,* punishing it.

62. See Person, *Dreams of Love and Fateful Encounters.* The aims and wishes of love are more complex than simply the gratification of half-buried wishes or the refinding of lost love objects. Love promises newness; it leads to separation from what has gone before, the formation of a new world and internal change if not transformation.

BIBLIOGRAPHY

Alexander, Paul. *Rough Magic: A Biography of Sylvia Plath.* New York: Penguin, 1991.

Alberoni, Francesco. *Falling in Love.* Trans. Lawrence Venuti. New York: Random House, 1983.

Alighieri, Dante. *The Divine Comedy.* Trans. John Ciardi. New York: W. W. Norton, 1977.

Alvarez, A. *The Savage God, A Study of Suicide.* New York: W. W. Norton, 1990 [1971].

American Psychological Association Commission on Violence and Youth. *Violence and Youth: Psychology's Response, vol. 1: Sumary Report.* American Psychological Association, 1993.

Ammaniti, Massimo. "Maternal Representations During Pregnancy and Early Infant-Mother Interactions." *Infant Mental Health Journal,* 12 (1991): 246–255.

Ammaniti, Massimo, E. Baumgartner, C. Candelori, M. Pola, R. Tambelli, and F. Zampino. "Rappresentazioni materne in gravidanza: Contributi preliminari." *Rivista di Psicologia Clinica,* 1 (1990): 36–50.

Ammaniti, Massimo, and Daniel Stern, eds. *Psychoanalysis and Development: Representations and Narratives.* New York: New York University Press, 1994.

Arlow, Jacob. "Conflict, Regression and Symptom Formation." *International Journal of Psycho-Analysis,* 44 (1963): 12–22.

————. "The Consecration of the Prophet." *Psychoanalytic Quarterly,* 20 (1951): 374–397.

————. "Ego Psychology and the Study of Mythology." *Journal of the American Psychoanalytic Association,* 9 (1961): 371–391.

————. "Fantasy, Memory and Reality." *Psychoanalytic Quarterly,* 38 (1969): 28–51.

————. "Metaphor and the Psychoanalytic Situation." *Psychoanalytic Quarterly,* 58 (1979): 363–385.

————. "Unconscious Fantasy and Disturbances of Conscious Experience." *Psychoanalytic Quarterly,* 38 (1969): 1–17.

Asbery, Marie, Peter Nordstrom, and Lil Traskman-Bendz. "Biological Factors in Suicide." In *Suicide,* ed. Alec Roy. Baltimore, Md.: Williams and Wilkins, 1986, pp. 47–71.

Atwood, Margaret. *The Handmaid's Tale.* Boston: Houghton Mifflin, 1986.

Baker, Susan. "Biological Influences on Human Sex and Gender." In *Women— Sex and Sexuality,* ed. Catharine R. Stimpson and Ethel S. Person. Chicago: University of Chicago Press, 1980, pp. 175–191.

Bergmann, Martin. *The Anatomy of Loving: The Story of Man's Quest to Know What Love Is.* New York: Columbia University Press, 1987.

Bernstein, Doris. *Female Identity Conflict in Clinical Practice,* ed. Norbert Freedman and Betsy Distler. New York: Jason Aronson, 1993.

Bettelheim, Bruno. *The Uses of Enchantment: The Meaning and Importance of Fairy Tales.* New York: Alfred A. Knopf, 1976.

Blum, Harold. "Chairman's Opening Remarks." Presented at the panel "Clinical Value and Utilization of the Daydream," Scientific Meetings of the American Psychoanalytic Association, New York City, December 19, 1993.

————. "Shared Fantasy and Reciprocal Identification, and Their Role in Gender Disorders." In *Fantasy, Myth and Reality,* ed. Harold P. Blum, Yale Kramer, Arlene K. Richards, and Arnold D. Richards. Madison, Conn.: International Universities Press, 1988.

————. "The Clinical Value of Daydreams and a Note on Their Role in Character Analysis." In *On Freud's "Creative Writers and Day-Dreaming,"* ed. Ethel Person, Peter Fonagy, and Sérvulo Figueira. New Haven: Yale University Press, 1995, pp. 39–52.

Bonaparte, Marie, Anna Freud, and Ernst Kris, eds. *The Origins of Psychoanalysis: Letters to Wilhelm Fliess, Drafts and Notes, 1887–1902.* New York: Basic Books, 1954.

Bornstein, Berta. "On Latency." In *Psychoanalytic Study of the Child,* vol. 6. Madison, Conn.: International Universities Press, 1951.

Brantley, Ben. "Sam Shepard, Storyteller." *New York Times* (November 13, 1994), p. B-1.

Brownmiller, Susan. *Against Our Will: Men, Women and Rape.* New York: Bantam Books, 1976.

Bruner, Jerome. *Acts of Meaning.* Cambridge, Mass.: Harvard University Press, 1990.

————. *Actual Minds, Possible Worlds.* Cambridge, Mass.: Harvard University Press, 1986.

Buka, Stephen, and Felton Earls. "Early Determinants of Delinquence and Violence." *Health Affairs,* 12, 4 (Winter 1993): 46–64.

Butscher, Edward, ed. *Sylvia Plath: The Woman and the Work.* New York: Dodd, Mead, 1977.

Calvino, Italo. *The Road to San Giovanni.* New York: Pantheon Books, 1993.

Campbell, Joseph. *Creative Mythology: The Masks of God.* New York: Penguin Books, 1968.

Cannon, Walter B. "The Role of Hunches in Scientific Thought." In *The Creativity Question,* ed. Albert Rothenberg and Carl R. Housman. Durham, NC: Duke University Press, 1976.

Capote, Truman. *Answered Prayers: The Unfinished Novel.* New York: Random House, 1987.

Chasseguet-Smirgel, Janine. "Creative Writers and Day-Dreaming: A Commentary." In *On Freud's "Creative Writers and Day-Dreaming,"* ed. Ethel S. Person, Peter Fonagy, and Sérvulo Figueira. New Haven: Yale University Press, 1995, pp. 107–121.

Chira, Susan. "When Hope Died." *New York Times Magazine* (June 6, 1994), p. 20.

Chodorow, Nancy J. *Femininities, Masculinities, Sexualities: Freud and Beyond.* Lexington: University of Kentucky; Great Britain: Free Association Books, 1994.

———. *The Reproduction of Mothering: Psychoanalysis and the Sociology of Gender.* Berkeley: University of California Press, 1978.

Chodorow, Nancy, and Susan Contratto. "The Fantasy of the Perfect Mother." In Nancy Chodorow, *Feminism and Psychoanalytic Theory.* New Haven: Yale University Press, 1989, pp. 79–96.

Coccaro, E. F., L. J. Siever, and H. M. Klar. "Serotonergic Studies in Patients with Affective and Personality Disorders: Correlated with Suicidal and Impulsive Aggressive Behavior." *Archives of General Psychiatry,* 46 (1989): 587–599.

Cooper, Arnold M. "Infant Research and Adult Psychoanalysis." In *The Significance of Infants Observational Research for Clinical Work with Children, Adolescents and Adults,* ed. Scott Dowling and Arnold Rothstein. Madison, Conn.: International Universities Press, 1989.

Dahl, E. Kirsten. "Play and the Construction of Gender in the Oedipal Child." In *The Many Meanings of Play: A Psychoanalytic Perspective,* ed. by Albert Solnit, Donald J. Cohen, and Peter B. Neubauer. New Haven, Conn.: Yale University Press, 1993, pp. 117–134.

Darnton, John. "A Scholar's Memoirs Raise Some Ghosts at Oxford." *New York Times* (November 18, 1994), A1.

Darwin, Charles R. *The Expression in Man and Animals.* London: John Murray, 1872.

de la Tour du Pin. *Memoirs of Madame de la Tour du Pin.* Trans. Felice Harcourt with an introduction by Peter Gay. New York: McCall, 1971.

de Rougement, Denis. *Love in the Western World.* New York: Pantheon Books, 1956.

De St. Jorre, John. "The Unmasking of O." *The New Yorker,* 70 (August 1, 1994), pp. 42–50.

Dowling, I. *Attachment and Love.* New York: Basic Books, 1969.

Dowling, Scott. "Fantasy Formation: A Child Analyst's Perspective." *Journal of the American Psychoanalytic Association,* 38 (1990): 93–111.

Easton, Nina J. "So You Think War Toys Are Bad? Well, Tell That to the Mother of a Four-Year-Old Ninja Turtle Who Longs to Fight the Bad Guys." *Los Angeles Times* (July 5, 1994), p. E-1.

Elich, Jaffa. *Hasidic Tales of the Holocaust.* New York: Vintage, 1988.

Emde, Robert N. "Fantasy and Beyond: A Current Developmental Perspective on Freud's 'Creative Writers and Day-Dreaming.'" In *On Freud's "Creative Writers and Day-Dreaming,"* ed. Ethel S. Person, Peter Fonagy, and Sérvulo Figueira. New Haven: Yale University Press, 1995, pp. 113–163.

Evans, Glen, and Norman Fanberow. *The Encyclopedia of Suicide.* New York: Facts on File, 1988.

Falk, Avner. *Herzl: King of the Jews: A Psychoanalytic Biography of Theodor Herzl.* New York: University Press of America, 1993.

Fiedler, Leslie. *Love and Death in the American Novel.* New York: Stein and Day, 1966.

Flaubert, Gustave. *Madame Bovary.* Trans. Francis Steegmuller. New York: Random House, 1957.

Foster, Hal. "Cult of Despair." *New York Times* (December 30, 1994), p. A-31.

Fraiberg, Selma, Edna Adelson, and Vivian Shapiro. "Ghosts in the Nursery: A Psychoanalytic Approach to the Problems of Impaired Infant-Mother Relationships." *Journal of the American Academy of Child Psychoanalysis,* 14 (1975): 387–422.

Freud, Anna. "Beating Fantasies and Daydreams." In *The Writings of Anna Freud, vol. 1, 1922–1935.* Madison, Conn.: International Universities Press, 1974.

———. "Denial in Fantasy." In *The Writings of Anna Freud, vol. 2: The Ego and Mechanisms of Defense* (New York: International Universities Press, 1966 [1936]), pp. 69–82.

———. *Normality and Pathology in Childhood: Assessment of Development.* New York: International Universities Press, 1965.

Freud, Sigmund. "Aetiology of Hysteria." *The Standard Edition of the Complete Psychological Works of Sigmund Freud,* vols. 1–24, ed. J. Strachey (hereafter *S.E.*). Vol. 3 (1896). London: Hogarth Press, 1953–1974, pp. 189–221.

———. "Beyond the Pleasure Principle." *S.E.,* vol. 18 (1920), pp. 1–64.

———. "Creative Writers and Day-Dreaming." *S.E.,* vol. 9 (1908[1907]), pp. 141–153.

———. "The Dissolution of the Oedipus Complex." *S.E.,* vol. 19 (1924), pp. 173–179.

———. "Dynamics of Transference." *S.E.,* vol. 12 (1912), pp. 97–108.

———. "Family Romances." *S.E.,* vol. 9 (1909[1908]), pp. 237–241.

———. "Female Sexuality." *S.E.,* vol. 21 (1931), pp. 223–243.

———. "Femininity," lecture 23 in "New Introductory Lectures on Psychoanalysis." *S.E.,* vol. 22 (1933), pp. 112–135.

———. "Formulations on the Two Principles of Mental Functioning." *S.E.,* vol. 12 (1911), pp. 215–226.

———. "Group Psychology and the Analysis of the Ego." *S.E.,* vol. 18 (1921), pp. 69–143.

———. "From the History of an Infantile Neurosis." *S.E.,* vol. 17 (1918[1914]), pp. 3–122.

———. "On Hysterical Phantasies and Their Relation to Bisexuality." *S.E.,* vol. 9 (1908), pp. 157–166.

———. "Interpretation of Dreams." *S.E.,* vols. 4, 5 (1900).

————. "Introductory Lectures on Psycho-analysis, Part III." *S.E.*, vol. 16 (1916).

————. "On Narcissism." *S.E.*, vol. 14 (1914), pp. 69–102.

————. "The Paths to the Formation of Symptoms," lecture 22 in "Introductory Lectures on Psychoanalysis." *S.E.*, vol. 15 (1916–17[1915–17]), pp. 358–377.

————. "Some Psychical Consequences of the Anatomical Distinction between the Sexes." *S.E.*, vol. 19 (1925), pp. 241–258.

————. "Totem and Taboo." *S.E.*, vol. 13 (1912–1913), pp. ix–162.

Freud, Sigmund, and Josef Breuer. "Studies on Hysteria." *S.E.*, vol. 2 [1893–1895].

Friday, Nancy. *My Secret Garden.* New York: Pocket Books, 1974.

Friedman, Richard C., and Jennifer Downey. "Biology and the Oedipus Complex." *Psychoanalytic Quarterly*, 64 (1995): 234–264.

Fuentes, Carlos. *My Self With Others.* New York: The Noon Day Press, 1990.

Gagnon, John H., and William Simon. *Sexual Conduct: The Social Sources of Human Sexuality.* Chicago: Aldine Publishing, 1973.

Gediman, Helen. "On Love, Dying Together and *Liebestod* Fantasies." *Journal of the American Psychoanalytic Association*, 29 (1981): 607–630.

Gibson, James William. "Paramilitary Fantasy Culture and the Cosmogonic Mythology of Primeval Chaos and Order." *Vietnam Generation*, 1, 3/4 (Summer/Fall 1981): 12–32. Special Edition "Gender and the War: Men, Women and Vietnam," ed. Jacqueline Lawson.

————. *Warrior Dreams.* New York: Hill and Wang, 1994.

Gilbert, Sandra M., and Susan Gubar. *No Man's Land: The Place of the Woman Writer in the Twentieth Century*, vol. 2, 1989; vol. 3: *Letters from the Front*, 1994. New Haven, Conn.: Yale University Press.

Gillman, Robert D. "Rescue Fantasies and the Secret Benefactor." In *Psychoanalytic Study of the Child*, vol. 47. Madison, Conn.: International Universities Press, 1992, pp. 279–298.

Goode, William J. "The Theoretical Importance of Love." *American Sociological Review*, 24 (1959): 34–47.

Gould, Madelyn. "Suicide Clusters and Media Exposure." In *Suicide Over the Life-Cycle*, ed. Susan J. Blumenthal and Donald J. Kupfer. Washington, D.C.: American Psychiatric Press, 1990, pp. 517–532.

Gregory, Robert. "Tactic of Evasion: A Review of *Male Fantasies.*" *American Book Review* (March/April 1990), pp. 6, 9.

Greenacre, Phyllis. "The Impostor." In *Emotional Growth: Psychoanalytic Studies of the Gifted and a Great Variety of Other Individuals*, vol. 1. New York: International Universities Press, 1971.

Haskell, Molly. "To Have and Have Not; The Paradox of the Female Star." *American Imago*, 50 (1990): 401–420.

Haynal, André, Miklos Molnar, and Gérard de Puymàge. *Fanaticism: A Historical and Psychoanalytic Study.* New York: Schocken Books, 1983.

Heath, Stephen. "Joan Riviere and the Masquerade." In *Formations of Fantasy*, ed. Victor Burgin, James Donald, and Cora Kaplan. New York: Methuen, 1986, pp. 45–61.

Hendin, Herbert. "Seduced by Death: Doctors, Patients, and the Dutch Cure." *Issues in Law and Medicine*, 10, 2 (1994): 123–168.

————. *Suicide in America.* New York: W. W. Norton, 1982.

Horney, Karen. "The Denial of the Vagina: A Contribution to the Problem of the Genital Anxiety Specific to Women." *International Journal of Psycho-Analysis,* 14 (1933): 57–70.

———. "The Dread of Women: Observations on a Specific Difference in the Dread Felt by Men and Women Respectively for the Opposite Sex." *International Journal of Psycho-Analysis,* 13 (1932): 348–360.

———. "The Flight from Womanhood: The Masculinity-Complex in Women as Viewed by Men and Women." *International Journal of Psycho-Analysis,* 7 (1926): 324–339.

———. "On the Genesis of the Castration Complex in Women." *International Journal of Psycho-Analysis,* 5 (1924): 50–65.

Hunt, Lynn. *The Family Romance in the French Revolution.* Berkeley: University of California Press, 1992.

Imperato-McGinley, J., R. E. Peterson, T. Gautier, and E. Sturla. "Androgens and the Evolution of Male Gender Identity Among Male Pseudohermaphrodites with 5a-Reductase Deficiency." *New England Journal of Medicine,* 300 (1979): 1233–1237.

Interbitzen, Larry, and Steven Levy. "Unconscious Fantasy: A Reconsideration of the Concept." *Journal of the American Psychoanalytic Association,* 38 (1990): 113–130.

Izard, Charles E. *Human Emotions.* New York: Plenum Press, 1977.

Jacobs, W. W. *The Monkey's Paw: A Story in Three Scenes.* Dramatized by Louis N. Parker. New York: Samuel French, 1910.

James, Henry. *The Altar of the Dead; the Beast in the Jungle; the Birthplace; and Other Tales.* New York: Scribner, 1909.

Jameson, Fredric. *The Political Unconscious: Narrative as a Socially Symbolic Act.* Ithaca, N.Y.: Cornell University Press, 1981.

Jankowiak, William R., and Edward F. Fisher. "A Cross-Cultural Perspective on Romantic Love." *Ethnology,* 31, 2 (1992): 149–155.

Johnson, Adelaide. "Factors in the Etiology of Fixations and Symptom Choice." *Psychoanalytic Quarterly,* 22 (1953): 475–496.

Johnson, Adelaide, and S. A. Szurek. "The Genesis of Antisocial Acting Out in Children and Adults." *Psychoanalytic Quarterly,* 21 (1952): 323–343.

Jones, Ernest. "The Early Development of Female Sexuality." *International Journal of Psycho-Analysis,* 8 (1927): 459–472.

———. "Early Female Sexuality." *International Journal of Psycho-Analysis,* 16 (1935): 263–275.

———. "The Phallic Phase." *International Journal of Psycho-Analysis.* 14 (1933): 1–33.

Joseph, Edward D. "An Unusual Fantasy in a Twin with an Inquiry into the Nature of Fantasy." *Psychoanalytic Quarterly,* 28 (1959): 189–190.

Jucovy, Milton E. "Initiation Fantasies and Transvestitism." *Journal of the American Psychoanalytic Association,* 24 (1976): 525–546.

Jung, Carl. *Psychology of the Unconscious.* New York: Dodd, Mead, 1957 [1916].

Kaplan, Linda Joan. "The Concept of the Family Romance." *The Psychoanalytic Review,* 61 (1974): 169–202.

Kennedy, Hansi, George Moran, Stanley Wiseberg, and Clifford York. "Both Sides of the Barrier." In *Psychoanalytic Study of the Child,* vol. 40. Madison, Conn.: International Universities Press, 1985.

Kern, Stephen. *The Culture of Love: Victorians to Moderns.* Cambridge, Mass.: Harvard University Press, 1992.

King, Robert A. "Cookies for the Emperor: The Multiple Functions of Play in the Analysis of an Early Adolescent Boy." In *The Many Meanings of Play: A Psycho-analytic Perspective,* ed. Albert Solnit, Donald J. Cohen, and Peter B. Neubauer. New Haven, Conn.: Yale University Press, 1993.

Klinger, Eric. *Daydreaming: Using Waking Fantasy and Imagery for Self-Knowledge and Creativity.* Los Angeles: Jeremy P. Tarcher, 1990.

———. *Structure and Functions of Fantasy.* New York: Wiley-Interscience, 1971.

Koestenbaum, Wayne. "Jacqueline Kennedy Onassis: Her Bouffant Magnificence." *The New York Times Magazine* (January 1, 1995), p. 40.

———. *The Queen's Throat: Opera, Homosexuality, and the Mystery of Desire.* New York: Vintage Books, 1993.

Kris, Ernst. "The Personal Myth: A Problem in Psychoanalytic Technique." *Journal of the American Psychoanalytic Association,* 4 (1956): 653–681.

Kurzweil, Edith. *The Freudians: A Comparative Perspective.* New Haven: Yale University Press, 1989.

Lahr, John, ed. *The Orton Diaries.* New York: Harper and Row, 1986.

———. *Prick Up Your Ears: The Biography of Joe Orton.* New York: Limelight Editions, 1978.

Lambert, Pam, and Ellin Stein. "Blood Memory: Writer Anne Perry Once Took Part in a Murder." *People,* September 26, 1994, pp. 57–60.

Laplanche, Jean, and Jean-Bertrand Pontalis. "Fantasy and the Origins of Sexuality." *International Journal of Psycho-Analysis,* 49 (1968): 1–18.

———. *The Language of Psycho-analysis.* Trans. Donald Nicholson-Smith. New York: W. W. Norton, 1973.

Laufer, Moses. "The Central Masturbation Fantasy, the Final Sexual Organization and Adolescence." In *Psychoanalytic Study of the Child,* vol. 31. Madison, Conn.: International Universities Press, 1976.

Laughton, Charles. *Tell Me a Story.* New York: McGraw-Hill, 1957.

Lebovici, Serge. "On Intergenerational Transmission: From Filiation to Affiliation." *Infant Mental Health Journal,* 14 (1993): 260–272.

———. "Le Nourisson, la Mére a te le psychanalyste." *Les Interactions Précoces.* Paris: Le Centurion, 1983.

Lemlij, Moisés. "Creative Writers and Day-Dreaming: A Parochial View." In *On Freud's "Creative Writers and Day-Dreaming,"* ed. Ethel Person, Peter Fonagy, and Sérvulo Figueira. New Haven, Conn.: Yale University Press, 1995, pp. 164–183

Lewis, C. S. *The Allegory of Love: A Study in Medieval Tradition.* New York: Oxford University Press, 1936.

Lewisohn, Ludwig, ed. *Theodor Herzl: A Portrait for This Age.* Preface by David Ben-Gurion. New York: World Publishing, 1955.

Lichtenstein, Heinz. *The Dilemma of Human Identity.* New York: Jason Aronson, 1977.

Lifton, Robert J. Presentation at the conference "Waiting to Die: Suicide in American Literature" organized by the American Suicide Foundation, New York City, November 11, 1994.

Lodge, David. *The Art of Fiction.* New York: Viking, 1992.

Loewenberg, Peter. "Theodor Herzl: A Psychoanalytic Study in Charismatic Political Leadership." In *The Psychoanalytic Interpretation of History,* ed. Benjamin B. Wolman. New York: Harper Torch Books, 1971.

Looser, Devoney. "Heroine of the Peripheral." *Auto/Biography Studies,* 5 (1993): 179–197.

MacKenzie, Norman. *Dreams and Dreaming.* New York: Vanguard Press, 1965.

Malcolm, Janet. "The Silent Woman." *The New Yorker* (August 23, 1993), pp. 84–159.

Martin, Douglas. "The X-Men Vanquish America." *New York Times* (August 21, 1994), p. B-27.

Martin, Jay. *Who Am I This Time? Uncovering the Fictive Personality.* New York: W. W. Norton, 1988.

Masson, Jeffrey Moussaieff. *The Assault on Truth: Freud's Suppression of the Seduction Theory.* New York: Farrar, Straus and Giroux, 1984.

May, Robert. *Sex and Fantasy: Patterns of Male and Female Development.* New York: W. W. Norton, 1980.

McCullough, Frances, and Ted Hughes, eds. *The Journals of Sylvia Plath.* New York: Dial Press, 1982.

Middlebrook, Diane Wood. *Anne Sexton: A Biography.* Boston: Houghton Mifflin, 1991.

Millett, Kate. *Sexual Politics.* Garden City, N.Y.: Doubleday, 1976.

Mitchell, Juliet. *Psychoanalysis and Feminism.* New York: Pantheon Books, 1974.

Mitchell, Stephen A. *Relational Concepts in Psychoanalysis.* Cambridge, Mass.: Harvard University Press, 1988.

Money, John. "Gender Role, Gender Identity, Core Gender Identity: Usage and Definition of Terms." *Journal of the American Academy of Psychoanalysis,* 1 (1974): 397–404.

———. "Sex Hormones and Other Variables in Human Eroticism." In *Sex and Internal Secretions,* 3rd ed., vol. 2., ed. W. C. Young and G. W. Corner. Baltimore, Md.: Williams and Wilkins, 1961.

Money, John, ed. *Sex Research: New Developments.* New York: Holt, Rinehart and Winston, 1965.

Money, John, Mark Schwartz, and Viola G. Davis, "Adult Erotosexual Status and Fetal Hormonal Masculinization and De-Masculinization: 46, XX Congenital Virilizing Adrenal Hyperplasia and 46, XY Androgen-Insensitivity Syndrome Compared." *Psychoneuroendochrinology*, 9 (1984): 405–414.

Morgenthau, Hans, and Ethel S. Person. "The Roots of Narcissism," *Partisan Review,* 45 (1978): 337–347.

Mundy, Chris. "The Life of Kurt Cobain: The Lost Boy." *Rolling Stone* (June 2, 1994), pp. 51–53.

Neubauer, Peter B. "The Clinical Use of the Daydream." Unpublished manuscript presented at the panel "Clinical Value and Utilization of the Daydream," Scientific Meetings of the American Psychoanalytic Association, New York City, December 19, 1993.

Newman, Charles, ed. *The Art of Sylvia Plath: A Symposium.* Bloomington and London: Indiana University Press, 1971.

Ovesey, Lionel. *Homosexuality and Pseudohomosexuality.* New York: Science House, 1969.

Ovesey, Lionel, and Ethel S. Person. "Gender Identity and Sexual Psychopathology in Men." *Journal of the American Academy of Psychoanalysis*, 1 (1973): 53–72.

———. "Transvestism: A Disorder of Sense of Self," *International Journal of Psychoanalytic Psychotherapy*, 5 (1976): 219–235.

Paley, Vivian G. *The Boy Who Would Be a Helicopter: The Uses of Storytelling in the Classroom.* Cambridge, Mass.: Harvard University Press, 1990.

Peller, Lili. "Daydreams and Children's Favorite Books: Psychoanalytic Comments." *The Psychoanalytic Study of the Child*, 14 (1959): 414–433.

Person, Ethel S. "Discussion of 'Initiation Fantasies and Transvestism,'" *Journal of the American Psychoanalytic Association*, 24 (1976): 547–551.

———. *Dreams of Love and Fateful Encounters: The Power of Romantic Passion.* New York: W. W. Norton, 1988.

———. "Male Sexuality and Power." *Psychoanalytic Inquiry*, 6 (1986): 3–25.

———. "The Omni-Available Woman in Lesbian Sex: Two Fantasy Themes and Their Relationship to the Male Developmental Experience." In *The Psychology of Men: New Psychoanalytic Perspectives*, ed. Gerald Fogel, Frederick M. Lane, and Robert S. Liebert. New York: Basic Books, 1986, pp. 236–259.

———. "Plagiarism and Parallel Process." In *Psychoanalysis: Toward the Second Century*, ed. Arnold M. Cooper, Otto F. Kernberg, and Ethel S. Person. New Haven, Conn.: Yale University Press, 1989.

———. "Romantic Love: At the Intersection of the Psyche and the Cultural Unconscious." *Journal of the American Psychoanalytic Association*, 39 (1991): 383–411.

———. "Sexuality as the Mainstay of Identity." In *Women—Sex and Sexuality*, ed. Catharine R. Stimpson and Ethel S. Person. Chicago: University of Chicago Press, 1980.

Person, Ethel S., and Howard Klar. "Establishing Trauma: The Difficulty Distinguishing Between Memories and Fantasies." *Journal of the American Psychoanalytic Association*, 42 (1994): 1055–1081.

Person, Ethel S., and Lionel Ovesey. "Psychoanalytic Theories of Gender Identity." *Journal of the American Academy of Psychoanalysis*, 11 (1983): 203–227.

———. "Homosexual Cross-Dressers" *Journal of the American Academy of Psychoanalysis*, 12 (1984): 167–186.

Person, Ethel S., Nettie Terestman, Wayne A. Myers, Eugene Goldberg, and Michael Borenstein. "Associations Between Sexual Experiences and Fantasies in a Nonpatient Population: A Preliminary Study." *Journal of the American Academy of Psychoanalysis*, 20, 1 (1992): 75–90.

Person, Ethel S., Nettie Terestman, Wayne A. Myers, Eugene L. Goldberg, and Carol Salvadori. "Gender Differences in Sexual Behaviors and Fantasies in a College Population." *Journal of Sex and Marital Therapy*, 15 (1989): 187–198.

Plath, Sylvia. "Daddy." In *Ariel*. New York: Harper and Row, 1966.

———. *The Journals of Sylvia Plath*, ed. Frances McCullough and Ted Hughes. New York: Dial Press, 1982.

"Proceedings of the International Scientific Colloquium on the Role of Fantasy in the Adaptive Process." *Bulletin of the Hampstead Clinic*, 7 (1984): 149–222.

Radway, Janice A. *Reading the Romance*. Chapel Hill: University of North Carolina Press, 1984.

Rangell, Leo. "Roots and Derivatives of Unconscious Fantasy." In *Fantasy, Myth and Reality,* ed. Harold P. Blum, Yale Kramer, Arlene K. Richards, and Arnold D. Richards. Madison, Conn.: International Universities Press, 1988.

Rapaport, David. *Organization and Pathology of Thought: Selected Sources.* New York: Columbia University Press, 1951.

Rich, Adrienne. *On Lies, Secrets, and Silence: Selected Prose 1966–1978.* New York: W. W. Norton, 1979.

Richards, David. "Boulevard of Broken Dreams." *New York Times* (November 18, 1994), p. C-1.

Rittenberg, Stephen, and L. Noah Shaw. "On Fantasies of Self-Creation." In *Psychoanalytic Study of the Child,* vol. 46. Madison, Conn.: International Universities Press, 1991, pp. 217–236.

Roiphe, Anne. *Torch Song.* New York: Farrar, Straus and Giroux, 1977.

Roiphe, Katie. *The Morning After: Sex, Fear and Feminism on Campus.* Boston: Little, Brown, 1993.

Rose, Gilbert. "Pre-Genital Aspects of Pregnancy Fantasies." *International Journal of Psycho-Analysis,* 42 (1961): 544–549.

Rose, Jacqueline. *The Haunting of Sylvia Plath.* Cambridge, Mass.: Harvard University Press, 1993.

Ross, Nathaniel. "On the Significance of Infantile Sexuality." In *On Sexuality: Psychoanalytic Observations,* ed. Toksov B. Karasu and Charles Socarides. New York: International Universities Press, 1979.

Rothman, Ellen K. *Hands and Hearts: A History of Courtship in America.* New York: Basic Books, 1984.

Ruddick, Sara. *Maternal Thinking: Toward a Politics of Peace.* New York: Ballantine, 1990.

Rushdie, Salman. "A Critic at Large: Out of Kansas." *The New Yorker* (May 11, 1992), pp. 93–103.

Sachs, Hanns. "The Community of Daydreams." In *The Creative Unconscious.* Cambridge, Mass.: Sci-Art Publishers, 1942.

Sacks, Oliver. "An Anthropologist on Mars." *The New Yorker* (December 27, 1993–January 3, 1994), pp. 106–125.

Sandler, Joseph. "Dreams, Unconscious Fantasies and 'Identity of Perception.'" *International Review of Psycho-analysis,* 3 (1976): 33–42.

———. "Reality and the Stabilizing Function of Unconscious Fantasy." *Bulletin of the Anna Freud Centre,* 9 (1986): 177–194.

Sandler, Joseph, and H. Nagera. "Aspects of the Meta-Psychology of Fantasy." In *Psychoanalytic Study of the Child,* vol. 18. Madison, Conn.: International Universities Press, 1963.

Sandler, Joseph, and Anne-Marie Sandler. "The Gyroscopic Function of the Unconscious Fantasy." In *Toward a Comprehensive Model of Schizophrenic Disorders,* ed. D. B. Finestein. New York: Analytic Press, 1986, pp. 109–123.

———. "On the Development of Object Relationships and Affects." *International Journal of Psycho-Analysis,* 59 (1978): 277–296.

———. "The Past Unconscious, the Present Unconscious, and Vicissitudes of Guilt." *International Journal of Psycho-Analysis,* 68 (1987): 331–341.

Sarnoff, Charles. "Narcissism, Adolescent Masturbation Fantasies and the Search for Reality." In *Masturbation from Infancy to Senescence,* ed. Irwin Marcus and John J. Francis. New York: International Universities Press, 1975, pp. 277–304.

Schimek, Jean G. "Fact and Fantasy in the Seduction Theory: A Historical Review." *Journal of the American Psychoanalytic Association,* 35, 4 (1987): 937–965.

———. "The Interpretations of the Past: Childhood Trauma, Psychical Reality and Historical Truth." *Journal of the American Psychoanalytic Association,* 23 (1975): 845–865.

Schneider, Keith. "Fearing a Conspiracy, Some Heed a Call to Arms." *New York Times* (November 14, 1994), p. A-1.

Segal, Hanna. *Dream, Phantasy and Art.* London: Routledge, 1991.

Sexton, Anne. "The Bar Fly Ought to Sing." In *The Art of Sylvia Plath: A Symposium,* ed. Charles Newman. Bloomington: Indiana University Press, 1971.

Shane, Morton, and Estelle Shane. "Unconscious Fantasy: Developmental and Self-Psychological Considerations." *Journal of the American Psychoanalytic Association,* 38 (1990): 75–92.

Shapiro, W. "One Went Right: Woes From Wall Street to the Gulf—But a Happy Ending in Texas." *Time,* 130 (1987), p. 30.

Showalter, Elaine. "Slick Chick." *London Review of Books* (July 11, 1991), p. 6.

Silverstein, Olga, and Beth Rashbaum. *The Courage to Raise Good Men.* New York: Viking, 1994.

Simpson, Eileen. *Orphans: Real and Imaginary.* New York: New American Library, 1987.

Singer, Jerome L. *Daydreaming: An Introduction to the Experimental Study of Inner Experience.* New York: Random House, 1966.

———. *The Inner World of Daydreaming.* New York: Harper and Row, 1979.

Slotkin, Richard. *Regeneration Through Violence: The Mythology of the American Frontier: 1600–1860.* Middletown, Conn.: Wesleyan University Press, 1973.

Smith, Theodate. "The Psychology of Daydreams." *The American Journal of Psychology,* 15 (1904): 465–488.

Spitz, Ellen Handler. "Picturing the Child's Inner World of Fantasy: On the Dialectic Between Image and Word." In *The Psychoanalytic Study of the Child,* vol. 43. New York: International Universities Press, 1988, pp. 433–447.

Spitz, Renée. "Hospitalism: A Follow-up Report on Investigation Described in Vol. 1." In *Psychoanalytic Study of the Child,* vol. 2. New York: International Universities Press, 1946, pp. 113–117.

———. "Hospitalism: An Inquiry into the Genesis of Psychiatric Conditions in Early Childhood." In *Psychoanalytic Study of the Child,* vol. 1. New York: International Universities Press, 1945, pp. 53–74.

Spitz, Renée, and Katherine Wolff. "Autoeroticism: Some Empirical Findings and Hypotheses on Three of Its Manifestations in the First Year of Life." In *Psychoanalytic Study of the Child,* vol. 3/4. New York: International Universities Press, 1949, pp. 85–120.

Stoller, Robert. *Sexual Excitement: Dynamics of Erotic Life.* New York: Pantheon Books, 1979.

Stone, Lawrence. "Passionate Attachments in the West in Historical Perspective." In *Passionate Attachments: Thinking About Love,* ed. Willard Gaylin and Ethel S. Person. New York: The Free Press, 1988.

Storr, Anthony. *Churchill's Black Dog, Kafka's Mice and Other Phenomena of the Human Mind.* New York: Grove Press, 1988.

Strauss, Neil. "The Downward Spiral." *Rolling Stone* (June 2, 1994).

Strich, Fritz. *Goethe and World Literature.* Westport, Conn.: Greenwood Press, 1971 (1945).

Styron, William. Presentation at the conference "Waiting to Die: Suicide in American Literature," organized by the American Suicide Foundation, New York City, November 11, 1994.

Symons, Donald. *The Evolution of Human Sexuality.* New York: Oxford University Press, 1979.

Tanner, Toby. *Adultery in the Novel: Contract and Transgression.* Baltimore, Md.: Johns Hopkins University Press, 1979.

Theweleit, Klaus. *Male Fantasies,* vol. 1: *Women, Floods, Bodies, History.* vol. 2: *Male Bodies: Psychoanalyzing the White Terror.* Minneapolis: University of Minnesota Press, 1987.

Tournier, Michel. *The Wind Spirit.* Trans. Arthur Goldhammer. Boston: Beacon Press, 1988.

Trosman, Harry. "Transformations of Unconscious Fantasy in Art." *Journal of the American Psychoanalytic Association,* 38, 1 (1990): 47–60.

Wakefield, Dan. "His 50's Then and Now: Robert Redford." *The New York Times Magazine* (August 21, 1994), pp. 26–29.

Wallerstein, Robert. "The Continuum of Reality, Inner and Outer." In *Fantasy, Myth and Reality,* ed. Harold Blum, Yale Kramer, Arlene K. Richards, and Arnold D. Richards. Madison, Conn.: International Universities Press, 1988.

Wangh, Martin. "The 'Evocation of a Proxy': A Psychological Maneuver, Its Use as a Defense, Its Purpose and Genesis." In *The Psychoanalytic Study of the Child,* vol. 1. Madison, Conn.: International Universities Press, 1968, pp. 451–472.

Weiss, Philip. "A Hoplophobe Among the Gunnies." *The New York Times Magazine* (September 11, 1994), pp. 65–100.

Wells, H. G. *H. G. Wells in Love: Postscript to an Experiment in Autobiography,* ed. G. P. Wells. Boston: Little, Brown, 1984.

Widzer, Martin E. "The Comic-Book Superhero: A Study of the Family Romance Fantasy." *The Psychoanalytic Study of the Child,* 32 (1977): 565–603.

Wolitzer, Meg. *Sleepwalking.* New York: Random House, 1982.

Wyatt, Jean. *Reconstructing Desire: The Role of the Unconscious in Women's Reading and Writing.* Chapel Hill, NC: University of North Carolina Press, 1990.

Yeats, William Butler. *Collected Poems.* New York: Macmillan, 1933.

Young-Bruehl, Elisabeth. *Anna Freud: A Biography.* New York: Summit Books, 1988.

Zilbergeld, Bernard. *Male Sexuality.* New York: Bantam Books, 1978.

Zweig, Stefan. *The World of Yesterday: An Autobiography.* Lincoln: University of Nebraska Press, 1964.

INDEX